PHILOSOPHICAL ESSAYS

in honor of Edgar Arthur Singer, Jr.

EDGAR ARTHUR SINGER, Jr.
Portrait by Harry Kidd

PHILOSOPHICAL ESSAYS

in honor of

Edgar Arthur Singer, Jr.

Edited by

F. P. CLARKE and M. C. NAHM

Essay Index Reprint Series

 BOOKS FOR LIBRARIES PRESS
FREEPORT, NEW YORK

B 21
P 43
1969

STANDARD BOOK NUMBER:

8369-1062-1

LIBRARY OF CONGRESS CATALOG CARD NUMBER:

78-80394

PRINTED IN THE UNITED STATES OF AMERICA

PREFACE

THE inception of this volume of philosophical essays in honor of Edgar A. Singer, Jr., Adam Seybert Professor of Philosophy in the University of Pennsylvania, lies in the desire of former students to express in an appropriate manner the respect and the affection in which they hold the man whose ideas have come to be integral to their own ways of thinking and the rigor of whose philosophical method has served as a too often unattainable standard for the evaluation of their own efforts to perfect techniques in various fields of research. It is because its beginnings do lie here that this book is, paradoxically enough, a *Festschrift* that required for its inauguration no merely external occasion of date or circumstance. Its publication, likewise, has awaited no specific occasion. The essayists who have contributed to the volume celebrate, rather, two integrated aspects of a life devoted to science: Professor Singer's long continuing contribution to technical philosophy in this country and his presentation of the historical "dialectic of the schools" and of systematic thought to generations of students in a university now entering upon the third century of its foundation.

That these aspects have been integrated remains true despite the fact that the rigor of the "logico-historical method," the pervasiveness of content, and the universality of application combined to present a systematic theory of evidence—all these have brought about in Professor Singer's Empirical Idealism that transcendence of immediate time and place which is one of the tokens of every profound philosophy. The import and value of this system of thought beyond the seminar and the classroom is evident to the philosopher who reads *Mind as Behavior, On the Contented Life, Modern Thinkers and Present Problems,* and the many technical papers which have appeared in the periodicals and learned journals devoted to philosophy. Professor Singer's contributions to speculation especially in epistemology and methodology in this country have long been known, not only through his publications but

v

through his activities in the American Philosophical Association, of which he is a former president, and in the American Philosophical Society.

There is, in addition to its purely technical side, the important function of philosophy which has made it central to the disciplines of the liberal college and has established its place in the curricula of the great universities which follow a tradition as old as the Academy and the Lyceum. To that tradition, firmly established at the University of Pennsylvania by Fullerton and Newbold, Professor Singer has contributed the talents of a profoundly influential teacher. Drawn to the lecture hall by word of the superbly-turned phrase and the classically-modeled sentence, many a beginner in the history of modern philosophy has verified the truth of the rumor and, at the same time, the further truth that the habiliments of Singer's style are integral to a dialectical skill whose employment upon historical and systematic material recasts not only the ideas but the mind of the auditor as well.

Not all of Professor Singer's academic career has been formed at, and devoted to, the University of Pennsylvania. A sojourn in France deepened a youthful but ranging interest in the literature and science of that country, an interest which has permeated both his style and thought. No less important in his philosophical training were the two years spent at Harvard University, where in 1895-96, he was Assistant to William James in the Department of Psychology. During those years the central problems of epistemology and the nature of mind came more clearly to present themselves as susceptible of solution by the refinement of technical and experimental method. Important as these influences were, it is nevertheless, primarily at Pennsylvania as a student under the influence of Fullerton and as a teacher that Professor Singer's career in philosophy was shaped and has had its most evident influence. As an undergraduate, he had studied engineering and had taken the degree of Bachelor of Science in 1892. His interest in mathematics and in exact sciences found its application in speculative philosophy, in which he took his doctorate in 1894. Upon his return to the University of Pennsylvania in 1896 as Senior Tutor,

Singer occupied successively higher positions in the Department of Philosophy until 1909 when he was appointed to a professorship. He has occupied the Adam Seybert Chair in Philosophy since the year 1929.

In the plan and structure of this volume of essays, the editors have taken full advantage of the twofold but related character of Professor Singer's philosophical influence. Papers upon specifically philosophical problems have been prepared not only by former students and by members of the Department of Philosophy in the University of Pennsylvania, but also by Professors A. O. Lovejoy, a former President of the American Philosophical Association, and John H. Randall of the New York Philosophical Club of which Professor Singer is also a member. To the pages of the book have been contributed, also, essays by former students whose interest in his philosophical system and method has been carried into the fields of their own research. It was not the assumption of the editors that each individual essay should apply the exact methodology of Professor Singer to the problem considered. Yet the diversity of the essays does indeed give evidence of the influence and suggestiveness of a systematic philosophy, the principles of which are formulated in the strictest mathematical and logical languages but whose elaboration has required analyses of the realms of art, morality, and religion. It may be, also, that the variety of the essays, particularly those prepared by Professor Singer's former students, touching as they do upon many interests, will aid in the fuller comprehension of a philosophy which insists upon sound empirical method through the technique of experimental science and upon the transcendence of the merely empirical in its reinterpretation of the *Grenzbegriff* and of the concept of progress inherent in Kantian Idealism. The full expression of that philosophy necessarily awaits the publication of *Experience and Reflection*.

It was partly with this end in view that the suggestion was made to the contributors to this book that they follow, in the preparation of their essays, certain general classifications corresponding to the well-defined divisions of Professor Singer's philosophy. These divisions and the writings in which the principles governing them principally appear are as follows: I. METHODOLOGY AND SCIENCE: the Postulates of Experimental Method and the Classification of Systems (*Mind as Behavior*, "The Philosophy of Experiment," *Symposium*, April, 1930); Logic ("Logic and the Relation of Function to Mechanism," *Proceedings of the Seventh International Congress of Philosophy and Religion*, and "The Construction of Functional Classes"); Biology (*Mind as Behavior*, "Beyond Mechanism and Vitalism," *Philosophy of Science*, July, 1934, "Logico-Historical Study of Mechanism, Vitalism, and Naturalism," in *Studies in the History of Science*); Psychology (*Mind as Behavior*, "On the Conscious Mind," "On Sensibility," and "On Spontaneity," *Journal of Philosophy*); II. ETHICS AND RELIGION: *On the Contented Life* and "On a Possible Science of Religion," *Philosophical Review*, March 1931; III. AESTHETICS: "Esthetic and the Rational Ideal," *Journal of Philosophy*, *On the Contented Life*; IV. HISTORY: *Modern Thinkers and Present Problems*.

To the contributors to this volume, the editors wish to express their appreciation for coöperation which has reduced their editorial task to a minimum. To two friends of Professor Singer, the late Professor Wendell T. Bush, of New York, and John Frederick Lewis, Jr., of Philadelphia, they are especially indebted for assistance and suggestions. To Mr. Lewis, in particular, they wish to express their gratitude for his subvention of the printing of this volume.

FRANCIS P. CLARKE, *University of Pennsylvania*
MILTON C. NAHM, *Bryn Mawr College*

CONTENTS

I

METHODOLOGY AND SCIENCE

ON THE CRITERIA AND LIMITS OF MEANING

ARTHUR O. LOVEJOY

Professor Emeritus, Department of Philosophy,
The Johns Hopkins University

NEARLY thirty years ago Professor Singer rather wistfully remarked in the course of a philosophical debate that "it
would be happier if men stood in closer agreement as to what
meaning meant." It can hardly be said that the subsequent
decades' philosophizing has brought us notably nearer to the
attainment of such happiness. The seemingly diverse meanings
of "meaning" have, on the contrary, multiplied without benefit
of birth control, so that recent attempted enumerations of those
which appear to be distinguishable in the writings of philosophers and others run to astonishing length. Yet in the same
period the feeling which apparently prompted Professor Singer's
wish has exercised an increasing influence in the movement of
philosophic and scientific thought—the feeling that the first
thing needful for philosophy and science is to determine what
are the *ungereimte Fragen*, the questions which are meaningless and therefore ought not to be and, indeed, logically cannot be, asked. The conviction that a general theory of the
nature of meaning, a formulation of the requisites to meaningfulness in terms and sentences, and a consequent preliminary
delimitation of the field of legitimate philosophical inquiry, is
a possible and necessary propaedeutic to philosophy—this conviction has spread more and more widely and manifested itself
in the most diverse quarters. The tendency to assume that the
theory of meaning is a major philosophical discipline, taking
precedence of all others, will probably be recognized by future
historians as one of the conspicuous and distinctive phenomena
in the reflection of this quarter-century. Most of the theories
actually produced that have dealt with this issue have been
variants of a single general type, which may be called radical

3

empiricism; the species includes pragmatism (in one of its senses), operationalism, behaviorism, the special theory of relativity (in its methodological premises) and neo-positivism. Some reflections on this problem which Professor Singer was a pioneer in raising may be a not unsuitable contribution to this volume in his honor.

Some preliminary observations by way of *Fragestellung* are necessary. The question: What is the meaning of "meaning"? would itself at first sight seem most obviously to be one of the questions that cannot be asked, since it is, by its very form, a question to which the answer must be known before it can be asked; or, to put it otherwise, one to which, if it *is* asked, i.e., is propounded as a genuine interrogation, no answer can be possible. One can imagine what complicated and amusing play with this question the Platonic Socrates would have made if it had come up in the course of one of the *Dialogues*. Yet I suspect that in the end Socrates would have been found maintaining that this question, which on its face cannot be asked, is one which contains its own answer within itself, and is therefore one which is especially suitable for asking. He would probably—after much dialectical banter—have persuaded one of the other interlocutors, perhaps a pupil of Gorgias, to admit that when he asked this question he was after all really thinking of something: that the word "meaning," when it first occurs in the question, was the expression of some concept already present to the interlocutor's mind; and he would have proceeded triumphantly to force the further admission that this concept is precisely *the concept of having a concept corresponding to, or expressible by, a given word*. People in general, then, the Socrates in my imaginary dialogue would have concluded, in truth know very well what they are asking when they ask: What is the meaning of "meaning"?—though a little philosophic midwifery is needed to enable them to bring forth what they know. They are asking a question about a word, the word "meaning," as it occurs the second time in the sentence; and they know that what they *want* to know about this word is, what specific thought, in their own or someone's, or perhaps everyone's, actual stock of thoughts, it stands for; and, precisely *be-cause* of the seemingly paradoxical circularity of the question, to know what they want to know about this one word "meaning" is to know what constitutes for them the attribute of meaning as a conceivable predicate of any other word in any language. A term, accordingly, has "meaning" if for someone who uses it there is back of it some actual *νόημα*, some thought-content, which the user intends to employ that word to express, an idea of a quality, object, event, or act, whether a particular or a universal, which the user would be willing to *name* by that word; only when this condition is not satisfied do words lack meaning. A word has *distinct* meaning in so far as the user or users are clearly aware just what idea it is that they are expressing by it; and the potentiality of meaning in words is limited only by the range of discriminable ideas which human minds are capable of entertaining.

If Socrates had reasoned in this manner, I suggest, he would have reasoned well. He would have correctly made explicit that *particular* meaning of "meaning" which all those who actually ask the question: What is the meaning of "meaning"? have in mind; the nature of the information they desire and therefore the only meaning of it which is relevant to the question asked, and the only one which permits other than an arbitrary and question-begging answer. Unfortunately Plato neglected to write a dialogue on this subject and, therefore, numerous later writers, especially in our own time, have, I think, been prone to lay down propositions about meaning without sufficient logical cir-cumspection, without making initially clear to themselves ex-actly what they were doing. Some of them have either proceeded to declare certain classes of terms or sentences to be devoid of meaning without first formulating any general answer to the question of the meaning of "meaning"; or if they have formu-lated such an answer, they have not observed how anomalous a question it is, and have not asked the prior question: What in fact is it that I seek to know when I ask *this* question? They have consequently presented a variety of answers which are not subject to control by any fact, but are merely verbal definitions from which only verbal conclusions can be drawn as to the meaningfulness of any terms or sentences, i.e., propositions which have, or should have, the form: If you happen to choose, as I do, to define the word "meaning" in a certain manner, then such and such a sentence, "S," is not, in that arbitrary sense, meaningful; but if you happen to mean something else by "meaning," then "S" *is* meaningful.

With these preliminaries, I turn to a consideration of a particular attempt to delimit the province of philosophy by means of deductions from a thesis, or assumption, about "meaning." For this purpose I choose a small volume by a distinguished representative of the school of logical positivism, Professor Carnap. It appears doubtful whether this volume, published in 1928, precisely represents the present views of its author.[1] Logical positivism seems to be a rather protean philosophy which, if the pronouncements of its best-recognized spokesmen are to be taken as defining it at any given moment, changes its shape frequently and rapidly. Nevertheless, the contentions of the volume in question—*Scheinprobleme der Philosophie: das Fremdpsychische und der Realismusstreit*—represent an influential phase in recent philosophical thought; they constitute a view which it is possible for acute reflective minds to hold and one which is, there is reason to believe, still current. It is therefore deserving of examination, apart from the purely historical question as to what changes may have taken place in the opinions of particular individuals or groups. It is in the question of the validity of a certain type of argument and conclusion that I am here interested, not in the historical question. But a philosopher is less likely to seem to be dealing with straw men, and also is less liable to unconscious falsifications of the grounds upon which a given conclusion rests, if he applies his scrutiny to the actual reasonings of individuals, whether in the present or past, who are recognized as especially competent and lucid expounders of those grounds.

The second part of the volume, entitled "Purgation of Philosophy from Spurious Problems" (*Reinigung der Philosophie*

[1] The present essay was written in 1938.

von Scheinproblemen), begins with a statement about "meaning."

The meaning of a proposition [Carnap writes] consists in its expressing a conceivable (not necessarily actual) fact (*Sachverhalt*). If a supposed proposition expresses no conceivable fact, it has no meaning, and is only seemingly a proposition (*Aussage*). If a proposition contains a concept of which the signification is in doubt, or about the legitimacy (scientific applicability) of which question has been raised, its meaning must be specifically stated. For this purpose it is necessary and sufficient to state in what cases—primarily merely conceived cases—of experience the proposition would be called true (*sie wahr heissen soll*), and in what cases it would be called false.

This is necessary in order to give the concept a meaning,

because if it were regarded as permissible in science to make assertions of which the validity cannot be definitely established or contradicted through experiences, there would be no way of preventing the introduction also of quite obviously meaningless propositions, or rather pseudo-propositions such as "bu ba bi," "this triangle is virtuous," "this rock is sad."

Already at this point an even slightly circumspect reader will find several questions forcing themselves upon him. In the first place: What is the author doing here? What kind of statement is his initial one about "meaning" supposed to be? Is it explicitly a verbal definition, an indication of the connotation which the author chooses to attach to the word "meaning"? If so, all that follows in the book—and much that follows in the general neo-positivistic doctrine—consists of particular verbal propositions deduced from this general one. If I choose to define the word "dog" as signifying exclusively "a metal contrivance designed to support logs in a fireplace," it follows that I cannot consistently call Fido a dog; but this deduction conveys no material information about Fido but only about myself—about one particular oddity in my use of language resulting from the peculiarity of my original definition of a general term. It is difficult to suppose that a philosopher setting out to "purge philosophy of spurious problems" intends nothing more than the conveyance of information about the eccentricities of his private terminology. It must, then, be assumed that Carnap's initial statement is put forward as an assertoric proposition possessing either truth or falsity, and itself capable of some sort of verification or control, presumably through comparison with some fact or set of facts. But if so, with what facts? Is it a proposition about what everybody already understands by "meaning," a fact of universal usage? We are not told; but if this is what is to be understood by the assertion, no evidence is offered to show that it accords with the fact with which it is intended to accord; and, indeed, it clearly does not do so.

And, in any case, precisely what *is* the definition or criterion of meaning propounded? Is it, perhaps, that which I have already suggested: "a proposition possesses meaning if, to every one of its terms, there corresponds, in the actual thought of someone using it, a specific idea of some thinkable object, or referent [or class of such objects], which the user would designate by that term"? In part, I think, and primarily, though not altogether unequivocally, this *is* what "meaning" means in the argument we are considering. In the definition one of the crucial terms is "experience"; and in the application of it elsewhere for the proof of the meaninglessness of particular questions or assertions, the general ground on which these are condemned is that they express nothing that is "experienceable," *erfahrbar*. But the notion of the *unerfahrbar*, which figures so largely in the argument, is an equivocal one. It may designate either of (at least) two deficiencies of a nominal referent.

1. In one sense such a referent is, in Carnap's usage, unexperienceable if the terms used in defining or describing it designate no qualities or relations of which our experience has enabled us to form any conception. Obviously, in such a case the definition would not tell us what the object or event nominally referred-to would be *like*; the terms would correspond to no idea actually possessed by the propounder and would evoke no such idea in the hearer. The definition would be meaningless because it would be a definition of the unthinkable. Such manifest meaninglessness of a sentence can in strictness, however, arise only in two ways: either because the sentence is composed

of what we call—and our use of this adjective is significant—nonsense syllables—marks or sounds with which no reader or hearer associates any ideas whatever; or because, though the separate terms in the sentence have ideas associated with them, these ideas are mutually contradictory and cannot be put together in the relation specified in the sentence. But there is a third type of case (mentioned by Carnap) of which the proper classification, as "experienceable" or "unexperienceable," is not immediately evident; it is exemplified by the expression: "the color-quality corresponding to infra-red or ultra-violet rays." For organisms having our type of visual apparatus the quality referred to is unexperienceable; nor have we any idea in what way our visual organs, peripheral and central, would need to be changed in order to give us this kind of experience. Nevertheless the expression mentioned is admitted by Carnap not to be completely meaningless, for the quality in question is not known to be *inherently* unexperienceable. It is the kind of quality which might be experienced by other creatures under partially definable conditions, namely, when rays of a certain wave-length were acting upon them, if their optical apparatus differed from ours in some way, by us, undefinable but not, by us, known to be impossible. Even the proposition: "There is a color, trumpet-red, which is terrifying to see," is said by Carnap to be meaningful. The term "trumpet-red" has no specific idea corresponding to it; we have never experienced such a color, and have no idea even of the conditions under which an experience of it could be attained. Nevertheless, "we can think of an experience by means of which the proposition would be empirically established (*fundiert*) and can [partially] describe the nature of this experience; it would, namely, be an experience which included the visual perception of a color which was some shade of red, the perception being accompanied by a feeling of terror." Similarly, a proposition about the landscape on the other side of the moon would presumably be meaningful, though admittedly destined never to be empirically verified.

This limitation of meaningfulness to terms referring to something experienceable seems, then, plainly to presuppose the meaning of "meaning" which Socrates formulated in our extra-canonical Platonic dialogue. Carnap assumes that we have no ideas not derived in some fashion from "experience," not gained through *Erlebnisse*, and he therefore identifies "meaning," as a property of terms and sentences, with: "expressing an idea with which somebody, or everybody, has, or might have, through experience actually been furnished"; but the reason *why* the realm of the *unerfahrbar* and the realm of the meaningless are regarded as coextensive is that the former is assumed to be the same as the realm of the *undenkbar*. Now it is in some sense true that we cannot have ideas which, or the elements of which, are not given us in experience; the proposition is, indeed, tautological, since to have an idea present for awareness is, precisely, to have just that kind of experience. But the empirical way to find out whether one has an idea is—simply to observe, by analytical introspection, whether one in fact has it. To argue that one cannot have it because some *other* kind of experience cannot have furnished one with it is to put the cart before the horse; it is to refuse to attend to the only relevant question of empirical fact.

2. A second sense of "experienceable," and consequently a second criterion of meaning, is used by Carnap as if it were interchangeable with the first. In this sense the experienceable is the "verifiable." If a sentence is to have meaning it must be one "of which the *validity* can be definitely established through experiences." This appears to mean that, at the moment of referring to the referent, the latter must, by anyone who asserts or denies the proposition, be *then* conceived as something of which the existence could by some investigator at some time be actually experienced under specifiable and practicable conditions. It is not the *what* but the *that* of the object-meant that is in question, not its nature but its being. This criterion of meaning, in short, is pertinent, not to terms or definitions, but only to sentences or questions concerning empirical matters of fact. Propositions which satisfy the criterion fall into two classes, (a) the previously verified and (b) the subsequently verifiable, defined respectively as follows: (a) "If an assertion *p* expresses the content of an experience (*Erlebnis*) E, and if

the assertion q is either equivalent to p or derivable from p or inferrible from p and previous empirical knowledge, either by deduction or inductive reasoning, then p [q?] is said to be established by (*fundiert durch*) the experience E. (b) A proposition p is said to be subsequently verifiable (*nachprüfbar*) if the conditions are specifiable [*angebbar*] under which an experience E would occur through which p, or the opposite of p, would be established. . . ." A further essential term in the definition of meaning given at the outset is defined thus: "An assertion p is said to be factual (*sachhaltig*) if experiences through which p or its opposite would be established are thinkable (*denkbar*), at least as experiences, and specifiable with respect to their character."[2] Only such assertions have meaning. But what is necessary in order that a proposition shall be capable of being "established through experience" and therefore *sachhaltig*? The hypothetical entities of theoretical physics are, in one obvious sense, unexperienceable, and propositions concerning them, Carnap grants, "are neither previously-established nor subsequently-verifiable." Are they, therefore, meaningless? It would seem to follow that they are; but our positivist's piety towards natural science is too great to permit him to accept this consequence. "If anyone wishes to be so rigorous as to banish such propositions from science, no conclusive objection to his doing so can be raised. Nevertheless it must be remembered that the customary method of the natural sciences, even of physics, does not regard such propositions as meaningless, but admits them as hypotheses. . . . We shall therefore not adopt this rigorous standpoint, but shall regard such propositions as meaningful (though not on that account necessarily true)." This concession is presumably not looked upon by the author as inconsistent with the general thesis about meaning which we are examining; and that thesis must therefore be construed as including, among propositions capable of empirical verification, not only those referring to objects or events which can conceivably be presented as actual data in perceptual experience, but also propositions referring to thinkable but not sensibly experienceable objects

[2] Carnap, *op. cit.*, p. 29.

or events, provided the propositions are in any way useful as hypotheses in scientific inquiry. "Empirical verifiability," or "testability," as Carnap prefers to call it in more recent writings, is thus a double-barreled criterion of meaning; and when it is taken in the second sense, it does not appear to restrict the realm of the meaningful within very narrow bounds.

In spite of the duality of the second criterion, the difference between it and the first is evident. By the first a term or sentence has meaning if its terms express any actual thought-content, if its referent is thinkable; by the second a sentence has meaning only if it expresses a judgment (or a question) such that there is a thinkable experience which would be so related to the judgment that it would *"establish the truth or falsity"* of the judgment, or give an answer to the question. Is there any reason for regarding the second criterion as inferrible from the first? The only reason, I believe, given in the *Scheinprobleme* is that if propositions not thus empirically verifiable were admitted into science, one would be unable to exclude from it "quite obviously meaningless propositions," such as collections of nonsense syllables, or sentences about virtuous triangles or melancholy stones. But the reason is manifestly question-begging. Nonsense syllables express nothing, and sentences about virtuous triangles contain combinations of predicates not thinkable together in the relation required by the grammatical form of the sentence. But it is not evident that all propositions not empirically verifiable are incapable of expressing thinkable ideas—that they are really of the same class as these *ganz offenkundig sinnlose (Schein-) Aussagen.* Whether assertions not in any sense sensibly verifiable should be excluded from natural science I do not, at the moment, discuss; but at all events they cannot be excluded for this reason, unless it is shown that such assertions are just like either nonsense syllables or formal self-contradictions. This is not shown, and, I suggest, it is not true. The realm of entertainable notions, questions, and hypotheses, is not identical or coextensive with the realm of propositions conceived as verifiable—verifiable either through the presentation in direct experience of the particular entities or events to which they refer or through inferences *to* the existence of such entities or events—inferences based upon the serviceableness of the resultant propositions for the explanation or correlation of the entities or events directly experienced. The two criteria, then, are not interchangeable.

But Carnap's procedure, it appears to me, when, on the basis of his doctrine about meaning, he set about purging philosophy of meaningless questions, consisted in interchanging the two; more specifically, it consisted in substituting a factual conclusion deducible only by the first criterion for a verbal conclusion reached by applying the second. This will, I think, become apparent if we examine the reasoning by which he seeks to show that two historic problems of metaphysics are pure *Scheinprobleme.* The first is that of the existence of an external world. The criterion applied here is the second. "Science cannot take either an affirmative or a negative position with respect to the question of the reality of the external world, because the question has no meaning";[3] and it has no meaning because no possible experience which would *settle* the question can be defined or conceived. If two geographers, one a realist, the other an idealist in philosophy, are asked whether a supposed mountain in Africa is merely legendary or actually exists, they know, as geographers, what *experiences* would give them an answer to the question, and how to go about getting these experiences; and if they apply, each for himself, the recognized empirical or scientific tests for the existence of the mountain, they will inevitably both arrive at the same conclusion. But as soon as they pass from the geographical to the philosophical question—or so-called question—the possibility of empirical verification vanishes. The opposing theses of the realist and idealist, since they lie "beyond experience" (*jenseits der Erfahrung*), have no factual content; neither makes any assertion whatever with respect to which the question whether it is true or false can be raised.[4] It is possible that "the realistic thesis" may have, for the philosopher who utters it, "a certain emotional concomitant"; he may have a feeling that the mountain

[3] *Ibid.,* p. 34.
[4] *Ibid.,* p. 36.

is in some sense alien to him, or the like. But this concomitant does not, we are told, lend meaning to the thesis which evokes it.

This reasoning may at first appear to make for peace among philosophers; and it is apparently as a means of enforcing peace that it is put forward. Realist and idealist are summoned to beat their philosophic swords into scientific ploughshares, on the ground that there is not, and never has been, any cause of quarrel between them. Since it is supposed to have been shown that neither ever means anything by what he says, they are manifestly in complete agreement. And, at the least, those who propound such reasoning appear thereby to proclaim their own neutrality—not, indeed, a benevolent but a malevolent neutrality—in these, and by implication in many other, ancient controversies. One who says that the dispute between realist and idealist is a dispute about nothing at all, seems to say that he takes sides with neither. But this air of being *au-dessus la mêlée* is entirely specious. The radical-empiricist theory of meaning as here applied simply results in subjective idealism. For the proposition which the idealist *asserts* is admitted to be both meaningful and true. That experiences, *Erlebnisse,* are real is not denied. But the proposition which the realist asserts is *not* admitted; and it is absurd to pretend that the realist is being treated no more harshly than the idealist, on the ground that the realistic thesis is pronounced, noi false, but worse— nonsensical. The authors of these doctrines, it is evident, sincerely covet the blessing pronounced upon the peacemakers, but their pacifism is of that thorough sort which seeks to annihilate one of the potential combatants before he has fairly appeared upon the scene.

It is true that Carnap and other neo-positivists have sometimes expressed their thesis about meaning in a qualified form in which it might seem to have less destructive implications. In stating it, namely, they often prefix the adjective "scientific" to the noun "meaning." If the adjective is taken as restrictive, the thesis would amount merely to the assertion that, in the general class of meaningful propositions, a species, to be called "scientifically meaningful propositions," may be differentiated; and that it is only to these that the requirement of empirical verifiability is to be applied. If it is so applied by definition, i.e., if "scientific" *means* "empirically verifiable," the thesis manifestly becomes a tautology. It would be another way of saying that the empirical sciences are empirical sciences. From this no consequence would follow as to the meaningfulness of the question about which the realist and the idealist disagree. It is obvious, and, I suppose, universally admitted that that question cannot be settled by the experimental method. You cannot through sensible experience determine whether there are existences independent of sensible experience. But the question, upon this interpretation of the positivistic thesis, would still be one which could intelligibly be asked and conceivably answered upon non-experimental grounds. This, however, does not appear to be all that the positivist intends to convey. He does not, I think, conceive himself to be enunciating propositions which nobody denies. To him "scientific meaning" and "meaning" are apparently synonymous and coextensive terms, as is indicated, *inter alia,* by the fact that he frequently employs the noun without the adjective. Certainly if his contentions are to be supposed to be of any philosophical consequence—to be important if true—it is in this sense that they must be construed. And so construed they manifestly have such hypothetical importance in the highest degree. *If* they are true, all philosophers ought henceforth to desist from either affirming, or denying, or even entertaining doubts about the existence of an external world. For you manifestly cannot even entertain doubts about a question of which the terms are meaningless.

Now this conclusion—benign or devastating, whichever you may choose to think it—could be established, as a factual and not merely a verbal proposition, only by applying the first criterion: by showing that the idea of an external world never has been, and cannot be, entertained, that nobody has any idea corresponding to the term "external world" or "objects existing when not perceived." But no attempt is made to show this; and it appears to me to be obviously false. I perceive a mountain, i.e., a certain complex of characters; I am aware that at the moment I *am* perceiving it. The word "mountain" expresses one idea, the word "perceiving" another. Since the ideas are distinct, they are presumptively not inseparable; and no evidence of their inseparability is offered. I can therefore think of the mountain as continuing to be there, in a certain region of Africa, after I shall have ceased to perceive or even think of it. The same is true with respect to the possible relation of the mountain to any other person's perceiving. By the first criterion, then, the conclusion that the *Realismusstreit* is meaningless does not follow. From the second criterion—at least in the first of *its* two senses—a conclusion does follow: but it is a different conclusion. It is merely the tautological proposition that I cannot by perception establish the fact that the mountain continues to be there while unperceived. This is a proposition which nobody denies. But it is not equivalent to the proposition that I cannot attach any sense to the *question* whether the mountain was there before it was perceived, or will be after.

It may, however, be urged that it is none the less an important proposition; for it means that the question, even though it can be asked, cannot be answered—that the continued existence of the mountain cannot be verified. I reply, in the first place, that this is, at any rate, a quite different question; and, in the second place, that the degree of importance of *this* proposition depends upon the prior settlement of the question whether no proposition that is incapable of perceptual verification may permissibly be believed. And that this prior question must be answered in the negative is by no means obvious. I am, for my own part, enough of a pragmatist to hold that meaningful (i.e., thinkable) propositions which I find any important advantage in believing, I am entitled to believe, unless there is some direct or inferential empirical evidence against them. And against the belief in the continuance of some kind of natural processes in space and time at times when no perception of them is occurring there obviously can be no empirical evidence. I have already suggested elsewhere that science itself rests ultimately upon beliefs having no different kind of basis, and that, in fact, the belief that there is such a thing as empirical verifiability is not empirically verifiable. One obvious reason for this is that science rests in part upon the postulate that past events (e.g., scientific experiments) have occurred. But the occurrence of a past event (when it *is* past) can never be empirically verified.

Let us now examine the application in the *Scheinprobleme* of its equivocal criterion of meaning to the second of the two questions which Carnap would expel, as meaningless, from the realm of legitimate philosophical consideration—the reality of consciousness or mental content in others. His reasoning here leads him first to behaviorism and through behaviorism to a solipsistic idealism. This "reduction" of the concept of "other's consciousness" (*das Fremdpsychische*) in Carnap's own words, proceeds as follows:

The knowledge of other minds in every case comes back to a knowledge of the physical. It does so not merely in the sense that there must always at the same time be a knowledge of some corresponding physical fact, but in the sense that the recognition of *das Fremdpsychische* entirely depends in every particular upon the corresponding known physical objects. Consequently, every proposition about any particular state of consciousness in another (*ein bestimmtes Fremdpsychisches*), such as "A is enjoying himself," can be translated into a proposition which is expressed in purely physical terms, namely, facial expressions, actions, spoken words, etc. . . . There are, then, available in such a case two fashions of speech, a psychological and a physical; and we affirm that they convey the same theoretic content. It will be objected that in the assertion "A is enjoying himself" *more* is expressed than in the corresponding physical assertion. And this is also correct. . . . But this more is not a "more" in the *theoretic content* of the proposition; it only expresses certain concomitant representations. And these are all simply representations which assert no matter of fact, and, therefore, cannot constitute the content of a proposition. When I say: "A is enjoying himself," instead of saying, "A has such and such a facial expression," I express the fact that *I* have the representation of a feeling of enjoyment—but a feeling of enjoyment *im eigenpsychischen Sinne* [i.e., in the sense that it is *my* feeling], for I assuredly am acquainted with no other. If, however, anyone supposes that, by using the psychological rather than the physical form of expression—by saying "enjoyment" rather than "a certain facial expression" he has referred to any fact over and above the physical fact he has confused the theoretic content of a proposition with its concomitant representation. Through this confusion . . . we are led, not to an erroneous proposition, but to a pseudo-proposition (*Schein-aussage*). For no fact [or state of things, *Sachverhalt*] exists, or can even be thought or expressed, which can connect the representation "enjoyment" (*im eigenpsychischen Sinne*, i.e., in the sense of *my* feeling of enjoyment) with the behavior of A.[5]

Carnap is not here asserting the banal proposition that people can, and sometimes do, observe other people's physical behavior without happening to think of it as accompanied by "enjoyment," or some other kind of sensory or affective content. He is asserting, first, that the only *possible* "concomitant representation" in any such case is of *my* enjoyment; and second, that this "representation" is not combinable in thought with the percept or concept of A's behavior. The first proposition seems to me false, as a piece of introspective psychology; but, for the moment, suppose it true. Then the second does follow. If by "my enjoyment" Carnap means "not another's"— or the "enjoyment associated with that other behavior out there which I am now perceiving"—then it is mere tautology to add: "My enjoyment is not associated with that other behavior." The question, then, concerns the truth or falsity of the first of these two propositions.

To make his meaning clearer, Carnap supposes a discussion to be taking place between two psychologists, analogous to that previously mentioned between two geographers. One of the psychologists *calls* himself a solipsist, the other, a "non-solipsistic idealist or realist." They raise the question whether A's pleasure is "real," just as the two geographers raised the question whether the mountain is real. So long as they confine themselves "to the empirical criteria of psychology," i.e., merely consider A's observable behavior, there is no possibility of disagreement between them: the solipsist's and the non-solipsist's assertions about A mean the same thing. If, however,

[5] *Ibid.*, pp. 36-38.

"they pass from psychology to philosophy, dispute arises. The solipsist affirms that only the physical behavior of A is real . . . his opponent declares that A not only manifests this particular physical behavior . . . but in addition actually possesses consciousness. . . ." But this difference of opinion, "since it relates to something beyond the factual (*jenseits des Sachhaltigen*), to that which is in principle unexperienceable, has, according to our criterion, no scientific meaning whatever."[6]

Here, as before, the ostensible result is, not the denial of the existence of other consciousnesses, but merely the discovery that the question whether they exist or not is devoid of meaning. The solipsist and his adversary are *both* using words without sense. But it must again be pointed out that the neo-positivist's air of neutrality is delusive. What the behaviorist (now quite correctly identified as a solipsist) asserts is admitted: A's observable behavior *is* an empirical fact. But what the anti-behaviorist asserts is *not* admitted, namely, that over and above A's behavior there is such a reality as A's consciousness or his mental content. It is not a way of avoiding the paradox of solipsism to say that no sense can be attached to such an expression as "another's consciousness," or *das Fremdpsychische*, unless it is translated into the expression "certain events observable by me which I *call* the bodily behavior of another organism." And this bodily behavior, it will be remembered, is not the behavior of a real physical body; for we have already seen that physical reals have similarly been exhaustively reduced to "my experiences." A's behavior, as well as his consciousness, becomes, when the "reduction" of these concepts is completed, *eigenpsychische*.

How definitely solipsism is affirmed by the spokesmen of this philosophy is shown further by their reply to an obvious objection, the "worm-objection," as Carnap calls it. The objector declares:

When I utter the proposition: "This animal—say a worm—has consciousness," I must intend to express something more than the fact that the animal, under a given stimulus, is exhibiting certain observable reactions; for the proposition has an influence upon my

[6] *Ibid.*, pp. 38-39.

conduct. If I know that the worm feels pain, I avoid treading on it; but the mere observation that it writhes when I tread on it would not deter me from doing so.

That there is such a difference between the practical effects of the verbal assertion and the verbal denial of consciousness in the worm our radical positivist admits; to that extent the objection is justified. But the difference consists only in the occurrence in my experience, when I say "the worm feels pain," of a certain affective concomitant, namely, a slight feeling of pain on *my* part; this, by a sort of empathy (*Einfühlung*), or pathetic fallacy, I ascribe to the worm. But such empathy "is not knowledge; it contains no theoretic content, *nothing that can be expressed*. It is an act (*Tun*), not a cognition, an act which puts a feeling in the place of a cognition, and can thus lead to a different mode of outward behavior."[7] The same explanation must, in accordance with this theory of meaning, be applied in all similar cases. Certain forms of expression, though they mean nothing, happen, mysteriously, to give rise to certain affective states; if a mother sees her child in tears, and thereupon *says* it is suffering pain or grief, *she* suffers, and consequently seeks to remove what she calls the cause of the child's distress; but she cannot be supposed to *think* that the child is suffering, since no one can really think anything expressed by a phrase without sense. A very great part, and, emotionally and practically, the most potent part, of human speech, therefore, is by this theory, expressly declared to consist of meaningless propositions. The most obvious reply to this is, of course, that the emotional efficacy of these propositions should, and would, disappear when and in so far as they were *recognized* to be meaningless. If I were a solipsist, and were therefore persuaded that a worm cannot intelligibly be said to have any feelings, I should assuredly not put myself to any inconvenience to avoid treading on it; nor would appeals for funds to relieve the hungry ever arouse in me any sympathy for those insensible automata.

The solipsistic consequence has similarly been drawn by Ludwig Wittgenstein:

[7] *Ibid.,* p. 40.

What we cannot think we cannot think; we cannot therefore *say* what we cannot think. This remark provides a key to the question, to what extent solipsism is a truth. The fact is that what solipsism *means* is quite correct, only it cannot be *said*, but shows itself. That the world is *my* world, shows itself in the fact that the limits of the language (the language which only I understand) mean the limits of *my* world . . . I am my world.[8]

The reason why solipsism cannot be "said," it will be observed, is that it cannot be thought. Since it cannot be thought, the proposition which it denies is meaningless. Nevertheless what it asserts is admitted somehow to have a meaning; and what it means is true.

The conclusion of this argument seems to most men too absurd to deserve discussion; nevertheless it is based on an argument which has been advanced by serious philosophers. I shall, therefore, take the argument seriously, and proceed to point out, not the absurdities in the conclusion, but the principal fallacy in the reasoning by which it is reached. The fallacy once more consists in confusing the two criteria of meaning. The conclusion asserted is the factual proposition that the existence of *das Fremdpsychische* is unthinkable, that a proposition referring to consciousnesses other than one's own "has no theoretic content." This could be established only as a consequence of the first criterion. But by that criterion the conclusion is simply untrue. Anyone who can count up to two can think of a perceiving or a thinking not his own. He observes his own behavior, he finds that *Erlebnisse* accompany it. Even by the positivist the two ideas are admitted to be distinct. They are therefore separable. It is, therefore, as possible to think of conscious experience as concomitant with another's observable behavior as to think of it as concomitant with one's own. In the first sense of meaning, therefore, propositions about my neighbor's sensations, opinions, feelings, and emotions are meaningful. The argument designed to show that they are not

---

[8] *Tractatus Logico-Philosophicus*, London, 1922, pp. 150-51. Wittgenstein later adds an interpretation of the first personal pronoun in the solipsistic theorem which nominally reverses the whole signification of the doctrine and makes it, when "strictly carried out, coincide with pure realism." But this remarkable transformation-scene in fact renders the original thesis itself pointless, by making the word "my" meaningless.

derives its appearance of logicality from the application of the second criterion—that of empirical verifiability; but from this the conclusion drawn does not follow. The major premise of *that* argument is that I cannot have as my own experience what by definition is not my own experience—which is true and obvious; the minor is the definition: "sentences referring to that which is by me unexperienceable are meaningless"—which is only a statement about the neo-positivist's taste in terminology; and the only conclusion which follows is that in that terminology sentences referring to what is not my own experience are (oddly) called meaningless. They remain none the less thinkable. And if for the question whether they have meaning is substituted the quite different question whether they may legitimately be believed, in the absence of empirical verification, the answer to the latter is, as before, that they may be believed if there is no empirical evidence against them— as, of course, there cannot be—and if there is any important advantage in believing them. And the advantages in this case are so great that the neo-positivist himself manifestly finds it unavoidable to postulate their truth. He believes, for example, that there is such a thing as science; he identifies science with the empirically verifiable; but he constantly betrays the fact that he means by science the socially verifiable (which should, by his reasoning, be a term without meaning). This is amusingly shown in Carnap's supposed proof that propositions about other minds and their contents are meaningless. The reason given for this was that the two psychologists differed as to whether the subject before them was or was not conscious. But neither the hypothesis that there are (or might be) two psychologists, nor the question whether the organism they were considering is conscious, could have any "meaning," by the second criterion, since the hypothesis and the answer to the question could not by either, or any, psychologist be "empirically verified" in the sense required. The reason given for the conclusion, in short, presupposes the falsity of the conclusion.

Nevertheless, in deducing solipsism from the "verifiability" criterion of meaning the radical positivist (in this phase of his reasoning) has done a genuine service to philosophy. He has reminded us of the fact that the existence of other conscious beings never has been, and never can be, verified *as* a direct experience of his own. No man has, or can hope to attain, literally empirical evidence that he is not the sole observer of the spectacle of nature, that anyone else has ever performed an experiment, that his own existence is known to any other being, that his thoughts and feelings, hopes and fears, are objects of understanding and sympathy for any other consciousness. Though this is by no means a recondite, it is an often forgotten fact; and it is, for philosophy, an important one. Its importance, however, is as a *refutation* of the seemingly plausible general theory of meaning which radical-empiricist philosophers of various types have propounded. It shows that empirical verifiability, in any exact sense of the expression, has nothing whatever to do with the meaningfulness of propositions and need have nothing to do with their truth, since no science and no philosophy would be possible if it were accepted as the sole and universal criterion of meaning and of truth. The *reductio ad absurdum* of that general theory is the apparently unconscious but useful achievement of the phase of recent positivism which has here been reviewed. But on the original question of "the meaning of 'meaning'" it has contributed only confusion, made manifest by self-contradiction.

POSTULATES OF EMPIRICAL THOUGHT*

HENRY BRADFORD SMITH†

Department of Philosophy, University of Pennsylvania

IN THIS brief survey of a problem, which will appear to promise more than the performance achieves, the procedure will be unsystematic and provisional because the intention is rather to furnish an illustration of method than to suggest that the results obtained correspond to any complete or final working out of the problem itself. The writer has small confidence that the postulates here set down possess strict independence of one another, far less that they are sufficient to exclude the paradoxes of historical points of view, or that they could have found no better mode of expression. We assume only that there are cases in which philosophical systems lead seemingly to contradictory or otherwise untenable results. These may be presumed to depend upon presuppositions either explicitly set down or tacitly assumed. If it be allowed that these results are forced, the method we shall adopt proposes to remove them as possibilities by excluding the foundation on which they rest. A denial of this kind takes the form of a demand that such and such be granted in advance; that is, it takes the form of a postulate. Ideally, then, the postulates of empirical thought should be independent of one another and sufficient not only to furnish the general basis of a theory of experience, but to exclude whatever assumption would lead to conclusions that are ultimately untenable. This ideal or methodological aim will be illustrated, but not adequately defended, at this time. The central question to be raised will concern only the truth of the postulates themselves. We begin, then, by stating our first assumption:

* Reprinted from the *Journal of Philosophy*, Vol. XXV, No. 12, June 7, 1928. By permission of the Editor.

† Died Nov. 14, 1938. This article is included because of the long association of the author with Professor Singer, and his coöperation in the initial planning of this volume.

1. *There is nothing to be found in the meaning of experience that is not already contained in the meaning of
experiment.*

This postulate proposes that we gain at the outset what advantage we can for analysis by replacing a term whose connotation is vague by one whose meaning is more precise. If our
postulate is true our problem is much simplified and might be
simplified still more if we were to choose for the purposes of
our analysis to consider the simplest experiment in the laboratory list. But we mean, besides, that there is more than an
analogy between the process that we call experience and that
other process that we call experiment. We mean to assume the
essential identity of the two. That is, just as experiments
methodically devised contribute to our experiential knowledge
of the world, so, conversely, experience of whatever sort is experimental in all of its characters. Or, otherwise, if these terms
be ambiguous, in that they connote both the method and its
results, the methodical procedure of experience in general is
experimental, and, in particular, the data of sense are the results as of an experimental process.

So much might indeed be deemed self-evident were it not
for the consequences that follow from such a view. For while
it would be generally agreed that any experiment may in the
nature of the case be repeated by any trained observer, it would
not be equally agreed that what is experienced may be shared
by all. For the mystics recognize certain private insights into
the nature of things, intuitions that have no public character,
the knowledge that each one is supposed to have of those things
that lie deepest in his own heart, and other revelations besides.
Our postulate, then, by implication asserts that mystical experience like any other, if it be real, must be experimentally
observable, that is, accessible to the observation of all; they must
be devoid of any sense or meaning, if they cannot be so shared.

It will be understood, then, that when we speak of the *given*,
we may have in mind either the datum of experience or the
fact of experiment, for we have postulated that these two have
a kindred nature and are not different in kind. As a particular

case, however, and one of commonest reference, the datum refers to a single character of the object given in experience. We mean quite literally that the apparatus of sense, physiologically considered, is more than analogous to the instruments employed in the laboratory. We mean that it is itself an instrument and is employed in essentially the same way, in the business of ordering and comparing data. The instruments of the laboratory are a part of the observer himself, the incarnation of his very soul, an elaboration or prolongation of devices already established in the apparatus of the organs of sense. Conversely, then, we might expect to gain some further insight into the physiological nature of man through a study of his instruments and tools. And, similarly, some understanding of his conscious and unconscious habits of perception by analyzing his methods of experience and experimental technique.

2. *There is nothing given in experience that has not been already related to experience in advance.*

This is not to imply that the datum may not become altered within the context of experience, or, by analogy, that the outcome of experiment can be determined in advance by analysis of the conditions that enter into the experiment itself. The datum, instead of being taken for what it is as given, is only the starting point of analysis, or of further experimentation, or of both. Further experimentation reveals it as something other than it was. On analysis it dissolves into its relationships. Thus, if it be a length that is observed, and the experiment be properly contrived, our data, this time our scale readings, will differ *inter se*. On analysis the length turns out to be nothing in itself, but always a *comparison* of lengths, the number of times the scale unit goes into the length observed. Or, to generalize, *every datum is a comparison of data*. The color red, as given in sensation, is only a comparison of data that have a like character, but which differ *inter se*, and beyond this it is nothing. What we do is to represent to ourselves any invariable condition by which we will experience some complex given as an objective property of the datum.

From all this it follows, of course, that there is no original datum, *no first sensation*, as our empirical-minded philosophers of the past have too often and too precipitately assumed. There was a time when this child who has but recently come to "the shores of light," there was a time we will be told, when this child was more like a bare possibility than an existing thing. In brief, there was a time when he was not. He now finds himself in the possession of certain data of sense, which others about him call, and which he will one day learn to call, his sensations. Ergo, there must have been an original datum, a first sensation.

But I wonder if the conclusion is forced, compelling as it has often seemed to that hard-headed empirical-minded past, to the psychology that traces its ancestry along the same long line of descent. Put the argument in somewhat different terms and see if our assent would be so readily given. If I say, more generally, a process that once was not, and now is, must have known a time when it first began, I only put the matter in more abstract terms. Any logician will agree with me, if I stop to point out that in order to invalidate a general case it will be enough to point to a special instance of its being untrue. I come downstairs of a Sunday morning, rather late as is my habit to do, and find that the family clock has run down. Rewound and the pendulum again in motion, the hands are soon judged to be moving over the face of the dial. There was a time, we may suppose, when they were *not* in motion, and they are in motion now. It follows, does it not, that there must have been a moment when they were in motion *for the first time?* No, it follows not. And because there never was such a moment, such a moment can never be pointed out. There are series that have no end and may have no beginning, and there may be a *before* where none of its terms are found, an *after* in which one may search for its terms in vain.

There is nothing, then, that is hard to grasp in the notion of a series of sensations that once were not, but which began at no set time, and the motives for conceiving the matter so, must now be clear enough. You can not build your experience of a world from data "immediately given" in analogy to the manner in which a child builds his castle from his pile of wooden blocks. The matter is not so simple as that. Is this surprising? What surprises us most, sometimes, is the way in which a logical simplification can often radically change for us the face of things.

3. *A judgment of fact that can receive no experimental confirmation is neither true nor false, because it is meaningless.*

This in essence was Kant's key to the solution of the antinomies of the reason. What he said, in effect, was that judgments involving terms that can never become the objects of a possible experience are illusory. The law of excluded middle is not applicable to the case of judgments about infinite wholes (cf. Brouwer). Such an illegitimate totality, for example, would be the concept of the world-whole, for the idea of such a totality is not even a limiting case.

It has been said there are relations which will always be found in experience, that analysis will always reveal, because they have been put there in advance. Such might be the relation of the "material" points that we find by experiment to lie on a line. Any point that is observed has its position in the number series, and if we imagine a material point to be somehow dropped at random on the line—for example, rolled down a rough inclined plane and allowed to skip about until it comes to rest on the base—and then its position observed, it must be assumed to occupy some position in a series of positions mathematically defined. This is what our postulate requires. Otherwise, the position of the point in question could not be observed because it would stand in no known, in no knowable, relation to the other points on the line. Or, more concretely, what we assert is that there exist no points on a line until they are ordered on that line, and because they can be ordered in different infinite series, we say that the number of points on a line is infinite.

The essence of the continuum was described by Anaxagoras in these words: "In the small there is always a smaller but never a smallest, for what is cannot cease to be by being

divided." The difficulty centers on the question whether the
infinite divisibility of the line implies the existence of an aggregate of infinitely small parts. Many thinkers there have been
who have sharply denied this. Euler says: "In spite of the fact
that bodies are infinitely divisible, yet the proposition that
every body is composed of an infinite number of parts, is absolutely false and actually stands in open contradiction to the
assumption of infinite divisibility." And Leibnitz in his correspondence remarks:

Let us assume that in the line there actually exists (every) division denoted (by the terms of an infinite series), then you conclude
that there is also an infinitesimal number; in my opinion it only
follows that there exists a small arbitrary length of any finite arbitrary size. The totality of all numbers [he continues], contains a
contradiction when one views this totality as a single whole.

These quotations we have taken from a recent work by Weyl.
The author himself puts the issue in the following way:

Der Sprung ins Jenseits will complete itself when the infinite,
law-determined, and still open series of numbers shall have been
made a closed totality of objects existing in themselves. The belief
in the absolute is planted deeply in our breasts. Small wonder if
the mathematician in all naïveté took the jump. *Das Zahlsystem ist
ihm ein Reich absoluter Existenzen geworden, das 'nicht von dieser
Welt ist' und von welchem nur tropfenweise ein Abglanz in unser
schauendes Bewusstsein faellt.*

A number is a place in the continuum, determined not by
an aggregate, but by its position in a defined series. The continuum is not an aggregate of existing elements, infinite in
number, but the medium of a free construction. Or, more
guardedly, if you like: because the points on a line can be ordered in different infinite series, it does not follow (it is at least
disputed) that an infinite totality of points or of parts exists.
For a certain kind of realism this infinite totality may be supposed to exist in independence of the observer and on such a
view it may well seem that the flying arrow can never pass
from point to point. It is just to avoid such paradoxes that our
postulate was introduced. The infinite exists not in being but

in becoming, that is δυνάμει, not ἐνεργείᾳ, for we have denied the existence of that which cannot in principle be observed.

4. *The existence of conflicting data points not to an absolute object, but to an observing mind.*

If each datum is a comparison of data which are presumed to have some character in common, but which differ *inter se*, we might be tempted to assume that the common character is contained among the presuppositions which the observer himself brings to his experiment and that the variations represent the unpredictable, that the one is a priori and the other a posteriori. Whether this condition would hold of the common character or not, it seems at least certain that the variations cannot be foretold in advance of experience, that they are independent of the rules of experimental procedure which brings them to light. If this be the case, then, it is clear that any method devised for resolving these differences into a unity will obtain a result as accidental as the constituents that make it up. The real datum cannot, then, be regarded as the limit of a series of approximations. What the existence of conflicting data points to is the being of an observing mind.

Moreover, it is clear that when we have spoken of minds, we have not prejudged the question as to whether these minds are individual minds or not. If two or more observers are in the private possession of data that by common presumption refer to the same object, but which differ among themselves, it may be that we are then dealing with a group-mind. Whether these data do actually refer to the same object or not is a matter of relative probability and one for experiment to decide.

THE DEVELOPMENT OF THE EXPERIMENTAL METHOD

Haym Jaffe

Penn Treaty Junior High School, Philadelphia

To puzzle out the riddles of Nature, we turn to Nature and ask the questions for which answers are wanted. Some of these are broad and general, as, for example, "What is the meaning of life?" Other questions are narrower and more specific, for example, "What is the melting point of tin?" We follow a definite procedure in asking a question: we order our experiences in such a fashion that they are exposed to an arrangement of certain natural elements. Then, like spiritualistic mediums, our voices utter and we write down the answer; not ours, indeed, but Nature's.

The answer to the question of the meaning of life involves a considerable quantity and every variety of experiences and experiencing. No matter how carefully we proceed in our questioning our "true" answer might, nevertheless, not seem so true to a fellow investigator with his differing experiences. Nature appears to explain "life" differently to him. We surmise that the complexity of experiences encountered, the ambiguous meanings of all human words, and the vague assumptions underlying their expressions are reasons for the varieties of replies. Added to these perplexities is the immensity of the problem of life. There is, therefore, little wonder that to many, all answers given and perhaps all possible answers that might ever be offered, will always prove to be unsatisfactory. The proffered solutions for the query of the meaning of life lie within the circle of interest of those investigators we call philosophers.

The narrower question is asked by the scientist. He recognizes it as one of a family of questions. The answers to these questions were at one time within the province of wise men who had accumulated much learning, or of travelers who had added the experiences of others to their own. Aristotle, by way of illustration, combined the quality of observing hard facts with a love of finding the abstract principles of their classification and arrangement. Hence he wrote the standard textbooks for the ancient and the medieval world. Furthermore, the travelers' lore was added to the storehouse of facts of an Aristotle or a Philostratus.

How true and how enlightening are the theories and experiences of these sages? Ptolemy owes an acknowledged debt to the data of Aristarchus and, even more so for his own cosmic theory, to the reckonings of Hipparchus. But was his discarding of the heliocentric theory in favor of a geocentric one the answer he obtained from mute Nature? There was nothing in the astronomical data added since Hipparchus' findings to force Ptolemy's rejection of the earlier theory. With triumphant hindsight, we point out that the arguments Ptolemy advances for the geocentric theory are extraneous to his data. We understand and appreciate the argument for the hypothesis of a fixed earth, since Ptolemy was misled by the data of the senses in dismissing a conjectured motion of the earth which, although not felt through the senses, yet simplifies the entire cosmic theory. We can also see how he would naturally assume the earth to be far larger than any of the heavenly bodies although scientific caution should have prevented him from doing this.

Nevertheless, why have the gods singled out the circle as the path of heavenly bodies? As does Ptolemy after him, Aristotle shows us by his discussion of the perfection of the circle in *Physics*,[1] the classical preference for a priori reasoning rather than for direct observations. Since the motion of any heavenly body is continuous, Aristotle reasons, its path must be circular. Since heavenly bodies have uniform velocities, Aristotle continues, the orbits must take the shape of that primary and perfect figure, the circle! This unsatisfactory method of deducing Nature's secrets is inherent in Aristotle's conception of science. In the *Posterior Analytics* we read:

[1] Book VIII.

Knowledge or Science and its Object differ from Opinion and its Object. Knowledge is commensurate, and rests on necessary grounds. Contingent truths cannot be objects of knowledge, else they would both be necessary and non-necessary: nor can they be objects of Reason, for Reason is the beginner of Science; nor of indemonstrative science, for this is the apprehension of immediate propositions: and as all apprehension of truth is either Reason, Science, or Opinion, it follows that Contingent Truths are the object of Opinion. This is confirmed by phenomena: the truth of Opinion is precarious: this is explained, if its object is the mutable. When a man regards a fact as necessary, he regards himself as possessed of Knowledge, not of Opinion: when he regards it as actual but contingent, he regards himself as possessed of Opinion, not of Knowledge: confirming our position, that the contingent is the object of Opinion, the necessary of Knowledge. . . . Knowledge and Opinion of the same fact cannot coexist in the same mind: for we cannot believe one and the same truth to be both contingent and necessary.[2]

For the ancients, the formulation of the physical theories of the universe was based on some series of Experiencing. The results of their Experiencings were classified according to some rational principle, and the whole scheme seemed to them a tight scientific system. A priori deductive reasoning and classification are the distinguishing techniques of the Greek scientific quest.

The ancient philosophers never had and perhaps never thought of laboratories. This was certainly true throughout the Dark Ages. "Dans les idées d'alors, la science et l'expérimentation étaient choses distinctes, presque opposées. L'idée de laboratoire était associée à celles de magie, de superstition, de charlatanisme."[3]

How much better are we faring in the experiments we make? Much has happened since the days of Aristotle and Ptolemy to our mode of questioning and to the answers we elicit from Nature. In the gropings of early Renaissance science, we can see the mixture of shrewd observation, curious superstitions, and naive travelers' tales. Although a chronicle of the advance of thought would show a grand array of men of talent, there was

[2] Chap. 33.
[3] M. Egger, "Science Ancienne et Moderne," *Revue de l'enseignment*, 1890.

nevertheless sufficient in all to stamp them as of the medieval mental-cast. Difficult as the early experimenters, the chemist-alchemist and the barber-surgeon, felt their tasks in distinguishing their truths from the tradition of the school to be, even harder was the goal of the scientist-philosopher. His plan was to organize the newly acquired knowledge so that it would be couched in the new mathematical language and would exhibit the new spirit.

It was not the neglect of fact as fact, nor was it that the fact's value was held in too low estimation for philosophical speculation: rather it was the lack of induction, with its fruitful method of classification, that prevented the growth of ancient science. Even Galileo, founder of the Experimental Sciences of today, relied mainly upon Deductive Reason. Experiment was secondary and subsequent to the careful logical thread found in the *Dialogues of the Two New Sciences*. An appeal to experiment was made only to confirm the results of his syllogistic conclusions. We make much today of Galileo's experiment of dropping various weights from the Tower of Pisa. Yet this was done primarily to confound those skeptical of his logic. And these skeptics were many. When he cautiously used the inductive method,

Vicenzio di Grazia objected to a proof from induction, which Galileo adduced, because *all* the particulars were not enumerated; to which the latter justly replies, that if induction were required to pass through all the cases, it would be either useless or impossible; impossible when the cases are innumerable; useless when they have each already been verified, since then the general proposition adds nothing to our knowledge.[4]

Nevertheless, Experiment in the modern sense of the word was already born and Galileo was truly its father. Contrast his scientific attitude with that of Aristotle. The Greek saw a downward tendency in a stone. A falling body seeks its resting place. For Aristotle motion, even mechanical motion, needed something like a life-force to push it at every instant along its path. The doctrine for almost two thousand years was this,

4 Whewell, *Philosophy of Discovery*, p. 118.

that "the moving body comes to a standstill when the force which pushes it along can no longer so act as to push it."

Galileo exorcised this animal spirit lurking in every mechanical motion. In his *Dialogues* he clearly proclaims:

. . . any velocity once imparted to a moving body will be rigidly maintained as long as the external causes of acceleration or retardation are removed, a condition which is found only on horizontal planes; for in the case of planes which slope downwards there is already present a cause of acceleration; while on planes sloping upward there is retardation; from this it follows that motion along a horizontal plane is perpetual; for, if the velocity be uniform, it cannot be diminished or slackened, much less destroyed.[5]

Measurement and observation were ready tools for his mechanical genius. His invention of the telescope, for instance, meant that the old theories could not contain the new observations. In this vibrant century, the discovery of the microscope relegated to a purely academic realm, with little meaning to the new world of Leeuwenhoek, the old arguments whether the infinitely small is ultimately a plenum or a void. This was the age when general experience gave way to specific experiment. Galileo showed how to resolve forces into their components. He was then able to focus attention upon isolated forces. His study of falling bodies not only convinced him that speed is a property of the inertia of a moving object, but also clarified his notion of acceleration. After this, it was a comparatively easy step to isolate an intended experiment from its surroundings and to simplify the conditions under which it was observed. As a consequence, the modern experiment was made possible. From such beginnings grew Blaise Pascal's experiments with atmospheric pressure and Robert Boyle's discoveries in physics.

A great deal of theoretical work was still required. René Descartes, in his first writings, *Regulae Ad Directionem Ingenii*, planned a method based upon the mathematical discoveries he had made. If one follow his prescription, he claimed, the principles of our complex universe can readily be found. The sciences should consider only those questions

[5] *Dialogue* III, Prop. XXIII, Scholium.

which can be stated in terms of number and measure. All problems of physics should be translated into those of quantitative mathematics. Neither first causes nor final causes are objects for scientific research. The sciences, instead of debating endlessly the "inherent qualities" in nature, should consider only the basic concepts: extension and magnitude.

Contrast this with the physics which Descartes studied in La Flèche. The Aristotelian "substantial forms" had almost become "occult qualities" with mysterious powers. Spirits seemed to lurk behind every motion in the physical universe. Natural phenomena were glibly explained away by the parading of a name or by some artificial classification. Molière's explanation of "virtus dormitiva" was a satire on current scientific definitions.

Descartes' writings follow a usual pattern of starting with simple propositions and stressing clear ideas. Therefore, some critics have hastily assumed that Descartes intended to write the *Regulae* as a well-defined philosophical system similar to his later *Meditations*, since both discuss our complex universe. A distinction must be made, however, between the method described in the *Regulae* and the exposition of the principles and truths in the philosophical system of the *Meditations*.

His mathematical discoveries had convinced Descartes that cosmic phenomena have simple relations between them analogous to the terms of an equation or to the lines in a geometric figure. The plan of procedure in the *Regulae* is to reduce all phenomena to laws of extension or to those of movement, to geometry or to mechanics. For instance, "What is the nature of the magnet?" is a meaningless question. This and every question must be couched in terms of measure and order. Measure relates all magnitudes into one unity, making it possible to compare phenomena and deduce universal laws. When one observes the first few terms in a mathematical progression, the other terms can be found. In like manner, order shows us how objects in nature are related to one another.

The nature of matter or of bodies in general, Descartes contended, is not found in the qualities of hardness or weight or color or in other sensible qualities, but only in that it is an extended substance. All properties of matter are only modifications of extension, and depend on the movement of its parts.

The *Regulae* leads to the experimental method, but because of Descartes' belief that all certitude can be deduced from first principles by the mind, it falls short of the modern experiment. Experience, for Descartes as for Aristotle, is a great help, indispensable in studying nature. Nevertheless, certitude does not proceed from experience, which yields "probable knowledge," but from reason, which gives us our truths. The "probable knowledge" with which Descartes was acquainted was that of indifferently verified opinions, and not the "probable knowledge" of today's science. His distrust of the common science of his day helped to develop in him the conviction that the way to truth must begin with doubting all things. Nevertheless, Descartes made a vastly important contribution to the development of the modern experiment when he replaced the current qualitative with his quantitative interpretation for all scientific descriptions of natural phenomena.

The development of the new science, with its astonishing discoveries, was welcomed by Francis Bacon. Although he stood apart from the actual work of experimenters and despite his lack of understanding of the importance of mathematics for science, he did clearly see that the new science needed a new logic. He insisted that from his accumulated facts his inductive logic could draw successive laws of greater and greater generality. The foes of induction do not understand its scheme when they represent it as attempting to draw the highest generalizations from a handful of special facts. Experimental science, such as the centuries following Bacon have developed, has closely followed the plan Francis Bacon traced and the procedure he recommended.

Gradually the experimental method was becoming more definite, both as to induction and to the resulting hypotheses. Even the champion of innate ideas, Leibniz, understood the character of an experimental hypothesis. In a letter to Conring, March 19, 1678, he wrote:

Une hypothèse est d'autant plus probable: 1) qu'elle est plus simple, 2) qu'elle explique un plus grand nombre de phénomènes par un plus petit nombre de postulats, 3) qu'elle permet de prévoir de nouveaux phénomènes ou d'expliquer de nouvelles expériences. Dans ce dernier cas surtout, l'hypothèse équivaudra à la verité, elle aura une certitude "physique" ou "morale," c'est-à-dire une extrême probabilité, comme est celle d'une clef presumée qui permet de déchiffrer entièrement un long cryptogramme en lui donnant un sens intelligible et suivi.

The title and description of a posthumous work of Robert Hooke may also be quoted as illustrative of the new spirit: *A general scheme or Idea of the present state of Natural Philosophy, and how its defects may be remedied by a methodical proceeding in making experiments and collecting observations, whereby to compile a natural history as the solid basis for the superstructure of true philosophy.*

During the ensuing years, many of the wonders of nature were discovered. The laboratory technique was yielding success. This technique was gradually being refined and it imperceptibly grew into a formula for success: the experiment must be isolated from the rest of the universe; the given must be explicitly stated and its limits for the experiment must be defined; the apparatus to be used, with an analysis of its influence on the results, should be written down; one must be able to state the purpose of the experiment as simply as possible; the observations and readings are to be stated in quantitative terms; and the conclusions are to be based solely upon the data, the probable errors of the observations, and upon the confining limits of the experimental range. On the basis of some fundamental observations, some postulates, and a series of theorems and consequences, systems such as Galileo's *Dialogues*, Newton's *Principia*, and Hertz's *Principles of Mechanics* have been erected, each as far-reaching and as astonishing as the geometry of Euclid.

Meanwhile, the underlying assumptions concerning the nature of the universe were being critically studied by such philosophers as Locke, Berkeley, and Hume. The solid facts of Substance and its Qualities, Cause and Effect, and Continuity became elusive, and began fading away. This analysis was crowned by the writings of Immanuel Kant. He asked: How is knowledge possible? He thought that he had written all the terms of the answer. The complete answer is, however, still for the future. Nevertheless, Kant did point out how we do bring our mental cast to Nature and that Nature's answers are couched in the form that our brains comprehend. For instance, we recognize the three-dimensional Euclidean space in which all material objects are contained because our minds clothe all objects in that form.

From such reflections, it follows that the experiment cannot be completely isolated from the mind of the experimenter. Kant's assumptions were phrased, however, both in terms of the science of his times and of its limitations. For instance, he assumes the completeness and the correctness of Aristotle's deductive logic. Francis Bacon had justly remarked that the deductive logic may be a vehicle for truth but that often we have isolated instances in nature which must be gathered into Universals, before the Aristotelian syllogism operates. The history of the experimental method shows many such instances.

Certainly there is no reason why one need agree with Kant that the Ancient Logic is the necessary and fundamental one for our experiences. The new symbolic logics are not curious intellectual exercises with no application in the world of experimental science. All logical systems have their interconnections. A series of glossaries between them can be set up, or else a vast portion of reasoning exists, unintelligible unless expressed in a particular logical system. On re-reading Kant and keeping in mind what we have learned since his day, we must modify his argument. Our minds do bring logic to the observation of phenomena but that logic need not necessarily be Aristotle's.

By the time of Newton, the advantages of the experimental method for the physical sciences were readily acknowledged, and the postulates of Isaac Newton were unhesitatingly used by Immanuel Kant. Newton assumed three-dimensional Euclidean space. Kant asserted that our minds comprehend natural phenomena through three-dimensional Euclidean space.

In his *Principia*, Newton introduces Absolute Time, a notion derived from common experience but never from experimentation. Absolute Time, instead of a coördinate, local time, was unguardedly subscribed to by Kant as fundamental for any experiment whatsoever. Not until Einstein analyzed the notion of simultaneity in his paper of 1905 on *Restricted Relativity* did the mysticism of Newton's Universal Time become glaringly apparent. We cannot know of an instant of time being experienced in some mysterious way throughout the entire universe. Yet the theoretical scientist forgot his methodology in talking about time, until Einstein awoke him to this fact.

Since three-dimensional Euclidean space is confirmed by our daily doings, who would have dreamed that the various non-Euclidean geometries would ever enter the domain of the practical physicist? Yet when Einstein found it necessary to replace our familiar geometry and the Absolute Time coördinate with a four-dimensional non-Euclidean space-time geometry, the effect has been to re-examine the physical nature of space and of time. Problems dormant for centuries again became vital. Is the universe an open or a closed one? Is Aristotle or Bruno right? What reasons are there, and how good are they, for assuming that there is Continuity in space? Large-scale phenomena in the universe demand such continuity but laboratory experiments in the electron-world deny it! In what way does the presence or absence of matter, the electrical and gravitational forces, and the various stresses and strains in this world of ours, modify our space-time continuum? The structures of the mechanical models for our universe have been undergoing extensive revision. Hence, a dogmatic attitude with reference to a priori postulates for any experiment whatsoever is not sound doctrine.

The experimenter is now more conscious than ever before of factors that persist in influencing his isolated experiment. Error, for instance, in a series of readings is now valued at its true significance. Error is of a variety of types and each type has meaning for the experimenter.

The Quantum Theory has introduced us to "h," whose very definition depends upon the assumption of error. When the scientist has gone beyond the threshold of observation, and has tried to impose his daily experience upon particles tinier than the wave length of light, the Heisenberg Uncertainty Principle warns us as we approach the lower limit of observation that our apparatus and we, the observers, interfere with the motions and behavior of the ultimate particles. A cautious experimenter can find nothing in this principle, which prescribes a limit for observations when using certain methods, to warrant him in deducing an ethical application. Eddington, like Lucretius of old, goes beyond the range of experiment to draw conclusions such as free will in man from the errant particles.

There is another type of error inherent in all experiments. The experimental method means that you, the experimenter, write a complete description of what you are doing, so that anyone else might repeat your procedure—to verify your work. But in the repetition of your experiment, whether you or someone else undertake it, the data obtained may vary in the last decimal place. There is a "variable error" and no series of experiments is conceivable in which the variable error can be reduced to zero. What does that seemingly insignificant fact mean? So far, it has meant the difference between the science of the ancients and that of today. Just as our "Laws of Nature" are determined by the data of our observations, so the variable errors have given us the choice of an infinite number of laws. For how can there be a unique mathematical curve when the condition is that this curve may be drawn somewhere within a broad region between $t+e$ and $t-e$, where e is a finite constant? We have an infinity of mathematical curves from which to choose. Usually, we take the one mathematically simplest and forget the existence of the others.

The observer first collects readings [writes Professor Singer]. Of these he obtains a mean and mean variation, such that if he plotted his finds, each set of readings would yield him not a point but a region (of dimensions depending on the nature of his problem); the fact would be an infinitely remote ideal, which we might think of as that dream of a mathematical point toward which the region shall shrink as with progress the experimental error is diminished. Through such regions the scientist may draw an infinity of curves; he does draw but one, and nothing in all his observation determines which one he shall choose. In the sense in which a choice once exercised is commonly said to have been determined, this choice must have been determined; namely, *by a motive*. It may be that part of the definition of exact science will lie in the motives which ought to determine its choices; but it is vain to propose that observation alone shall eliminate all need of choice.[6]

Instead of holding the old belief that once you get your data, you deduce *the* universal principle, experimenters are now more cautious. Data might be arranged in innumerable ways and not all are of equal weight. Newton, for instance, felt that there are more ways than one to express "Nature's Laws." In the third book of the *Optics*, Question XXXIII, he writes: "By what efficient cause these attractions be effected, I ask not. What I call attraction, may well enough be brought about by impacts, or in some other way unknown to us."

Whether due to faulty perception, or to an error of judgment, or to a lively imagination, or even to some conceptual opacity, the user of any experimental method errs. Yet with the progress of scientific knowledge we have narrowed to within the variable error the range of error which is due to mal-observation. If we obtain a larger error, we are at once aware of a grave fault in our reasoning.

Let us now consider another aspect of the experimenter's technique. He *interpolates* and *extrapolates* constantly as he works. How legitimate are these processes? The reply that the scientist makes is significant. We might phrase it somewhat as follows: "What do I mean by interpolation, you ask? Well, there are countless points of observation. No human being can possibly gather all the data. Provided the readings are arranged in some order, and I can conjecture that any intermediate value lies between the limits of error, it is not necessary for me to set down the value at every point."

The scientist's statement seems reasonable enough when he draws his continuous curve and explicitly assumes that within the domain of his observations each region is analytic. Even in the Quantum Theory, interpolation is used in the arrangement of the data. The continuity or discontinuity of the ultimate

[6] "Experience and Reflection" (in manuscript).

motions of quanta is a totally different problem. Only confusion results when the two problems are treated as one.

Not only is the experiment assumed to be valid within the range of the data but, for the results of the experiment to have utility, we extrapolate. That is, the meaning of the experiment is assumed to be valid beyond the range of the actual data. The extension takes place at both ends of the range, below the lower limit, and beyond the upper limit, of actual observation.

Forces from beyond the upper limit of observation have brought new concepts to the scientist. Speeds within the ordinary range of experience hardly prepared the experimenter to expect the Fitzgerald Contraction for the staggering speeds actually in nature nor for the construction of the new world models upon non-Euclidean geometries. How can we be certain that our experiments have validity beyond the upper range of observation? Examples from the history of science show how easy it is to err in reasoning from the known to the unknown. Nevertheless the sweep of the region beyond the range of observation is needed in constructing any mechanical model of nature.

Similarly, from below the lower threshold of observation come the answers to the questions of continuity and discontinuity, of the effects of electrical forces, of gravitation, of the repulsion of particles, of our geometrical space perhaps distorted by the presence of such high velocities. These and many other problems that our ordinary experience ignores, now loom large.

The validity of experimentation rests upon measurement and measurement rests upon our number system. The concept of number has grown beyond that understood by Aristotle or by Ptolemy. Despite the protests of many to the numbers the Greeks used, the incommensurable was added. Then, in the course of centuries the validity of negative numbers was questioned. The complex numbers are fairly recent arrivals. The experimenter today, however, uses unhesitatingly all and every type of number in his calculation, ranging from simple fractions to transcendental and complex numbers. The pleasant story told of Sir William Hamilton that when he discovered quaternions he remarked, "Thank God, they are useless," can be repeated of practically all branches of mathematics; and in all cases, the physicist has been finding mundane uses for them in his cosmic theories.

We have seen then that our experimenter's brain sees the world through the forms Kant described. These forms, however, must not be dogmatically expressed in the language of the restricted and limited sciences that Kant knew. This means that the geometry is to be the most general, the logic the broadest, the coördinate time must be considered solely on the basis of empirical findings, and the measuring system must be as wide as all of mathematics.

Physical experiments can never give us the *ding an sich*. They do permit, however, an approach to the limiting case of the phenomena, even if the final decimal in any reading has not been and cannot be reached. Hence the results of observations yield probability, not certainty. Nevertheless, for most uses this probability plays as important a role as if it were certainty itself.

In each generation, builders of cosmic systems have been able to take the same data and build theories completely different. The theory may depend for its characteristic uniqueness, as in Schelling's theory of polarity or as in any type of Monism, upon a particularly striking emphasis that a set of observations has for the philosopher. There was an obvious demonstration for Leibniz's entelechies as he peered through the microscope and saw the newly discovered animalcules. Similarly, the mechanical forces, the forces of gravitation and of electricity, of light waves, of light rays—these dynamic agents are the units which the scientist uses to build his world-image. Within the restricted field of the experiment, there are often coincident or parallel theories. Idealism and Realism have no practical differences within the laboratory of physics, even if they differ in their psychologies.

Constant analysis has made the scientist alert both to what he presupposes when he uses the experimental method and to the limits of his conclusions. His greatest danger of error in the past has been, and is most likely to be in the future, in the unhesitating acceptance of the "climate of opinion" of his time. The terminology and the scientific slang of his age contain within themselves the seeds of error. This fact makes it of utmost importance that any expression of an experiment be translatable into an empirical "logical language."

We have seen that the notion of an Experiment, with its definite limited measurable objective, was foreign to the minds of the ancients. To them Experience had a qualitative ring and classification was the procedure of their science. With the growth of Renaissance science, however, the present day idea of an experiment began with emphasis on quantitative measurement and with the further insistence that the experiment be isolated from the rest of experience. Kant pointed out that the scientist brings to every experiment certain presuppositions: space and time dimensions, the number system, and a logic. Subsequent history has shown that Kant too was caught in the climate of opinion of his day and that his concepts of space, time, logic, and even of mathematics, have to be extended and loosened from the limitations imposed by the thought of his times. The ideas of upper and lower limits are a subsequent development of placing the experiment on a quantitative basis. Many times, when physical theories that have been verified for the mean values are unwarrantedly extended beyond the limits of observations, errors arise. The scientist must therefore take into account the forces and new ideas that arise from phenomena from above the upper limit of observation and those from below the lower limit. These modify profoundly, and occasionally overthrow, the already accepted physical hypotheses.

The scientist has become conscious of the Experiment and he has refined it. It is now his surest instrument for proving the outside world.

TOWARDS A GENERAL LOGIC OF PROPOSITIONS

C. WEST CHURCHMAN

Department of Philosophy, University of Pennsylvania

LOGIC is the basic science in that it is presupposed by all sciences; an illogical science is no science at all. This truism may be used for the purpose of definition, for we may define (the general) logic as that science whose laws are applicable to all sciences. This preliminary definition leads to a bisection of the science of logic and a more accurate definition of the subject; for all sciences necessarily make use of terms or substantives, and all sciences make use of propositions. Hence logic must be separated into two divisions[1]: (1) the science which determines all statements about propositions which are true independently of the meanings or forms of these propositions (the so-called propositional calculus) and (2) the science which determines all statements about objects ("things," "nouns") which are true independently of what these objects may be (the substantive calculus). Thus the statement "p implies q," where p and q are propositions, is not a law of logic since its truth depends on what is meant by p and q, but the statement "p implies p" is true *independently of the meaning of p*. We are interested here in the calculus of propositions.[2]

It is to be noted that in defining logic in the above manner we have excluded a great deal which has often been regarded as a part of this science. Thus the most general logic has no regard for the form of the propositions in question; it is searching for statements about propositions which hold regardless of the form or content. Hence the calculus of propositional functions, which

---

[1] Into three, if we include the calculus of relations.

[2] The solution of the general problem outlined here is essentially that of H. B. Smith, though the present treatment goes beyond Smith's developments in several respects. That the philosophy of logic and the general method of solution are Smith's will be clear to anyone familiar with his "Abstract Logic," *Philosophy of Science*, vol. 1, pp. 369–97, and "The Algebra of Propositions," *Philosophy of Science*, vol. 3, pp. 551–78.

deals with propositions of the form "x is related to a" and asks such questions as whether "$\phi(x)$ is always true" implies "$\phi(x)$ is sometimes true," is not a part of this logic; it is a science which comes above logic in the scale of sciences, in that it presupposes logic but logic does not (apparently) presuppose it.

To elucidate better our present problem, let us suggest how a classification of the sciences might be made with respect to their order. Our simple calculus of propositions and calculus of classes would come first. Like the general calculus of propositions, the fundamental calculus of substantives would not specialize the meanings of its terms; thus, "all a is a" is true no matter what substantive a represents, be it a class or an individual. Between these two fundamental sciences and the most elementary science of mathematics, arithmetic, would come a great deal of what is ordinarily regarded as logic, the calculus of propositional functions, the calculus of classes and individuals, etc. Arithmetic is fundamental to all post-logical sciences, since these all presuppose the concept of number; on the other hand, of course, logic does not presuppose arithmetic, since presumably it does not make use of arithmetical terms or laws. Singer has actually worked out a scheme of the sciences along these lines. The plan necessarily becomes more complicated as we advance, and it often becomes convenient to divide into parts what has traditionally been accepted as one science, as we have already done in the case of logic, since a part of one science may presuppose another science, while another part of the former is presupposed by the latter.

From the above discussion, we may conclude that the terms of the science under consideration represent propositions in the most general sense, i.e., any meaningful statements of any science. What are the relations of the science? The following criterion seems to follow from our definition: the relations of the calculus of propositions must apply only to propositions, must not restrict the meaning or form of the propositions to which they are applied, and, finally, must be such that, when applied to any propositions whatsoever, the result is a proposition. Thus the relation "says" is not a relation of tne general logic of propositions, for in the expression "A says B," A cannot be a proposition; similarly, "is true for some values of its variables" would be excluded, since when this is applied to propositions without variables, the result is meaningless. The following are certainly relations of the calculus:

1. Conjunction   "*p* and *q* are both true"   *pq*
2. Disjunction   "*p* or *q* is true" $p + q$
3. Implication   "If *p*, then *q*" $p \angle q$
4. Negation   "*p* is false" p'
5. Equivalence   "*p* and *q* are equivalent" $p = q$

Whether this list be sufficient or not is much more difficult to determine and, indeed, cannot be determined rigorously. At any rate the list is certainly necessary and if new relations are added, the calculus will merely be extended, not altered.

Important in the general logic are the concepts of "asserted" propositions and their denials. Since our interest here lies in the construction of a logic which shall have application to all sciences, it seems reasonable to interpret the symbol "1" as any proposition of any formal or deductive science whatsoever that is an "asserted" truth, i.e., a definition, postulate, or theorem. "0" stands for any proposition which is the contradictory or contrary of some asserted truth of a given science. We speak here of "formal" truth, since logical laws may be applied to the postulates and theorems of any deductive science, regardless of whether they have been "verified" by some scientific method. In the system of general logic below we shall regard all such truth-assertions as equivalent, whether they be postulates or theorems in a deductive system of logic or a deductive system of sociology. This attitude towards such propositions, necessitated by the generality of the logic, will cause important differences between the formal system developed below and C. I. Lewis' System of Strict Implication. In this respect, the system is much closer to the two-valued logic of Russell and Whitehead's *Principia Mathematica* than Lewis'. It differs from the two-valued calculus, however, in distinguishing between implication ($p \angle q$) and the disjunction ($p' + q$). The philosophical reasons for insisting on this distinction in general have been explained in another paper.[3] We assume that these reasons are cogent and merely state the resulting char-

---

[3] "The General Problem of Logic," to appear in *Philosophy of Science*. The philosophical arguments have also been presented in many of H. B. Smith's articles.

acteristic, namely that the system of the general logic shares with Lewis' the property of being a non-truth-value system. A truth-value system of logic is any system whose laws are said to be verified *in general* if they are verified when their variables take on all permutations of a certain set of values; i.e., a truth-value system of logic is any system capable of being represented by "truth-tables."[4]

The distinguishing characteristic may be seen in the following manner. In the two-valued logic, an expression of the form $p \cdot \supset \cdot q \supset p$ ("*p* implies that *q* implies *p*") is simply a shorthand representation of a set of "concrete"[5] propositions: " 'Today is Monday' implies that '2 + 2 = 4' implies 'Today is Monday,' " " 'Caesar died' implies that 'Grass is green' implies 'Caesar died,' " etc. Hence, the expression is called "valid" or "universally true" if it becomes true for every concrete value of *p* and *q*. Since any concrete value of *p* has the value of 0 or 1, the truth of a given expression is tested by these substitutions. The present system, on the other hand, does not regard its expressions as representations of concrete propositions. The "meaning" of a given expression is not given by exhibiting (if that were possible) all concrete examples. This does not make the logic "intensional" in the usual sense of the term "intensional logic," since no attempt is made here to specialize the meanings of the variables. The necessity of so viewing the general logic arises from the necessity of avoiding the Theory of Types, which seems forced on all truth-value systems. The Theory of Types as applied to the propositional calculus would seem to deny any solution of the general problem we have proposed, since there could be no law which held for all possible propositions, the law itself being excluded as a value of the variables. The above manner of viewing expressions of the general logic enables us to solve the difficulties which the Theory of Types was constructed to solve, without the aid of this theory.

Because of the distinction between implication and disjunction, certain "modal functions" occur in the calculus. We cannot identify the implication ($p \angle 0$) with the simple negation p', for

[4] Cf. E. L. Post, "Introduction to the General Theory of Elementary Propositions," *Amer. Jour. of Math.*, vol. 43, pp. 163–85.

[5] Where "concrete" means that there are no real variables in *p* and *q*; if *p* is "All *a* is *b*," then it also represents a set of concrete propositions where *a* and *b* are definite nouns.

such an identification reduces the algebra to a two-valued calculus. There are, then, at least six distinct modes of assertion and denial, none of which can be equated to any of the others: p, p', $(p \angle \text{o})$, $(p \angle \text{o})'$, $(p' \angle \text{o})$, and $(p' \angle \text{o})'$. These do *not* represent the modes of "possibility" as expressed in the intensionalist logic. They are simply formal expressions resulting from the assumptions of the system. Their meaning will become clearer in the sequel. It will be convenient to use some sort of abbreviation for these modal functions and others which may arise. Smith used the very simple $|p|$ or $p|$ to represent $(p \angle \text{o})'$ ("p" does not vanish). Then $(p \angle \text{o})$ is $p|'$, etc. This symbolism is far more convenient than Lewis', and also will serve to distinguish the modal functions here from those of the System of Strict Implication, since the two are quite distinct in meaning. A modal function is said to be "affirmative" if it contains an even number of "primes" or negations; "negative" if it contains an odd number. Thus $p'|'|$ is affirmative; $p'|'|'$ is negative. More precisely, a function is affirmative if, when applied to a true proposition, the result is true; negative if, when applied to a true proposition, the result is false (cf. below).

Our problem is to determine all propositions involving the above five relations which are true independently of the meanings of the variables. We may restate the problem in the following, clearly equivalent, way: To determine all statements about propositions involving the above five relations that "vanish identically," i.e., that are false for all values.

Owing to certain complications that result, the general problem has not been solved completely. Our aim here is to give an exposition of the development as far as it has proceeded and to suggest certain ways in which the end might be reached.

First of all, a set of assumptions will be given which, while not complete, will provide us with a method for testing whether any given expression always vanishes. This method may be described as follows: Suppose that we are given some meaningful expression involving the five relations of logic. If the expression contains no "principle" implication-relation, i.e., is not of the form $p \angle q$, we merely deny the entire proposition, and by successive applications of De Morgan's Laws: $(pq)' = (p' + q')$ $(p + q)' = p'q'$, the Law of Double Negation, $p'' = p$, the commutative, associative, and distributive laws for multiplication and addition, $pq = qp$, $p + q = q + p$, $p(qr) = (pq)r$, $p + (q + r) = (p + q) + r$, $p(q + r) = pq + pr$, $p + qr = (p + q)(p + r)$, and the Law of Absorption, $pq + p = p$, we may determine whether the given expression "vanishes" by determining whether each product in the sum of products that results contains a contradiction, i.e., a term of the form pq, where $p \angle q'$ is true in the science. If the negative of the given expression vanishes, the expression is true in the science. If the expression is of the form $p \angle q$, then we determine by the above laws whether pq' vanishes or not. If $pq' = 0$, then $p \angle q$ is true. Our preliminary task will consist in constructing a set of assumptions, as "economic" as possible, which will enable us to apply this method to any given expression, i.e., a set of assumptions sufficient to prove all the laws mentioned above. We say "preliminary task," since other difficulties still remain to be solved.

All symbolic systems of logic require a so-called "non-formal" or "non-symbolic" basis that sets down the method of procedure. The present system differs from most in that, besides the usual Rules of Substitution and Inference, a few other non-formal rules are required that express the properties of "asserted" propositions. We cannot formalize the concept of an asserted proposition for reasons which will become apparent. Hence the rules governing the use of such propositions are partly non-formal. "p is asserted" may be abbreviated by Russell's $\vdash p$, but $\vdash p$ is not a formal symbol of the system, and means simply "p is a definition, postulate, or theorem." In other words, we consider the premise of some such expression as $\vdash p \cdot \angle \cdot p + q$ to be verified (asserted) if p is a definition, postulate, or theorem. In these non-formal rules expressing the properties of asserted statements, "if, then" may be expressed by the formal symbol for implication, " $\angle$ "; as is well known, the implication in the Rule of Inference cannot be stated in terms of the formal symbol for implication without involving an infinite number of symbols and rules.

Indefinables: p, q, r, etc.; p'; pq; $p + q$; $p \angle q$; $p = q$; 0; 1.[6]

[6] To avoid the ambiguities involved in using " = " as both a definitional-equivalence-sign and a sign of mutual implication, no definitions are made in this system, all statements that might appear to be definitions appearing as postulates The method is not required but seems philosophically "neater."

Non-formal Assumptions ($\vdash p$ is short for "p is asserted."):

1. If $\vdash p$ and $\vdash (p \angle q)$ or $\vdash (p = q)$, then $\vdash q$.

2. The variable elements p, q, r, etc., in any asserted expression may be replaced throughout by any "meaningful" expression and the result is still asserted. A "meaningful" expression is any expression appearing in the list of indefinables, or anything derived from this list by similar substitutions.[7]

3. If $\vdash (p = q)$, then any asserted statement containing p or q will still remain asserted if any instance of q is replaced by p or any instance of p is replaced by q.

4. $\vdash (p \angle q) \cdot \vdash (q \angle r) \cdot \angle \cdot \vdash (p \angle r)$

5a). $\vdash p \cdot \angle \cdot \vdash (p = 1)$

5b). $\vdash (p' = 1)' \cdot \angle \cdot \vdash p$

Formal Assumptions:

6. $(p + q) = (p'q')'$

7. $1 = 0'$

8. $(p \angle q) = (pq' = 0)$

9. $(p \angle q) = (pq = p)$

10. $pq = qp$

11. $p(qr) = (pq)r$

12. $(p = q) \cdot \angle \cdot (p \angle q) \; (q \angle p)$

13. $(p \angle q) \, (q \angle p) \cdot \angle \cdot (p = q)$

14. $p \angle p''$

15. $pp' = qq'$

16. $0 = pp'$

Abbreviation: $|p|$ is to be written for $(p \angle 0)'$.[8]

17. $p \angle |p|$, ("The Modal Law")

Space does not allow a detailed development of these fundamental assumptions. Suffice it to say that all the above-mentioned laws may be deduced. Some remarks concerning (5) and its consequences seem necessary. By means of this rule and the other assumptions, we can show (1) that all asserted propositions are equivalent, and (2) if p is asserted, then all affirmative modal

---

[7] The author is aware of H. B. Curry's work in making this rule more precise, but has avoided his formulizations since additional explanations would have been necessary.

[8] One might be inclined to assert that $p + q$ is an abbreviation for $(p'q')'$, but such an assertion would be misleading. Actually, conjunction and disjunction are quite distinct relations; e.g., the Law of Duality does not necessarily hold in the general logic.

functions of p: $p'|'$, $p'||'$, $p'|'$, etc. will be asserted, and conversely, if any affirmative modal function of p is asserted, then p (and hence all affirmative modal functions of p) will be asserted. In the System of Strict Implication neither of these assertions would seem to hold in general. There are many cases in such a system in which we cannot assert that a given proposition is necessary but we can assert that it is true. Thus "Wilson is not President of the United States" is true, but is not necessary, since its contradiction is not a logical absurdity. This illustration clearly indicates the difference in viewpoint between Lewis and Smith. In the general logic, laws are true independently of the meaning or content of the propositions which form their elements; hence we cannot distinguish between a proposition which is true for logic (a logical necessity) and a proposition which is true for some other science, for such a distinction demands a knowledge of the meaning or form of the propositions in question. Incidentally, it is not clear what is meant by saying that an asserted proposition is "true but not necessarily true" for, if to apply the adjective "true" to a proposition means that the proposition is a definition, postulate, or theorem in a deductive system, then the contradictory of a true proposition is always a logical absurdity.

Some justification, perhaps, is required for asserting that if any affirmative modal function of p is asserted, then all affirmative functions are asserted. For example, if $|p|$ or $(p \angle 0)'$ is asserted in any deductive system, then p must be asserted, for if $(p \angle 0)'$ is asserted, then p can never be false or else we would have $(0 \angle 0)'$, or an asserted contradiction. Hence p must always be true. Put otherwise, since the general logic does not have regard for the content or form of p, it cannot assert that p holds for some of its values but not all, since such an assertion makes use of terms and relations which do not belong to the general logic. Hence, we cannot assert that a proposition does not vanish and yet is not true without making use of terms beyond the scope of the science. It may be important at a later stage to make such distinctions, just as it is important to develop the science of arithmetic, but they cannot be made in the fundamental science without specializing the form or content of the propositions. The existence of this rule in the calculus will become important in the formal development.

For many, this rule would be equivalent to denying all modal distinctions, but such is not the case. Even though a given proposition holds for both truth-values, it cannot be said to hold in general. Hence, though $p = |p|$ is true when $p = 0$ and $p = 1$, it is not true in general.

A defence of our procedure with regard to the non-formal rules seems necessary in view of the fact that some logicians have come to regard the method as unsound.[9] According to them, we cannot assume as a basis for deduction in a formal system of logic the very principles we later pretend to deduce. It is true that the non-formal rules above form a part of the general logic. How, then, can we use a part of the formal system in deducing theorems of the formal system?

The present method is a result of formal procedure, i.e., it is a result of the attempt to formalize the science of logic by constructing definitions and postulates and deducing theorems. All systems of logic must include, besides their formal (symbolic) expressions, certain "rules of procedure," i.e., certain rules which tell us how to operate on these expressions in order to deduce theorems. It seems evident enough that these rules cannot themselves be purely formal; they must, then, be phrased at least partially in a non-symbolic language. The Rules of Substitution and Inference are the usual examples, but here an additional set of non-formal rules are required because of the structure of the general logic. We must first have the laws governing asserted statements (definitions, postulates, and theorems) of a formal system before we can deal with the general laws whose elements are not restricted to truth-values. These laws must be stated non-formally in part. For example, an attempt to symbolize $\vdash p$ by $p = 1$ would lead to something false, for we could then deduce "$p \angle (p = 1)$," which fails in the general logic, since it reduces the entire logic to the (restricted) two-valued system. In general, the development of the system depends on our being able to consider any postulate or theorem as an expression

---

[9] I have not mentioned names here, since the criticisms have only been expressed in informal correspondence. But whether there exist logicians holding these views or not, the matter seems to demand explanation.

satisfying the premise of any rule of the form "⊢ $p \cdot \angle \cdot$ - - - -."
Hence, we cannot consider ⊢ p as a formal symbol without
asserting a non-formal or verbal sentence which will attribute to
the symbol this property. Hence, since (1) in order to complete
the system we require laws governing asserted statements in a
formal system and (2) these statements cannot be completely
symbolized, the result is that (1) we are forced to assume certain
special laws of our logic at the beginning as laws of procedure and
hence, (2) the non-symbolic language is larger than that ordinarily
used. Much the same procedure seems to be necessitated in the
case of Lewis' system which is also a non-truth-value logic.[10]
Truth-value systems of logic, of course, can avoid this secondary
non-formal language.

There is nothing fallacious, however, in assuming certain laws
of the general logic as a basis of procedure.[11] All sciences introduce
methods of procedure for deducing theorems that are peculiar
to the science, e.g., Mathematical Induction in arithmetic, and
the construction-theorems in geometry. Nor can we claim that
these non-formal rules are more "basic" than the general logic;
rather, the former is merely a proper part of the latter, but in
formal procedure it becomes either necessary or highly convenient to assume this sub-part first.

It has also been objected that the non-formal language, which
contains such words as "if," "then," "and," etc. must remain
vague, or a new logic must be constructed to make them precise.
In reality, however, these words are made precise by the formal
system itself. There is no distinction between the "p and q" of the
non-formal rules and the "pq" of the formal (symbolic) rules,
provided the symbols of the system are given an interpretation in
the science of logic. The reason we write "p and q" in our non-
formal rules is that we wish to restrict the interpretation of the
conjunctive symbol to one meaning (logical conjunction); such
restriction is necessary for the deduction of theorems in the sys-

[10] Cf E. V. Huntington, "Postulates for Assertion," etc., *Proc. Amer. Academy of
Arts and Sciences*, vol. 72, No. 1 (1937).

[11] It is not clear that any great advance is made in calling the non-formal rules
"sub-languages," as though the propositions there expressed belonged either to a
different science or a different sphere from the formal assumptions. The language-
distinctions only become useful in discussing the nature of symbols and the symbolic method, and hence are not distinctions of logic; logic is not a science of languages.

tem, but it does not imply an essential distinction between the symbolic and non-symbolic expressions. If the variables of the system were interpreted as numbers and the relations were given new meanings, then "*pq*" and "*p* and *q*" would be distinct, since the variables in "*p* and *q*" would represent propositions of arithmetic, but the variables in "*pq*" would represent numbers. In short, the need for writing "*p* and *q*" or "if *p*, then *q*" in certain places is a need arising from the abstract nature of the symbolic method. The distinction between the formal and non-formal in our symbolic method is not a logical distinction.

We shall call a modal function of a single variable a "single-order" function; thus $p|$, $p'||'$, $p'|$, etc. are single-order functions. A multiple-order function will be a modal function of a conjunction (or disjunction) of two or more variables: $|(pq)'|$, $||pq'|'|$, etc. An expression will be a single-order expression if it contains only single-order functions. Our preliminary problem will be to determine all valid single-order expressions. The multiple-order problem presents certain further difficulties and will be treated separately.

The above set of assumptions is not sufficient for the complete solution of the single-order problem since the Modal Law, $p \angle p|$, is not enough to establish all modal relations. Thus the relation between p and $p|'|'$ is undetermined. Here a number of choices are open, each giving rise to a different modal system. For convenience' sake in the discussion of these systems, we introduce a new notation. Any modal function may be represented by n numbers:

$$(a_1, a_2, \cdots, a_n),$$

where a_1 represents the number of "bars" between the variable and the first prime, a_2, the number of bars between the first and second primes, etc. Thus (3, 2, 1) represents the modal function $p|||'||'|'$. If no prime appears on the last bar, a final 0 is added: $p'||'||$ is represented by (0, 2, 2, 0), since the modal function can also be written $p'||'||''$. By convention, all numbers other than the first and last must be greater than 0, i.e., 0 never appears between two numbers greater than 0. If the number of numbers within the parenthesis-sign is even, the function is affirmative;

otherwise it is negative. Adding two zeros to the end of any function does not alter the "value" or "meaning," since $p = p''$:

$$(a_1, a_2, \cdots, a_n) = (a_1, a_2, \cdots, a_n, 0, 0).$$

The simplest modal system contains but six "irreducible" elements; all complex modals may be equated to one of the following: $p|, p|', p, p', p'|', p'|$. This system may be deduced from the above postulates if we add the additional assumption:

A1. $p| \angle p|'|'$, or

$\qquad (1, 0) \angle (1, 1)$

A1 and the Modal Law give

$\qquad (1, 0) = (1, 1)$.

All modal functions of the form $(0, a_2, \cdots, a_n)$, where $a_2 > 0$, are equivalent to $p'|'$ or $p'|$, depending on whether n is even or odd. All modals of the form $(a_1, a_2, \cdots, a_n)$, where $a_1 > 0$, are equivalent to $p|$ or $p|'$, depending on whether n is even or odd. There are no modal functions of p equivalent to p other than p itself.

This system is extremely simple, but very restricted, in that multiple implications become reduced to single implications. For example, the double implication $(p \angle q) \angle r$ becomes, if r is 0, $[(pq' \angle 0) \angle 0]$, or $|(pq')|$, or $(p \angle q)'$. Such restrictions seem to make the system only slightly more general than the two-valued logic.

The simplest modal system making a distinction between all modal functions was given by Smith.[12] Such a system is called "infinite" because of the infinity of distinct modals that result. An indefinite number of postulates are required for completeness; these may be summarized by the general notation as follows:

$$(0, 0) \angle (1, n),$$

where n is any positive integer (when n is 0 we have the Modal Law).[13]

This formulation is somewhat cumbersome in that (1) it does

[12] Cf. H. B. Smith, "Abstract Logic," *loc. cit.*

[13] It is recognized that the general logic makes use of the concept of number in this formula, as it does in the general notation, but the use is so far a matter of convenience, i.e., the concept of number is not required as an indefinable but is very useful in presenting the subject simply. It may be that in the solution of the multiple-order problem, the concept of number is required. This would merely mean that logic cannot be completed without arithmetic, though the latter would presuppose some non-arithmetical part of logic in its development.

not show, what is a fact, that a (non-reversible) implication can be proved between any two affirmative (and hence any two negative) modal functions, and (2) it is redundant, since if it holds for a certain number n it will hold for all numbers less than n; e.g., if $(0,0) \angle (1,1)$, then $(0,0) \angle (1,0)$, since $(1, 1) \angle (1, 0)$ or $p|'|' \angle p|$. These difficulties may be obviated by asserting an equivalent postulate in the general notation which will also exhibit the character of the system:

Postulate: A necessary and sufficient condition that

$$(a_1, a_2, \cdots, a_n) \angle (b_1, b_2, \cdots, b_n)$$

be true is that either (1) $a_i = b_i$ ($1 \leq i \leq n$), or (2) there exists a_ν such that if $a_i = b_i$ ($1 \leq i < \nu$) and $a_\nu \neq b_\nu$, then for n even and ν odd or n odd and ν even ($n - \nu$ odd)

$$a_\nu < b_\nu$$

and for n even and ν even or n odd and ν odd ($n - \nu$ even)

$$a_\nu > b_\nu.$$

A few examples will help clarify the postulate. For instance, we know that $p'|' \angle p'|'|$, which is expressed in our notation by $(0, 1, 0, 0) \angle (0, 1, 1, 0)$. Here $n = 4$ and is even; $a_1 = b_1, a_2 = b_2$, but $a_3 \neq b_3$, and hence $\nu = 3$ and is odd. Hence we should have $a_3 < b_3$ by our postulate, which is actually the case. Again "Brouwer's Axiom," $p \angle p|'|'$ in our notation becomes $(0, 0) \angle (1, 1)$. Here $a_1 \neq b_1$ and hence $\nu = 1$ and is odd, while $n = 2$ and is even. Hence we should have $a_1 < b_1$, which is the case. Again, take any two random modal functions $p'|'||'|'|'$ and $p'|'||'|'|'|$, which become $(0, 1, 2, 2, 1, 0, 0)$ and $(0, 1, 2, 1, 1, 1, 0)$ respectively. Here n is odd and $a_i = b_i$ for $i < 4$, but $a_4 \neq b_4$. Hence ν is even, and we have $b_4 < a_4$; therefore, by the postulate, the second modal function implies the first.

It is clear that between any two affirmative modal functions an implication always exists,[14] and also that from the postulate we cannot have $p \angle q$ and also $q \angle p$, i.e., the postulate does not yield any equivalences. Whether any equivalences can be proved by means of the remaining assumptions of the system would be extremely difficult to determine, but the writer thinks not. If the

[14] Such systems are called "complete" modal systems.

non-reversibility of the modal implications is to be maintained, certain well-known expressions of the propositional calculus will fail to hold. These chiefly fail because a basic non-formal rule also fails. This is called Becker's Rule and may be stated as follows:

If $\vdash (p \angle q)$, then $\vdash (|p| \angle |q|)$.[15]

As an instance of the failure of this rule, let q be $p|'|'$, or $(1, 1)$. Then $p \angle q$ is asserted, but $|p| \angle |q|$ or $(1, 0, 0, 0) \angle (1, 1, 1, 0)$ is not asserted, since its converse is asserted.

Since Becker's Rule fails in this system, so does the following formal expression:

$$(p \angle q)(q \angle r) \angle (p \angle r) \text{ ("Syllogism")}[16]$$

Syllogism does not hold when thus formally expressed, but it is valid as a non-formal Rule (cf. above). The following also fail:

$$(p \angle q) \angle (pr \angle qr)$$
$$(p \angle q) \angle [(p+r) \angle (q+r)]$$
$$(p \angle q) \angle [(q \angle r) \angle (p \angle r)], \text{ etc.}$$

Becker's Rule and, hence, Syllogism, however, do not fail simply because of this Modal System. If this were the case, we might have a valid argument for rejecting the system, since Becker's Rule simplifies the calculus. But the fact of the matter is that any modal system of the general logic which contains the above assumptions must deny Becker's Rule. The proof is as follows: Suppose Becker's Rule holds. Now by the postulates above we have

$$p \angle (p+q) \quad \text{and} \quad q \angle (p+q).$$

Hence, by Becker's Rule, we would have

$$|p| \angle |p+q|$$
$$\text{and} \quad |q| \angle |p+q|$$
$$\text{or} \quad |p| + |q| \cdot \angle \cdot |p+q|[17]$$

Now let q be the modal function $|p|'$: $|p| + ||p|' \angle |(p+|p|')|$.

<hr>

[15] This rule is far weaker than the purely symbolic

$$(p \angle q) \angle (|p| \angle |q|).$$

Becker's Rule holds in the System of Strict Implication, but this does not. Cf. "On Finite and Infinite Modal Systems," *Jour. Symbolic Logic*, vol. 3, No. 2.

[16] For the formal proof, see "On Finite and Infinite Modal Systems," *ibid.*

[17] If $p \angle q$ is asserted and $r \angle q$ is asserted, then $(p+r) \angle q$ is asserted by virtue of the non-formal rules.

But $|p| + ||p|'|$ is true (its negative, $|p|' \cdot ||p|'|'$, vanishes). Hence $|(p + |p|')|$ is true. Hence $p + |p|'$ must be true, since if $|p|$ is asserted, p is asserted. But if $p + p|'$ is true, then $|p| \angle p$ and all modal distinctions are erased. It follows that even the simple system A, containing six irreducible modals, must deny Becker's Rule.

In any system, such as the present one, that recognizes complete modal distinctions, if Ap is any affirmative modal function of p, then if $p \angle q$ is asserted, we cannot necessarily assert $Ap \angle Aq$. This may be shown by two cases:

1. Suppose $p \angle Ap$. Then, as above, if the non-formal rule holds, $(Ap + Aq) \angle A(p + q)$. Now let q be $(Ap)'$ (or $A'p$): $[Ap + A(A'p)] \angle A(p + A'p)$.
But, since $p \angle Ap$, then $A'p \angle p'$; hence, writing $A'p$ for p: $A'(A'p) \angle Ap$, which implies $A(A'p) + Ap = 1$.
Hence, since $1 \angle A(p + A'p)$, $A(p + A'p)$ must be asserted. Hence, $p + A'p$ is asserted, which yields $Ap \angle p$, and this gives the modal equality $Ap = p$.

2. Suppose $Ap \angle p$. Then, if the generalized Becker's Rule holds, $Apq \angle Ap$, and $Apq \angle Aq$, since $pq \angle p$ and $pq \angle q$. Hence, $Apq \angle ApAq$, or $A'p + A'q \angle A'(pq)$. Letting q be $A'p$, we have: $A'p + A'(A'p) \angle A'(p \cdot A'p)$. But since $Ap \angle p$, $A(A'p) \angle A'p$ or $A'(A'p) + A'p = 1$. Hence, $A'(p \cdot A'p)$ is asserted. Since A' is negative, this means that $p \cdot A'p = 0$ is asserted, or $p \angle Ap$, which again gives $p = Ap$.

Of course, one might deny one or more of the above assumptions in order to save Becker's Rule, but the resulting systems become quite complicated.

In the present system, the only change which may be made in an asserted "modal" implication $(p \angle q)$ that will not alter its validity, is to "strengthen" p or "weaken" q.[18] This may be shown by means of the general notation.

Modal functions in this system have interesting mathematical properties, quite apart from their applications to logic. We may talk of "infinite" modal operators, some of which "converge," some "diverge." Thus the operator $(1,x)$ converges as $x \to \infty$; i.e., $\lim_{x \to \infty} (1,x) = (0,0)$, since, given any modal function implied

---

[18] x is stronger than p if $x \angle p$, and y is weaker than q if $q \angle y$.

by $(0,0)$, we can find an x such that $(1,x)$ implies this function also. If we abandon logical terminology for mathematical, we may say that one series $(a_1 - - - - a_n)$ is "less than" another $(b_1 - - - - -b_n)$ if the conditions of the Postulate above are satisfied. Then, the convergence of one variable towards a "constant" may be expressed, as in mathematics, as follows: $(a_1, - - - , x, - - - a_n)$ $(a_1, a_2, - - - - a_n$ are constants) approaches $(b_1 - - - - - b_n)$ as $x \rightarrow \infty$, if, given any "constant" $(c_1 - - - - c_n)$ greater than $(b_1 - - - - b_n)$, there exists an x such that $(a_1, - - - - , x, - - - a_n)$ is less than $(c_1 - - - - c_n)$.[19] The variable approaches its limit" monotonically" if $(a_1, - - - , x, - - - , a_n)$ is less than $(a_1, - - - - , x + 1, - - - - , a_n)$ or $(a_1, - - - - , x, - - - - - , a_n)$ is less than $(a_1 - - - - , x - 1, - - - - a_n)$. Other convergent variables are the following:

$$\lim_{x \rightarrow \infty} (1, 1, x, 0) = (1, 0, 0, 0)$$

$$\lim_{x \rightarrow \infty} (1, 2, x, 0) = (1, 1, 0, 0)$$

In general, we may say

$$\lim_{x \rightarrow \infty} (a_1, a_2 - - - - - a_m, k, - - - a_n) \doteq (a_1, a_2 - - - - a_{m-1}, 0, - - - a_n),$$

where the constant on the right must be rewritten to eliminate the 0 between two significant numbers.

An example of a divergent variable is $(x, 0)$. One might feel inclined to assert that $\lim_{x \rightarrow \infty} (x,0) = 1$, i.e., that if we apply enough (affirmative) modal operators to any statement, we will eventually have a true statement; this is not the case. If $(x,0)$ operates on $(1,1)$ we have $(1, x + 1)$ as a result, and the limit here is $(0,0)$ as above, which is not necessarily a true statement. Divergent variables here do not approach "infinity," i.e., do not approach 1, but are merely indeterminate. There is also the possibility of considering variable series such as $(1, 1, 1, 1, - - - -)$ where the number 1 is repeated an indefinite number of times, or rather, the pair $(1, 1)$ is repeated, since otherwise the variable would oscillate between positive and negative values. Though no limit can be assigned to such variables, we can indicate their upper and lower limits or bounds. A lower bound of the above

---

[19] Where $(a_1, - - - , x, - - - a_n)$ is always greater than $(b_1 - - - b_n)$.

would be $(1, 1, 1, ---2, 1, ---)$, where 2 is in an even place. If 2 is in an odd place we have an upper bound, for, by the postulate, $(1, 1, 1, 1, ----)$ is greater than the first and less than the second. Also $(1, 1, 1, 0)$ is an upper bound. Similar series could be constructed by taking the pairs $(1, 2)$ or $(2, 3)$ or $(1, 3)$, etc., and repeating them.

Other infinite modal systems would be given by the following assumptions:

C 1.　$(0, 0) = (1, 1)$　　　$(p = p|'|')$
D 1.　$(1, n) \angle (0, 0).$　　$(p|'|_n' \angle p)$

C 1 would reduce to A1 if Becker's Rule held, as Parry has shown.[20] D 1 would reduce to a system of material implication if the Rule held. But since the Rule fails, it is not apparent that such reductions could take place, though the method of demonstrating this fact is not clear. In general, there seems to be no adequate method at present of showing that a given modal system must be infinite.

If C 1 cannot be reduced, the resulting system is infinite, though it contains modal equivalences as well. By virtue of the non-formal Rule: "If $p = q$ is asserted, then $|p| = |q|$ is asserted," which holds because of the Rule of Substitution. C 1 and the Modal Law are sufficient to establish the law $(0, 0) = (1, n)$ and ultimately to make the system complete. There is no very simple way of describing this system by the general notation, but the following show some of its important characteristics:

(1)　$(0, 0) = (n, n)$ (for all n);
(2)　$(0, 0) = (n, n, n, n, ----),$

where the number of integers within the parenthesis signs on the right is even, of course;

(3)　$(1, 0) = (n, n - 1, n, n - 1, ----);$
　　$(2, 0) = (n, n - 2, n, n - 2, ----)$, etc.

System D, like B, has no modal equivalences, but is more complicated than B in that D 1 is not sufficient for completeness. In

[20] Cf. "Modalities in the Survey," *Journal of Symbolic Logic*, vol. 4, No. 4. The reduction in particular depends on the law 14.2 $|p + q| = |p| + |q|$, which is not true here.

the first place, we must set a "lower" bound to $(1, 1)$. This may be done by asserting

D 2. $(0, 1) \angle (1, n)$, for all positive integers n.

The system cannot be summarized in a simple manner by a postulate analogous to that given for B above, since in the determination of the validity of an implication we cannot ignore all the numbers after the nth as we do in the case of B. Thus, there are cases where $a_1 > b_1$, but $(a_1 \text{-} \text{-} \text{-} \text{-} a_n) \angle (b_1 \text{-} \text{-} \text{-} \text{-} b_n)$, e.g., $(3, 1, 0, 0) \angle (2, 1, 1, 0)$, and there are cases where $a_1 < b_1$, but $(a_1 \text{-} \text{-} \text{-} \text{-} a_n) \angle (b_1 \text{-} \text{-} \text{-} \text{-} b_n)$, e.g., $(0, 1, 2, 0) \angle (1, 2, 1, 0)$.

We should mention a "non-complete" modal system, E, which asserts no implication between $p|'|'$ and p. This system may be simpler than B or D, because the multiple-order problem may be easier to solve (cf. below). The only modal implications which exist in this system follow from the Modal Law, $p \angle |p|$.

The above analysis is not complete, though it does represent the important infinite systems.[21] There is another absolutely incomplete system in which the Modal Law also does not hold. This is perhaps the simplest as far as the solution of the multiple-order problem is concerned, but does not yield a very satisfactory interpretation of $(p \angle 0)'$.

There remains one other question with regard to the single-order problem: Must we assert the non-reversibility of certain modal implications? In particular, must we add a postulate asserting that $|p| \angle p$ is not true in general? Both Lewis and Smith have done so in their systems. Thus, Lewis asserts:

$$(\exists p, q) : \sim(p \dashv 3 q) \cdot \sim(p \dashv 3 \sim q) ;\text{[22]}$$

and Smith asserts: "Let P stand for a certain (propositional) function of the (traditional) class calculus, A (ab) (all a is b). Then P is not a solution of the equation

$$|p| \cdot |p'| = 0".\text{[23]}$$

---

[21] For examples of finite systems, cf. Parry, *op. cit.*, and O. Becker, "Zur Logik der Modalitäten," *Jahrbuch für Philosophie*, etc., vol. 11, pp. 496–548. These systems must be modified somewhat in the general logic, since here Becker's Rule does not hold.

[22] *Symbolic Logic*, p. 179.

[23] *Abstract Logic*, p. 373. Smith seems to take propositional functions of this type as exceptions to the statement $p = |p|$. But it is evident that we need not find specific cases where the proposition fails. We need only point out that if it holds, the two-valued logic and the Epimenides paradox result.

It is clear, however, that we cannot assert these non-equivalences in the general logic, for such assertions require concepts which specialize the meaning or content of the variables, p, q, r, etc. We cannot, of course, assert $(|p| \angle p)'$, for if p is 0 or p is 1, we have the contradiction $(0 \angle 0)'$ or $(1 \angle 1)'$.

But in view of the statement of the general problem given above, it does not seem necessary for the general calculus of propositions to include a postulate such as Lewis' or Smith's, i.e., it is not necessary for this calculus to point out propositions which do not hold true in general; it is only interested in expressions which do hold (or fail) for all values; in Smith's system at least, to set down enough assumptions to determine all non-general propositions would seem to be an endless task.

Now there is one difficulty which occurs if we omit from our calculus a postulate of the nature of those described above. Suppose we have reduced an expression to one which apparently does not vanish by our postulates; how can we determine whether this expression does or does not vanish in general? E.g., if one of the products in our sum of products is $p' \cdot |p|$, we cannot determine by our postulates whether this might not be equal to 0, though the previous discussion has indicated that it is not. Our answer is that such a question does not fall within the scope of the general logic, but is nevertheless a question of value, to be solved by other branches of logic or even by other sciences. The general logic must be sufficient to establish all the laws of the general calculus, and it must not include among its laws ones, such as $p = |p|$, which destroy its generality; but it need not go outside its field and point out non-general laws.

However, one might add a "Completeness Axiom," though such an axiom would not be a part of the general logic:

Axiom: If a given expression does not vanish by virtue of the postulates of the general calculus, then it does not vanish identically in this calculus.

There remains the difficulty of a method for determining whether a given expression does or does not vanish by the postulates; here, I think, Huntington's matrix-method[24] for determining the independence of a symbolic set of expressions would work;

[24] Cf. E. V. Huntington, "Sets of Independent Postulates for the Algebra of Logic," *Trans. Amer. Math. Soc.*, 1904.

it is true that such a method could not be used on the postulates of the general calculus, since the method presupposes these assumptions, but it could be used here in a field beyond the general logic, in a field which presumably it does not presuppose. In sum, the equivalence of $|p|$ and p is not a law of the general logic. The actual cases in which the equivalence fails must be given by other sciences. But even though no case can be found, the equivalence still does not hold, since if $p = |p|$ is asserted, a restricted (two-valued) logic occurs which contains all the difficulties of the Epimenides paradox.

We now consider the multiple-order problem. If we can reduce all multiple-order modal functions of the type $|pq|$ or $|p + q|$ to single-order functions by "expansion" formulas, then the problem will be solved, since the single-order problem is solved. Our first problem, then, is to find such formulas.

The "meaning" of the expression $|pq|$, "The conjunction 'p and q' does not vanish," seems to indicate that $|p| \cdot |q|$, "p does not vanish and q does not vanish," is the required expression. Let us suppose, for the moment, that $|pq| = |p| \cdot |q|$ holds in general. Then we can reduce some such expression as $|p|'|pq|$ to $|p|'|p| \cdot |q|$ and this does vanish by virtue of the contradiction $|p|'|p|$.

But this simple solution is inadequate, for $|pq| = |p| \, |q|$ is not true in general in that it fails if q is the contradictory of p; in this case the left-hand side vanishes (it reads $(p \angle p)'$), while the right-hand side ($|p| \, |p'|$) does not vanish in general, i.e., "p does not vanish" and "p is false does not vanish" are not contradictories. Other simple formulas for the expansion of $|pq|$ meet this same fate.

Similar remarks apply with regard to an expansion formula for the disjunction $|p + q|$. Here the obvious solution is to let

$$|p + q| = |p| + |q|^{25}$$

But the formula fails in some cases where p and q are contraries; e.g., suppose q is $|p|'$:

$$|(p + |p|')| = |p| + | \, |p|'|.$$

The right-hand side is a truth of logic (since $|p| + |p|'$ is a truth,

[25] This formula does hold in Lewis' system: cf. *Symbolic Logic*, p. 176, 19.82.

a fortiori $|p| + ||p|'|$is). Hence the left-hand side must be. As above, it follows that $p + |p|'$ is a truth of logic, a result that leads to the equivalence of p and $|p|$.

These examples indicate the difficulty of the problem. The solution might also vary according to the single-order modal system that is chosen, but the following solutions are perfectly general and may be applied to any of the systems. We note first that under certain conditions expansions may be made quite readily. Thus, $|pq|$ will expand to 0 if $pq = 0$, to $|p|$ if $pq' = 0$ or $p \angle q$, to $|p|$ if $p'q = 0$ or $q \angle p$. Again $|(pq)'|$ or $|p'| + q'|$ expands to 1 if $p'q' = 0$, to $|p|$ if $p'q = 0$, to $|q|$ if $p\,q' = 0$. Hence, the only cases of difficulty arise when $p'q' = 0$ or when no implicative relation exists between p and q. Second, the expansion of $|(pq)'|$ or $|p' + q'|$ when $p' + q' \neq 1$ or $pq \neq 0$ must not be 1, or else we would have $|p' + q'|$ asserted but $(p' + q')$ not asserted. That is, the modal operator must not "stretch" the expression to 1. The simplest solution, perhaps, is to say that in the case where $p'q' = 0$, or no implicative relation exists, no expansion of a sum takes place, i.e., here we have

$$|p' + q'| = p' + q'.$$

In the case of systems A, B, or C above, the product expansion must be $|pq| = pq$.

For we cannot say that in the case $p'q' = 0$, $|pq| = |p|\,|q|$. For we have $|p' + q'|' = pq$, by the above. Applying the modal operator to both sides of this (which is permissible, the equality being asserted), we obtain $||p' + q'|'| = |pq|$. This becomes, if $|pq| = |p|\,|q|$: $\qquad ||p' + q'|'| = |p|\,|q|$.

If we "multiply" both sides of (3) by $(p' + q')$, the left-hand side vanishes in all these systems, since it is a special case of $p\cdot||p|'|$. But the right-hand side becomes $p'|p|\,|q| + q'|p|\,|q|$ which does not (necessarily) vanish. Hence, along with (1) above, we must have

$$|(p' + q')'| = (p' + q')' = pq$$

It will be simpler if we extend these results to any modal function of a product, $M(pq)$. Let us assert, then, as an additional postulate, the following (where M is any affirmative modal operator; e.g., $M(pq)$ might be $||pq|'|'$, or $|(pq)'|'$, etc.)

a) $\vdash (pq = 0) \cdot \angle \cdot \vdash M(pq) = 0$
     $\vdash (pq = 0) \cdot \angle \cdot \vdash M(pq)' = 1$
b) $\vdash (pq' = 0) \cdot \angle \cdot \vdash M(pq) = Mp$
     $\vdash (pq' = 0) \cdot \angle \cdot \vdash M(pq)' = Mp'$
c) $\vdash (p'q = 0) \cdot \angle \cdot \vdash M(pq) = Mq$
     $\vdash (p'q = 0) \cdot \angle \cdot \vdash M(pq)' = Mq'$
d) $\vdash (p'q' = 0) \cdot \angle \cdot \vdash M(pq) = pq$
     $\vdash (p'q' = 0) \cdot \angle \cdot \vdash M(pq)' = (pq)'$
e) $\vdash (pq \neq 0)(pq' \neq 0)(p'q \neq 0)(p'q' \neq 0) \cdot \angle \cdot \vdash M(pq) = pq$
     $\vdash (pq \neq 0)(pq' \neq 0)(p'q \neq 0)(p'q' \neq 0) \cdot \angle \cdot \vdash M(pq)' = (pq)'$

The formulas for negative functions will follow from these.

The *Entscheidungsproblem* seems to be solved by such an additional postulate. Suppose, by way of illustration, we determine for what values of M and N the expression NpMpq vanishes in general. Evidently there will be no cases where M and N are both negative, for if p is 0 the resulting expression is always 1. Again, if M is negative and N affirmative, the expression will always be 1 (no matter what M and N are) if p is 1 and q is 0, and when M and N are both affirmative, the values $p = 1$ and $q = 1$ will always yield 1. Hence, if the expression ever vanishes in general, M must be affirmative, N must be negative. Examining the given expression under our postulate, we have:

1) $\vdash (pq = 0) \cdot \angle \cdot \vdash (NpMpq) = 0$
2) $\vdash (pq' = 0) \cdot \angle \cdot \vdash (NpMpq) = (NpMp)$
3) $\vdash (p'q = 0) \cdot \angle \cdot \vdash (NpMpq) = (NpMq)$
4) $\vdash (p'q' = 0) \cdot \angle \cdot \vdash (NpMpq) = (Np[pq])$
5) $\vdash (pq \neq 0)(pq' \neq 0)(p'q \neq 0)(p'q' \neq 0) \cdot \angle \cdot \vdash (NpMpq) = (Np[pq])$

Restrictions are imposed on M and N by 2), 3), 4), and 5). Taking 3) first, we ask for what values of M and N, NpMq = 0 when $p'q$ = 0 is asserted. That is, we wish to know for what values of M and N the expression: $(q \angle p) \cdot \angle \cdot (Mq \angle N'p)$ is true. From the above discussion of Becker's Rule in Smith's modal system, this will only be the case when M$q \angle q$ and $p \angle$ N'p. Hence 3) has imposed certain necessary restrictions on N and M. These restrictions are actually sufficient, for NpMp will vanish in 2) if

$Mp \angle p$ and $p \angle N'p$, and $Np[pq]$ will vanish in 4) and 5) if $p \angle N'p$. Hence $NpMpq$ vanishes in general if, and only if, N is negative, M affirmative, and $Mp \angle p$ and $p \angle N'p$.

The method outlined seems applicable to any given expression. But it is certainly not the best method conceivable. In the first place, because of its elimination of modal functions, it appears "loose." But attempts to construct more rigid formulas have in general either failed or been too complicated to be practical. Second, since the validity of a given expression must be examined under a number of "cases" ($pq = 0$, $pq' = 0$, etc.), we require some such non-formal rule as the following:

If when $\vdash p_1$, $\phi = 0$, and if when $\vdash p_2$, $\phi = 0$, and if when $\vdash p_3$, $\phi = 0$, ..., and $p_1 + p_2 + p_3 + \cdots = 1$, then $\phi = 0$ is true (in general).

The necessity of this non-formal rule is the strongest objection to the method of solving the problem of expansion formulas which has been outlined above, for the rule has a "truth-value flavour" which is contrary to the philosophy of the general logic. The ideal solution would involve expansion formulas which held in general, i.e., which held in all cases; under such a solution the inconveniences of the non-formal rule required here would disappear.

TWO APPLICATIONS OF LOGIC TO BIOLOGY

ELIZABETH F. FLOWER

Department of Philosophy, University of Pennsylvania

THE significance of biology as a formal science has lately been emphasized, especially by von Uexküll and Woodger. This development points with increasing clarity to the fact that not all the issues of experimental science are to be solved by experiment alone, and to the part that logic must play in the refinement of a science. It is the purpose of this paper to develop this theme by indicating two instances, the mechanist-vitalist controversy and the definition of life, in which considerations of logic contribute to the science of biology. What follows is by way of illustration of the method and theory advanced by Professor Singer in his studies in "The Analysis of Concepts."

Every deductive (formal) system has a set of indefinables in terms of which all other terms and relations are defined and which are contained in a postulate set for that system. An examination of the indefinables of various formal sciences shows a peculiar relationship existing between them. Each science introduces at least one new term and presupposes those of the sciences which are more primitive. Thus a linear arrangement of the sciences will indicate precisely what the presuppositions of any given science are. The following, of course, does not include all sciences, but it will serve as a preface to the matter at hand.

In a schemata of the sciences, logic may be considered as basic since it introduces the idea of thing, of substantive. One of the new concepts that arithmetic adds is number, but it also utilizes the indefinables and postulates of logic. Geometry adds uniquely either distance, length, or direction while, of course, building upon arithmetic and logic. Kinematics introduces time or motion; and mechanics, the proximate in complexity, velocity or charge of mass, i.e., the motion of particles of matter. Physics may be considered as that science which adds to the indefinables—substantive, number, length, time and mass—the concept of the properties of groups of points (temperature). A problem arises in the classification of chemistry: unless valence is a unique concept chemistry is not an independent science but a part of physics.

The particular concern of this paper is the indefinable of biology, life. All the properties mentioned up to this point have been ateleological and the mechanists take biology to be no exception; that is to say, they conceive it to be a branch of physics introducing no new concept, much less one of a different order. The vitalists, on the other hand, insist that life is unique, so unique in fact, that it is of a different (teleological) order than the indefinables characterizing the more primitive sciences.

To complete the scheme it is suggested that the indefinable of psychology, which obviously presupposes biology, is the concept of mind; and, of sociology, the group mind. The manner in which this concept is considered is important; for the "life" of biology, further modified, is the key to psychology, and sociology, and whatever other science there may be. If this notion is altogether covered by physics, if biology is but a branch of physics, then the way is open for tremendous precision in the more advanced sciences. This is, however, at the expense of teleological, or purposive, character. The historical alternative, at least until the time of Kant, is not more inviting, for it finds life inexplicable in terms of mechanical law. The controversy lies between the dignity of man and his opportunity for precision of knowledge.

All possible positions toward this indefinable have been classified by Singer in terms of the proponents' attitude toward these three propositions:[1]

D. The Democritean Postulate: Everything in Nature is structural (independent of environment) in nature.

[1] E. A. Singer, Jr., "Beyond Mechanism and Vitalism," *Phil. of Science*, I, p. 273 (1934). Also E. A. Singer, Jr., "Logico-Historical Study of Mechanism, Vitalism, and Naturalism," in *Studies in History of Science* (Univ. of Penn. Press).

A. The Aristotelian Postulate: Some things in Nature are non-structural (dependent on environment) in nature.

C. The Classic Logician's Postulate: Nothing non-structural in nature is structural in nature.

A mystic neither affirms nor denies any of these postulates. His grasp on truth depends upon an ineffable experience. In Hegel's terms he is *ein musikalische Bewusstsein*. History amply provides examples, St. Paul, St. Theresa, and Cusanus, but unfortunately no implications can be derived from them that can be incorporated in propositions. Of those positions whose negations and affirmations are greater than zero there are two possibilities: either only denials are made, in which case the view is skeptical, or some affirmations are made.

It is this latter, or non-skeptical, instance which contains the fruitful points of view. A position which affirms but one postulate is ill-defined, and takes as its name the name of that postulate. A well-defined position makes two affirmations and perforce denies the third, for if any two of the propositions be taken as premises of a formally valid syllogism, the conclusion will be the contradictory of the third. The mechanist holds that the existence of living beings may be accounted for by the same kind of laws which determine non-living objects. He would affirm the Democritean postulate (D) and deny the Aristotelian (A). The vitalist proposes a unique factor in living organisms that differentiates them from physical phenomena, and implies a function. He affirms (A) and denies (D). Both of these accept the Classic-Logician's postulate. We shall postpone a discussion of the position that affirms (D) and (A) and denies (C) until we have drawn upon the wealth of historical illustration.

Parmenides' immutability of nature and Leucippus' universe of homogeneous particles moving in empty space anticipated Democritus; but it was left to the latter first to formulate a completely mechanistic view of life by postulating the existence only of space and atoms. These atoms are infinite in number and differ only in size and shape. They are forever moving and by occasionally impinging upon one another set up transient vortices out of which worlds are built. The soul is composed of the lightest and most refined atoms spaced throughout the body, and when they leave death ensues.

Epicurus and Lucretius escape this severe mechanism of Democritus by their doctrine of the swerving atom, moving without cause a distance less than any given distance. In like manner the mechanism of Descartes breaks down in the soul points, although it might be expected that the animate would be reducible to matter or motion. Among others who have supported the Democritean hypothesis are Booerhaave, Hoffman, Verworn and Loeb, but they lack the vigor of our final and modern example. The views of Haeckel and Roux are similar, but the latter states his case more precisely. According to Roux, biology admits of exact formulation because matter alone exists; there is no ground for a fundamental distinction between the living and non-living. The animate, appearing as cells with nuclei, developed from the inanimate by the operation of mechanical laws, and is governed by them. Roux emphasized the problem of development, as have both recent mechanism and vitalism, and it was on his interpretation of the growth of rudimentary organs that he denied all purposive activity.

The tradition of vitalism is quite as well established as mechanism. Although it probably derives originally from the Hippocratic writings, it was Aristotle who first formulated the theory with precision. Aristotle's well-known definition is the antithesis of that proposed by Democritus. Things are living by virtue of an activating principle, form, or entelechy which endows the non-living with vital warmth and completes it. The purposive character of everything appears in the search for a higher form. Many have followed Aristotle, though with varying degrees of originality. Paracelsus spoke of a *spiritus vitae* that governed the organism; Van Helmont, of *archai*; and Stahl, of *phlogiston*. Leibniz reduced the dualism of Descartes to a world comprised of soul points, and Buffon postulated unique, eternal molecules of an organic nature. In modern times Reinke proposed diphysical forces; Bergson, the *élan vital*; and Driesch, entelechies.

The views of Roux concluded our statement on mechanism

and so it is fitting that those of Driesch should close the discussion of vitalism. Driesch never loses sight of the contrast between a machine, and a living entity. The one exhibits only chemical and physical processes, the other contains its laws and purpose within itself. These are incompatible; the choice of one demands the rejection of the other.

Both of these men are interested in the problem of development, but their experiments and subsequent conclusions are antithetical. Where Roux destroys half of a frog's egg and then develops a partial embryo (which later regenerates the rest), Driesch splits a sea-urchin egg in half and gets two small but complete embryos. Roux infers the preformation or the early determination of parts; Driesch infers the existence of potentialities which are coördinated and actualized in terms of an entelechy or completed whole.

Emphases arising out of the controversy between vitalism and mechanism have profited biology. On the one hand, mechanism has limited itself to experimental research directed toward comprehensive consistent explanation in physico-chemical terms, but it does not adequately account for organization and unity. On the other hand, vitalism supplies the grounds for functional interpretation but often is tautological or mystical. It would be of the utmost importance, then, if the values of both could be reconciled. However, the Democritean postulate and the Aristotelian postulate have long been thought to be contradictories; the affirmation of both together would necessarily imply the denial of the classic-logician's postulate: "Nothing non-structural in nature is structural in Nature."

If, however, the concept of a universe of discourse be utilized, a possibility appears for denying the truth of the classic-logician's postulate. Formally stated the postulate reads: "No X is non-X"; or, as here, "Everything is structural in nature" and "Some things are non-structural in nature" cannot be true simultaneously. These are certainly contradictories in some sense, but not in every sense, since contradictories established in one universe of discourse do not necessarily apply in a second, and the assumption that they do, involves an equivocation. Thus structural and non-structural are negative terms only as long as the "thing" of the subject is the same in both instances. Logic has exposed a fallacy and provided thereby the formal grounds for showing the resolution of mechanism and vitalism. Such a discussion is valuable because it expresses definitely and in non-vitalistic terminology a compatibility which many apparently have felt.

The case is excellently illustrated by J. S. Haldane in *The Philosophical Basis of Biology*.[2] Explanation of a physical order in terms of matter and energy is there distinguished from that of a biological order in terms of life and its maintenance. Haldane states that the one is not inconsistent with the other if the deeper insight of the biological order is recognized. He offers, however, no demonstration of this. Biology, then, is an independent science because it uses concepts not comprehended by physics. The case is somewhat like Bergson's philosophy in which life is understandable only in terms of environment, of a struggle against chaos, and of the relation of part to whole, and the relation of these to the maintenance of a characteristic structure and activity.

Haldane's view misses narrowly, if it does at all, being vitalistic, and yet it is obvious that he has accepted some such resolution of the Democritean and Aristotelian postulates as has been proposed. We agree that the biological sciences initiate a new kind of definition, namely the teleological, but it must be so rigorously stated that it is shown to be consistent with and intimately related to a mechanically interpreted universe.

Bertalanaffy and Woodger[3] approach the problem of teleology first logically and then experimentally. They point out that the mechanists assume the analogy between an organism and a machine, and then are forced continually to invent new machines to patch it up. The vitalists, noting the failure of the machine theory, merely invent a vital force to support it. They, too, seek a "Beyond Mechanism and Vitalism" and find it in "organismic biology." Three levels of explanation are distinguished. On the systematic level objects are classified and their

[2] J. S. Haldane, *The Philosophical Basis of Biology*, New York, Doubleday, Doran and Co., 1935. Especially 2d Lecture.

[3] Ludwig von Bertalanaffy, *Modern Theories of Development*, London, Oxford University Press, 1938. Translated and adapted by Woodger.

distribution in time and space noted. The causal phase uses physico-chemical terms. The final or organismic stage considers objects in a uniquely biological and teleological light. The wholeness of the organism and its other properties are studied as they contribute to its maintenance.

Woodger's conclusion[4] is the same as ours, that there is a biological category consistent with the causal. The logical demands of the situation, however, have not been met. Biology has gone beyond the point where it must choose either a mechanical or vitalistic explanation before it proceeds with experiment. Yet, without such an analysis as Singer's, the ground seems questionable; with it the logical aspect of the question is solved. It has been demonstrated that it is logically sound to affirm the Democritean and the Aristotelian postulates, that there need be no inconsistency in asserting the structural nature of organisms without denying them function.

A fundamental problem in the non-formal science of biology is the determination of a criterion for membership in the class *life* (or *living beings*), since the science, as previously defined, concerns the propositions which can be made about living things. An intuitive or aesthetic element has figured in the definition of life. It is often assumed that the distinction between organic and inorganic is known and that all that is needed is to delineate sets of properties expressing something which everyone feels, and to adjust these sets as test cases develop. Early discussions centered upon the intrinsic nature of life, but Wöhler's synthesis anticipated a more subtle problem now focused upon the filterable virus: When is a given X to be called living?

The property (or properties) that define this membership has (or have) seldom been agreed upon with any encouraging unanimity. It is no mean task to distinguish the essential from the accidental. The qualities by which life is generally recognized are often present in objects that we are not wont to call living. Sometimes they are not present in objects admittedly animate. Since centuries of thought have not produced a neces-

[4] J. H. Woodger, *Biological Principles*, New York, Harcourt, Brace and Co., 1929.

sary and sufficient criterion, it is possible that logic may make a second contribution to biology by indicating an alternative approach, as yet untried.

All possible definitions of life are either teleological or ateleological, but our particular interest is in those to which recent biological progress has contributed. The ateleological classification includes criteria of substance and of structure; the teleological, obviously, of function.[5]

It has often been held that life depends on the presence of some vital material. We have already had occasion to refer to one interpretation of this as heat. Lavoisier showed that this property, believed to be peculiar to the living body, was due to the combustion of ordinary hydrogen and carbon. Buffon, under the influence of Leibniz, was one of the first in modern times to attribute life to the presence of biological particles. In our time Verworn developed the biogen molecule as the chemical unit and Altmann elevated the granules he had found in the plasma to the elementary organisms of all life. Just three years ago, Guye proposed a similar notion but he supported it with a laboratory vocabulary. Later, he assumed a large asymmetric molecule which could activate the immediate inorganic environment and by reaction with it form a larger and larger aggregate which eventually began life.

Several instances of the defining of the vital material are implications of theories whose primary consideration was the origin of life. As such they stress the necessity of a substance but not its uniqueness and thus, even were they experimentally valid, they would be inadequate as criteria. Troland, for example, believed that life was inaugurated by the fortuitous presence of an autocatalytic enzyme. Others have felt that the enzymes are responsible for life-giving properties, but this is scarcely possible. Although the composition of enzymes has not been determined, Buchner showed that their action was not dependent on living protoplasm nor conversely.

Pflüger, also seeking the origin of life, thought that the proteins were labile and auto-oxidizable and therefore living

[5] Cf. Huxley, *On the Physical Basis of Life*. A threefold unity characterizes living objects: a unity of substantial composition, of form, and of power.

because of a cyanogen radical $\begin{array}{c} C\equiv N \\ | \\ C\equiv N \end{array}$. His theory studied the decomposition products of living and dead proteins. The former are definite compounds containing cyanogen, in creatine, uric acid, etc., while the latter are indeterminate and lack the radical. The theory is obviously lax not only because protein cannot be so oxidized, but also because cyanogen may not be necessary at all. As a matter of fact, quite as good a case could be made for carbon. Its universality and asymmetrical properties qualify it immediately. In addition it has other recommendations. Analogous compounds do not have analogous properties. For example, the chlorides of metal react with aqueous silver nitrate and are decomposed by concentrated H_2SO_4, but the chlorides of carbon are relatively inert. In addition, carbon is the backbone of the protein molecule. Far from being the criterion of life, however, it merely indicates a distinction between organic and inorganic reactions generally, the one largely ionic and the other molecular.

Other chemicals such as nitrogen, phosphorous, magnesium, and calcium have at one time or another been thought to be indispensable to life; but in no sense do they, any more than cyanogen or carbon, uniquely define it. After protoplasm was accepted as the physical basis of life, it was recognized that its elements were not equally vital. The search for the important phase continued. Proteins in general, the nucleoproteins, nucleic acids, histone, the sterols, and even the fat globules have been proposed as the life-giving elements.

Attempts to differentiate animate from inanimate by a special vital molecule simply have no support in experiment. Chemical composition is no more satisfactory. The synthesis of urea was the initial blow to this latter conception and the large number of organic compounds that have already been prepared indicate no unique chemistry of biology. It is the protoplasm as a whole that is alive, and not the particle.

A more adequate criterion might be developed in terms of structure, the second type of ateleological theory. Structure and composition, it is true, are not very different in modern science, and it would be difficult to classify Carl Kraft's theory which replaces the usual polypeptide chains by a helical spiral. The distinction is, however, clear in the instances we cite.

The emphasis on chemical entities and configurations is overcome by the field theory of Burr and Northrop.[6] The wholeness and pattern of an organism is maintained by the factors of an electro-dynamic field in the face of considerable chemical exchange and physical activity. This field of force is derived from potential gradients, polar charges, and other electrical phenomena. By means of it, problems of development and organization may be understood. The same laws govern fields of force in animate and inanimate realms; the only difference between them, and the criterion of their differentiation, is the degree of complexity.

A bold theory is advanced by Dr. William Seifriz of the University of Pennsylvania.[7] The attribute, living, is dependent upon a specific state of matter. Protoplasm is characterized by a dynamic invisible structure. This theory, consistent with the known properties of protoplasm, is built about the long-chain molecules of protein. These molecules have chemically active poles which allow for the increase in size and, possibly, linear side chains. A three dimensional fibrous lattice is thus formed which satisfies the demand for a perpetuated system and for quick readjustment by mere transfer of the chemical affinities of the termini.

This hypothesis is particularly inviting because it provides for so many of the physical properties of protoplasm. Elasticity is due to the arrangement of the fibers resembling the construction and the give of a brush heap. Its viscid flow and tensile strength are likewise easily explained. The fact that protoplasm can pass through the pores of a fine filter and retain its vital properties but cannot be forced through larger pores indicates that the structure reorients itself in the first instance and is destroyed in the second. And even further, this theory would allow for the variety of composition and structural organization

[6] Burr and Northrop, "The Electro-dynamic Theory of Life," *Quarterly Review of Biology*, 10, pp. 322-33 (1935).

[7] W. Seifriz, *Protoplasm*, New York, McGraw-Hill Book Company, 1936.

while showing a common property. It would also explain how so many reactions can occur simultaneously by assuming enclosures set off by the structure.

The theory accounts for newer developments. Viruses, which seem to have the same chemical composition, have different properties. This would be explicable in terms of structure. A similar development in chemistry indicates the importance of structure rather than of atomic weight in the periodic table.

This level of organization is not different from the physical but it is more complex. The operation of a clock is dependent upon the placing of a last cog, a cog exactly like the others, but one which gives the clock a set of new properties.

It is evident that this is a most convincing theory but its value as a criterion of life must be questioned. Its necessity, like that of the chemical element, may be obvious, but its sufficiency is not. Seifriz does not state quite clearly enough what the significance of this theory is in distinguishing life, for he says in one place: "Fully to interpret protoplasmic organization in physical terms is impossible; it is too intricate—it is life itself."[8] Later, he says that "the harmonious functioning of a cell is but another name for life."[9]

Peters arrives at a structure similar to Seifriz's while trying to account kinetically for the speed of local and general responses.[10] Neither he nor Needham, however, seem to consider structure as the criterion of life.

To say that these theories are inadequate as tests of life is not to deny their manifest virtues. The physical and chemical properties as well as the peculiarly biological owe their definiteness to theories of this nature. It is possible that some non-living proteins might exhibit the rudiments of such a structure, or possibly even a model cell such as Dr. George Crile's, formed by a few drops of brain ash in a solution of the phospholipin, lecithin.

It is in the teleological theories that we find the most profitable suggestions for a criterion of life. Let us begin by defining

[8] *Ibid.*, p. 264.
[9] *Ibid.*, p. 267.
[10] R. A. Peters, "Proteins and Cell Organization," *Perspectives in Biochemistry,* Cambridge, Cambridge University Press, 1937.

function as that property which a set of morphologically different classes has in common.

Historically, it has been most usual to propose certain functions as differentiating the animate from the inanimate. If there be such properties they must be common to all objects known to be living and must include no object which is non-living. A word of warning is necessary; we shall rarely consider the highly developed forms such as man but shall restrict ourselves to the lower forms.

Perhaps the earliest criterion which man used was that of movement. It is well known that ancient peoples distinguished, although not always correctly, the living from the not-living by this property. The stream, the fire, and the cloud were all alive. This is not an adequate test for not only are there forms which are not motile, but motion is only a kind of energy resulting from the oxidation of fuel. There are many other examples of motion in the inorganic world which approximate the movement of protozoa. These have been developed through the study of the mechanics of motion. Spontaneous movement is largely the result of surface forces and osmotic change. Quincke found that the difference of molecular tension between the surface of a body and water at different points resulted in movement toward the lesser tension. He has remarked on the streaming movement of water and alcohol.

Another often suggested criterion is that of irritability and, at first sight, it seems satisfactory. However reaction by a change to an external stimulus is a general phenomenon of Nature. The expansion of metal in heat is just this. Sensibility does not satisfy even when further modified. If it is suggested that external stimulus be changed in favor of internal stimulus we have the osmotic growths to consider. If a greater disproportion between action and reaction be suggested we need only to be reminded of the difference between the force necessary to detonate dynamite and its resulting force. Like movement, irritability appears to be negligible in some plants and bacteria, while models such as Lillie's nerve cell duplicate it.

The next criterion may be considered under the broad heading: the functions of nutrition. This is defined as the phenomenon by which a living organism absorbs material from its environment, subjects it to chemical change, utilizes it and disposes of its waste products. This also is an ancient theory. Aristotle had said that life is nutrition, growth, and decay, having for its cause a principle which contains its end. It is fitting that this should be placed here, for irritability is associated with permeability, and the latter with the selectivity of foods. An interesting example of this selectivity is shown by the well-known ingestion by a drop of chloroform of a waxed glass filament and subsequent ejection of the glass.

Having considered the absorption of nutritional material, we now consider its utilization. Life is said to depend on the process of metabolism, the constant chemical activity which synthesizes relatively specific material. It is to this end that all nutrition is devoted. Anabolism is the constructive phase. The energy which it provides is responsible for maintenance and growth. The destructive phase, katabolism, is responsible for degeneration and death. There seems to be no reason for assuming that viruses have metabolisms of their own. In addition, the case of suspended animation of bacteria and spores seems to indicate that this faculty is not unique. Loeb thought that metabolism was adequate for defining life, yet it is significant that neither maintenance nor growth, neither reproduction nor death is an adequate criterion of life. Bichot defined life as the ensemble of the functions which resist death; but this defines life in terms of death, yet death is the end of life and cannot be defined without first defining life.

Repair and growth are intimately related and those two inorganic examples that effectively rule out the one serve likewise to exclude the other. We refer of course to the growth and repair of crystals and of semipermeable membranes. The objection commonly brought against these examples, that the growth here is by simple accretion not at all like living growth, is scarcely fair. It is not too broad an interpretation to say that when a piece of calcium chloride is put in a sodium carbonate solution the calcium absorbs the carbonic ion, incorporating it in calcium carbonate, and ejects the chloride ion. Thus, one may describe the systems composed of semipermeable mem-

branes as growing by intussusception. This objection bows
before another point of criticism. It assumes the chemical identity of the organism independent of its food, but protoplasm
has only a limited power of imposing a specific chemical form
on the nutrient.

Finally we turn to the function of reproduction. A variety
of non-living models illustrates this: simple fissure occurs in
crystal and osmotic activity or when an oil globule suspended
in water is touched on opposite sides by particles of soda. Le
Duc has shown that even saline solutions of different concentra-
tions approximate karyokinesis.[11] It is quite possible, without
too wide an interpretation of the terms, to say that pepsin and
trypsin are self-producing in the presence of pepsinogen and
trypsinogen respectively. It has even been suggested that the
origin of periodicity, no uncommon phenomena of colloidal
behavior, may be the same: a progressive change of concentration at an available surface.

The suggestion has been made that life be defined in terms
of a twofold rhythm of nutrition and/or reproduction. Dr.
Pennypacker has discussed this criterion but it, too, seems in
the last analysis to be inadequate. It is still an open question
whether any more satisfactory criterion would emerge by using
the more usual properties of living things in combination or as
terms in a Boolean expansion, i.e., a definition stated in a disjunction of the product of properties or the negatives of properties having the form $A = a_1 a_2 \ldots a_n b_1 b_2 \ldots b_m k_1 k_2
\ldots k_g$. N. W. Perie remarks: ". . . combinations of two or
three qualities, though they might easily be drawn up to exclude all obviously non-living systems, will also exclude some
which are, if not typically living, at least generally included in
that category."[12]

The discussion so far has shown the inadequacy of the usual
definitions of life; instances under the teleological and the
ateleological did not promise success. A logical possibility, however, still exists under the teleological classification. In closing

[11] S. Le Duc, *The Mechanism of Life*, London, Rebman, 1911.
[12] N. W. Perie, "The Meaninglessness of the Terms Life and Living," *Perspectives in Biochemistry*, Cambridge, Cambridge University Press, 1937, p. 21.

we should like to indicate this alternative in anticipation of Singer's contribution to the problem. Here, as before, it may turn out that an issue of experimental science hinges upon a matter of logic; a sufficient logical technique may explain the difficulty and perhaps resolve it. Definitions usually state that all life has at least one of a number of properties: p_1, p_2, . . . p_n. The "all" is generally taken distributively, but a definition may make use of a collective "all." Thus it may be that a sufficient definition of lives must have some reference to a concept of the domain of life, "Nature," as a collective term.

Singer develops the idea of collective definition by distinguishing three kinds of structural classification. The objects of a mechanical class have the same configuration and have properties at analogous points; these objects differ *inter se* only by their position. (Thus x_1 belongs to the same mechanical class as does x_2 if $x_1 - x_2 = 0$.) Two elements, x_1 and x_2, belong to the same physical class if $f(x_1) - f(x_2) = 0$. Morphological classification is expressed mathematically $f(x_1) - f(x_2) = k$ (where k is a fixed quantity). Biology is concerned with objects of this last category. Living things, though lacking mechanical and physical identity, conform to a certain morphology, for they can only vary within definite limits defined by parentage and ancestry.

In addition to structural properties, biological entities also possess nonstructural properties. The compatibility of these has already been demonstrated; it was there apparent that the use of functional classes did not necessarily imply vitalism since the classes are not in any sense unique to the biological level. The class of timepieces is teleological, for it contains objects of different morphology related by the common difference, a function of time, which each produces in itself. The producer-product relation is significant in biology; Singer formulates the conditions of this relation and then develops a class having the function of reproducing.

A description of the *producer-product* relation may best be effected by reference to a mechanical image representing individuals and classes found in Nature. This image, composed of a manifold of points individuated by space-time coördinates and in one to one correspondence with the points of a natural system, is subject to a law such that, if the conditions at all points were given for a value t_1, of an independent variable t, they are determined for any second value, t_2. "The t for which these requirements hold is true in the time-dimension of its space-time coördinates." That point manifold of S which is at t_1 may be called S_1; that at t_2, S_2; etc. The cause-effect relation maintains between S_1 and S_2 if the system is closed; the producer-product relation holds only between a detail of S_1 and of S_2, for the producer is only a part of a cause and a product only a part of an effect.[13]

The conditions for defining the producer-product relation are four in number. An acorn, a_1, may be said to *produce* an oak, o_1, if a_1 belongs to a morphological class a, in S_1, and o_1 belongs to a morphological class o in S_2; and if a_1 is removed from a then no o_1 exists in o. This bionomic condition serves further to differentiate the producer-product relation from cause-effect: the cause of the oak's existence is a state of nature having an acorn in it. The second condition may be stated: a_1 is said to be a *nonproducer* if a_1 belongs to a class a some of whose members are producers of o's, but a_1 is not a producer of an o. a is said to be a *potential producer* of an o if it belongs to a class a at least one of whose members is a producer of an o and at least one is a nonproducer. a is said to be the *reproducer* of an o if there is an o which is the producer of o. *Nonreproducer* and *potential reproducer* may also be defined according to this pattern. These terms pertain to other morphological classes, for example, eggs and birds. An egg, by the conditions laid down, may be defined as a potential reproducer. Then the acorn and the egg are members of a class not having the same morphology, but having the same function, that of reproducing.

The existence of a functional class established, the next step is the definition of membership in a sequence; this is distinct from membership in a class because it uses the concept of individuation. Suppose four (or more) structural objects each the necessary condition for the next; it is evident that the second

[13] The cause-effect relation is reflexive, transitive, and not symmetrical; the producer-product relation is reflexive, transitive, and asymmetrical.

and the third are reproducers in the sense that they produce in the sequence the same kind of thing that produced them. The fourth is a potential reproducer because the second and the third are producers and the first is not. The fourth is the first to have the function of reproduction, but the whole sequence has the potentiality of producing itself in the geometrical sense of producing a line. This is a sequence of objects whose function is reproducing.

So also, suppose a sequence of n (four or more) bodies, the (n — 1) and (n — 2) are reproducers and the n, a producer of a body of different morphology which inaugurates another sequence of at least four of the same morphology. Thus the function of type-reproduction has been introduced, for there are now two parental lines differing in morphology but having the same function. The same holds for a sequence of n parental lines; the last body in this instance has acquired the function of type-variations and now has the double function of continuing its past history and of change.

It is not necessary to hold that every living thing possesses these two functions, but the class of living beings cannot exist unless some bodies have them. Just so, all the members of a family are not fathers. The existence of a class of living beings, then, implies a body having the function of type-reproduction and of type-variation; a parental line, an ancestral line, and finally of a group possessing these functions.

The series of groups, each composed of bodies of the same morphology, will increase with the number of variations. There develops a cone of life, and to it all living things are said to belong since they are members of groups composed of the ancestors and progeny of the ancestors and progeny of all things having the properties of type-reproduction and type-variation. All lives are fragments of this collection, Life, and are defined as living by their participation in it.

BIOLOGICAL PHENOMENA WHICH A DEFINITION OF LIFE MUST INCLUDE

MIRIAM I. PENNYPACKER

Department of Zoölogy, University of Pennsylvania

ALTHOUGH the problem of determining the fundamental differences between living and nonliving matter is a very old one, it still holds the interest of a large number of people who would like to have it solved or at least receive adequate reasons why no satisfactory solution can be given. This request seems to me to be a reasonable one, but one which has not so far been satisfactorily answered. Many attempts have been made by biologists to distinguish living from nonliving phenomena, but none of them hold absolutely for all possible cases; and I doubt that their proponents had the idea that they should. One finds more frequently the statement or its implication that no satisfactory definition can ever be made. Perhaps it may seem entirely superfluous to many biologists to give any detailed explanation of the nature of the impossibility of constructing a definition of living phenomena, at least to enlighten other biologists; but one can easily see why this state of affairs is not satisfactory to the thoughtful non-biologist.

The present paper is not an attempt to define life nor can it claim to give a complete statement of the reasons why such a definition is impossible. It is my aim, rather, to indicate the wide range of phenomena which would have to be covered by such a definition and to point out what appear to me to be some of the most obvious difficulties. There are, scattered in many of our general textbooks on biology, suggestions of this nature, but nowhere, so far as I can discover, have they been gathered together into a single text. To assist such gathering of material in preparation for defining may have its justification. As J. Gray, in *A Text-Book of Experimental Cytology* (1931, p. ix), says, "Whatever viewpoint enables us to establish new facts, that viewpoint is the one we should cherish: if it stimulates others to frame hypotheses more fruitful than our own we may rest content."

One of the questions likely to arise early in any attempt made to define life, is whether a definition can be constructed which will embrace all cases to which the term "living" is commonly applied. Not only must we include all organisms, from the simplest to the most complex, but there must also be included certain individual parts, such as organs, tissues, cells, capable of an independent existence in an appropriate medium. It seems to me that this difficulty of including parts of organisms is not an unsurmountable one. It can be diminished by constructing a somewhat analogous problem. If all of an individual's dwelling except two or three rooms had been carried away by a tornado or some other catastrophe and we tried to answer the question whether or not the individual had a home, we should first have to decide what we considered essential to a home. Similarly, in defining life, our definition must be strictly limited to the minimum essential to that state. The definition must then be applied to all cases which appear, for possible solution.

If, in dealing with the problem just mentioned or with any other phase of the larger question, it is necessary to use and define "individual organism," a new obstacle may arise. There are cases in which it is difficult to determine either in time or in space the exact limits of certain organisms. Organisms with complicated life cycles, animals in which encystment takes place, and even those, such as amoeba, undergoing fission, are examples in which it is difficult to determine the life-span of the individual. The plasmodia of Mycetozoans illustrate the class with indefinite boundaries for the individual in space.

The objection has been raised: "How can we define life when we cannot determine the death-point of an organism?" That it is difficult and sometimes impossible to discover the death-point of whole or parts of organisms has long been known to experimental scientists. Nevertheless, to see in this circumstance a real obstacle to the construction of a definition of living things is similar to the statement that one cannot tell red from blue until the relative proportions of red and blue in all shades of purple can be indicated exactly. We should expect the determination of the death-point to be facilitated by a clearer demarcation of living and non-living. That it is so difficult at present is due to the fact that we cannot clearly state the essential differences between the two states.

Extreme diversity in form, certain fairly constant structural elements, and complicated chemical composition of living matter have proved tempting features upon which to base theories of life. Theories of this kind utilize characteristics of whole organisms and parts, down to, and including, their constituent molecules. R. Beutner (1938) gives the ability to develop diversified forms as one of two distinct general characteristics of life. In order to serve as a distinguishing characteristic of life, the statement that living matter appears in the form of organisms must be accompanied by a definition of organism which does not use the terms "life" or "living."

When we read Gray's (1931) statement that from a mechanical viewpoint, cellular structure, or its equivalent is required, if life is to take the forms which actually exist in nature, we seem to have something which will be of real service to us. But this hope is dispelled upon learning further that his criterion has some exceptions. Fragments of amoebae without nuclei, or enucleated sea urchin eggs possess for some time the typical properties of living matter. Bacteria, while not having the structure of typical cells, are alive. So are fungi, which lack cell structure in the strict sense of the word.

It is difficult for the cytologist to picture an organism possessing even a relatively small number of distinguishing characteristics and yet not having some self-perpetuating mechanism, such as chromosomes. Although recent cytological studies continue to add to our list of species in which such a mechanism is found, it is probably too much to hope that all forms will eventually be included. If, therefore, we must assume that certain primitive forms of what we now call "life" have no special mechanism for perpetuating characteristics, we must be prepared to accept the idea that there may be just as great a gap between these lowest forms and the rest of the living world as there is between the inanimate and the primitive animate forms.

At this point we are led naturally to a consideration of protoplasm as a special substance peculiar to living organisms. If we are to say that all living things can be distinguished from non-living by the fact that the former possess protoplasm and the latter do not, we are constrained to explain what we mean by protoplasm. We may turn, first of all, to the cytologists to determine whether there are any visible characteristics which will enable us to say what is and what is not protoplasm. E. B. Wilson (1925) wrote that, "Up to the present time no single theory of protoplasmic structure has commanded general acceptance, and it is more than doubtful whether any universal formula for this structure can be given." He said that many reasons caused us to believe that protoplasm has a perfectly definite organization, but its visible expression is in many kinds of structures, none of which can be regarded as universally characteristic of living substance. As regards visible structure no valid distinction, either practical or logical, can be made between a "primary" or "fundamental" structure and a "secondary" structure. The "fundamental" structure of living material is beyond our present limits of microscopical vision, so can only be inferred. The only element of protoplasm which all cytologists describe as omnipresent is the "homogeneous hyaloplasm," in which can be seen no structure.

The observations of the protozoölogist, G. N. Calkins, seem to confirm Wilson's statements concerning the need to go beyond the range of visible structure to determine the nature of protoplasm. Calkins has written (1926, p. 38):

In its last analysis form depends upon the chemical and physical make-up of the protoplasm and its polarity which signifies a specific protoplasmic organization and interaction of different protoplasmic substances. A minute fragment of Uroleptus mobilis is difficult to distinguish from a similar fragment of Dileptus gigas, yet the former develops into a perfect Uroleptus, the latter into Dileptus. The encysted forms of many types are impossible to identify until the cysts are opened and vital processes begin again.

B. J. Luyet (1934, p. 1) has made some different assumptions from those of Wilson. He says:

It is generally agreed that the entire cellular mass, exclusive of some evident inclusions, is living matter, but in the last analysis this is a mere assumption, although supported by some observed facts. It is possible, as well, that the only living elements of the cell are the chromosomes or the genes, and that all the rest of the cellular content is a product of their activity but is not alive. Possibly also, the formed elements of the cell, such as the chromosomes, the nucleoli, the centrosomes, the plastids, the chondriosomes, etc., are the living units, and the ground substance is of the nature of an elaborated culture medium allowing the life of the formed ele ments to be carried on. Another possibility is that all the so-called granulations or microsomes of which the protoplasm seems to con sist are the living units. The hyaline protoplasmic mass would be then an elaborated medium. And there are, of course, many other possibilities that I do not intend to develop here.

I assume as a working hypothesis, that the processes that we cal life take place in some formed components of the cell, such as the genes or the chromosomes, possibly the centrosomes, the nucleoli or some of their constituent parts, the plastids or some of their struc tural elements, the chondriosomes, the nucleoplasmic and cyto plasmic granulations, etc., and that the fundamental hyaline mas of the cell is not living matter. The living units would then con stitute only a relatively small fraction of the entire cell. . . . assume, as one of my working hypotheses, that the cell is a symbi otic colony of biological units which possess life in different degrees

W. Seifriz (1938) believes the differentiation of protoplasm to be due to structural characteristics. He writes:

All fundamental properties of living matter are due to the struc ture of its protein constituents, and the two chief characteristics o this structure are its specificity and its continuity. Thus may th conclusion be drawn that structural organization is responsible fo the physical properties of living matter, and for the specific prope ties which elevate living matter above the non-living.

L. W. Sharp, in his *Introduction to Cytology* (1921, p. 49) expresses some further views on this subject. He writes:

By most modern biologists such attempts to assign the principle of life to any particular constituent unit of protoplasm or of the cell, whether this unit be an observed structural component or a purely imaginary one, are regarded as not in harmony with an adequate modern conception of the term "living." It has been repeatedly emphasized that life should be thought of not as a property of any particular cell constituent, but as an attribute of the cell system as a whole (Wilson 1899); or, as Brooks (1899) put it, not merely as a property but as a relation or adjustment between the properties of the organism and those of its environment. This recalls Herbert Spencer's characterization of life as a "continuous adjustment of internal relations to external relations." As Sachs (1892, 1895) and others urged, the various elements in the cell should be referred to as active and passive rather than living and lifeless. These elements play various rôles in the cell's activity: each contributes to the orderly operation of the whole. When any part fails to function properly, or when the proper adjustment is not maintained, the whole system of correlated reactions, the resultant of which we call life, must become disorganized. As Child (1915) remarks, the theories postulating vital units only transfer the problems of life from the organism to something smaller; the fundamental problem of coordination is no nearer solution than before, and the whole question is placed outside the field of experimentation. Harper (1919) also points out that modern cytology no longer looks upon protoplasm as a substance with a single specific structure, or as one made up of ultimate fundamental units of some kind, but rather as a colloidal system or group of systems of varying structure and composition. "The fundamental organization of living material is expressed in the structure of the cell." The cell itself, and not some hypothetical corpuscle, is the unit of organic structure. Protoplasm is accordingly not made up of structural units arranged in various ways to form the cell organs, but is rather a colloidal system in which special processes and functions have become localized and fixed in certain regions; and this in turn has resulted in the evolution of organs possessing more or less permanence.

There are some biologists who, failing to find a satisfactory basis of separation of living from non-living in the visible structure of organisms, go on to the chemical realm. As these attempts are so far theoretical explanations, only a very brief mention will be made of them here.[1]

Gray appeared to be convinced that the ultimate criterion for the animate would be revealed by a knowledge of the molecular state. He thought that it seemed more rational to consider living material as a state of matter in which the constituent molecules are organized in a different way from those of inanimate objects. This organization has yet to be disclosed. Gray believed that the study of protoplasmic structure clearly illustrated the limitations of a simple physical approach to biological problems and that the underlying mechanism of cytoplasmic differentiation is atomic or electronic in nature. Therefore, until we have the means to determine the answer to this problem a confession of our ignorance is our best asset.

Among biologists who resort to a special kind of molecule to explain protoplasm are some, who like Verworn (1903) depict "peculiarly labile protein molecules called 'biogens.' The molecule itself was not thought of as alive, but its constitution was held to be the basis of life, which 'results from the chemical transformations which its lability makes possible.' "[2] The change from the labile to a stable condition is death.

Adami (1908, 1919) attributed life to "the function, or sum of functions of a special order of molecules," called biophores (not the same as the biophores of Weismann), which are proteidogenous in nature.

They compose an active substance which takes the form of relatively inert proteins when subjected to chemical analysis. The biophore is conceived by Adami to have the form of a ring or a ring of rings of the benzene type—a ring of amino-acid radicles with many unsatisfied affinities or bonds. The biophore grows in a manner analogous to that of the inorganic crystal: ions and radicles from the surrounding medium become attached as side chains to the free bonds of the central ring and take on a grouping similar to that of the latter; in this way the biophoric molecules are multiplied. Since side chains can be detached and new ones of other

---

[1] Sharp, from whose *Cytology* (1921) most of the following remarks have been taken, gives a fuller account and a bibliography of the literature. Also see his 1934 edition.

[2] Quoted from *Introduction to Cytology*, by L. W. Sharp, p. 49.

kinds added, the biophore is changeable and may exist in many different forms. Although the central ring is thought to be relatively stable and fixed, the variety of side chains and their many possible arrangements probably give to each species a distinct kind of biophore. On this hypothesis the molecule of living matter (biophore) is one of extraordinary complexity, and in a state of constant unsatisfaction, built up by linking on other simple molecules, and as constantly, in the performance of function, giving up or discharging into the surrounding medium these and other molecular complexes which it has elaborated. . . . Accordingly, life is a state of persistent and incomplete recurrent satisfaction and dissatisfaction of . . . certain proteidogenous molecules.[3]

A. P. Matthews, in his account of the "General Chemistry of Cells,"[4] says:

The great difference between living and dead is a difference in the energy content of the molecules and atoms in the two states. All substances, electrons, atoms, and molecules can and do exist in two forms: energy-rich and energy-poor forms. . . . The former is the living; the latter is the dead form.

He goes on to relate the method by which this energy is derived originally from the sun, passes on to earth, water, and air, raising the energy content of their molecules, and then passes on to plants and animals.

Not all of the chemical theories to explain living matter are dependent upon the postulation of a special form of protein or protein-like molecule. P. H. Mitchell writes in his *Textbook of General Physiology* (1938, p. 417):

The properties of living matter are due in part to structure, in other words, to the manner in which the components are put together. The chemical constituents may not be different from substances producible by non-living agencies. Many of them, indeed, have been artificially synthesized. . . . But even if all the different proteins, fats, carbohydrates and other substances of living structures could be artificially synthesized, it would still be impossible, in the light of our present knowledge, to put them together in such

[3] Quoted from *Introduction to Cytology*, by L. W. Sharp, p. 50.

[4] A chapter of the *General Cytology*, edited by E. V. Cowdry, Univ. of Chicago Press, Chic., Ill. 1934.

a manner as to produce life. The architecture of living matter is exceedingly complex.

Luyet has assumed (1934, p. 5) that

vital phenomena are due to a special and exceptional arrangement of the atoms, or other structural elements, according to a type of "architecture" different from any actually known in chemistry [and] therefore that the exceptional type of "architecture" supposed in the living units is such that more atoms or more structural elements are concentrated in living matter than in the same volume of dead matter.

Höber (1911) explained life as the result of many correlated processes occurring between many substances under certain conditions. Child (1915) wrote:

Protoplasm, instead of being a peculiar living substance with a peculiar complex morphological structure necessary for life, is on the one hand a colloidal product of the chemical reactions, and on the other hand a substratum in which the reactions occur and which influences their course and character both physically and chemically. In short, the organism is a physico-chemical system of a certain kind.[5]

One thing upon which all of these investigators seem to agree has been summed up by Sharp in these words: "It is with protoplasm that the phenomena of life, in so far as we know them, are invariably associated." They probably would agree with his further statement:

The complex behavior of the living organism can receive scientific explanation (i.e., be fitted into an orderly scheme of antecedents and consequents), if at all, only on the basis of the constitution and properties of the materials composing protoplasm; the structural organization of protoplasm; the relation of the reactions and responses of protoplasm in the form of organized units or cells to the environmental conditions; the chain of energy changes occurring in connection with all of the organism's activities; and the correlation of all these conditions and events.

But the exact determination of this basis must await the discovery of better methods, methods which will not result in

[5] Quoted from *Introduction to Cytology*, by L. W. Sharp, p. 51.

the death of the subject and the consequent invalidation of the results. We must conclude, therefore, that any justifiable use of the statement, "living can be distinguished from non-living because the former is composed of protoplasm and the latter is not," lies in the future.

The use of certain functions of living organisms as distinguishing processes peculiar to them alone has thus far not been very successfully employed, although it is not infrequently the case that a number of functions are listed in general texts as characteristic of life. Metabolism (including growth), reproduction, and irritability are probably those most often mentioned. Adaptation, rhythmicity, and contractility are given in a long list of characteristics, submitted by C. G. Rogers in his *Textbook of Comparative Physiology*. He says (1938, p. 73), "It may be said that certain of these properties appearing alone would not be sufficient to determine a given structure as living rather than dead, but it may be held that if all or any considerable number of them can be demonstrated the material would be classed as living matter." Previously, in this chapter, there is given the means for distinguishing protoplasm. "Protoplasm exhibits a few characteristics by which it may always be recognized and distinguished from other material substances. These are its chemical composition, metabolism, its tendency to undergo cyclic changes, and its power to produce its own catalytic agents."

W. J. V. Osterhout, in a series of lectures on *The Nature of Life*, considered in turn growth, reproduction, motion, irritability, metabolism, and selective permeability. He did not indicate that he found any one of them sufficient to characterize living phenomena. He wrote (1924, p. 88):

What shall we conclude f om our survey of the tests of life? Certain of them can be imitated to a remarkable degree and seem to be reducible to mechanism. In other cases we have not yet reached this stage but we are making continual progress toward a physico-chemical explanation, so that many investigators are convinced that such an explanation must eventually be reached. It is certainly true that all biologists agree that the organism is in some respects a machine but to what extent it is a machine, is still a matter of controversy.

Beutner considers self-reproduction, i.e., "the power of chemically transforming the material of their environment (or food material) into their own substance" as one of two distinct general characteristics of living organisms. The questions arise: "How much does Beutner include in the term, 'self-reproduction'; does it include repair and growth of the individual alone, or does it also include reproduction as the term is generally applied in biology?" As he has used this term in connection with viruses and enzymes, which are formless, one cannot tell the extent to which he would apply it in organisms with form. If the ability to reproduce new individuals is made the determining factor, many hybrids are excluded from the class of the living. Here again may arise the difficulty of having to define the term "individual organism"—a problem which we have already discussed. In some stages, such as the seed, the spore, or even the adult stage of certain species, there is no intake of food and very little evidence of metabolism.

Some experimental work, such as the formation of individual animals by joining two halves of different species of eggs and allowing them to develop (Hadorn, 1937), stimulation of the development of unfertilized eggs by artificial means (Loeb, 1913), and the substitution of parts of another individual in replacement of the organism's own parts in the embryo (Spemann, 1938), impedes any definition of living organisms based upon their derivation by the usual means of reproduction.

L. V. Heilbrunn gives irritability as the most important distinguishing characteristic of life. He has written that (1937, p. 397),

exposed to a sudden change in its environment, a living system typically shows a reaction or a response. As will be noted more fully later, this response is not so much dependent on the nature of the environmental change as on the nature of the living system. In general, practically all living systems are very sensitive to sudden alterations of their environment; to such changes they respond by showing activity of one sort or another. This characteristic of living material is called "irritability" and, perhaps more than any other vital characteristic, serves to distinguish living systems from non-living. A simple inanimate system such as a block of wood resting on a table is moved when force acts upon it. The nature of this reaction and the extent of the movement is a relatively simple function of the magnitude of the force involved, and the frictional resistance. In living systems, however, the reaction to a change in environment or to an external force may be extremely complicated, and typically bears very little relation to the nature of the force or its magnitude. This type of behavior is not unknown in complicated inanimate systems. Thus when the trigger of a gun is pulled, or the throttle of a steam or gasoline engine, the changes that ensue bear no very direct relation to the original force. From the standpoint of the mechanist, the only difference between the inanimate engine and the living system lies in the fact that the latter is vastly more complicated. It is, indeed, of a different order of complexity.

One might ask at this point for a comparison in the degree of complexity of some of the simplest living organisms, such as bacteria and viruses, with some of the most complicated inanimate systems. Should we still find the former vastly more complicated? It seems likely that as yet no answer can be given to this question. Heilbrunn says (p. 397):

Because of the fact that man constructs his own machines, he is in a good position to know how they work, and he can if he pleases state exactly the various physical and chemical changes that follow the pull of a trigger or a throttle. The changes produced by outer environmental forces on living systems are for the most part mysterious and unknown. We perceive the end-result of the response, but at the present time it is very difficult to be certain of any of the physical and chemical changes which intervene between the external force and the discernible response.

It is obvious that a satisfactory comparison cannot be made of the degree of complexity of two systems, one of which is "for the most part mysterious and unknown." It follows that, whatever may be the physiologist's reasons for regarding irritability as a distinguishing characteristic of living organisms, those of us less favored with opportunities for studying living processes at first hand must await more conclusive evidence before taking the same stand.

The foregoing account is sufficient to indicate the problem, as it appears to me, of defining living organisms. Some of the obstacles which biologists see in this connection may turn out, as I have indicated, to be only temporary. The preponderance of theory over fact in the claims of biologists who would use the possession of protoplasm as their criterion at present prevents its acceptance. The effort to attach the identification of the living to some characteristic structure or arrangement of parts shifts the field of exploration constantly toward the more and more minute, until it is finally lost in the haze of theory. Functions and properties as now described are not serviceable even if biologists themselves could agree concerning which are most characteristic of life.

It may be well to repeat here that I do not claim to have given a complete account of the difficulties which biologists may see in the task of defining living things: I know that there are many more. I have indicated briefly what appeared to me to be some of the most important. Certainly, they are sufficiently serious to keep investigators occupied for a long time. Even after all of these obstacles will have been removed, there is no assurance that the solution to the problem of the differentiation of living from non-living matter will be unmistakably obvious. It will simply mean that the problem will be ready to be passed along to the philosophers, for as D'Arcy W. Thomson expressed it:

While we keep an open mind on this question of vitalism, or while we lean, as so many of us now do, or even cling with a great yearning, to the belief that something other than the physical forces animates the dust of which we are made, it is rather the business of the philosopher than of the biologist, or of the biologist only when he has served his humble and severe apprenticeship to philosophy, to deal with the ultimate problem.[6]

BIBLIOGRAPHY

All quotations from this Bibliography are used by permission of the Publishers.

Beutner, R. "The Independent Nature of Morphogenesis and Self-

[6] Quoted from *Introduction to Cytology*, by L. W. Sharp, p. 52.

Reproduction and Its Significance for the Cosmic Development of Life," *Biodynamica*, No. 38 (1938).

Calkins, G. N. *The Biology of the Protozoa*. Lea and Febiger, Philadelphia, 1926.

Gray, J. *A Text-Book of Experimental Cytology*. Cambridge Univ. Press, The Macmillan Company, New York, 1931.

Hadorn, E. *Archiv fuer Entwicklungsmechanik der Organismen*, 136 (1937), pp. 400-89.

Heilbrunn, L. V. *An Outline of General Physiology*. W. B. Saunders Co., Philadelphia, 1937.

Loeb, J. *Artificial Parthenogenesis and Fertilization*. Univ. of Chicago Press, Chicago, 1913.

Luyet, B. J. "Working Hypotheses on the Nature of Life," *Biodynamica*, No. 1 (1934).

Mitchell, P. H. *A Textbook of General Physiology*. McGraw-Hill Co., New York, 1938.

Osterhout, W. J. V. *The Nature of Life*. Henry Holt and Company, New York, 1924. Colver Lectures, Brown University.

Rogers, C. G. *Textbook of Comparative Physiology*. McGraw-Hill Co., New York, 1938.

Seifriz, W. "The Structure of Living Matter," *Biodynamica*, No. 32 (1938).

Sharp, L. W. *Introduction to Cytology*. McGraw-Hill Co., New York, 1921.

Spemann, H. *Embryonic Development and Induction*. Yale Press, New Haven, 1938.

Wilson, E. B. *The Cell in Development and Heredity*. The Macmillan Company, New York, 1925.

THE PRINCIPLE OF ASSOCIATIVE LEARNING

Edwin R. Guthrie

Department of Psychology, University of Washington

SOME form of the principle of association has been held by all psychologists. That it is included in the essential nature of mind is inescapable, whether we are concerned with action or with thought. Creatures with mind profit from experience, but profiting from experience requires first that there have been experience and second that something of that experience be revived by signs or marks that originally accompanied it. The profit must lie in improved action in a real situation, and it must be certain features of the situation that elicit the proper action.

The limitations of profit by experience lie in the limitations of our original repertoire of action. Only such actions as are provided for in our muscular and glandular equipment of response are available for the re-alignment that constitutes learning. We can only contract what muscles we have and in the patterns of contraction provided for in our nervous equipment. The difference between the minds of animals and of man lies mainly in a difference of original equipment of separable muscular contractions. Any movement once produced may be attached to an indefinite variety of signals or combinations of signals.

In the realm of thought, association is equally prominent. The rule of the syllogism, that the mark of a mark is a mark of the thing, is but a statement of the associative process. The signal of a signal is a signal for the perceptual response. Modern psychology is gradually recovering from the dualism introduced into the science of mind by theology and medieval soul-theory. Mind is regaining its Greek unity with the rest of nature. The essential likeness of thought and action, the realization that thinking is a special form of action, is gaining ground.

Dualism made quite impossible any satisfactory attack on the problem of association. Separation of thought and action as distinct, description of thought as an event outside the natural world order and as unrelated to physical events in sense organs, muscles, and nerves made the association of ideas an insoluble problem because it removed the objects associated and the conditions of association from observation. The modern conception of thinking as minimal action, an event in the physical world, growing out of overt action and taking its place in a series of physical events which includes physical stimuli to sense organs as the occasion for thought and physical stimuli to sense organs as one of the important results of thought, makes possible a new attack on the nature of the thinking process.

The motor theory of consciousness makes possible a great clarification of the questions: "What are the items that are associated? Are these ideas; stimuli; feelings; movements?" Before there can be any successful attack on the problem of association by the acknowledged scientific methods of observation and verification this question of what is associated must first be answered.

Science aims to furnish rules and generalizations about the world we live in. These rules derive from observation. But they must be communicable in language. The terms in which they are stated must be public and objective. The weather signs of events must be weather signs open to the observation of many persons. Only public experience can be dealt with by science because science is essentially a publication, a making common, a communication. Ideas, in so far as these are conceived as private events open only to the experiencer, are not stuff that science can use.

This difficulty the motor theory of consciousness overcomes. It limits the events to be clarified and publicized to the events open to public naming and public recognition, the first and most important requirement of science. Ideas as ideas are not thus open to the public. But the stimulation of sense organs, neural activity, and movement are observable and recordable. Of these three classes the second, nervous activity, is the least important for a theory of learning. Nervous activity is observable, but not, as a rule, in the cases in which learning is to be studied. Men will probably always be recalcitrant toward too close an inspection of their brain pathways when they are awake and in their right minds, which means when they are proper subjects for the observation of learning at its best. Our observations of nerve impulses and brain events are, thus far, limited to animal experiment and to medicine. We may relate disturbances of mind to brain pathology and thus realize that the brain is essential to learning. We may extend our knowledge of the roles played by brain structures through such ingenious experiments as those of Loucks, but a useful and verifiable theory of learning must be stated in terms of weather signs that can be observed without damaging the subject.

The objections of Köhler and Koffka and other Gestalt psychologists to association theory center about the truism that any act or any thought is the product of a total situation and not of one part or item of that situation. With this in mind they object to any rule that attempts to predict an action from some detail of the situation. Just as Bosanquet pointed out many years ago that the whole history of the world is the ground of every judgment, so it is true that every action of an individual is a part of a total experience that includes his whole past and his whole present.

But to make this an objection to the use of association as a principle is to misconceive the nature of scientific rules and the purpose of science. A scientific rule must enable its user to name and recognize some feature of the situation and as a result of this recognition enable him to anticipate through a named consequence what will be the following event. There are no names for total situations or total experiences and there will never be names for these. Names apply only to public, recurring features, to details, to parts of situations. Obnoxious as it may be, whenever a Gestalt psychologist talks about the world he must recognize partial features of that world. He is compelled to select and analyze. The Gestalt psychologist, if

he is consistent, must simply refuse to speak and content himself with an inarticulate gratification in the succession of name-
less dynamic totalities.

In the meantime practical persons, and science is either practical or it is nothing, will continue their search for recognizable antecedents of behavior, for the weather signs that enable
them to anticipate what is coming. And they will continue to
search for the items that are associated and for the conditions
under which association may be expected.

The association in which psychologists are interested is obviously an event that attaches to the individual person. Hol-
lingworth and Köhler have allowed themselves to slip into a
consideration of association as between events of the physical
world-order independent of the organism. The physical *Ges-
talten* in which Köhler is occasionally interested lie outside
the field of mind and are independent of the observer. Their
problems interest the philosopher and not the psychologist.
The problem of psychological association attaches to a person
or to an organism.

Pavlov's studies of association marked a real advance because
they made explicit what was being observed and they conformed to the requirement that this be public material. He
presented food to a dog and together with this stimulated some
sense organ or group of sense organs and observed a fraction
of the response, namely, the flow of saliva from a salivary duct.
Before Pavlov, association had labored with the handicap of a
theological dualism and attempted to deal with a strange
mélange of physical and mental events, of stimuli to sense
organs, contractions of muscles, secretions of glands, ideas,
thoughts, feelings, emotions. Some of these could be recorded
and were open to public inspection. Some were not. The only
previous laboratory observation of association which had been
systematic and extensive had been the work of Ebbinghaus
with nonsense syllables. But Ebbinghaus' method and reports
left the question of what he was observing quite unsettled.
Ebbinghaus thought of his work in terms of ideas and of the
associations established as between ideas. He was his own subject. Pavlov was working with dogs and speculation concerning

the ideas of the dog when the bell rang or saliva flowed was obviously dangerous and quite unverifiable. These were physical events and both were open to public observation and to instrumental recording. The supposititious ideas were not necessary to a description of what was found or to the formulation of the events into rules. Men now knew what to look for and this was reflected in the astonishing volume of research that has followed Pavlov's lead.

Pavlov's work was an advance toward clear scientific method. But there are reasons for judging that it suffered in one respect from the dead hand of the old tradition. Pavlov assumed from the beginning that the association was between two stimuli, using that word as Robinson used the word "stimulation" to indicate the activation of sense organs by a physical change. In the strict sense, food is not a stimulus to the dog. The stimulus is the action of food on the dog's sense organs, his taste, and touch, and temperature receptors. The association was, Pavlov assumed, an association between two stimuli, the old and the new. One had been previously an occasion for the reflex. This was the unconditioned stimulus. The other, the conditioned stimulus, had previously been ineffective in producing the particular response of salivary secretion.

Probably the reason why Pavlov assumed the association to lie between the two stimuli was that he still tended to think in terms of the association of ideas and conceived the real association as being between the idea of the bell and the idea of the food. He seems at least to have been strangely content to leave unexamined the details of the food stimulation and he records the time at which food was *presented*, not the time at which it affected sense organs. Nor was he interested in the question of just what action of the food constituted the stimulus. There is some evidence that the movements of chewing activate the salivary glands. This did not interest Pavlov. He is content to speak of food as the stimulus. It is enough for him that the dog perceives food and that he perceives the bell. The fact that the perception of the bell involved action and a sustained complex of self-stimulation, movement-produced stimulation, Pavlov found without interest and he expresses some impatience when attention is called to it.

What are the items most available for observation and record in dealing with association? In my own judgment these are the new signal, the stimulus that is to become an associative cue, and the resulting movement. One reason for ruling out the unconditioned stimulus as the important second item of the association is that this is often unobserved in behavior. Action cannot always be related to one detail of the antecedent situation. There is always a complex of stimuli of which the unconditioned stimulus is only a part. The dog does not secrete saliva as a result of food alone; also essential are hunger, freedom from distraction, posture, and many other determiners. To observe association it is necessary only to observe the response and the association of this response with new determiners. How the response was produced is irrelevant except in so far as this affects the nature of the response.

To observe an association, then, it is required that we observe some action of the person or animal and the circumstances of this action. We must also observe this action again in altered circumstances and on another occasion. If the circumstances are exactly repeated we have no evidence that learning has occurred. Bricks and other mindless objects will behave as they behaved before if the circumstances are the same. To qualify as associative learning an action must be observed twice; but there must also have been a third observation. Usually many more are taken for granted because the final observation must consist in noting that the action follows a situation including a cue, a situation that it has failed to follow when this cue has not been previously associated with the action.

This means that the situation including the new cue must not contain elements that would give rise to the response without the cue.

We must observe:

(1) A situation (A) including the cue is followed by behavior that does not include the response in which we are interested (saliva flow, leg flexion, naming—any action whatever).

(2) Situation (*B*) including the cue is followed by the response.

(3) Afterward, situation (*A*) including the cue is followed by the response.

If we have observed this succession of events we say that the cue has become a conditioner of the response, a new signal for the response, that learning has taken place, that mind is in evidence. This is the essential of mind.

The position of association in current experimental programs is a curious one. Experiments in simple conditioning aimed at discovering the circumstances of association, the effect of unsupported repetition of the signal, the more precise description of the evoked response, the effect of different patterns of stimuli, etc., abound in the current literature. This is reassuring because for many years experiments in animal learning have not been concerned with association and the analysis of habit. The thousands of recorded experiments with maze learning have almost without exception been so planned and so recorded that association could not enter the record. The number of trials required to reach a certain criterion of success, the number and position in the series of alleys of errors made by the animal, are entered in the record, but these are usually entered in the form of averages and smoothed curves and the nature of the changes in the successive runs of individual animals is not noticed. I am not familiar with any maze experiment in which association would show in the record. The experimenters have been interested only in determining the general conditions of success. This is in spite of the fact that all give a certain lip service to the facts of habit and associative learning. So far as I know Muenzinger is the only psychologist working on the problem of animal learning, as distinct from the traditional Pavlovian experiment, who has shown any interest in the details of the animal's movements. And Muenzinger's interest has been confined to an occasional departure from expectation or regularity rather than to their repetitiousness. The phenomenon of association would demand close examination of the successive performances of individual animals.

The facts of association have been confused by another recent tendency, namely, to introduce some element of reward or punishment or "reinforcement" into the experiment and to observe that this affects the process of learning. One lamentable feature of these experiments with reward or reinforcement is that the new feature has so distracted the attention of experimenters that they have failed to notice just what are the changes in action brought about by the reward and so have made impossible any record of whether or not association has taken place. Until it becomes fashionable to observe what the animal does in response to reward or reinforcement these experiments will not contribute to our knowledge of association. Skinner insures that the experimenter will remain in ignorance of possible association of cue and movement by having his animals perform in closed boxes, protected from the "subjective" descriptions of the experimenter, recording being done automatically by some end-product of the animals' movements.

Culler has, by an ingenious distortion of the observation, succeeded in obtaining results that lead him to re-formulate the rule of association in teleological terms. After practice with a cue the dog will not do what he previously did at the cue but "something adaptive." Culler arrives at this failure to predict what the dog will do by allowing the dog to escape punishment (a shock) by flexing his leg at a signal. As unconditioned stimulus Culler used a shock to the foot, producing leg flexion. As "motivation" he used a shock applied to the thorax on those occasions when the dog failed to flex the leg to the signal. Under these circumstances variation in response is to be expected, just as any animal will vary its behavior under sharp punishment and resulting excitement. If the dog eventually crouches instead of flexing his leg at the signal this is because the punishment has introduced new behavior to be conditioned to the cue.

A study of the phenomenon of association must undertake to observe just what response follows the new signal. If the experiment is complicated by reward or punishment or "reinforcement" after the act, association should be looked for between the signal and the action caused by the reward or punishment.

The reason for searching for a principle of association in the bewildering variety of experimental results of learning experiments is not that we believe nature to be following a few simple word formulas. Nature is indefinitely complex and can get along very well without rules. There is no compulsion that drives the universe to be simple. But human beings in discussing the world are limited to their own speech, to words to which certain common experiences have attached (by association) at least a bit of common meaning. Human beings themselves are not simple, but the human science of psychology must be simple or it can not be discussed among psychologists or taught to college freshmen. No science can attempt a detailed description of the phenomena in its field. The stargazer's notations of the positions of the planets taken over a series of many years are valueless for general use. They must be reduced to simple rules. They never make an exact fit to these rules. But without rules there is no teachable science of astronomy.

The rules that embody the widest and most fundamental generalizations, those essential to the initial arrangement and classification of facts, we call the principles of a science. They should conform roughly to observation but they are assumed in spite of exceptions and we look for explanation of the exceptions. Boyle's law of gases to the effect that pressure times volume is a constant is "obeyed" by no known gas. Yet it is made an assumption on which the physics of gases is based. With a set of detailed observations of pressure-volume changes in one hundred different gases, the freshman student would be only bewildered and there could be no science of physics.

In my own opinion the general facts of association justify the assumption of a principle analogous to the principle of gravitation. Once assumed, such a principle becomes a basis for ordering the facts and directing observation. I have previously suggested that the statement of this principle might take the form: *A stimulus pattern acting at the time of a response tends on its recurrence to elicit that response.*

I have elsewhere suggested a number of difficulties in the use of such a principle. We may first consider its advantages. One of these is that, so far as I know, it has no demonstrated exceptions in which there is not a possible explanation of the exception, just as the failure of a falling body to conform to the law of gravitation exactly might be explained through the resistance of the atmosphere. Bodies have no *exact* mass or *exact* position. These are only determinable by a number of observations with a variance not reducible to zero.

An instance of such an apparent exception would be the result in an experiment by Yakorzynski and myself which conditioned a voluntary arm flexion to the sound of a buzzer and discovered that occasionally the buzzer elicited a slight extension of the arm instead of the response practiced with the buzzer. We explained this by assuming (with introspective evidence) that the subject, who was instructed to flex his arm at a shock to the other arm, set himself against flexion as well as for it. After one experience of buzzer and no shock the subject realized that he had been "fooled" and attempted not to let this happen. He prepared to resist flexion with extension. This set instead of the flexion was occasionally released by the buzzer.

The facts are that no associative response is an exact duplicate of the practiced associative response. But it is also true that no actual mass was ever observed to follow exactly the principle of gravitation. The psychologist is, of course, faced with anomalies greater in number and extent than is the physicist, but this is inherent in his subject of study.

Just as no mass is determinable without error, so no stimulus pattern satisfies the requirements of the principle by being an exact duplicate of any other. The question is, however, can two stimulus patterns be sufficiently identified to be recognized by observers as the same, and can two responses be in practice identified, one as the repetition of the other? The principle of association does not settle these problems of identification. That is a question to be settled in practice. The principle is a guide to this practice and does indicate, although only

roughly, what to look for. It is an admonition to look for the
weather signs of behavior among the physical changes affecting sense organs; and to look for the predicted behavior not
in success or failure, but in actual muscular contractions.

It is my own conviction that the principle can be very use-
fully applied to the analysis of success and failure; but this
application requires active and sustained interest on the part
of the psychologist. A principle is like a tool which can be
used or neglected, and rather few modern psychologists have
made any effort to use this particular tool. They are like a
conservative workman offered a new hammer who skeptically
picks it up and gives a few half-hearted blows without the
desired result and lays down the tool in disgust. Tolman,
Köhler, and Lewin have all argued against the use of association without trying it. In general the animal experimenters,
who record only success or failure or the attainment or non-
attainment of a goal, find in their results no evidence for habit
and associative learning because they omit from their records
all possible evidence on that point. The use of the principle
would add very substantially to the predictability of the behavior in which they are interested.

A psychologist who is interested in and records only goal-
attainment must necessarily confine himself to rules of goal-
attainment. These are quite legitimate where they can be discovered. We can predict many goal-attainments without the
use of association. We know, for instance, that a cat turned
loose in the woods will probably discover food and eat by
some means or other. Mr. Horton and I in working with cats
in a puzzle box can predict that they will eventually discover
an escape, although on some occasions we have not had the
patience to wait for this. But we can, after we have observed
a cat a number of times in the puzzle box, predict not only
that it will escape and escape in less and less time with practice: we can also predict, and lay heavy odds on our prediction, that a particular cat will use this or that method, nor-
mally the one last used. One cat will wander about, then lie
down, then after a few seconds paw the release mechanism.
Another will bite it; another will back into it.

In our opinion the explanation of the preservation of success, which Köhler would dismiss as a preservation of insight, can be best stated in associative terms. If we assume that any series of movements performed in a general setting like the puzzle box tends to be fixed through association so that one action and its movement-produced stimuli make up the cue for the next action, the learning having taken place on this first occasion, we shall expect on the second occasion a repetition of the behavior of the first.

Failures of this repetition are often understandable as the situation is observed. The cat repeats the first action substantially but this does not release the mechanism. For instance the cat that lies down and then after a few seconds paws the release-stick repeats this but its path has varied a few inches so that the pawing movement does not reach the stick.

Now the situation is altered. The cat remains in the situation *after* the previously successful movement. It remains in the box and must do something new. It had previously at this point in its action left the box. That is now impossible. It now *does something else* in the puzzle-box situation and the puzzle box acquires new associations. All that is necessary to change the associative habit success of any cat is to render this act useless. The cat is forced to new behavior (except where a state of excitement and "breakdown" is followed by indefinite repetition of the old) and a new solution will be found.

The new solution, like the old, remains a habit because a solution *removes the animal from the situation* and thus the situation cannot acquire any new associations. It is now gone. Even months later a cat may give a remarkably exact duplication of a performance which had been fixed in just a few trials.

The principle of association has as its chief defect its indefiniteness in indicating what constitutes a repetition of a stimulus pattern. This is a great weakness and accounts for the unwillingness of many writers to adopt it formally. All are forced by this refusal to adopt it in some disguised and still more indefinite form. Köhler's "retention of insight," Tolman's "sign gestalt," Wheeler's "conditioning" and "association" are all vague and unformulated principles of association which they are forced to use. Association is inescapable if one attempts to describe learning. In some form it underlies the goal-abilities of all animals that have mind. It is essential to an understanding of the effects of practice, the acquisition of skill, the phenomenon of forgetting.

We can predict behavior in many ways without its use. We can predict in terms of physics and gross structure. One glance at an elephant betrays that it would be a poor flier. We can predict from past observations of a species. We identify birds' nests in this fashion and know in advance the rough form that the oriole or the robin or the woodpecker will construct. We may call such patterns of behavior instincts and they are not only legitimate but necessary in the science of behavior.

We can predict human behavior from knowledge of the culture in which a man has been reared. Knowing only this we know his language and his food tastes, the limits of his devices for living. We can predict roughly in terms of Lewin's vectors and barriers and know in advance that the child in a barred pen will be found next to the wall through which the desired toy is visible. This is not to agree that Lewin's diagrams of organism, field, barrier, and goal-object can apply to such behavior as nausea or bladder-emptying in which the goal is not on one side of a fence and the child on another.

But we can also predict the behavior of animals and man in terms of our observations of their individual past experience. Mr. Horton and I know not only what the species "cat" will do in our puzzle box. We know in advance what cat number 52 will do, and this prediction is in terms of the observed past association of 52's actions in a particular situation. If one wishes to train a dog to lie down on command we can give adequate instructions in terms of association. First compel the desired behavior. This could be done by running the leash under our foot and pulling on it. Associate this with the desired signal. Eventually the desired signal (which, to the dog, includes the owner, his stance, his tone of voice, etc.) will produce the desired response. These directions could be deduced from the principle of association and I am not aware of any other general principle in psychology from which they could be deduced.

The limitations of human discourse drive us to the use of principles even though we recognize that these are over-simplifications of the information we wish to convey. Hull and his associates at Yale have in recent years given way to this demand for principles and published a great many of them as psychological postulates. Most of these are generalizations from one or a few special experiments and are of very questionable general application. With these postulates as a basis they are attempting to reduce psychology to formal theories with proofs like those of Euclid. This valiant enterprise has certain drawbacks. Even if they were rigorous in their proofs (and even mathematical rigor is not too rigorous) they would produce a system like the system of freshman physics which applies to a fairy world of ideal gases and liquids, not to the real world. It is a pedagogical device which is used only for beginners in the science. But their extreme readiness to make any generalization a postulate insures that the resultant system will apply to a fairy world of the mind much more ill-fitted to the actual world than is the system of physics. Their assumption of extinction, for instance, as a simple and universal postulate will encounter difficulties because of the phenomena we class as extinction—the tendency for a conditioned response to diminish and disappear with repetition of the conditioned signal unsupported by the original eliciting stimulus and to recover after an interval of time. In all probability the actual laboratory phenomenon of extinction is the result of a variety of causes. Razran, in a recent article in the *Psychological Review* on "The Nature of the Extinction Process," lists some six different factors operating in conditioning, from a general rule that there is a decrement in unreinforced responses to an associative stimulus, to the effects of temporary emotional states which are only sometimes involved. That all the phenomena of extinction can be subsumed under one general law and this used as a principle, he would not agree. I am quite in accord with this and by no means intended to suggest in my *Psychology of Learning* that there was one explanation of extinction. The only generalization applicable to all learning that appears to me acceptable is the general principle of association.

This applies also to McCulloch's recent criticism of my account of learning published in the *Journal of Psychology* (1939). He quotes my attempt at a generalized description of learning which made use of the notion that the removal of a drive, such as hunger, leaves the drive associated with the act which removed it. This is to account for the preservation of the successful act, which remains associated with the drive because re-association can not be effected in the absence of the event, the drive.

McCulloch's objections to this as a universal account of learning are valid. Learning occurs when a very small reward follows success, a reward that by no means removes the hunger. But I had not intended this as a statement of a universal rule of success learning, and must readily grant McCulloch's point that success interrupts the behavior of pursuit or search (so-called even though it be blind and consist only of restless exploration). In terms of association, success removes the animal from the situation of search or removes this situation from the animal. The successful act thus remains associated with the situation that last gave rise to it, and "purposeful" behavior has been accounted for in non-teleological terms.

Several have made the objection to the principle of association as formulated in this paper, that it is merely the principle of the uniformity of nature in disguise. It predicts that an animal in a situation will do what it was last observed to do in that situation.

This bears a superficial resemblance to the assumption of the uniformity of nature, that the same causes will have the same effects. But there is an essential difference. The principle of association implies that the animal will, in a situation, not do what it would have done before the last association took place; that the signal would have been ineffectual without a preceding occasion on which the signal happened to be included in a situation which resulted in the response in question. It is equivalent to holding that in creatures with mind there is continuous change in the effects of stimuli, depending on the association of these stimuli with new responses.

THE CONCEPT OF VOLITION IN
EXPERIMENTAL PSYCHOLOGY

FRANCIS W. IRWIN[1]

Department of Psychology, University of Pennsylvania

FOR the general inadequacy of the experimental study of volition a number of reasons are assignable. Chief of these is the frequently described flight of experimental psychology from "philosophical" or "metaphysical" concepts. It will not be denied that few notions are more thoroughly tarred with the philosopher's brush than that of the will, with its long history of fruitless disputation and its association with vitalistic and other contra-scientific attitudes. The experimentalist, in his attempt to avoid those aspects of the concept which would hinder him or even be opposed to his program, has gone to such lengths as either to use terms with inadequate analysis of their meaning, or to avoid the problem altogether. The unfortunate results of this will be made abundantly clear in what follows. Definitional analysis having been slighted, it has come about that problems have been determined by methods rather than methods by problems. It is illustrative of this state of affairs that Ach (1), in introducing his well-known work on volition, blames for the undeveloped state of research on the topic the lack of suitable methods, and that he grasps at the already well-established reaction-time method for his experiments although apologizing for its shortcomings. The conclusion that Ach's work, interesting as it is, has not led to any very profound understanding of the problems of volition may be generalized to apply to much that has been done in a field largely investigated at an opportunistic level.

A related consequence of the neglect of clear definition is

[1] The writer is indebted to Mrs. Jane Alben Shepherd for much helpful criticism.

the presence of sharply divergent trends of thought and experiment within the small body of accomplishment. While
some psychologists have defined voluntary behavior by the
existence of a distinctive conscious experience, others have
confined themselves to specific features of behavior-acts without reference to consciousness, and still others have denied
that it can be defined in either way. Appropriate to this
conflict of definitions is the lack of community of subject
matter among experiments conducted ostensibly with common
aims. In one experiment only characteristics of the subject's
behavior, such as can be read from kymograph records, have
been given attention; while in another this kind of data was
valued so little that subjects were required to decide between
two or more possible lines of behavior but were not even
permitted to carry their decisions into action, the results
being restricted to introspections upon the consciousness of
decision. Investigators of volition have thus not only failed
to speak a common language but in some cases have not been
treating the same fundamental problems.

If this diagnosis is correct the remedy becomes obvious.
Evidently there is needed such an analysis of the concept of
volition as will lead to a definition which is scientifically
meaningful and amenable to experimental handling. In attempting this task we may well be guided by a survey of the
losses and gains of previous thinking and research. Since explicit definitions of volition are not commonly found in
the experimental literature it will sometimes be necessary
for our purpose to extract from an author's writings what he
appears to imply, thus running a serious risk of misinter-
preting his opinions. With the hope that little injustice of
this sort has been done, we select for discussion the following
six definitions.

I. Volition consists in a characteristic unanalyzable mode
of conscious experience. (Michotte and Prüm)

II. It is the acceptance and carrying out of a conscious
resolve or intention. (Ach)

III. It is a behavior-pattern conditioned to an antecedent
behavior of a "symbolic" nature. (Hull, Hunter)

IV. It is a behavior-pattern distinguished by certain descriptive features such as a characteristic latent period and degree of modifiability by instructions of an experimenter, or by the manner in which these features vary with variations in experimental conditions. (Wickens, Peak)

V. It is behavior in which the self plays a dominant or controlling role. (Lewin)

VI. It is behavior following from the (teleologically defined) nature of the living being. (Singer)

I. The first definition is of a kind which for a quarter of a century has appeared unsatisfactory to a large number of psychologists. It sprang from an introspective and essentially non-biological tradition in psychology. As typical adherents to such a definition may be mentioned Michotte and Prüm, who maintained that: "La conscience d'action est la caractéristic qui différencie l'action volontaire de toute autre." (12, p. 194. Italicized in original.) This opinion derived from an experiment in which subjects were required to make a decision "for serious reasons" between, say, adding and subtracting two numbers exposed to them, and to give an introspective account of the process of decision. A "consciousness of action" was regularly present in those instances in which the subjects reported that they had acted voluntarily, and absent when the behavior appeared to them to have been involuntary or automatic. The experience itself was unanalyzable, i.e., irreducible to kinesthetic or other sensory data.

The logic of this argument seems simple enough: it is evidently implied that volitional acts are whatever properly trained subjects say they are, and that since the subjects in this experiment reported a consciousness of action to be characteristic of volitional behavior, volition must be defined by the presence of this consciousness. But beneath the first implication lies the assumption that the subjects somehow knew when they were acting voluntarily and when they were not—an assumption which begs the question. When, in addition, the subjects' differentiating criterion is seen to be a private experience which we cannot share with them, nor even they with each other, and which is therefore a scientifically unverifiable and meaningless entity, we need not wonder that history shows the definition based upon it to be sterile.

II. Dissatisfied with definitions of this sort, we turn to a somewhat different point of view. No survey of the psychology of volition can afford to neglect the work of Ach (1), which may perhaps still be accounted the most influential experimenting in the field. As stated above, when Ach came to study volition the most expedient method seemed to him to be that of reaction-time. To this he added "systematic experimental introspection"; and the outcome was what might be expected—a conception of the problem that we are likely to find too confining for our taste. In the familiar reaction-time experiment the subject is instructed to make a certain movement at the appearance of a signal. The behavior of a subject carrying out these instructions has generally been accepted by psychologists as voluntary. So it was by Ach, who made a thorough investigation of the conscious experience occurring during this process, and who invented the ingenious method of the "associative equivalent" in going so far as to attempt to measure that aspect of will which may be called its strength. With criticisms of the latter effort we are not now concerned; but the point of view which his work expresses is of some importance to us. The behavior which results from the conscious acceptance of a task, or the conscious formulation of an intention or resolution may be called volitional; but those who wish to convert this proposition into a definition restrict the area of the concept to an unnecessary degree.

If we ask what is excluded from such a definition that we should like to see incorporated into it, there comes to mind the whole domain of animal psychology, so diligently cultivated since the turn of the century, with its evidences of continuity in kind between the psychologies of man and of other living creatures. Are we to limit the application of the concept to man and only those other animals, if there be any, to whom conscious intentions can be ascribed? Who, when dealing with an obstinate pet dog or cat has failed to experience the pitting of another will against his?[2] Yet one would scarcely desire to impute to the animal a conscious intention of the kind described by the reaction-time experimenters. Again, we review our own daily behavior, our rising in the morning, our turning from one task to another, putting a query to one person, answering one put to us, eating our three meals a day:[3] it is clear that appropriate conscious intentions are not invariably antecedent to such acts, which, nevertheless, common sense tells us we perform voluntarily. Science is not to be bound by the dictates of common sense; but here we have a question of choice between traditions: a narrow, though reputably scientific one, which is known to have little in the way of productivity to recommend it; and a broader one, not yet developed into a large body of verifiable fact, which stands behind what comprehension we have of much that we and our fellows do. The latter alternative invites exploration. Rather than looking further into conscious experience of any kind for a defining criterion of volition, we shall search elsewhere for a solution which, without loss of scientific rigor, will yet permit us to take the wider view.

III. Whatever may be said of our reasons for it, we are not alone in the avoidance of unanalyzable experiences and conscious intentions. Those who are called behaviorists, with all their divergences of opinion, agree with each other and with us on this point at least. An illustration of what they have to offer instead is Hull's definition. For him, a voluntary act is the execution in a continuous sequence by the same individual of a "symbolic" act and its "instrumental" sequel, where symbolic acts are those which function purely as stimuli for other acts, and instrumental acts are those which produce "physical effects" (5, pp. 395-96). A statement in some respects similar to this has been made by Hunter and Hudgins: ". . . the hypoth-

[2] If charged with anthropomorphism we should reply that there are involved here two questions: first, what *is* volition, and second, do animals exhibit it? Our statement does not assume that animals act volitionally. It merely implies that it would be well to take account of this possibility suggested by casual observation, in order that it shall still exist as a possibility when we have decided what volition is. Whether animals exhibit it will then be a question to be decided by experiment.

[3] Cf. Lewin (10, p. 376), whom we paraphrase here.

esis is offered that so-called voluntary behavior is essentially a conditioned response having a characteristic latency and temporal course and under the control of self-excited receptor processes" (6, p. 204). This may be taken to be a definition rather than an "hypothesis"; and although it contains more than one criterion of volition, we wish at the moment to point out the resemblance of "self-excited receptor processes" to Hull's "symbolic acts." That this resemblance is a real one is evidenced by the fact that both parties have found in the same experimental data a critical opportunity for the application of their definitions. The data in question are those of Hudgins' recent but already well-known experiment on conditioning the pupillary reflex.[4] A good deal of light should be shed upon both definitions by an examination of these data and the way they have been used to support the definitions.

The essentials of the facts reported by Hudgins can be outlined briefly. Having conditioned the constriction or dilation of the pupil of the human eye to the sound of a bell, he was able in successive stages to establish this conditioning to hand contractions made by the subject at the experimenter's verbal signal, then to the experimenter's verbal signal, and finally to the subject's own vocal and even "subvocal" repetition of the verbal signal. The usual conditioning phenomenon of experimental extinction did not occur in the last stages of the experiment, and the conditioning was describable as "relatively permanent." Thus, by applying the familiar methods of conditioning, the experimenter produced individuals able to vary the diameter of their pupils, which they formerly were unable to do, by "saying to themselves" or "thinking" whatever word was used in the conditioning process. This is interpreted by the experimenter, and by Hunter and Hull as well, to mean that the subjects had acquired voluntary control over pupillary action.

When we ask ourselves why such behavior has been taken to be voluntary, we cannot escape the conclusion that it is because

---

[4] Hudgins (4). For the purposes of our discussion we shall assume the existence of the facts reported by Hudgins and neglect such criticisms as those of Steckle and Renshaw (20). None of our ultimate conclusions will depend upon the validity of Hudgins' experiment.

of similarities it exhibits to the behavior of subjects in a reaction-time experiment. It is a behavioristic analogue of the volitional act of Michotte and Prüm, or James, or McDougall, or any of the older psychologists whose concept of volition involved the notion that it was an action appropriate to some antecedent conscious process, the place of the conscious process being taken in the behavioristic formulation by the subvocal act (or self-excited receptor process or symbolic act). Now, if this subvocal act is defined objectively, as the behaviorists hope that it is, criticism on the basis of the introduction of private and unverifiable experience is avoided. But we shall not be obliged to consider this question, since, whatever the answer, we must still oppose this conception of volition on other grounds.

Put in the most general way, our objection is that the nature of the behavior of Hudgins' subjects, far from being the archetype of that behavior which has led men to develop the concept of volition, is its very antithesis. It is interesting to compare with Hudgins' work that of an earlier experimenter, Bair (2), who also set out to discover how voluntary control over a previously uncontrollable muscle-group might be established. Selecting the retrahens muscle of the ear for his purpose, Bair discovered that control over this muscle, which previously could not be contracted "at will" by his subjects, was achievable. The process involved, first, a violent voluntary attempt to contract the muscle which led to its being contracted as one of a group of muscles including those of the forehead and jaw, and second, a gradual exclusion of the accessory muscles by "attending to" the contraction of the retrahens and "forgetting about" the others. Facilitation of this process by electrical stimulation of the retrahens was believed by Bair to be due to the fact that the subjects more easily differentiated the desired movement from the others when they knew how the former "felt." Woodworth (24) was able to confirm these observations. Now, while Bair and Woodworth conclude, contrary to some prevalent opinion, that a motor or kinesthetic *image* of the movement to be made is neither a necessary nor a sufficient condition for the making of the movement, they likewise agree in stressing the necessity of the subjects' being able to *attend* to the desired movement, which presumably means that they must be aware of it through the sensations it arouses. Returning now to Hudgins' experiment, we find, first of all, that some emphasis is laid upon the very fact that his subjects could not be directly aware of the movements of their irises since the iris possesses no afferent fibers. (One of his subjects was able to report with some accuracy the occurrence of such a movement, but this capacity could be explained by the indirect cue afforded by variations in the illumination of the retina produced by the pupillary changes.) Furthermore, Hudgins makes a point of his subjects' behavior not being intentional, since they were quite unaware of the purpose of the experiment. We remember also that the pupillary responses became uninhibitable. Thus, the "voluntary behavior" of Hudgins' subjects, from his own description of it, consisted in their unintentionally doing something which they did not know they were doing and which they could not have prevented themselves from doing if they *had* known it. Since Bair's subjects acted with the most obvious intention; were the more successful when the more aware of the desired movement; and were under no compulsion to make this movement at an arbitrary signal, the contrast is complete— so complete, in fact, that we find it impossible to consider both behaviors as subsumable under a single class to be called voluntary. If either is to be so classified, and if at the same time we wish to conserve as much as possible of the spirit of the term "voluntary" as it is found both in common and in general psychological usage, our choice must rest with Bair. Hudgins' work is interesting and ingenious enough to deserve all the attention it has received among psychologists, but it should be classified in some field other than that of volition. At the same time we exclude from the realm of desirable definitions any, like those of Hull and of Hunter and Hudgins, which would compel us to regard the behavior of Hudgins' subjects as a classic example of volition.

IV. A fourth type of definition has arisen as a by-product of the activities of those who adopt a physiological attitude toward psychological problems. The physiological psychologists tend to study behavior at what may be thought of as a lower level than that of volition; but now and again they use the term "voluntary" and wish to distinguish such behavior from the reflexes they are wont to investigate. Thus we find Wendt (22), for example, comparing the latent times and muscle-contraction curves of the knee-jerk and the conditioned knee-jerk with those of voluntary leg kicks, the last-named being responses made by subjects according to instructions of the experimenter. In such experiments the various kinds of responses are found to have different mean latencies and distinguishably different contraction-curves. The discovery that these voluntary responses can be conditioned somewhat in the same way as reflexes has called attention to the desirability of considering more closely certain matters of definition. How this has led to a definition of voluntary behavior can be made clear by the examination of two recent experiments.

Marquis and Porter (11) have studied the differences found when voluntary and reflex eyelid responses were conditioned. Conditioning of lid-closure to a light was successfully established both when the response was made by instructions to the sound of a click (voluntary) and when it was produced by a puff of air against the eye (reflex). A number of differences between the two kinds of conditioned responses and the courses of conditioning they followed were observed; but most impressive to the authors was the relative ease with which the conditioned voluntary response was affected by instructions and the subjects' attitudes. On this point they say:

"In speaking of a conditioned response as voluntary, it is not implied that a reportable intention is necessary, but rather that the response is highly susceptible to the effects of instructions in contrast with the relative dependence of involuntary responses upon objective stimulus conditions" (11, p. 363).

We are not sure whether Marquis and Porter would wish this to be used as a defining criterion, or whether they imply only that when a response is found to vary easily with instructions its possible voluntary character should be looked into by other means. Probably the latter is the case, since they suggest that the finger-retraction from electric shock, which has frequently been dealt with as a reflex movement, is considerably modified by changes in the subject's attitude and may, therefore, be a voluntary rather than a reflexive movement.

This hint has been taken seriously by Wickens (23) in an experimental attack upon the question. Certain peculiar features of the logic of his experiment seem to us to illustrate the need for clearer definition as a prerequisite of incisive experimentation. His procedure was in many respects like that of Marquis and Porter. Of three groups of subjects, one retracted the finger from an electric shock; another responded similarly at the appearance of a light, by instructions; and a third also responded by instructions to the light, but in addition was threatened by a shock if they failed to respond (a threat which was, however, not carried out). A buzzer was used as the conditioned stimulus in all cases. The three groups exhibited differences in the obtained percentages of conditioned responses, in the nature of the finger-retraction curves, in the form of the curves of acquisition of conditioning, etc. The results of the third group could in general be ordered between the results of the first two, although overlapping was present. From these results Wickens concludes that the finger-retraction from shock is not "basically" voluntary, since when conditioned it displays so many differences from the conditioned voluntary response. "Basically" appears to mean "in large part," since Wickens uses a concept of "degree of voluntariness"; he holds that his experiment ". . . emphasizes the necessity of thinking of voluntary and involuntary as extremes of the same series rather than all-or-none phenomena" (23, p. 137). This series is essentially a continuum of degree of susceptibility of the response to variation of the stimulus conditions.

Several comments can be made upon this experiment and its interpretation. First, the experiment is well designed to describe the progress and nature of the *conditioning* of the various responses, and the nature of the responses once they have been conditioned; but the question at issue is the nature of the responses *before* the introduction of conditioning, which the results bear upon only indirectly. Would it not be much more direct and conclusive to introduce the attitude variable with the original responses without modifying them by conditioning? On the validity of Wickens' definition it must be observed that if degree of susceptibility to instructions or to irrelevant stimuli is to be used as a defining criterion, there is needed a unit or scale of measurement of susceptibility which has not yet been supplied. But even if such a unit or scale were obtained, it would be quite inadequate to the problem. Either all behavior whatsoever would have to be arranged on a single continuum between the extremes of reflex and volition, and no other coördinate classes of behavior would be available to the psychologist; or further defining criteria would have to be developed. The first would exclude most of the subject matter of psychology; and the second leaves our problem still unsolved.

Peak (14) has criticized the attempts to distinguish volition from other kinds of behavior by means either of its antecedents or by specific descriptive features. She points out that these criteria are frequently ambiguous: that, for example, the same conscious experience may precede behaviors between which we wish on other grounds to differentiate; or long reflex latencies may overlap short voluntary latencies (as Wickens and many others have found). However, if one determines the manner in which the descriptive features of reflexive and voluntary behavior vary *as functions of varying experimental conditions* it may be possible, she believes, to use these functions themselves as distinguishing criteria. Helpful as it might be if our problem were already settled, this suggestion begs the question of definition, since without previously formed concepts of volition and reflex we obviously should not know how to allot the obtained functions between them.

A reader sensitive to the variety and purposefulness of behavior can only have been disappointed by a review of one definition of volition after another which succeeds in setting technical limits without managing to catch the whole potential significance of the term. The facts available for discussion have been too often either trivial in themselves, or if interesting, then irrelevant to the psychology of volition. We observe that one of the most pressing problems turns out to be the distinction between volition and *reflex*; and we begin to wonder how we can have departed so far from the spirit of what once was regarded as willed or voluntary that it is now difficult or crucial to distinguish voluntary behavior from the simplest and most mechanical of behaviors. Must we consider this the natural result of the application of scientific thinking and method to the problem, or have we not perhaps overlooked something of which even the affairs of daily living might remind us? Let us hear the answer of one who has looked in the latter direction.

. . . There is still another general fact that must be adduced. The fact is somewhat over-stated by saying that there is no such thing as voluntary bodily movement. The emphasis is on *bodily*. There is such a thing, but it is a rarity, seldom occurring in practical life. Instances of it are found in "free" gymnastics, in the tricks children love to play with their fingers, and in such movements as psychologists make when they are exemplifying to themselves the process of voluntary movement. In these cases the bodily movement is willed for its own sake; there is no resulting motion of external things. . . . But the great majority of purposive movements are executed for the sake of some effect they produce beyond the mere movement. . . . It would be much truer to speak of our voluntary movement of physical objects than to speak of voluntary bodily movements. If I wish to cut a stick, my intention is not that of making certain back and forth movements of my arm, while simultaneously holding the fingers pressed tightly towards each other; my intention is to cut that stick (24, pp. 374-75).

These simple statements of Woodworth's open a window through which some of the stuffiness of the discussion may be permitted to escape. No longer are we progressing in the direction of physiological minutiæ which can apparently end only in more and more elaborate descriptions of the movements of members of the body, perhaps eventually of muscle fibers themselves.[5] Our plea here is not, of course, for less physiology, but only for more psychology. Our quarrel is not with physiological psychology, but with those critics who would raise the cry that we are becoming the less scientists the more we become, as we think, psychologists. Let us then take up Woodworth's clue,

[5] An eloquent criticism of the state of affairs arising from exclusive adherence to this line of progress has come recently from Köhler (7).

and search for a definition which will make volition independent of particular muscular contractions or movements of parts of the body, as well as of those private mental states we have already rejected.

V. Satisfactory from this point of view, at least, is the concept of "controlled behavior" used by Lewin (10). His criticism of the associationistic attitude toward intention is, in fact, closely analogous to our criticism of definitions depending upon specific bodily movements, since he attacks most severely the notion that the carrying out of an intended act is due to an associative coupling of the idea of the act and the idea of the occasion upon which the act is to be performed. How, he asks, can we reconcile such a theory with the simple fact that an intention may be satisfied by a substitute act? To use his own favorite illustration, the intention to drop a letter in a mailbox may be so thoroughly satisfied by the act of giving the letter to a chance-met friend to deliver that the future appearance of a mailbox may arouse no impulse to post a letter therein. Or, if the expected occasion fails to present itself—no mailbox comes within range—one may be discovered *seeking* an occasion. The fact that an intention can be fulfilled by any of a varied assortment of acts, planned or unplanned, cannot, Lewin thinks, be accounted for by a theory of associative connections. He thus aligns himself with Woodworth's emphasis upon the relative importance of the end pursued by an individual as against the means by which the end is sought.

Lewin takes the stand that the work on intentional behavior which he has criticized, and which bulks large in the experimental psychology of volition, is less important than it has been thought to be. Earlier in the discussion we have had occasion to use his opinion that an actual consciousness of intent is found relatively seldom in daily experience; but aside from this, he contends that when it does occur it does not have in general the characteristics of the "controlled act" (*beherrschte Handlung*) which seems to him the typical willed action. What is the typical laboratory instance of the performance of a consciously intended act if not the reaction to a signal in the reaction-time experiment? and what is more typical of such reactions than that they soon become so automatized as to be carried out even when they are no longer appropriate? In such experiments it is common to find *Vexierversuche* necessary to maintain the behavior at a relatively controlled level. Whatever "will" may mean, Lewin believes we must distinguish between controlled and uncontrolled behavior.

This distinction can be understood only in the light of some acquaintance with his general theory, in which he envisages the psychological individual as a complex system of psychological fields of force, the more superficial fields being those of the experienced environment, the deeper-lying those of the self. Not all acts which are without intention are to be considered instinctive or impulsive (*triebhaft*); the reply one makes to a question, for example, partakes more of the voluntary than of the impulsive. Now, any behavior whatsoever is the resultant of the action of the forces operating in the whole psychological field; but in some acts, says Lewin, one does not submerge oneself completely, but maintains a certain reserve or objectivity (*Reserviertheit, Ueber-der-Sache-stehen*); or, in other words, the system of forces comprising the self is relatively independent and dominant. Such acts may be said to be *controlled* (10, p. 378, foonote). If one accepts the distinction between controlled and uncontrolled behavior one may then dispense with the terms voluntary and involuntary.

The enormous gulf separating this whole attitude from those attitudes previously discussed might well dismay any reader expectant of a miraculous reconciliation among them. Lewin has not only discarded as irrelevant to questions of volition much of what experimental psychology has so far achieved but, with the reintroduction of the self, he has intruded where angels have for years feared to tread. This "dynamic" point of view cannot, however, be dismissed as "so much futile speculation which serves only to revive antiquated notions" (as we can hear some of our tougher-minded colleagues saying). On the contrary, it has led at the hands of Lewin's students to a remarkable series of experiments, the influence of which is already easily seen in experimental and clinical psychology.[6]

There are, however, two difficulties which confront us. The more superficial of these arises from our not wishing to make the thoroughgoing distinction that Lewin has made between controlled and intended acts. We wonder whether he would have made this distinction if the *consciousness* of intent had not been so predominant a feature of the earlier psychology of will. Let us suppose (as we believe) that an adequate behavioral definition of intent can be arrived at without the implication of a specific type of conscious process. Dashiell (3), although he does not offer such a final definition as can be used in experimental work, nevertheless shows clearly what all can recognize: that the presence of a certain conscious state is a highly artificial criterion of intent; and that, as a matter of fact, intent can be and is judged from the observation of another's behavior, non-verbal as well as verbal. If this be admitted Lewin's distinction no longer carries the weight originally put upon it. A much larger proportion of intentional acts may be subsumed under the concept of volition than Lewin seems to wish to classify there, although automatized behavior remains still to be classified.

We are concerned more seriously over Lewin's concept of needs and the identification of controlled acts. He and the closely related Gestalt psychologists have developed systems which represent the most fruitful attempts to handle the *purposive* nature of behavior which have yet appeared. The concepts of purpose and goal are used constantly by Lewin and his students; yet both he and the Gestalt psychologists heartily disclaim teleology, as their general theoretical positions oblige them to do. It is our opinion, however, that the wide influence of Lewin's work is due largely to the opportunity he has afforded the laboratory man to use experimentally these very concepts of goal and purpose. From this contact with a real and much-avoided aspect of behavior his ideas derive their

[6] Cf. Lewin (9). In this work will be found discussions of the experiments referred to here. Particularly interesting in connection with problems of volition are the experiments of Karsten, Zeigarnik, and Hoppe.

enormous vitality and significance. We should like to preserve the teleology without assuming an underlying theory which disclaims it.

Lewin seems to have been led to his dynamic theory specifically by the phenomena which he has called "equivalent acts"—the observation that a "need" may be satisfied by more than one specific activity. This characteristic of behavior has often been noted as an important though difficult problem. Lashley, to mention only one instance, has described

. . . the functional equivalence of responses, where various motor organs may be used interchangeably to produce the same end-result. . . . A familiar example is the capacity to form letters of an unaccustomed size without special practice for each new combination of movements. The most striking instance of the sort that has come to my attention is that of a student of piano who, in the stress of a public recital, unknowingly transposed one-half tone upward an entire movement of a Beethoven sonata, a feat which she had never attempted before and could not duplicate afterward even with some practice.[7]

Such cases always offer hindrance to strictly mechanistic theories. May we not, as Lashley does, define equivalent acts by their common function, without assuming their satisfaction of a *need* which can only be inferred from, or defined by, this function? We shall then be free to use or to avoid the concept of need, as we choose; and we shall not be obliged to accept Lewin's dynamic system and his concept of the self.

VI. Teleological concepts are not popular in contemporary psychology. Their use is likely to be regarded with the suspicion that under their guise some form of vitalism is being introduced. A notable example of the fact that this need not be so is the system so ably developed by Tolman (21). Another instance, and one backed by a penetrating theory of knowledge, is the point of view of Singer,[8] from whose writings we take

[7] Lashley (8). See also Murray (13) who, in defending the concept of need, argues that classifying behavior by its effects often leads to better comprehension than does classifying by the various means by which the effects are produced.

[8] See particularly 16, 17, 18, 19. The remainder of our argument rests upon the possibility of a teleology both objective and non-vitalistic. Since the development of such a position would, of course, be too long a story, we shall have to content ourselves with making these references to Singer's writings. It is to be

our sixth definition. Having defined living beings in purpose-ful terms which yet do not violate the mechanical nature of the world in which such beings are found, and having postulated that "the nature of the members of a class is the sum of the qualities belonging to them by definition," Singer continues:

When this definition is teleological these qualities would include end and typical means. No gesture of a member of a class could be said to follow from its nature unless the gesture were recognized as well-calculated to accomplish the defining end.

The subject of an act thus following from that subject's nature is said to act *sua sponte* (spontaneously or voluntarily). (17, p. 428)

Since on this view all living beings are members of classes defined teleologically, any living being which behaves may exhibit spontaneous behavior. Singer is thus ready to recognize spontaneity in the behavior of the simplest of animals; and an illustration of his is that of the swimming of a paramecium in a trough of water toward a region of optimal temperature. But here 'we find ourselves hesitating. If the animal is acting *sua sponte* in this situation, what, we wonder, is the implication of *sua*? Perhaps the paramecium is fulfilling a purpose of his *species* but not of his *own*. Has, as a matter of fact, a paramecium an "own" at all? If not, we ask once more, should we wish to consider its behavior volitional?

We suggest here one final distinction. Let us agree that the paramecium's behavior is spontaneous if the purpose of the behavior can be shown to be one which helps to define the paramecium as a living being and a member of a particular class or species of living beings. But for an act to be regarded as volitional we shall require that it be shown to display some purpose of the creature *as an individual*. Such purposes would be experimentally demonstrated from the observation of a number of acts of one living being, with the exclusion of all purposes which belonged to this being as a member of any

emphasized that the term "purpose," as used hereafter in this paper, always refers to a descriptive, and not an explanatory, feature of behavior; and that it does not necessarily imply the existence on the part of the subject of an awareness of his own purposes.

structurally defined class. No amount of knowledge of races, species, or other structurally defined classes of animals will enable us to call his behavior volitional; we must know also something of his individuality or personality. It goes without saying that a given behavior-act may be expressive of more than one purpose. It results, then, that we know (or for the purpose of argument assume we know) the class called paramecia well enough to grant spontaneity to the specimen described by Singer; but we do not know that particular paramecium well enough (since Singer has told us nothing of the little animal's individuality) to say whether or not the behavior could also be classed as volitional. We define volitional behavior, then, as *any behavior which exhibits a purpose ascribable to the behaving creature as an individual.* This definition avoids the criticisms we have levelled at Ach, Hull, and the physiological psychologists by relying neither upon the existence of characteristic antecedents of the behavior to be called volitional, whether these are defined introspectively or behavioristically, nor upon structurally descriptive features of the behavior itself. By its teleological nature it conserves an important aspect of the notions of Woodworth and Lewin. In its dependence upon the nature of the individual it admits the spirit of the tradition embodied in Lewin's use of the concept of the self.

There remains the necessity of considering, with this definition in mind, how we should classify the various kinds of behavior which have at different times been considered as constituting volition. Intentional behavior is surely such a candidate, whether or not the term implies the individual's awareness of his intent. It is doubtless a feature common to members of the human race to display intents of many sorts, and in a hierarchy of goals many of the goals may be shown to be common to the race. But although a man may work with the intention of eating, and eat in order to preserve himself as a living being, it is also true that he may work at a job he has chosen from a certain range of alternatives and which gives him a measure, greater or less, of satisfaction for its own sake. One could then describe laying-bricks-to-see-a-house-grow, or for that matter, laying-bricks-to-put-in-time, as volitional, even if it should be shown to be "instinctive" to work-to-live. However intent be defined, unless it is to lose its present connotations we believe its existence must be determined by a study of the purposes characteristic of an individual and hence denoting volition.

Many unnecessary difficulties have been raised by failure to recognize that the same behavior may be classed as "instinctive" in so far as it exhibits a purpose common to the species, and volitional to the extent that it has purposiveness for the individual. If it be allowed that seeking a mate is instinctive, the love of a man for one woman above all others must nevertheless always show itself in behavior that also exhibits purposes of that man as an individual. He may, for example, be expected to act in a way which he believes will favor that woman's happiness. But any man to whom the woman's happiness or individuality is insignificant, who seeks her only as a female of his species, can be said in the old-fashioned phrase to be acting like an animal, and to that extent his behavior would be purely instinctive.

Behavior under hypnosis has always provided borderline cases for testing definitions of volition. It is remarkable that although in the layman's eyes the actions of a hypnotized person are the antithesis of voluntary, the processes of re-definition have led some psychologists to regard hypnotic behavior as the example *par excellence* of a willed response. They have been driven to this by attempting to define volition as behavior resulting from a characteristic conscious process. We have already argued against the use of this or the analogous behavioristic definition. But by our own definition the hypnotic phenomena must be subjected to the same scrutiny as any others. What is peculiar about the behavior of the hypnotic subject, and what leads to the layman's reluctance to regard it as voluntary, is the tendency for the subject to carry out commands of the hypnotist even where the ensuing behavior is at variance with what would be expected of the subject in the normal state. Rowland's (15) subjects, who attempted under hypnosis to pick up an active rattlesnake, and to throw a fuming beakerful of acid at the experimenter, constitute an extreme example. Remembering that nothing is implied as to their awareness of their own purposes, we are of the opinion that their behavior must be regarded as purposeful, and probably not following simply from their structurally defined nature. The question is, *what* purpose was exhibited? We do not believe that the subjects were voluntarily attempting to kill themselves or the experimenter. Their purpose, judged from what is known about hypnosis, would better be described as that of obeying the experimenter. This follows from the assumption that if the same subjects had been commanded to perform an action *beneficial* to themselves or to the experimenter, instead of a very dangerous one, they would have done so. But if a subject were found who did his best to throw acid at the experimenter no matter what the latter's commands, and who, when prevented from doing this, took yet other means of harming him, one could then with some right describe the behavior as a series of voluntary attempts to injure the experimenter. From a single act, such as the throwing of a beaker of acid, with no knowledge of what was to be expected under other conditions, no determination could have been made with respect to the voluntary or nonvoluntary nature of the act. In any case, the decision must ultimately rest upon experimental evidence.

Reflexes, conditioned reflexes, and automatized habitual acts must in general by our definition be classified as involuntary. However, it is necessary to do this on the basis of the opinion that such acts, to the extent that they are purposive at all, fulfill purposes of the individual not as an individual but as a member of a class of organisms defined by their possession of certain structural features in common. No knowledge of the personality of an individual will, we believe, throw any light on what purposes may be fulfilled by his knee-jerk or pupillary reflex; a full description of such purposes could be obtained by regarding the individual merely as an animal of a certain kind. In the case of intentional activity which with repetition becomes automatized, the behavior can be regarded as voluntary until it becomes uninhibitable by the subject, even though in the meantime it may sometimes have been unsuccessful in fulfilling the subject's purpose. Thus, in a reaction-time experiment a response made to the wrong signal by a coöperative subject, who understands what signals are to be responded to and what are not, would be classifiable as voluntary until the point is reached at which, even with the knowledge in advance that a signal is not to be reacted to, he still responds. As long as the response can be thought of as a response to a *signal mistaken for a correct signal* it must be described by the purpose of obeying the instructions of the experimenter. When it becomes uninhibitable, and occurs even contrary to instructions and to the perception that it is the wrong signal, it then appears (in the absence of further knowledge) no longer to be characterized by a purpose of the subject as an individual, and hence no longer to be volitional.

The experimental determination of the voluntary nature of an act becomes in part, then, a matter of the diagnosis of personality. It requires the fullest possible knowledge of the purposes which an individual exhibits. This is to admit, in view of the difficulties confronting the scientific study of personality, that it will seldom be easy to make this diagnosis with a high degree of precision. Furthermore, since acts of the individual as such must be distinguished from acts performed as a member of a structurally defined class, we shall need also the fullest resources of genetic, comparative and physiological psychology—or, shall we not confess, of psychology as a whole. We are ready, however, to rest our case with research men, who do not ask for ease nor for facile answers, but need rather to know how to discover that they are moving in the right direction.

BIBLIOGRAPHY

1. Ach, N. *Ueber die Willenstätigkeit und das Denken.* Göttingen: Vandenhoeck & Ruprecht, 1905.
2. Bair, J. H. "Development of voluntary control." *Psychol. Rev.,* 8 (1901), 474-510.
3. Dashiell, J. F. "The objective character of legal 'intent'." *Psychol. Rev.,* 38 (1931), 529-37.

4. Hudgins, C. V. "Conditioning and the voluntary control of the pupillary light reflex." *J. Gen. Psychol.*, 8 (1933), 3-51.

5. Hull, C. L. *Hypnosis and Suggestibility.* N. Y.: Appleton-Century, 1933.

6. Hunter, W. S. & Hudgins, C. V. "Voluntary activity from the standpoint of behaviorism." *J. Gen. Psychol.*, 10 (1934), 198-204.

7. Köhler, W. *The Place of Value in a World of Facts.* N. Y.: Liveright, 1938.

8. Lashley, K. S. *Brain Mechanisms and Intelligence.* Chicago: Univ. of Chicago Press, 1929.

9. Lewin, K. *A Dynamic Theory of Personality.* N. Y.: McGraw-Hill, 1935.

10. Lewin, K. "Vorsatz, Wille und Bedürfnis." *Psychol. Forsch.*, 7 (1926), 330-85.

11. Marquis, D. G. & Porter, J. M. "Differential characteristics of conditioned eyelid responses established by reflex and voluntary reinforcement." *J. Exper. Psychol.*, 24 (1939), 347-65.

12. Michotte, A. & Prüm, E. "Étude expérimentale sur le choix volontaire et ses antécédents immédiats." *Arch. Psychol.*, Genève, 10 (1911), 113-299.

13. Murray, H. A. "Facts which support the concept of need or drive." *J. Psychol.*, 3 (1937), 27-42.

14. Peak, H. "An evaluation of the concepts of reflex and voluntary action." *Psychol. Rev.*, 40 (1933), 71-89.

15. Rowland, L. W. "Will hypnotized persons try to harm themselves or others?" *J. Abn. Soc. Psychol.*, 34 (1939), 114-17.

16. Singer, E. A., Jr. *Mind as Behavior.* Columbus, O.: Adams, 1924.

17. Singer, E. A., Jr. "On spontaneity." *J. Phil.*, 22 (1925), 421-36.

18. Singer, E. A., Jr. "Logic and the relation of function to mechanism." *Proc. VII Internat. Congr. Phil.*, Oxford: Oxford Univ. Press, 1931, pp. 47-56.

19. Singer, E. A., Jr. "Beyond mechanism and vitalism." *Phil. Sci.*, 1 (1934), 273-95.

20. Steckle, L. C. & Renshaw, S. "An investigation of the conditioned iridic reflex." *J. Gen. Psychol.*, 11 (1934), 3-23.

21. Tolman, E. C. *Purposive Behavior in Animals and Men.* N. Y.: Appleton-Century, 1932.

22. Wendt, G. R. "An analytical study of the conditioned knee-jerk." *Arch. Psychol.*, N. Y., 1930, #123.

23. Wickens, D. D. "A study of voluntary and involuntary finger conditioning." *J. Exper. Psychol.*, 25 (1939), 127-40.

24. Woodworth, R. S. "The cause of a voluntary movement." In *Studies in Philosophy and Psychology*. Boston: Houghton Mifflin, 1906, pp. 351-92. [Reprinted in: *Psychological Issues*. N. Y.: Columbia Univ. Press, 1939, pp. 29-60.]

THE EXPERIENCE THEORY OF THE SOCIAL ATTITUDES

MALCOLM G. PRESTON

Department of Psychology, University of Pennsylvania

I

A PROMINENT feature of the history of psychology during the last twenty-five years has been the general attack which has been developing upon the doctrine of past experience. This doctrine, in its most general form, asserts that modes of response are to be understood largely on the basis of the past experience of the organism. Its acceptance often leads to the view that conduct is to be understood entirely on the basis of the occurrence of previous stimulus conditions, a view, of course, which implies that learning is the fundamental psychological process, and as has frequently been remarked, that frequency of repetition of experience is an important key to the understanding of a psychological event.

The recurring use of the doctrine of past experience as a principle of explanation is a striking feature of psychological theory. The conventional theory of tactual space localization, for example (6), explains the development of the ability to localize contacts on the skin on the basis of the integration of a perceptual pattern which progresses with practice. A well-known theory of the appearance of instinctive action (no longer seriously entertained) assumed that the inheritance of skills acquired from the experience of progenitors explained the remarkable adjustive reactions so characteristic of the insect. Indeed in recent years Rhine and McDougall (28) have entertained an identical hypothesis to account for the increased speed with which later generations of rats escaped from a water maze. Those psychologists who have attacked the validity of the concept of insight have not infrequently fallen upon a frequency theory of learning when they have attempted to cope with those facts of thinking and problem solving which appear to demand the concept of insight (16). The same type of attack has been characteristic of those psychologists who have failed to be attracted to the concept of general intelligence. The variability of the I. Q. among children of differing richness of experience has led some to conclude (31) that differences in mental ability are but a function of differences in the experiences of those whose mental abilities differ. Finally, it may be mentioned that not only the psychology of the normal but also the psychology of the abnormal offers illustration of the use of this doctrine. In illustration may be cited the Freudian view of the inter-relation of repression and forgetting.

Perhaps the most striking and certainly the most telling of the attacks on the doctrine of past experience have been those which have been made on the primary and secondary laws of association, in particular the laws of contiguity and frequency. These criticisms have been important because they have extended to learning theory itself, a fact which endows them with more than passing interest. Characteristic of those who have been brave enough to doubt what appears at first sight as axiomatic, is the view that a distinction must be made between experience as an occasion in the development of behavior of a given kind and experience as a condition necessary and sufficient to the development of the given behavior. As it will appear in the sequel, those who recognize the function of experience as occasional must look to the psychological processes of the individual for an understanding of conduct; while those who accept the experience itself as a condition necessary and sufficient for the appearance of the conduct are prone to turn either to a stimulus or to a frequency theory for its understanding.

A distinction similar to the one just mentioned was implied by Meumann (25) in his classic treatment of the psychology of learning and, indeed, as we shall show in a moment, in the same place Meumann came very near questioning explicitly that kind of explanation with which we are concerned here. Meumann was interested in pointing out that contiguity in and of itself had little effect upon the observer in the memory experiment. He wrote, in this connection:

> Of all those laws of association only that of contiguity is admitted by most modern psychologists; but it is easy to show that this law too is *wholly inadequate* [italics ours] . . . It may be readily shown that all ideas which were present in consciousness simultaneously or in immediate succession do not by any means become associated and do not subsequently reproduce one another.

The problem of learning, according to Meumann, was the identification of the special conditions under which the association and reproduction of ideas take place. Such conditions of course would include the well-known secondary laws of association among which is the law of frequency. But this law was formulated by Meumann not as a law depending upon frequency of repetition unqualified, but rather as the law of attentive repetition. Meumann never stated explicitly what he thought of repetition per se as a factor in memory; he built his theory rather on a view of frequency which confused its effect in the learning situation with effects which can only be understood by a consideration of what the observer himself brings to the learning situation.

Among those who have paused to question the effect of frequency in isolation is Thorndike. This investigator has shown in a large number of experiments on memory (34) that mere frequency of repetition of word lists contributes little to the later recollection of those items which the subject did not intend to remember. An important observation of Thorndike's is the fact that many repetitions can be given under conditions which lead in the sequel to no retention and that again a single repetition can be given under conditions which lead in the sequel to no forgetting. From these data Thorndike has been willing to conclude that frequency of repetition, in isolation, has very little to do with those lasting impressions which we describe as memorial. Like Meumann, Thorndike finds subjective factors to be decisive in the conditions of impression.

Thorndike's experiments in learning run parallel with a large number of learning experiments produced by the Gestalt psychologists to whom the primary and secondary laws of association have been the bête noir of psychology. These experiments have exerted a profound influence upon the psychology of memory because they have employed concepts and techniques which permit the analysis of subjective factors. Among these may be mentioned the celebrated experiment of Zeigarnik (36) who showed very clearly in one of her control experiments that a change in the dynamics of the subject *after impression* makes a considerable difference in later recall.

Zeigarnik required her subjects to perform a number of tasks. Some of the tasks were completed while others were interrupted before completion. At a later time the subjects were asked to recall the tasks and it appeared in the results that it was generally true that more of the interrupted tasks were recalled than of the completed tasks. Zeigarnik's observation has been confirmed separately by Marrow (22) and by Martin (23). In a control experiment Zeigarnik reported that some time after the original period devoted to the performance of the tasks a later period was used during which the subjects were permitted to complete the tasks previously interrupted. On recall, this group showed no significant difference between the number of completed and the number of interrupted tasks recalled. The difference in the relative number of interrupted tasks recalled (comparing the results of the control with the results of the main experiment), suggests that the completion of the task in the instance of the second group operated to accelerate the rate of forgetting for the interrupted tasks. As Lewin has pointed out, this fact is a fact of common experience; who does not proceed to forget an item, such as the mailing of a letter, once the need to remember has disappeared? Zeigarnik's experiment is celebrated because it was among the first to demonstrate conclusively the role of dynamic factors like needs in retention and recall.

Somewhat apart from the experiments of Thorndike and Zeigarnik but in the main tradition of the revolt against associationism is the work of von Restorff. This investigator (27) was interested among other things in analyzing the contribution made to the difficulty value of nonsense syllables by the lack of association which is characteristic of material of that kind. The conventional theory of the difficulty of the nonsense syllable ascribes that difficulty to its novelty in the experience of the subject. Von Restorff attacked the conventional theory by demonstrating that it was quite easy to memorize a nonsense syllable if it appeared among a series of meaningless geometrical figures rather than among a series of nonsense syllables. To the two conditions of presentation correspond two perceptual conditions: in the case of the nonsense syllable presented among a series of geometrical figures, the series may be said to be perceptually heterogeneous; in the case of the nonsense syllable presented among a series of nonsense syllables, the series may be said to be perceptually homogeneous. Not degree of association but homogeneity of the series is to be regarded as the fundamental condition for the appearance of the phenomenon of difficulty.

The investigations enumerated thus far have by no means been confined to any single era in psychology, nor to any single school. Meumann and Thorndike have little in common and neither shares his general orientation with the Gestalt psychologists. Belonging to a quite different school of psychology from any of them is the English psychologist Bartlett. Bartlett (3) has shown that recollection is affected not only by what happened at the time of impression and during retention, but also by the activity of the subject at the time of recall. Subjects in recalling a story recall it with a different point, add details consistent with the viewpoint, and furnish it with an increased plausibility. In general, the recall is not only a recall but in many respects a new creation, subject to the influence of factors deriving from the action pattern at the time of recall. This finding of Bartlett's, supported by a long series of investigations, has required among other things the redefinition of the problem of remembering. By definition, memory today is no longer merely the study of the consequences of the stimulus conditions obtaining at the time of impression.

The important features of the work of Meumann, Thorndike, Zeigarnik, von Restorff and Bartlett may be summarized in two conclusions. First may be mentioned the conclusion suggested by the work of all of these investigators, namely that the recall which at first glance appears to be only a reflection of the occurrence of the event or of the repetition of that occurrence may conceal the operation of factors contributed by the organism itself. That the organism must be regarded as a system governed by laws peculiar to it, rather than a static mechanism functioning only on the basis of stimulation imposed from without is indicated clearly by the work of Zeigarnik. Finally, there must be mentioned the conclusion suggested by the work of Bartlett, that the recall itself is in many respects an original creation of the imagination subject to the laws of imagination as well as the laws of memory. Bartlett, of course, is not alone in this view of mental activity. The Gestalt psychologists hold as a cardinal principle that the arbitrary division of the mental processes by the systematic psychologist into perception, memory, and imagination does violence to the facts of mental life as they are observed in practice.

These conclusions are not limited to the study of memory in their application. The views which they summarize may indeed be extended to any problem in which past experience itself has been the principal condition specified for the appearance of a psychological datum. It is the purpose of this paper to consider the grounds upon which it may be concluded that the social attitudes are so conditioned. It has been the purpose of the introduction to inform or remind the reader of experiments which suggest an analysis which might be applied to this task.

II

Of the various problems treated by social psychology the social attitude is perhaps the most significant. According to Allport (1) the attitude is probably the most distinctive and indispensable concept in contemporary American social psychology. Bogardus (5) and Folsom (12) define social psychology as the science of attitudes. While the attitude undoubtedly involves questions of the greatest systematic and theoretical importance, it is also the locus of problems of the greatest practical importance. The origin and development of attitudes is tangential to the problem of coping with propaganda (9). Many psychologists regard the development of attitudes as closely allied to the problem of the development of character (33). Sociologists find the social attitude to be the locus of an important problem in the history of social change (15). It follows, therefore, that the testing of the theories which have been devised to explain the origin and development of the social attitudes is an important undertaking both on the practical as well as the theoretical side.

Perhaps the most striking fact, indeed it has frequently been taken to be the most important fact, concerning the social attitude, is the fact that the behavior it denotes is characteristic of large numbers of people who have had uniform life experiences. The *attitude* of the Southerner towards the Negro, of the Californian towards the Mexican, of the conservative towards the radical, of the Hindu towards the Moslem, possesses no meaning as a social attitude unless it be understood to characterize the action of a large number of Southerners or Californians or conservatives or Hindus, the members of each group having had substantially the same life experience. It is convenient to examine the theories which have been developed to account for the origin and development of the social attitude in the light of this central fact.

Even a superficial consideration of the examples which have been given will suggest the fact that they illustrate not one, but two properties of the social attitude. In the first place they illustrate the fact that a group of people, the members of which respond in the same way to a social stimulus, frequently have had much the same past experience. Easy to overlook is the second fact that not only is the stimulus situation relatively constant for these people, but so is the response. An important characteristic of the social attitude is the apparent stereotyping of the response among large numbers of people. In the developing of a theory to account for the facts of the social attitude it is relatively easy to cast the facts into one of two molds, depending upon which of these two sets of facts one prefers to emphasize. Thus Allport and Schanck (2) point out in an important paper on this problem that theories of the

origin and development of the social attitude are of two principal kinds, the cultural theories on the one hand and the
biological theories on the other; the one as it will appear later
emphasizing the uniformity of the milieu in which the phenomenon makes its appearance, and the other emphasizing the
uniformity of the response to the stimulus conditions.

The cultural theory of attitude formation finds an explanation for the appearance of the social attitude in the effect of
culture upon the individual. It is a favorite theory of the cultural anthropologists and sociologists. Despite the fact that the
theory appears on the surface to be exclusively a sociological
theory it is not difficult to show that important assumptions
concerning human behavior are concealed in it. To that extent, of course, the theory is not only one which reflects the
fundamental conceptions of sociology but it is also one which
must find support or stand criticism from the fundamental
conceptions of psychology.

An important assumption which appears in variations of
both the cultural and the biological theories of the social attitudes characterizes all theories of behavior which treat reaction to stimulation as a phenomenon in which only two terms
are important, namely the stimulus and the response. Fundamental to the stimulus-response psychology is the assumption
that the organism is a kind of mechanism prepared either by
reason of its biological inheritance or its training to respond
in a standard manner, provided an appropriate stimulus is
applied. To the awareness of the subject at the time of response or to the significance which that awareness may find in
the lability of the subject's responses to the conditions of
stimulation, the stimulus-response psychologies tend to be
blind. The stimulus-response theory of conduct does not of
course stand or fall with a habit theory, since it finds explanation not only in the facts of training but also in the facts of
maturation. However, it is an important question, no matter
which of these alternatives is accepted, whether the facts warrant the conclusion that the responses follow machine-like upon
the stimulating conditions. In the event that they do not, a

serious impediment exists to the acceptance of either of the theories.

Concealed in the cultural theory of attitude formation, in the second place, is the assumption that attitudes are learned. It is characteristic of the proponents of the cultural theory that they point to the fact that variation in the cultural environment brings with it variation in the attitude. An infant raised in the North will not entertain the same notions toward the Negro upon reaching adulthood as will an infant raised in the South. As an example of the evidence upon which the cultural theory rests we may take Mead's frequently cited observation (24) of personality differences among the Arapesh, the Mundugumur, and the Tchambuli of New Guinea. In the case of the Arapesh, both men and women exhibit a gentle and humane attitude towards life. In the case of the Mundugumur, both sexes exhibit a violent, active attitude towards life and finally in the Tchambuli, we observe the women preserving a violent, active attitude towards life while the men are humane and gentle in their life attitude. On the basis of this observation the author concludes that "the differences between individuals who are members of different cultures . . . are almost entirely to be laid to differences in conditioning, especially during early childhood, and the form of this conditioning is culturally determined." The learning theory of the origin and development of the social attitudes is not confined of course to the sociologists and cultural anthropologists. Krueger and Reckless (19) define the attitude as a species of learned response.

As we have already shown in the Introduction to this paper, the use of the doctrine of past experience as an explanatory principle has met with increasing skepticism in recent years. In particular, it will be remembered that learning theory is in the process of undergoing radical changes, the changes running parallel with the growing skepticism of the influence of contiguity and frequency of stimulation (in isolation) on human conduct. It will be recalled in particular that the theory of learned behavior which rests its case on the study of stimulus conditions is now engaged in a serious competition with a set of theories which account for learned behavior on the basis of a consideration of the psychological forces operating within the individual at the time of impression, during retention, and at the time of recall. The remarkable similarity of the cultural theory of attitude formation to what might be described as the stimulus theory of learning, cannot fail to suggest the application of a criticism following the model of that reviewed in the Introduction. As will appear shortly each of our criticisms of the cultural theory will be found to have its analogue in the criticism of the Introduction.

To begin with, we should like to proceed on analogy to the theory developed by Bartlett, who showed that many of the problems encountered in the study of remembering cannot be treated unless attention be devoted to certain activities of the subject which are completely independent of the conditions under which the material, subject to recall, was committed to memory. In similar vein we shall attack the assumption that the behavior denoted by the social attitudes may in any sense be regarded as a stimulus-response form by considering the characteristics of the subject's conduct when he is responding in an apparently stereotyped fashion to a stimulus in a social setting. The assumption that the behavior in this instance is of the stimulus-response variety may appear to be well founded since much has been made of the fact that reaction on the basis of attitude is antithetical to rational behavior, not only being highly stereotyped but also notoriously not amenable to logical persuasion.

An important attribute of an habituated response is the fact that it will persist upon presentation of the stimulus despite changes in the general field in which the response is made. This is not only a fact of everyday knowledge, but also one to which convincing experimental proof may be given. Watson, for example (35), trained rats to traverse a maze. He then subjected the animals to a variety of surgical procedures by means of which they were systematically deprived of most of the avenues of sense experience. The rats continued to traverse the maze despite the radical change in the field. MacFarlane (21) trained rats to run through a maze. The rats with little change in their error score were immediately able to swim through the same maze pattern. An examination of the evidence on this point in the case of the social attitude begins with an investigation conducted by Schanck (30) on the differences in expressed attitude which depend upon whether the attitude is expressed publicly or privately. The investigator in this case settled himself as a member of a small community as a preliminary step to the study of the social psychology of that community. After his acceptance by the community he undertook a series of studies, among them being one which was aimed at comparing the viewpoints of members of the community when the opinions were collected by personal interview and when the opinions were collected in open meeting. The attitude of the members of a church congregation towards a wealthy member of the congregation, for example, differed quite widely under the two conditions. Most important in connection with the differences was a radical change in the nature of the curve describing the attitudes. When the frequency of opinions for each level of preference was plotted as a histogram it was observed that under the condition of private expression an approximation to a symmetrical distribution occurred. The great majority of opinions might be described as being moderate in degree, while extreme opinions in either direction were infrequently observed. In the case of the attitudes publicly expressed, the curve disclosed an enormous piling up at the one extreme with a rapid decrease in frequency through the range from the one extreme to the other. Reflection on the data of Schanck's investigation, in particular on the radical change in the type of the distribution curve which he observed, suggests the conclusion that a change in the conditions under which the question is asked results in a radical change in the character of the response.

This conclusion finds support from another source. In a recent experiment reported by Corey (8) scores on a highly reliable questionnaire probing the attitude of the student towards cheating were compared with the extent to which the student cheated in an examination situation. The extent to which cheating occurred could be ascertained without the knowledge of the subjects. Comparison of the scores on the questionnaire with the extent of cheating indicated that the coefficient of correlation between the two sets of scores was of the order of $+ .13 \pm .12$. From this fact of course the conclusion was drawn that the validity of the scale was highly questionable. The observation must suggest another conclusion than this however if it is placed in a somewhat different universe of discourse. The additional conclusion is obviously suggested that the same stimulus results in widely different responses depending again upon the conditions under which the response is to be made. If the attitude is limited to verbal expression, one kind of response is observed. If it is possible to express the attitude as overt behavior another kind of response, qualitatively different from the first, is observed. From the two studies it is apparent that the attitudes studied exhibited a remarkable lability to the field in which they made their appearance.

If we inquire why the change in the field is followed by a change in the nature of the response it is difficult to conclude that the answer can be made without reference to forces in the experiment contributed by the subject at the time the stimulus is offered. That subjective factors exercise an important influence upon behavior under the guidance of attitudes has been frequently recognized. Some writers on the topic like Kirkpatrick (18) define the attitude as a stereotyped form of response to a social stimulus in which the response is accompanied by a characteristic feeling tone. Indeed some writers have gone so far (10) as to define the attitude as a species of feeling tone and have made of the problem a problem in the affections. We are not disposed to go this far because of the many instances with which psychology abounds of attitudes for which no accompanying feeling tone can be specified. But the tendency to define attitude in such a way as to identify it closely with the feelings is important, not because the tendency leads to a fruitful or sterile treatment of the problem, but rather because it demonstrates the considerable importance given to subjective factors in this kind of behavior.

An important fact about the attitudes in general, and one which again distinguishes them from habituated responses, is the fact that they bear a special relationship to imagination and thinking. The setting in which the attitudes are studied is frequently a setting which requires the subject to solve a problem, or at least to make a choice, and the existence of the attitude is demonstrated by some characteristic of the end-product of thinking. This fact is illustrated by the nine dot problem exploited by Fernberger (11). In this problem three rows of three dots, the dots being approximately a half inch apart and the rows an equal distance apart, are given the subject, who is required to connect all dots, using not more than four straight lines with no retracing permitted. The problem is an impossible problem if the subject restricts his attempts at a solution to the area enclosed by the figure; to solve it the subject must use the area surrounding the figure. This type of problem conceals a principle which finds extensive application in the construction of puzzles, the principle involving the fact that the solution of the puzzle is made to depend upon an operation the possibility of which, for one reason or another, is not perceived by the subject.

The fact that the subject does not think of a solution, which he recognizes instantly once he is acquainted with it, is obviously not a consequence of any instructions given him by the one who sets the puzzle. A convenient way of regarding the subject's action is either to suppose that it is governed by instructions which he has given himself, perhaps explicitly, or by a suggestion which is contained implicitly in the form of the figure used in the puzzle. Whatever the theory developed to account for the action however, there remains an aspect of the situation which merits more than passing attention. In the first place, the function of the attitude (whether it be due to self instructions implicit or explicit) is to narrow the spatial field within which the subject will search for a solution. And in the second place, a characteristic of the behavior under the guidance of the attitude is the fact that the subject is not aware of this restriction of the field. Subjects who have failed the nine-dot problem not infrequently exclaim that they did not realize it was permitted to go outside the field. The limiting of the area within which choices will be made in the presence of at most an imperfect understanding of the fact that such a limitation exists is a characteristic not only of thinking in the laboratory, but also of thinking subject to the restrictions of a social attitude.

Not a few experiments on the social attitudes are designed to test an hypothesis by requiring the subjects to make choices. Illustrative of experiments of this kind is one performed by Hartmann (14) by means of which he was able to show the extent to which emotionally toned arguments surpass rational arguments in effectiveness during political campaigns. Hartmann was candidate for the mayoralty of Allentown, Pennsylvania, on the Socialist ticket. Prior to the opening of the campaign he divided the city of Allentown into districts, and selected three, equated roughly for relevant variables, as experimental and control areas. In the first experimental area he distributed a rational appeal for support of his candidacy. In the second experimental area he distributed an emotional appeal for support of his candidacy. In the control area he made no formal call for support. The election disclosed a greater gain in vote (on the basis of a comparison with the returns of a previous election) for the Socialist ticket in the second experimental area than in the first, and a greater gain in the experimental areas than in the control. From this fact it was concluded of course that an emotional appeal exerted a stronger influence upon the political attitudes of the voters than did a rational appeal.

While the arguments advanced by Hartmann in his campaign for the mayoralty of Allentown were unquestionably properly classified as emotional on the one hand and rational on the other, they might also be classified in another fashion, namely on the basis of the extent to which they were directed at the ego of the voters. Those arguments which Hartmann classified as emotional were appeals to the voter to cast his ballot in the interest of his home, the future of his children, and his own old age. It is a serious question whether the limitation on the choices of the voters was a consequence of the emotional quality of the appeal as the one classification suggests, or the fact that the one appeal was directed at the ego while the other (the rational) was not.

A common viewpoint appearing in the writings of investigators of widely differing training and convictions regards the attitude as closely related to the ego. Mead, already mentioned (24), has treated personality as it is observed among primitive people as a species of attitude. Spranger (32) regards the fundamental life values as attitudes. Upon a conception similar to Spranger's the Allport-Vernon test of values was developed (13), a test designed to distinguish people according to the fundamental life-purposes which they find meaningful. Baumgarten (4) has suggested that the attitudes of workers towards their work is in part determined by fundamental values which they find in the materials with which they work.

Consistent with the conception of attitude as a reflection of the fundamental character of the ego is the practice of caricaturists who delineate the ego by an exaggeration of one or another social attitude. Thus the professional radical, the professional Tory, the professional carpetbagger or the professional Southerner take the structure of their existence from an accentuation of well-known social attitudes. Experiment has shown (29) that what is true of the caricaturist is true also of all of us in our everyday thinking; our recollections of people are frequently recollections of a stereotype in the case of which the ego of the subject of the recollection is represented by an exaggeration of his social attitudes.

Observations such as these suggest that an important element which establishes limitations on the thinking of people who are affected by one or another social attitude is the ego. The suggestion finds confirmation in the well-known fact that rational argument is singularly unpersuasive in instances where deep-seated religious, political, or social attitudes are involved. The solution of a problem which involves the contradiction of an attitude intimately related to the ego not only is not made, it does not even occur to the subject. The person whose conduct is guided by genuinely religious attitudes not only does not steal to reconcile his financial difficulties, he does not think of stealing.

Bartlett showed that recall was to a considerable extent a function of the dynamic state of the subject at the time of recall. Our analysis of the conditions under which we observe that a subject is acting under the guidance of attitude brings the same situation to light. The extreme lability of the attitude to the field conditions, the close relation between attitude and thinking, the enormous importance of ego factors in the action involved are not characteristics of a stimulus-response psychology nor of habituated behavior. Rather they suggest a category of behavior having properties of its own, requiring its own definitions, experimental techniques and concepts, and leading perhaps to a fresh view of human nature.

Our second and final general attack is one which perhaps the reader has been awaiting impatiently, since it goes to the heart of the question whether the social attitudes, whatever is true of their nature after they are well formed, are in their origin and development to be regarded as a consequence of stimulus conditions alone. In analogy with the criticism of the Introduction it is our purpose here to show that frequency of repetition in particular has little to do with their origin and formation and that the true story cannot be understood unless the dynamical state of the individuals involved be thoroughly explored.

The experiments on the basis of which Thorndike, Zeigarnik, and others have shown that frequency as such is relatively ineffective in the development of memories are of a number of different kinds. In some, like Thorndike's, evidence is given that very little learning takes place, even on the basis of large numbers of repetitions, unless the subject is set in a given manner. In others, like von Restorff's, it has been shown that the influence of the primary and secondary laws of association on the difficulty of nonsense syllables and geometrical figures may be confused with the difficulty in memorization due to their perceptual homogeneity. The conventional theory of difficulty of nonsense syllables states that the less frequently we experience a nonsense syllable the more difficult it is. Not lack of experience with a given nonsense syllable but rather a characteristic of the figure-ground relationship in which the syllable appears, is the important factor which determines whether it is or is not difficult, according to von Restorff. We may mention a final kind of experiment, namely that performed by Zeigarnik, in which it was shown that whether or not an event is remembered depends upon whether the individual possesses any special needs depending upon that event. Despite these differences among the experiments reported by Thorndike, von Restorff, and Zeigarnik they have in common a certain principle of experimentation. In these experiments not only were the experimental conditions varied in order to provide grounds for comparison between experimental and control groups, but the variations in experimental conditions were such that the subjects' performances could be compared on the basis of changes in their internal conditions as well as on the basis of changing frequencies of presentation of the materials to be learned. Thus Thorndike's results permit the comparison of results when the subject intends to learn with the results when he does not intend to learn. Von Restorff's experiment permits the comparison of the difficulty of learning nonsense syllables when the crucial syllables are presented among a series of nonsense syllables on the one hand, and among a series of meaningless geometrical figures on the other. An important requirement therefore of any set of observations in social psychology, from which it is desired to conclude that frequency of repetition is the essential condition for the appearance of a social attitude, is that the observations be sufficiently extensive (in the sense of including satisfactory experimental variation) to show that the effect of frequency persists through changes in conditions calculated to affect the internal conditions of the subject. It is not enough to report the rate of onset or of change with increasing frequency, nor to report the remarkable similarity in attitudes among people of the same experience. From this latter kind of experiment we might equally well conclude that the appearance of the social attitude was a function, not of identical experience but of identical needs, identical responses to the same pressures or identical characteristics of the process of thinking. The interesting psychological fact is not that the Negro is the focal point of attitude development among people in the South, but rather that the general details of the pattern of the attitude towards the Negro, as the attitude is concerned with the right of the Negro to hold property, with the inter-marriage of Negroes and whites, with the type of education to be afforded the Negro, with the political rights of the Negro, repeats itself over and over again in human society. We may mention in illustration the attitude towards the Mexican and the Japanese in California, towards the Jew in the Third Reich, towards the Hindu as his life is affected by the English social classes in India.

While there have been a large number of experiments on changes in attitudes there are relatively few in which the in-vestigator has been permitted by his materials to put the ques-tion of the operation of the stimulus conditions (in isolation) to the crucial test. Investigations of attitude change are of course subject to certain definite limitations which affect them almost without exception. In the first place in very few cases are they experimental in design. This fact prohibits, in many instances, the variation of stimulation in such a way as to meet the conditions already established in the experiments on mem-ory as the minimum for the crucial testing of the question. A means of coping with this problem is to compare the results of large numbers of experiments carved out under two sets of conditions, the conditions being such that they may be said to excite differing internal conditions in the subjects. Murphy, Murphy, and Newcomb (26) report a series of thirty-eight studies which may be scrutinized according to this plan. Of the thirty-eight, twenty-five may be regarded as yielding a change in attitude consistent in direction with the type of propaganda used to effect the change.

Perhaps the most striking difference in experimental tech-nique among these various studies is the fact that in twenty-one of the studies, the agency utilized to effect a change in the atti-tudes was used in the classroom, while in seventeen of the studies, the agency utilized to effect a change was used outside the classroom. We may therefore compare the effectiveness of the propaganda in the two situations. In the instance of the first set of twenty-one studies, eleven produced results favorable to the direction intended by the investigator. In the instance of the second set of studies, change favorable to the direction intended by the investigator occurred in fourteen of the seventeen studies. The conclusion is of course suggested that the use of propaganda under conditions where it is apt to be recognized as such is less efficient than under conditions where it is disguised. Such a conclusion bears no air of novelty since it is confirmed by the experience of advertising experts and other propagandists. The facts which support it make useful the distinction which students of the effect of propaganda have made between explicit and implicit propaganda (9).

But it must also be noted that the two sets of conditions correspond to two sets of internal conditions. And if we observe the results in the instance where the internal conditions are least favorable it is obvious that the number of experiments in which the results were favorable in direction is almost exactly what would be expected if chance alone were operating. Finally it should be emphasized that over this long series of experiments although the internal states were quite different among the two groups, frequency of repetition of the propaganda was substantially the same.

That the effectiveness of propaganda is conditioned by the extent to which it matches the structure of the attitudes of the group against whom it is directed parallels a phenomenon noticed by J. F. Brown (7) and Kurt Lewin (20). These writers, in particular J. F. Brown, have observed that rapid changes in attitudes towards minority groups are a consequence of serious economic and political pressures being exerted on the majority group. The intensification of a prejudiced attitude towards a given minority is always accelerated whenever the minority is placed in a position of competing with the majority for a livelihood. Thus the attitude of Northerners towards the Negro has changed in communities where the Negro has limited the opportunity of the Northerner to find work. The source of specific instances of racial difficulties in the South has not infrequently been attributed to the same economic conditions. While evidence of this kind cannot be taken to be crucial for the question at issue in this paper, we may note with interest the fact that accelerated changes in social attitudes occur under conditions where a concept of frequency or quantity of experience is completely inapplicable to the facts. What it is which makes the mere presence of a member of the hated minority a stimulus to unregulated action is not made understandable by an account of the stimulus conditions, as such, affecting the majority. Rather must the response of the majority be clarified by a recognition of the fact that their action in a case of this kind is a consequence of the same kind of phenomenon observed by Zeigarnik. Whether or not an event is remembered depends upon whether or not a need exists which depends upon that event; in similar vein we may say that the attitude of a member of the majority is not understandable unless we take into consideration the psychological needs of the members of the majority. As those needs accelerate in intensity, so does the attitude.

III

At the outset of our discussion we remarked on the fact that the problem of attitude development was tangential to the problem of coping with propaganda. In conclusion we should like to point out that the answer to the question whether frequency of repetition is the basis upon which attitudes develop has an important bearing upon the selection of measures to be taken in dealing with the effects of propaganda. Two general techniques may be utilized in dealing with propaganda, the one consisting in the use of counter-propaganda, the other consisting in the exposure of the original propaganda as such. The use of counter-propaganda is of course predicated upon the frequency theory of attitude formation. The exposure of the propaganda as such is predicated upon a theory of attitude formation which finds an explanation for the phenomenon in the psychological forces at work in the individual. From our consideration of the psychological theory affecting the origin and development of the social attitudes it follows that if the exposure of the propaganda as propaganda affects the internal forces of the individual, in particular his recognition of vital needs to be fulfilled, it must be a more effective means of abating the influence of the propagandist than the use of counter agents. Propagandists and students of propaganda (9) are in general agreed that the most efficient method to use is to expose the propaganda as such. Whether this method will work effectively among peoples who feel no vital need to acquaint themselves with facts instead of fancies is of course another question, to which another answer must be given. The exposure of the propagandistic methods which have been used to fix the attitudes of the people of a nation like present-day Germany could scarcely be expected to be effective unless the need to base individual action upon a knowledge of facts transcends those needs which appear to have developed as a consequence of post-war European diplomacy.

BIBLIOGRAPHY

1. Allport, G. W. "Attitudes," in *A Handbook of Social Psychology*, ed. by Carl Murchison. Worcester, Mass.: Clark Univ. Press, 1935.
2. Allport, G. W. & Schanck, R. L. "Are attitudes biological or cultural in origin?" *Character & Pers.*, 4 (1936), 195-205.
3. Bartlett, F. C. *Remembering.* New York: Macmillan Co., 1932.
4. Baumgarten, F. "New aspects of job analysis," *Occupations*, 12 (1934), 79-85.
5. Bogardus, E. S. *Fundamentals of Social Psychology.* New York: Century & Co., 1931.
6. Boring, E. G., Langfeld, H. S. & Weld, H. P. *Psychology.* New York: John Wiley & Sons, 1935.
7. Brown, J. F. *Psychology and the Social Order.* New York: McGraw-Hill, 1936.
8. Corey, S. M. "Professed attitudes and actual behavior," *J. Educ. Psychol.*, 28 (1937), 271-80.
9. Doob, Leonard. *Propaganda.* New York: Henry Holt & Co., 1935.
10. Ewer, B. C. *Social Psychology.* New York: Macmillan Co., 1929.
11. Fernberger, S. W. *Elementary General Psychology.* Baltimore: Williams & Wilkins Co., 1936.
12. Folsom, J. K. *Social Psychology.* New York: Harper, 1931.
13. Freeman, F. N. *Mental Tests.* Boston: Houghton Mifflin Co., 1939.
14. Hartmann, G. W. "A field experiment on the comparative ef-

fectiveness of 'emotional' and 'rational' political leaflets in determining election results," *J. Abnorm. (Soc.) Psychol.*, 31 (1936), 99-114.

15. Herskovits, M. J. "Social history of the Negro," in *A Handbook of Social Psychology*, ed. by Carl Murchison. Worcester, Mass.: Clark Univ. Press, 1935.

16. Hunter, Walter S. "Learning: IV. Experimental Studies of Learning," in *A Handbook of Experimental Psychology*, ed. by Carl Murchison. Worcester, Mass.: Clark Univ. Press, 1934.

17. Katz, D. & Schanck, R. L. *Social Psychology*. New York: John Wiley & Sons, 1938.

18. Kirkpatrick, C. "Assumptions and methods in attitude measurement," *Amer. Sociol. Rev.*, 1 (1936), 75-88.

19. Krueger, E. T. & Reckless, W. C. *Social Psychology*. New York: Longmans, Green, 1931.

20. Lewin, Kurt. *Topological Psychology*. New York: McGraw-Hill, 1936.

21. MacFarlane, D. A. "The role of kinaesthesis in maze learning," *Univ. Calif. Publ. Psychol.*, 4 (1930), 277-305.

22. Marrow, A. J. "Goal tensions and recall," *J. Gen. Psychol.*, 19 (1938), 3-64.

23. Martin, John, *Reminiscence and Gestalt theory*, Ph.D. thesis, Univ. of Penna., accepted for publication in *Psychol. Monogr.*, 1940.

24. Mead, Margaret. *Growing Up in New Guinea*. New York: Morrow, 1930.

25. Meumann, E. *The Psychology of Learning*, trans. by J. W. Baird. New York: D. Appleton & Co., 1913.

26. Murphy, G., Murphy, L. B., and Newcomb, T. M. *Experimental Social Psychology*. New York: Harper, 1937.

27. von Restorff, H. "Über die Wirkung von Bereichsbildungen im Spurenfeld," *Psychol. Forsch.*, 18 (1933), 299-342.

28. Rhine, J. B. and McDougall, W. "Third report on a Lamarckian experiment," *Brit. J. Psychol.*, 24 (1933), 213-35.

29. Rice, S. A. "Stereotypes, a source of error in judging human character," *J. Personnel Research*, 5 (1926), 267-76.

30. Schanck, R. L. "A study of a community and its groups and institutions conceived of as behavior of individuals," *Psychol. Monogr.*, 43 (1932), #195.

31. Skeels, H. M., Updegraff, R., Wellman, B., and Williams, H. M.

"A study of environmental conditions," *Univ. Ia. Stud. Child Welfare,* 15 (1938), #4.

32. Spranger, E. *Types of Men,* trans. by P. J. W. Pigors. Halle: Max Niemeyer Verlag, 1928.

33. Stagner, Ross. *Psychology of Personality.* New York: McGraw-Hill, 1937.

34. Thorndike, E. L. *Human Learning.* New York: Century & Co., 1931.

35. Watson, J. B. "Kinaesthetic and organic sensations, their rôle in the reactions of the white rat," *Psychol. Rev. Monogr.,* 8, #33.

36. Zeigarnik, B. "Uber das Behalten von erledigten und unerledigten Handlungen," *Psychol. Forsch.,* 9 (1937), 1-85.

II

ETHICS AND RELIGION

TOWARD AN EXPERIMENTAL DEFINITION OF CRIMINAL MIND

THOMAS A. COWAN

Department of Philosophy, University of Pennsylvania

INTRODUCTION

IN THE 17th year of the reign of Edward IV, Brian pronounced his celebrated dictum that a man is responsible only for his words and deeds and not for his thoughts, because "the devil himself knoweth not the mind of man." What the learned judge apparently took to be an axiomatic rule of evidence has become a part of the substantive law of contracts in the form of the doctrine of objective intent. Contract law is now taken to be concerned only with intent as outwardly manifested by the conduct of the parties.

Similarly, the law of torts is almost exclusively occupied with the external behavior of the parties. Only in the case of intentional wrongs does it purport to refer to states of mind as qualifying responsibility. The great body of non-intentional torts applies what are called "objective standards." In determining negligence, for instance, the law does not inquire whether the harmful act was accompanied by a culpable state of mind. On the contrary, it merely decides whether the defendant failed to conform to external standards of reasonably expectable conduct. His state of mind is immaterial. Anglo-American *civil* law, therefore, has from the earliest times indicated that, with certain few exceptions, objective intent is the only kind of intent with which it is prepared to deal.

The theory of the *criminal* law is different. Here it is still felt necessary to investigate a man's secret thought, or absence of thought, whenever intention, or malice, or even negligence is an element of the crime in question.

It is the purpose of this essay to lay the foundation for an objective or experimental interpretation of criminal mind. Our theory, following Professor Singer,[1] is that mind is a form of behavior, and that "states of mind," if they are to have any meaning, must gather their meaning from observation and experiment in the same way as do other types of human conduct. It is part of our general thesis that criminal mind is criminal behavior; that criminal intent, one of the aspects of criminal mind, is therefore also a form of criminal behavior; and that malice, criminal negligence or inattention, and similar concepts are not subjective states of mind, but rather are aspects of ways of acting. Criminal intent, because it is the most important form of criminal mind, will occupy our attention very largely in the sequel. Yet nothing we shall say respecting it will be inapplicable to criminal mind generally.

We have said that criminal intent must be defined objectively. Accordingly, the sense in which the terms "subjective intent" and "objective intent" are here employed should be explained. Subjective intent refers to an internal state of mind, called variously by law writers "advertence coupled with high degree of expectancy," "inward awareness," or merely "state of mind accompanying a forbidden act." Objective intent, on the other hand, makes no reference to internal states of mind but is gathered solely from the legal behavior of the accused, that is, from all the aspects of his conduct and its attendant circumstances that come legally to the attention of judge and jury. Intent so defined may be the subject of observation and experiment. It should be noted that this distinction is not the same as that often made between subjective and objective standards of conduct for determining tort liability for negligence. A subjective test of negligence is one which takes into consideration the peculiar abilities and disabilities of the defendant, while an objective criterion requires all or nearly all to conform to the same standards without reference to variations in physical or mental capabilities. In our use of the term "objective," each of these tests of tort liability is objective because each refers only to external conduct and not to internal states of mind. At a later point we shall have occasion to discuss this problem somewhat at length.

[1] *Mind as Behavior* (1924).

ORIGIN AND DEVELOPMENT OF THE DOCTRINE OF THE "MENS REA"

Actus non facit reum, nisi mens sit rea. Anglo-American law has come a long way since the concept of the *mens rea* first appeared in it. The phrase itself probably originated with St. Augustine who says in one of his Sermons, *"Ream linguam non facit nisi mens sit rea."* The doctrine has been attributed to the influence of Christianity which introduced difference in degrees of guilt according as the wrongdoer was or was not regarded as being possessed of an evil mind.

The earlier law was simpler. The perplexities attendant upon an inquiry into the state of mind of the evildoer were none of its concern. Its maxim *Qui inscienter peccat, scienter emendet* was easy to apply. However, ease of application is only one advantage to a theory of law; and, when it is attained by ignoring differences so great as to shock the moral sense of the community, then refinements are properly called for. The doctrine of the *mens rea* constituted precisely such a refinement.

Historians are not in agreement with respect to whether the concept of the *mens rea* had a counterpart in Roman law. Professor Albert Lévitt,[2] who has given the matter much thought, states the belief that the origin of the doctrine of the *mens rea* is to be found in the interaction of Christian theology and Anglo-Saxon law, and that the doctrine was not a part of Roman law. In Roman law, he says, no inquiry into the state of mind of the accused was ever instituted. This was true even in the case of homicide.

It was really the justification for the killing that was inquired into and not the mental state of the killer. And the same holds true of crimes based upon fraud. The fact that there was fraud was all that was necessary. The law did not ask whether the accused had a guilty mind.

Those who subscribe to the subjective theory of the *mens rea* may well wonder how a system of law so advanced as the Roman could have dispensed with what seems to be an essential

[2] *The Origin of the Doctrine of the Mens Rea* (1922) 17 Ill. L. R. 117.

part of the law of crimes—the mental element. Professor Lévitt answers, "The [Roman] law did not ask whether or not the accused had a guilty mind. It *presumed* from the circumstances that he had." Professor Lévitt need not have said that intent was *presumed*. He could have said that the Romans did not regard intent as one of the elements of a crime and that hence they did not find it necessary to presume it. It is entirely gratuitous first to assume that the Romans were faced with the problem of *mens rea*, and then to say that they solved the problem by ignoring it, that is, by presuming the existence of the *mens rea*.

Regardless of its origin, however, the doctrine of the *mens rea* became firmly embedded in our law at an early date. The classic view of its nature is stated by Bishop:[3]

There can be no crime large or small without an evil mind. In other words, punishment is the sequence of wickedness. Neither in philosophical speculation, nor in religious or moral sentiment, would any people in any age allow that a man should be deemed guilty unless his mind were so. It is therefore a principle of our legal system, as probably it is of every other, that the essence of an offense is the wrongful intent, without which it cannot exist.

Bishop, however, finds it difficult to defend this broad assumption. The doctrine of ignorance of the law rises to plague him. Although no evil state of mind exists, punishment nevertheless is often meted out for the innocent violations of legal rules. Bishop explains the inconsistency by calling the doctrine "arbitrary, compelled by necessity, the master of all things."

Coercion is another admitted exception. In many instances, a crime committed by a wife in the presence of her husband is as a matter of law presumed to have been done through his coercion. What, then, of the necessity for the existence of an evil mind in the husband? Bishop says, "The doctrine and reasoning of this chapter are partly artificial."

Still another exception is the application of the criminal law to corporations. Says Bishop, "If [a corporation] can level mountains, fill up valleys . . . , it can intend to do it, and can act

[3] 1 *Criminal Law* (9th ed. 1923), Sect. 287, *et seq.*

therein as well viciously as virtuously." And so it can, we may say, but not with a vicious or a virtuous mind.

Other law writers are more cautious than Bishop. For example, Wigmore[4] says,

The state of mind accompanying a forbidden act is *frequently* an element material to make the act a crime.

Mikell's edition of Clark on Crimes states the matter in this wise:

It is true, indeed, that most, if not all, acts which are criminal at common law are *mala in se*, and hence that to a greater or less extent the voluntary commission of the act presupposes a guilty mind. Yet in the case of some of the minor common law offenses it can hardly be said that the commission of an act presupposes any such state of mind, *except in a purely technical sense*; and, if the act is prohibited, the bare intention to commit it is enough to supply the requisite intent.

Still other writers have gone so far as to reject the distinction between *mala prohibita* and *mala in se*. Holmes did so because, as he said, the distinction is based on the supposition of the special heinousness of certain crimes. Archbold rejected it as an attempt to substitute the law of nature or some such moral standard, for the law of England, his position in this matter being in accord with the imperative theory of the nature of law expressed by Bentham, Austin, and Holland. Numerous judges have repudiated it in round terms, the following extract from the opinion of Best, J. in *Bensley* v. *Bignold*[5] being a forceful example:

The distinction between *mala in se* and *mala prohibita* has been long since exploded. It is not founded on any sound principle, for it is equally unfit that man should be allowed to take advantage of what the law says he ought not do, whether the thing be prohibited because it is against good morals, or whether it be prohibited because it is against the interest of the state.

In addition to the above, the doctrine of constructive intent has been widely discarded. This fiction was invented to supply

[4] 1 *Evidence* (2d ed. 1923), Sec. 242.
[5] 5 B. and A. 335.

the requisite guilty mind when an accidental injury is caused in the pursuit of certain crimes of violence. The theory is that the accused "constructively intended" the accidental harm.

The case of statutory crimes presents another difficulty. It is frequently said that intent is not an element of a statutory crime if the statute does not require it. *United States* v. *Balint*[6] is a typical case in point. That case involved the construction of a federal statute which prohibited the sale of certain drugs except upon conditions outlined in the act. Defendants, indicted for failure to comply with these conditions, demurred on the ground that the indictment failed to allege that the prohibited sale had been made with *knowledge* that it was illegal. The demurrer was overruled. In the opinion Mr. Chief Justice Taft said:

> While the general rule at common law was that the scienter was a necessary element in the indictment and proof of every crime, and this was followed in regard to statutory crimes even where the statutory definition did not in terms include it, there has been a modification of this view in respect to prosecutions under statutes the purpose of which would be obstructed by such a requirement.

So far as present-day writers are concerned, therefore, the older view that every crime involves *mens rea* has undergone modification. The doctrine is admitted to be inconsistent with the absence of intent as a requirement of certain statutory offenses, with the nature of corporate crime, and with the defenses of ignorance of the law and of coercion. In all these instances, however, the only thing that the writers as quoted above have said is that a criminal state of mind is not an element of all crimes. There remains, therefore, that large class of crimes in which a state of mind is still regarded as a necessary element.

In attacking this problem some writers have arrived, either by necessary implication or by express admission, at an objective definition of criminal intent or *mens rea*. Thus, Wigmore[7] defines criminal intent as a subjective state of mind, but the means he adopts for determining this state of mind turns out

[6] 258 U. S. 250.
[7] 1 *Evidence* (2d ed. 1923) Sects. 242, 498.

to be objective. He says, "the state of mind accompanying a forbidden act is frequently an element material to make the act a crime." Yet when he comes to indicate how such intent should be determined, the method is clearly objective. Let us analyze the following statement at some length:

To prove intent, as a generic notion of criminal volition or wilfulness, including the various non-innocent mental states accompanying different criminal acts, there is employed an entirely different process of thought (from evidencing knowledge). *The argument here is purely from the point of view of the doctrine of chances,*— the instinctive recognition of that logical process which eliminates the element of innocent intent by multiplying instances of the same result until it is perceived that this element cannot explain them all. Without formulating an absolute test, and without attempting by numerous instances to secure absolute certainty of inference, the mind applies this rough and instinctive process of reasoning, namely, that an unusual and abnormal element might perhaps be present in one instance, but the oftener similar instances occur with similar results, the less likely is the abnormal element likely to be the true explanation of them. Thus, if A while hunting with B hears the bullet from B's gun whistling past his head, he is willing to accept B's bad aim or B's accidental tripping as a conceivable explanation, but if shortly afterwards the same thing happens again, and if on a third occasion A receives B's bullet in his body the immediate inference (i. e. as a probability, perhaps not a certainty) is that B shot A deliberately; because the chances of an inadvertent shooting on three successive similar occasions are extremely small. . . . In short—the recurrence of a similar result . . . tends . . . to negative accident . . . and to establish the presence of the normal, i.e. criminal, intent accompanying such an act; and the force of each additional instance will vary in each kind of offense according to the probability that the act could be repeated, within a limited time and under given circumstances, with an innocent intent.

This account of the procedure employed in evidencing intent is of course purposely oversimplified. It might have been said that nothing less than the whole experience of the race has entered in this "calculation" of the probability of harm resulting from the forbidden acts. The circumstances may well be such that *one* bullet from B's hunting gun may be the basis of a charge of murderous assault. However, even though we reject the test for evidencing criminal intent here proposed, the method interests us. It is expressed in terms of probability, and the categories of probability are nothing if not objective. If we take Wigmore's analysis of the theory of evidencing intent as correct, then no mention need be made of the accused's subjective state of mind. Criminal intent, which is a part of the crime, is no more than an expression of the degree of probability of harm which society expects from the forbidden act. Criminal mind is here certainly defined objectively.

Wharton[8] is another writer who ascertains intent objectively. Impressed by the incomplete nature of even the most careful induction based upon evidence of facts, he reasons that every evidentiary conclusion must be reached as a *culmination* of probabilities. The determination of intent is no exception to this rule. For Wharton all intent is based on circumstantial evidence. However, by circumstantial evidence he does not mean evidence for which on some occasion confirming testimony has not been found, but rather evidence which is based on the outward behavior of the accused and upon the physical factors surrounding the commission of the crime. That is, Wharton bases intent wholly upon circumstances, and in this sense intent for him is circumstantial. It is true that for Wharton a state of mind may be inferred from the circumstances surrounding a crime. To this extent he admits the possibility of inferring criminal mind from criminal behavior. But he is careful to point out that there is at least a logical difficulty in inferring behavior from mind. The process is circular.

It may be said that intent is to be inferred from an intelligent act, and so it is; but so far as concerns the question before us, this is a petitio principii; because if you ask the witness how he knows the act was intelligent, or if you ask yourself why you infer it was intelligent from what the witness says, the answer is circumstances.

The foremost proponent of the doctrine that criminal mind must be interpreted objectively is Holmes. The statement of

[8] 1 *Criminal Evidence* (10th ed. 1912) 13 et seq.

his theory is contained in Lecture II, of his treatise on the Common Law where he examines the basis of punishment for a crime. After rejecting revenge and reformation as adequate explanations, he considers and accepts the theory of prevention as the proper foundation for punishment. This theory he bases on the observation that society is ever willing "to sacrifice individual welfare to its own existence." In so doing, society promulgates external standards of conduct to which all its subjects must conform at their peril. These external standards take account only of gross mental and physical differences or deficiencies.

Now, it is quite difficult for Holmes to depart from the learning of the past respecting the mental element in crime. He knows the traditional doctrine of the *mens rea* only too well, but all his experience with the actual administration of the criminal law seems to be in the very teeth of this theory. However, his distrust of it becomes stronger as he goes on. The following are running quotations from pages 49-50 of Lecture II:

If we take into account the general result (public policy, sacrificing the good of the individual for the general good), we shall see that *the actual state of mind accompanying a criminal act plays a different part from what is commonly supposed.*

For the most part, the purpose of the criminal law is only to induce external conformance to rule.

Considering this purely external purpose of the law (general welfare) . . . we can see more readily that the actual degree of guilt involved in any particular transgression cannot be the only element, *if it is an element at all,* in the liability incurred.

So far from its being true, as it is often assumed, that the condition of a man's heart or conscience ought to be more considered in determining criminal than civil liability *it might almost be said that it is the very opposite of truth.*

So far Holmes has not said that it is unnecessary to refer to states of mind to determine degrees of guilt. He has merely pointed out that for the most part the law has, in actual practice, disregarded the state of mind of the accused. For him, however, the standards of the criminal law are objective because the purpose of the criminal law is the protection of society. Hence he feels that society must condemn conduct inimical to itself without considering the state of mind with which an anti-social act is committed. That is, he believes that only the behavior of the criminal is of interest to society which regards a man as guilty or innocent according as he has or has not conformed to external standards of conduct. Holmes also believes that these standards must necessarily be broad and general as well as being external. Whether there is anything in the nature of an external standard which necessitates generality of application will be discussed later. Suffice it here to say that there does not appear to the writer any necessary connection between the two.

II

CRIMINAL MIND AS CRIMINAL BEHAVIOR

We have said that in the classic view of the nature of the *mens rea* the degree of criminality attached to a forbidden act varies with the state of mind deemed to accompany the act. Now this doctrine of the law depends upon that almost universally accepted psychology which assumes that knowledge of another's state of mind may be inferred from knowledge of one's own.

It may be recalled that the older law rejected this argument by "induction from a single instance." One accused of crime could be convicted only after he had confessed, because he alone possessed the requisite knowledge of his "state of mind." No matter that at times the faintest groan extracted under torture was taken as an admission of guilt. It was still felt preferable to agonize the victim rather than to allow the inquisitor to commit the fallacy of inferring the contents of another's mind from those of his own.

To be sure, the law has come to doubt very seriously the wisdom of relying upon confessions of either criminal state of mind or criminal act. If only those who confess to crime might always be members of the class "those who could have done it!" But, unfortunately, confession is nothing but a "conclusion of law," the legal result of verbal or written conduct of the accused viewed in the light of all other factors in the case. The prisoner's utterance with respect to his state of mind is not the last and unalterable test of what this "state of mind" was, particularly if the prisoner "confesses" that in his mind or heart or conscience he was innocent. Confession of one's state of mind must take its chances with every other piece of legal evidence, and submit to an "experimental" test to determine its meaning. And yet the old law long continued to crack bones in order to elicit sounds that satisfied its logical resolve to punish only those wicked in their hearts.

The newer law is more humane. No longer need prosecutors extort confessions. External evidence may now be adduced in the attempt to ascertain the prisoner's state of mind. And so, comforted with the thought that at least one individual knows what state of mind accompanied the commission of a forbidden act admitted to be his—the accused himself—the law infers what that state of mind was by examining his behavior.

We have already seen that at least one noted writer on the criminal law observed that the process of inferring criminal mind from criminal behavior involves a *petitio principii*. In a passage already cited, Wharton shows that if intent is to be inferred from the doing of what is ordinarily called an intentional act, one cannot then say that the mental element of intent is what makes the act intentional. In other words, to argue that mental intent must be inferred from conduct, and that conduct regarded as intentional must be inferred from mental intent, is to reason in a circle. Wharton was content to point out this fallacy, and having done his job as critic, to continue to assert that intent may be inferred from circumstances. He did not suggest that the process of inferring mind from circumstances and circumstances from mind is at least a work of supererogation.

Professor G. H. T. Malan[9] has made just such a suggestion. Conceding that states of mind "are much the best creators and private supports of meaning," yet since jurisprudence is an ob-

[9] *Behavioristic Basis of the Science of Law* (1922), 8 A. B. A. 737 (1923) 9 A. B. A. 43.

jective science, he states that in it "an additional inference as to states of mind though not wrong is supererogatory."

Thus it is argued that even though it is unnecessary to make inferences from conduct to mental element and from mental element to conduct, yet there is nothing formally fallacious about the procedure. That is, in making these inferences, the law is doing only what every science does in inferring mind from behavior. This is so. However, it merely puts the jurist in company with the large body of learned men who make the same kind of inferences whenever they are called on to explain their "psychology." And if it be shown that such inferences are not merely unnecessary, but are also logically impossible, then we might expect the law to abandon a position which is at once theoretically indefensible and practically unnecessary.

The theory that mind may be inferred from behavior is based upon the psychology of introspection. Its argument has been briefly stated by Professor E. A. Singer, Jr. in his study on *Mind as Behavior*[10] as follows:

I am aware, and I alone am aware that certain of my bodily acts are accompanied by mental states. When I observe similar acts in other bodies I infer that they are accompanied by like states of mind.

This argument involves the formal fallacy of induction from a single instance. To continue with Professor Singer's analysis of it:

[This] argument calls its procedure an inference. Now, everybody knows an inference from a thousand cases to be more valuable than one drawn from a hundred, an anticipation based on a hundred observations to be safer than one with only ten to support it. But there are those who, knowing all this, would conclude that an inference from one instance has *some* value. If in my case mental states accompany my body's behavior, there is at least some ground for supposing like acts of another's body to be in like manner paralleled. This illusion, for it is one, springs I think from a failure to catch the meaning of inference. An inference from a single case, has exactly no value at all. No one would be tempted to attribute eight planets to every sun because our sun has eight such satellites.

[10] Pp. 3 et seq.

The reason a single observation is sometimes correctly assumed to have weight is that the method of observing has been previously tested in a variety of cases. The shopkeeper measures his bit of fabric but once; he has however measured other fabrics by the same method numberless times, and has a fairly clear idea of the probable error of his result. But the principle holds absolutely of all results; no series of observations, no probable error; no ground for inference; no meaning as a datum.

This analysis of mind has a direct application to the criminal law. The more recent theory of the nature of criminal intent, it has been said, is that states of mind differ in the several types of crimes. ". . . Having in view the diverse states of mind which in different crimes are sufficient to constitute the mental element, it is hardly possible to define criminal intent more narrowly than by saying that it is the particular state of mind, differing in different crimes, which by the definition of the particular crime must concur with the criminal act." According to this theory, if one were given an insight into the mind of the accused he could hope to fix with some degree of accuracy the kind of criminality attached to the prohibited act. Now, it is admitted on all sides that no one can thus make himself privy to another's mind. Only the accused himself, it is said, can testify concerning the state of mind with which the act was presumed to have been done, and if he refuses to do so his behavior may be examined in an effort to discover his state of mind.

It is quite clear that this position is open to the objection that has just been urged against the argument for the existence of minds other than one's own. If one assume the existence of internal states of mind, then one is forever barred from offering objective evidence to determine such a state of mind. And objective evidence is the only kind of evidence with which the law is prepared to deal.

Following the method of *Mind as Behavior*, it may now be said that the *mens rea* is not something to be inferred from criminal behavior; it is criminal behavior. Every criminal case which purports to throw light on the nature of subjective criminal mind merely adds to the definition of criminal behavior.

If this is so, it may be asked whether the law faces the problem of re-defining criminal behavior from the very beginning by throwing into the discard all the learning of the past on the criminal mind. No theory of criminal law which made such a demand could be seriously entertained. Every case which in the past has discussed criminal mind subjectively has in fact been concerned only with criminal behavior. So far then, this essay has simply attempted to square the law's account of what it says it has been doing, with what it has in fact been doing.

III

TENTATIVE APPLICATIONS OF THE METHOD OF MIND AS BEHAVIOR

While it might be admitted that the foregoing analysis is an accurate account of what courts have always done when the inquiry before them involved a state of mind, yet it might further be asked what practical difference an objective interpretation of intent makes in the law in action. Can not the law continue to speak of subjective states of mind, provided its method of procedure is objective? The answer is clear. The law may indeed continue to ask meaningless questions about subjective states of mind, but it is the function of jurisprudence to call attention to this inconsistency, and to substitute questions which the law's theory of evidence will permit of answering. One may not meaningfully question another's secret intention; he may question to the limit of scientific knowledge another's behavior. Only in this way can the law's theory be squared with its practice. Again, even though explanation of past decisions cannot affect such decisions, nevertheless the pursuit is not academic. As Pound[11] says, ". . . Juristic theories come after lawyer and judge have dealt with concrete cases and have learned how to dispose of them. But it is also true that such theories go before our law-making, as they precede law-making elsewhere." Let us consider an example of an attempt to reconcile legal theory and practice drawn from the law of contract. The concept of the "meeting of the minds" has generally been abandoned in contract law. Now this was not made necessary

[11] Introduction to trans. Saleilles, *Individualization of Punishment* (1911) xi.

by any one decision or group of decisions whose results would vary depending on whether the subjective or the objective standard of ascertaining contractual assent were applied. The fiction of meeting of minds could have been retained to this day, undergoing modifications and restrictions as it became more and more difficult to explain cases where juries would insist that contractual agreement was found, yet a meeting of minds seemed lacking. But the time had come when the principle of meeting of minds outwore its usefulness as a means of reconciling conflicting cases on mutual assent. Hence, it was abandoned in favor of a principle which makes a much more satisfactory explanation of these contradictions, namely, the doctrine of objective intent. So, even though one felt impelled to reject the psychological analysis of *Mind as Behavior* which denies meaning to subjective states of mind, nevertheless, scientific ease of explanation should force him to accept as a postulate this objective definition of legal intent.

If the analysis of legal intent made in the last section be acceptable, many of the doctrines of the criminal law require restatement in the interests of simplicity. In a very tentative way we may indicate the direction this restatement should take.

The theory of "general intent" is usually stated as follows: a man is presumed to intend all the natural and probable consequences of his voluntary acts. If this is a complete statement of the doctrine, then it might well be accepted as a very crude formulation of objective intent. The inquiry into intent would then narrow itself down to a determination by judge and jury of the question of the natural probability of consequences without regard to internal states of mind. In point of fact, the dogma is usually restricted to those cases in which serious harm results from the use of objects dangerous to human life. In such instances, one will seldom be heard to say that he acted with good will, or without malice. The theory is that the chances of innocence are so slight that the court may disregard its avowed effort to fathom secret intent and try the accused on the natural and probable consequences of his acts. That is to say, it gathers his intent only from his behavior. In situations of this sort, courts admit that they are dealing only with objective intent.

The relation of the criminal law to corporations illustrates the utility of the method of mind as behavior. The sanctions of the criminal law were devised to apply only to human beings. Fines theoretically are not merely a deprivation of a certain amount of wealth but are inflicted to cause pain. This being so, the criminal law has felt that its theory and its procedure are inadequate to deal with insensible corporations. If a corporation is a juristic person, then its harmful acts should be punished as nearly as may be in the same manner as those of real persons. No embarrassment is felt in levying a fine against a corporation because it is in effect only a financial structure. More than one court has referred to money as the very life-blood of a corporation. But when the corporation has committed an act which if done by a private individual would be punished by imprisonment or death, the law is faced with a more difficult problem. Obviously, corporate death or dissolution is not an adequate punishment. Resort is then had to fiction and the corporate guilt is "imputed" to the corporation's agents, its responsible officers. The difficulty does not become acute until there arises the question as to whether a corporation may be guilty of an intentional offense. Classic theory must answer in the negative. Although a corporation is a person, it is a person without a mind. Therefore, it cannot be guilty of a crime, one of whose elements is the *mens rea*. Yet corporations have been held liable for malicious prosecution, for libel, for assault and battery, for manslaughter. The law has been able to rest content with these contradictions only because the number and gravity of cases of this nature are slight.

Now, if criminal behavior alone be regarded, then the difference between the criminal intent of an individual and that of a corporation is not one of kind, but only of degree of complexity. A corporation as well as a natural person may be guilty of intentional crimes, and the intent will be gathered from its behavior. It is true that the final analysis of corporate responsibility must await an investigation into the nature of group mind. But investigation can bring to light a satisfactory explanation of group mind, only if it defines group mind in terms of group behavior. And corporate crime must consist of criminal corporate behavior, regardless of what analysis may disclose concerning the relation of individuals to groups.

The application of the method of mind as behavior to the doctrine of Statutory Intent is quite simple. If the statute contain, or be construed to contain, the qualification "knowingly," "intentionally," or "maliciously," then the usual investigation for determining criminal intent must be instituted. If it be decided that the mere doing of the act is prohibited, then of course, no such inquiry is necessary. The criminal behavior to be punished is the mere doing of the act. So, in neither situation is there a question of a subjectively guilty mind.

Criminal negligence is best explained on the objective theory of criminal mind. It is common to say that in crimes of negligence, the necessary mental element consists in the criminally negligent state of mind which accompanies the negligent act. However, as Mr. Justice Stephens is careful to point out in *Regina* v. *Tolson*,[12] the definition is self-contradictory.

In some cases it (*mens rea*) denotes mere inattention. For instance, in the case of manslaughter by negligence it may mean forgetting to notice a signal. It seems contradictory, indeed, to describe a mere absence of mind as "mens rea" or "guilty mind."

The test for determining criminal negligence must be objective, just as is the one for determining civil liability for negligence. Of course, this does not mean that the degree of inattention which suffices to constitute civil liability for negligence will be enough in every instance to establish criminal negligence. Indeed, what is ordinarily called the subjective test of negligence in tort law comes very close to being the proper criterion for determining criminal negligence. This may be stated to be the amount of care it is reasonable to expect from such a person as the defendant. This is the kind of "subjectivity" the law can deal with. The test is not based on the subjective state of mind of the accused. His conduct is measured by external standards, yet these standards are not such as bind

[12] L. R. 2, C. C. R. 154 (1875).

all members of the community indiscriminately. That is to say, the test is not subjective in the sense that it postulates a negligent state of mind, as Austin does. Neither does it accept the broad generalization of tort law, that every man acts at his peril when he departs from standards of conduct to which all are expected to conform. The test calls for a refinement of objective standards of due care, as now applied to determine negligence in civil cases. The lines along which this refinement must proceed are indicated in the next section.

Finally, the problem of "constructive intent" illustrates the desirability of the objective method. For example, it is usually said that an unintentional killing which occurs in the course of the commission of an unlawful act is criminal since the unlawful act supplies the criminal state of mind. Now, it need scarcely be said that many unlawful acts do not supply criminal states of mind. One who accidentally killed another while engaged in the infraction of a minor ordinance could hardly be held for murder, especially if the connection between the unlawful act and the accidental killing is difficult to establish. Again, one who causes accidental injury may be held even though the primary crime does not involve intent. For example, one who accidentally maims in the commission of statutory rape would be guilty of mayhem, even though mayhem requires intent and statutory rape does not. To say that the unlawful act supplies the intent is misleading. This theory is responsible for distinctions like that which divides criminal acts into acts *mala in se* and *mala prohibita*, a distinction now generally abandoned. If criminal behavior alone be regarded, the purposes which this doctrine seeks to accomplish may more easily be effected. That is to say, certain types of criminal behavior (the serious felonies) are so reprehensible that the law holds one who commits them responsible for all the harm he does in the course of their commission. Other types of criminal behavior are punished less severely, and one of the mitigations is the willingness of the law to inquire into "state of mind" with respect to extraneous harm done by one engaged in the less malevolent pursuits. In general, some relationship, causal or otherwise, should be established between the unlawful act and the accidental harm, before responsibility for the latter should attach. If criminal behavior alone be regarded, it is much easier to determine whether or not such relationship exists.

IV

MIND AS BEHAVIOR AND CRIMINOLOGY

In his *Criminal Justice in America,* Pound discusses at length the essentially conflicting interests which the criminal law attempts to reconcile. Briefly put, the conflict is the following: On the one hand "criminal law involves the most insistent and most fundamental of social interests." It aims at general security. On the other hand, criminal law presupposes a free moral agent and attempts to mete out punishment in accordance with individual demerit. The dilemma arises when general security and individual interest appear in conflict. In a sense this antinomy is a basic problem of the whole of jurisprudence. We have already seen in a previous section, that the standards of the criminal law are external. Holmes, emphasizing the fact that the criminal law aims at the general security but ignoring the equally important fact that it likewise protects individual interests, insists that its standards must be external. We too have seen that these standards must be external, not however for the reason that Holmes assigns, namely, that it uses the individual as a tool to increase the general welfare, but because external standards are the only ones the law's theory of evidence permits it to apply.

Criteria of criminal responsibility are not only external. According to Holmes,[13] they are also of general application, and necessarily so.

They not merely require that every man should get as near as he can to the best conduct possible for him. They require him at his peril to come up to a certain height. They take no account of incapacities, unless the weakness is so marked as to fall into well-known exceptions, such as infancy or madness. They assume that every man is as able as every other to behave as they command.

Thus, for Holmes, the test to be applied in determining crim-

---

[13] *Common Law* 50.

inal intent is the familiar one used in ascertaining tort liability for negligence. The jury is asked to consider the difference between the conduct of the accused and that to be expected under similar circumstances from the average man of ordinary intelligence.

Now, however adequate this account of the objective test of intent or negligence may be in explaining tort liability, it does not suffice for the criminal law. Forces at work since the time of Bentham tending toward the individualization of criminal law and administration have compelled the law to recognize incapacities far beyond the few "well-known exceptions." Tulin[14] states the difficulty with Holmes' view.

. . . Courts and juries are supposed to project themselves, being reasonable men, into the position of the defendant and to determine whether they would in fact have anticipated the consequences that did in fact occur [sic]. Utter discord is thus achieved between the viewpoint of the psychologist, the psychiatrist, and criminologist who assert that society must focus on the *individual*, and the theory of the law.

Here, then, is the dilemma of the criminal law. The cases reveal to Holmes that in the application of broad, general standards individual differences are ignored, and it seems that this must necessarily be so, since the test of criminal intent must be objective. To Tulin, however, this sacrifice of the individual to the general rule is morally devastating. His refusal to accept the objective test of criminal intent is expressed in the following excerpt:

Even though it may be demonstrated beyond the slightest possibility of doubt that the particular individual whose "mind" is being probed by the mental fluoroscope of court and jury did not anticipate the consequences for which society is now seeking to charge him, he will nevertheless be held to have "intended" them if a reasonable person in his position would have anticipated them.

This is a picture of a defendant who did not "really" intend the consequences of his act, but since a reasonable man would have, the defendant is not heard to say that he did not. The

14 *The Role of Penalties in Criminal Law* 37 Yale L. J. 1048.

objection urged by Tulin is a good statement of the problem, but no solution of it. He feels that the difficulty with Holmes' theory lies in the fact that its test for determining intent is objective. This is not so. It is rather to be found in the fact that the objective test as outlined by the two writers is not objective enough. This will be explained a little later, when it will be shown that an objective standard is not synonymous with a broad standard. A necessary preliminary to this explanation is an analysis of the objections to the generalizations of all science including the science of jurisprudence on the ground that science ignores essential individual differences.

Naive reflection regards the conflicting claims of society and of the individual as insoluble. Mature philosophical thought often fares no better. Renouvier says that science, in abstracting from the meanings of its terms, falsifies to the extent that it abstracts. For him, any attempt to express the complete meaning of a particular object in general terms is doomed to failure. Thus, the individual eludes classification, or as it is sometimes said, dissection. Without pursuing the matter further it may be said that this is the basis of vitalism and the reason for the revolt of Renouvier and Bergson from the psychological determinism of Auguste Comte.

We have already intimated that this problem is basic to all law. For Pound it is inherent in the nature of justice according to law, being a necessary incident to the rule element in law. In the history of Jurisprudence the conflict is revealed in the controversy respecting equity.

In the Fifth Book of the *Nicomachean Ethics*, Aristotle says that the function of equity is to mitigate the inequalities resulting from the necessary generalities of the law. The law is general; equity, individual. The Roman praetor occupied a similar position in Roman law. For example, he had power to give equitable enjoyment to an heir when a will was informal, or, under certain circumstances, invalid; or, to give the inheritance in case of intestacy to certain persons not entitled to it by *jus civile*.

Whether or not Anglo-American equity jurisprudence has a similar function has long been the subject of dispute. Story, following Blackstone, denied that it is the duty of equity to correct, mitigate, or interpret the law. Equity may supplement, but may never change the law. This is generally taken to be the attitude of the Romans toward equity; yet it would seem that their own understanding of its nature is at best confused. There is a section of Gaius' *Institutes* which illustrates this lack of clearness. Discussing intestate succession in the third book, Gaius points out the strictness of the Twelve Tables with regard to this branch of law. Emancipated children, agnates who have undergone adoption, and female agnates beyond the rank of sister are barred from inheritance by the Tables. Yet the edict of the praetor emends the inequalities. He gives "bonorum possessio" to these people. Now Gaius maintains that this procedure is not contrary to the law.

Those whom the praetor calls to the inheritance are not made heirs at law, for the praetor cannot make heirs; only by a statute or similar constitution of law are heirs made, as for example through a decree of the senate or an imperial constitution. When the praetor gives them "bonorum possessio" they are put in the position of heirs.

Here it is apparent that the praetor is not merely interpreting the Twelve Tables, but is actually giving possession, as it is said, *contra tabulas.*

Modern equity jurisprudence does not attempt to follow the ideal of *jus naturale* and settle each individual case on the basis of natural justice. Neither has it become as crystallized as Blackstone intimates. Modern writers on equity take a middle ground as instanced by Pomeroy.[15] He says in effect that there is in equity an essential capacity for orderly and systematic growth, based on settled principles of justice and morality. While the basic rules or principles of equity are fixed, the chancellor's application of them may vary to fit the circumstances of the case. However, in spite of the chancellor's margin of freedom in applying the rules, equity is a closed system and "it is impossible that any new general principles be added to it."

So, according to Pomeroy, equity must always face the diffi-

---

[15] *Equity Jurisprudence* (4th ed. 1918) Sect. II.

culty of applying general rules to individual cases. The chancellor has an area of free movement. He may adapt the prevailing morality to particular cases, provided he be careful to move within the fairly well-defined limits of statutes, settled precedents, and general principles.

In the criminal law, proposed solutions of the antinomy have taken the form of attempts to individualize punishment. Unfortunately, modern criminology has continued to deal with this problem from the point of view of the ancient ethical dispute between libertarianism and determinism. In its philosophical aspects, the question is as old as the atomism of Democritus, and its thread runs clearly defined through the entire course of the history of philosophy.

Even to the present day the ethical problem of freedom of the will is confused with the postulate of mechanism. The scientific ideal of a world consistent in every respect with mechanism is taken to be incompatible with human freedom of the will. As has just been said, the difficulty is old. Descartes, following Democritus, admitted the all-pervading influence of mechanical law, but excepted from its operation the human soul. Spinoza made mechanism complete.

Nineteenth century natural science was mechanical in the same way. Laplace's hypothesis typified it. If one be given the mass, position, and velocity of every atom in the universe at the present moment, he may completely predict the future and reconstruct the past. It has been stated above that modern criminologists have continued the old dispute. Present-day determinists insist that the criminal's behavior must in every instance be subjected to experimental control. They find that all scientific procedure attempting to deal with crime must employ the objective or experimental method. This necessitates a demand that no element of criminal responsibility be beyond the reach of experiment. The determinists think, then, that they are committed to the ethical doctrine of determinism, and to its physical counterpart, complete mechanism.

Now, experimentalism does not rest solely on mechanism. To be sure, the universe, including man, is governed by mechanical law. This is a necessary postulate of all experimental science. It is the ideal which draws the physicist on in constructing a mechanical image of nature. This does not mean, however, that purposive conduct can be adequately explained in terms of mechanical law. Mechanical law has reference only to points and their movement within a system. It cannot explain the behavior of groups. For example, let us consider a group of mechanisms which have the common purpose of telling time. They may differ widely in physical composition. Now, suppose the most complete mechanical description of them to be made. There will still remain one characteristic not described, indeed, not at all describable, in mechanical terms, namely the timepieces' purpose. Teleology is a necessary supplement to mechanism. And experimental science need only demand that purpose be experimentally defined. Freedom of the will may remain as a necessary moral principle. Freedom may be defined as persistence in one's purpose in a variety of mechanical situations. And since purpose does not violate mechanism, freedom of the will likewise does not.

Hence, if criminologists could come to regard themselves as experimentalists, they would avoid the difficulties both of determinism and libertarianism. They could then admit with the libertarians that man is not merely a machine and that not even an indefinitely complete knowledge of mechanical law would suffice to explain his behavior. But they could insist with the sturdiest of the determinists that only experimental science, applying objective methods, may attack the difficult problem of explaining man's behavior.

The necessity for legal individualization is stressed by a French writer, Saleilles, in his book entitled *Individualization of Punishment*. Here Saleilles has subjected the theory of individualizing punishment to a searching analysis. In passing, he points out the defects in the Italian school of criminology. It is "objective" in the sense that it deals only with the "materiality" of crime. Hence, it ignores the personality of the criminal. It treats man, not as a person, but as a thing. This doctrine results, says Saleilles, in the same inequalities implicit in any system of jurisprudence which attempts to deal with crime alone, and not with the criminal. The solution, according to this writer, lies in the individualization of criminal law and criminal procedure. The possible types of individualization of punishment are these: legal, judicial, and administrative. A brief summary of his criticism respecting these types follows:

Legal or legislative individualization is false individualization, because the law (enactment) can distinguish only classes of cases, not individuals. Of course, it is not to be supposed that legislation cannot effect reforms in the criminal law. However, it does not reach the heart of the problem.

Judicial individualization is the most effective type. The judge has the offender before him and can determine what type of punishment is best suited to the case. Punishments should not be standardized according to type of crime; rather, they should be uniform according to the type of criminal. One who kills for honor should not be punished to the same degree as one guilty of cold-blooded, intentional murder. Finally, there must be individualization of administration. If the criminal reforms, he should be freed. The "indeterminate sentence" is an attempted response to this demand.

Now, there can be no objection to reform of the criminal law in its legislative, judicial, or administrative aspects. However, it is difficult to see why Saleilles calls his project *individualization*. It seems obvious that he is dealing with classes, not with individuals. In the case of legislative individualization, he has already admitted this. But it is equally true of judicial individualization. Ascertaining whether one who has committed homicide belongs to the group of honor slayers, or to the group of wanton murderers, is classification. And it is the same type of classification as is employed in determining whether a criminal homicide is murder, or only manslaughter.

We are now ready to attempt a reconciliation of the demands of law for generality, and of morality for attention to the individual. It has already been anticipated in the discussion of the foregoing comments on criminal responsibility. To begin with, no system of jurisprudence can have as its ideal an individual solution for each particular case based on arbitrary rulings of the judge. This would be what Geny calls a jurisprudence of sentiment. The criminal would be wholly at the mercy of judicial prejudice. Each decision must invoke general rules, and only general rules; general, in the sense that they apply alike to every individual within the class or field of their application. Thus, the ideal of criminal equity cannot be a small number of fixed *general* principles whose application depends upon the moral sentiment of the judge and jury. The difference between a general rule of law and the most specialized ruling of a trial judge is not a difference in kind, but one of degree—the number of times it is invoked, say, either implicitly or explicitly in courts of law. The settled rules of any special branch of law are those which have been conventionalized through countless applications. They become *hornbook* law, which confines itself to principles enunciated a very great number of times by important judges, and makes no mention of implicit rules of law, seldom cited by courts, although these may be of even more general application than the conventional settled rules. Neither does it take into account principles of less importance.

In what way, then, may law proceed toward the ideal of an individual solution for each particular case? It may be helpful here to draw an analogy from the science of logic on the meaning of definition. "A relationship is defined when enough of its properties are set forth to distinguish it from whatever other relationships are in question."[16] Each quality predicated of the relationship in question is a universal. And when the relationship is described as possessing a unique collection of these general attributes, it is defined, or set apart from all other possible relationships. So too with treatment of the criminal. The ideal toward which criminal justice must work is the formulation of more and more rules of general applicability.

The criminal law, then, may not continue to ignore all but a few well-known differences in insisting that all measure up to objective standards. Criminal behavior must be the subject of classification and sub-classification whenever the results of the social sciences show experimentally that such sub-classification is desirable.

[16] Smith, *Symbolic Logic* (1927) p. 21. This is quite different from the problem of individuating the objects of a natural system, and in particular is to be dis tinguished from Leibniz' *principium identitatis indiscernibilium*.

Saleilles suggested a number of these sub-groups. Examples of re-classification mentioned by him are the following: differentiation between political and other prisoners, provision for uniform punishment, parallel punishment, distinction between static and dynamic criminality, indeterminate or modified indeterminate sentences.

It has already been said that criminology must classify and re-classify indefinitely the groups with which it deals, as science furnishes it with the bases for such classifications. At the outset it may be objected that such minute classification is foredoomed to failure. The experience of the past has been that criminologists are compelled to abandon all such classificatory schemes.

Indeed, it seems that one need only point to such failures as that of Lombroso, with his discredited criminal types. The very nature of human behavior, it is often said, makes such classification useless. Human behavior is capable of infinite variation. Hence, a comprehensive and definitive table of its categories is impossible. Now, this difficulty arises from a failure to understand the nature of scientific classification. Lombroso's types failed of practical application, not because classification is useless, but because his were based upon insufficient evidence.

He made a prediction that criminal tendencies would always be closely associated with easily recognizable physiological and especially physiognomic characteristics. Experience did not justify the prediction. Later research showed that Lombroso's types were of little use. However, this does not mean that the criminologist may cease scientific prediction. It merely shows that Lombroso was on the wrong track.

The solution of the difficulty is not complete individualization of the treatment of crime. The demand for individualization is essentially negative in character. When we demand individualization we are merely calling attention to the fact that existing rules of law do not take care of some important difference between one individual and another. But we do not mean that the remedy be unique. On the contrary, when the remedy is applied, we insist that it be applicable not only to the individual in question, but to any other who may be found to be in similar circumstances, that is to say, we insist that it be a *rule* of law. Criminal jurisprudence will grow according as it learns how to take account of differences in individual cases, and all the conclusions of the social sciences are its materials to be used in formulating its rules.

Saleilles called criminology "sociology applied to crime." The phrase is somewhat restrictive. Criminology is the application of all the social sciences to the treatment of crime. The old broad classifications of the criminal law must go in the light of the progress of the social sciences. Criminology must subject its methods of treating crime and criminals to continual experiment and research. Then and only then will it take its place among the experimental sciences.

REFLECTIONS ON CONTEMPORARY
SCIENCE AND ETHICS

WILBUR SPENSER SHERIFF

Pastor, The First Baptist Church, Cooperstown, New York

THE turmoil which exists in the world about us in spite of the almost incredible accumulation of the elements of civilization gives pause to any informed and reflecting person. In the midst of the uncertainties an ethicist can hardly set pen to paper without feeling the greatest possible sense of responsibility, to say nothing of occasional but severe attacks of despair. Only by recalling that far-reaching developments in ethics occurred during such unpromising historical periods as the decadence of Greece and the disorganization of medieval life can the moralist of the present have the heart to express himself at all. For his reference to history is likely to bring to him the conclusion that it is quite possible for the confusion in contemporary ethics to stimulate remarkable growth in the field. The ethicist, accordingly, may venture to voice a thought or two in the hope that something, however little, may be contributed to this growth.

Against the background of contemporary chaos two matters of concern for the ethicist stand out.

One is the astounding rapidity of progress in the sciences. Not only is pure scientific knowledge accumulating rapidly, along with corresponding activity in the history of science and in the philosophy of science, but the application of scientific knowledge to everyday living through industrial research, organization, and production has brought about hitherto unbelievable alterations in the conduct of human affairs. So great has the power of science become that in the dictatorships the ruler feels compelled to curtail and control scientific endeavor very markedly if he is to remain assured that his grip on the populace by force and propaganda will not be loosened. The ethicist is compelled by the very human reference of his task to recognize these alterations in conduct which science is bringing about, but he is disturbed to an even greater extent by the immensity of the problems being posed to philosophy as a result of the onward sweep of scientific achievement, in particular, by the questions being put to the philosophy of science. For ultimately it is to the intellectual aspects of the contemporary growth in science that the ethicist must directly adjust his work.

The other outstanding matter of concern for the contemporary ethicist is the moral uncertainty of our time. Some long accepted standards have fallen into disrepute. Some anciently conceived principles are in question, and others are in the ascendency. Above the sordid shouts of the moral quacks is heard the clash of seasoned thinkers upon the agelong problems of right and wrong. So uncertain are the voices of the ethicists, so unimpressive the preachers of morals, that organized science is expressing itself by addresses before learned societies and by articles in its journals as being very deeply concerned lest its immense power be used not for the enrichment and completion of a civilization but for the aggrandizement of ruthless individuals with a lust for power. In fact, there are leaders in the sciences who are looking to ethics and its foundations for guidance in assuring the best possible use of the discoveries and the products of science. This guidance appears none too certain, and we seem to be living in a confusion of ethical tongues, a moral Babel.

Out of reflection upon these two phenomena of contemporary existence grows a persistent question: Can ethical certainty and moral stability be restored in time to assure the world that the achievements of science will be used for the common good, however good may be conceived, and that science itself will be guaranteed the freedom to grow in whatever direction truth leads it and with whatever speed it can command?

Against the background of these observations and under the pressure of this question the ethicist of this generation must work.

Two parts of the moralist's task require special consideration: his principles and his methods.

The principles of ethics must, if they do not grow out of
scientific endeavor, at least be in accord with the results of
scientific investigation. No moral principle or precept that is
at variance with scientifically tested fact seems to endure. The
task of keeping his principles from clashing with psychologically established fact is particularly difficult for the ethicist.
In all of the sciences discoveries and emphases shift with amazing swiftness, but in psychology the subject matter of investigation is so intricate and the science itself is in such a formative
stage that the ethicist is hard put to it to keep his deliberations
and conclusions beyond challenge by some colleague in psychology. And yet of all his scientific neighbors the ethicist finds
the psychologist the nearest, and peace is a desirable condition
in any neighborhood. This situation in which the moralist finds
himself with respect to his psychological neighbor is bound to
become no easier in the immediate future. For the reason that
mental disease, for example, is now conceded to be a major
problem for medicine and the next public health problem to
be attacked by organized medicine, the amount of additional
information and insight to be gained from the medical point
of view toward certain aspects of the mind will become even
greater than it has been by means of developments in psy-
chiatry. A considerable portion of this information and insight
may be expected to have a bearing upon the mental background of morality, and if so, the ethicist will have to take
cognizance of these relations when he strives toward principles
of human conduct. It is conceivable, for one thing, that further researches in criminal psychology as far as it relates to
mental disease may give considerable illumination for the psychological bases of morals and thus for principles in ethics.
Developments of this kind in psychology and its related fields
will serve not to decrease but to make greater the anxiety of
the ethicist to keep his principles, and of the moralist his precepts, beyond accusations of groundlessness in mental bases, or
even of abnormality.

That growth of this nature in psychology does not simply

make the ethicist's task more terrifying than it has been but also affords him hints of forthcoming aids and even of implements for his work will be made clear when this discussion moves on to a consideration of his methods.

While particular reference must be made by ethics to psychology, special regard must also be had for the results of social scientific investigation apart from that carried on by social psychology. Anthropology, sociology, political science, and their kindred are steadily uncovering such a wealth of data in regard to mores, customs, sentiments, attitudes, groups, societies, and governments, of the present as well as of the past, that the attention of the moral philosopher is drawn to them. Such a study as that of Westermarck on marriage has made necessary the consideration of a mass of data like that which Hobhouse gave to moral problems in general in his *Morals in Evolution*. As the contemporary ethicist moves in his work toward the problems of social ethics and of political ethics he must keep himself sufficiently informed of tendencies in social theory and in political theory to escape attack from his fellow investigators who are nevertheless the specialists in sociological and other social scientific facts even though they are not sole rulers in their respective realms of theory.

Less directly but with equal sureness the moral philosopher is influenced by the biological and the physical sciences. They touch his thinking as a rule at the point where he investigates the relation between ethics and its metaphysical foundations. It is by way of the metaphysician, particularly the philosopher of science, that the ethicist encounters the philosophical adjustments made imperative by the onrush of physical and biological research and reflection.

The necessity which has been felt with special strength in the history of modern philosophy for ethics to conform to the demands of science is keener than it has ever been before because the ethicist of today finds he can do nothing in the matter of principles without having to weigh, either directly or indirectly, their various scientific relations and implications.

With regard to ethical principles another observation may be made than that these principles must not run contrary to the conclusions of the sciences. It is felt by some individuals that the moral principles of the present and the future may grow out of scientific endeavor and its results. Professor Max Schoen has recently contended[1] that the basis of moral action must be scientific. He holds that that action is right which is intelligent. Intelligence, he points out, is a generally accepted datum of human existence. Indeed, it is measurable. An ethic based on the employment of one's intelligence, he concludes, is on scientifically solid ground, in fact, on ground provided by psychological science. He is particularly delighted to find on investigating the history of ethics that this ethic is the very moral philosophy of Socrates himself.

The position taken by Professor Schoen is clearly open to several criticisms. The measurableness of intelligence, although in a fairly satisfactory state, is acknowledged as a fact, but the implements for it are as yet by no means refined. Indeed, the Thurstones of the University of Chicago, who know a great deal about these implements, are convinced that intelligence has more dimensions than they used to think it had, and they further hold that the discovery of additional dimensions has called for revisions in the measuring devices. Further, Professor Schoen seems to have overlooked the differences between the present concept of intelligence and the Socratic concept of knowledge. Again, he seems to have missed the complexity of moral action, and hence of ethical reflection. Moral action and the principles guiding it involve not only intelligence, but also the feelings, the emotions, conation, sentiments, and attitudes. One wishes at times that morality were simply a matter resting upon intelligence, but to wish is not to make true. Also, one feels on reading Professor Schoen that he has missed the difference between what *is* and what *ought to be*. That intelligence *is* an accepted datum of human existence is no guarantee that intelligence *ought to be* the criterion of morality. He falls into the same error made by the early English hedonists who attempt to turn the fact of pleasure into a principle of morality. Lastly, one cannot help thinking that what Professor Schoen

---

[1] "A Scientific Basis for Moral Action," *Scientific Monthly*, March 1939, pp. 246-52.

has done, after all, is to take a glimpse at the history of ethics, to choose the Socratic principle of morals, then to identify it with the concept of intelligence, and then to infer that the Socratic principle has come from his investigation of psychological data.

And yet, whatever the criticisms to be offered of Professor Schoen's contentions, his proposal does illustrate the expectation of some contemporaries that science will furnish the ethic of today and tomorrow. Further, his argument serves to indicate the extreme closeness with which the ethicist is expected by many investigators to work with scientific results, in particular with those of psychology.

Leaving the observations on principles, discussion may move on to methodology in ethics as it is confronted by contemporary science.

The urgency for ethical certainty and the confusion in present morals unite to exert such pressure upon the ethicist, if he is not wary, that he may be thrown off balance. The need for perspective on his part is essential to the value of his work. Perspective can be gained in no better way than by the study of the history of ethics. His familiarity should extend into ancient and medieval as well as into modern ethics, and he will do well to have some acquaintance with moralities and moral philosophers of the Orient as well as with those of the Occident. Not only will his knowledge of history give him encouragement for his task, as has been intimated earlier in these pages; but his too ready acceptance of some suggestion or solution proposed by persons enthusiastic enough but quite unlettered in moral philosophy will be prevented. If to the study of the history of ethics there is added careful attention to the history of science with particular reference to the occasions when it has markedly influenced ethics, the background of the contemporary ethicist will be considerably improved. His mind, thus furnished with history, will be able the better to distinguish between problems which are recent in origin and those which are simply recurrent; and if they are recurrent he will be better fitted to avoid mistakes in their solution which he knows have been made earlier in history. The ethical problems of the present are such that they demand a minimum of mistakes in handling them.

Affected by contemporary science in the examination of the history of moral philosophy, the ethicist finds also that the precision and the thoroughness of the surrounding scientific atmosphere demand accuracy and thoroughness of him when he approaches the problems of ethics as they exist today. Accumulation of data, observation, analysis, reflection are the ingredients of his procedure. An indispensable part of his methodology is the analysis of ethical concepts in general. Involved are the assembling of the concepts in array and the systematic reduction of them to their essentials, and then the comparative evaluation of the essentials in the search for ultimate principles.

That this analytic procedure based on a thorough assembling of the materials is valuable finds attestation in significant periods in ethical history. In the ancient world this method was used by Aristotle. In all of his studies, especially those in the sciences as he knew them, he proceeded to reflection and generalization only after he had accumulated a comparatively large amount of data upon which his mind could work. In the medieval period it can be remarked that Aquinas moved to thought in ethical matters only after he had amassed in his mind the data of ethics of his time with all the thoroughness he could command. The panoramic view, the encyclopedic content, the almost matchless perspicuity of the reflection of his richly furnished mind evidence the value of the method for his age.

In modern ethics this procedure of exact observation and analysis has found masterful use in the magnificent work of Henry Sidgwick, a most thorough and a most systematic investigator. *The Methods of Ethics* is a kind of encyclopedia of ethical terms and concepts as well as a masterpiece of ethical analysis. Acquaintance with it gives one a grasp of the general field, and familiarity with it gives one a sense of matters exceedingly important for the contemporary ethicist, a sense of where the boundaries of ethics coincide with those of other fields and a feeling, as it were, for the problems growing out of these mutual relations between fields. It is of interest, too, to observe that Sidgwick developed his procedure by returning in a critical period of his intellectual development to the work of Aristotle and by determining as a result to "do the same for *our* morality here and now, in the same manner of impartial reflection on current opinion."[2]

The world has moved a long way, however, since April of 1901 when those words were ready for publication. This onward movement has brought to light through the efforts of mathematical science and psychological research new devices for handling opinion, even current opinion. Opinion is not merely gathered and sifted any longer. It is measured. For some years the measurement of intelligence has been quite widely known, and of recent years its implements have reached a stage of considerable refinement, and they are due for even more precision. Nevertheless, wide cognizance has not been taken until fairly recently of the fact that psychological measurement has invaded interests to a considerable extent and attitudes to some degree. The attitude scales edited by L. L. Thurstone for such attitudes as those toward war, patriotism, and the law are examples of devices being used. The section on attitudes done by Hornell Hart and his associates for President Hoover's famous investigating commission is an example of a large-scale program in the measurement of attitudes successfully carried to a point permitting a reasonably satisfactory report for wide publication. More recently the public has seen this developing skill in measuring mental material extending itself even to the measurement of current opinion and the prediction on this basis of outcomes in such events involving current opinion as elections. Gallup's Institute of Public Opinion is a widely known and an amazing institution the mechanics of which is made up solely of devices for psychological measurement.

Now it is clear that if the contemporary ethicist is to be thorough in assembling data in order that his analysis may be thorough, he will not be able to avoid giving attention to the morality of common sense, or, if he prefers to call it so, the common morality. And contemporary science has such a strong

[2] H. Sidgwick, *The Methods of Ethics* (7th ed., 1922), pref. 6th ed., p. xx.

hold on life and thought that the moralist needs to use the implements of science in this part of his work. He may, to be sure, find himself faced by an immense task, and, of course, he has no Institute of Moral Opinion whose regular bulletins he may receive in his journals or directly from the Institute. If, on the other hand, he tries to substantiate his own work, he will doubtless find the measuring apparatus of the present quite inadequate for the highly specialized task of estimating moral opinions or the drifts in the social conscience. It is highly questionable just how much progress can be made before the Institute of Moral Opinion or its equivalent begins to operate and before suitable devices for gauging moral opinion can be invented and manufactured. In any case, the ethicist of today is faced by the necessity of taking cognizance of the possibilities for employing scientific techniques in those parts of his work which demand them. He may be encouraged to find at this point, moreover, that scientific advances have not simply made his task more complicated and more exacting, but they have also furnished him with the possibilities for aid in some aspects of his work.

There has thus arisen the possibility of using techniques of measurement for refining the age-old method of such widely separated thinkers as Aristotle and Sidgwick, the examination of common sense and reflection upon the findings. Of course, Aristotle and Sidgwick were to derive from the method different conclusions. Sidgwick was to forge from it an intuitionism which was to help him to fill in the gaps of utilitarianism as he saw them. His conclusions might not be reached by employment of the method with the suggested refinements and by contemporary reflection upon the data thus amassed by accurate investigation. And yet this method in ethics is the only one in history which appeals very strongly as capable of adjustment to the present demand for the use of precision instruments seen particularly in the social sciences. For in the matter of methods as in that of principles, the ethicist must take into consideration the procedures and the results of scientific investigation.

The reader may now, perhaps, find before his mind the question raised in the early pages. Can ethical stability be achieved in contemporary life in time to assure the use of scientific accomplishment for the general welfare?

He may be alarmed by reflecting that an examination of the historic methods and systems of ethics discloses many which give no satisfaction to the contemporary mind, athirst for accuracy and factualness. Revelational ethics have for the most part no appeal. Intuitionism appears to fare little better. Utilitarianism seems too often to be rather pointless. Evolutionary ethics, quite promising to many thinkers for a generation, have appeared too flabby. Persistent study of the history of ethics cannot help but impress one with the lack of ethical systems adequate to the demand voiced on every side by serious-minded people today. Nevertheless, as one ponders the course of ethics through the centuries one cannot help being fascinated by the possibility that there is an ethic which by its recurrence, its richness of content, its rooting in human nature, its wide spread in current opinion (a spread perhaps demonstrable by the precision instruments of social and psychological science) may contain the answer to our pressing question, and in the affirmative. It is the ethic which was brought to the surface along with the ethic of intelligence by Aldous Huxley in 1937 in his *Ends and Means*: the ethic of love.

The ethic of intelligence as proposed by Professor Schoen we have seen to be open to various objections. Among the most serious criticisms of it are the ancient ones made to the Socratic principle of knowledge. Mr. Huxley did well in facing the moral issues of our time to sense the inadequateness of intelligence alone as the basic principle of a sound ethic and to add the principle of love. But it may be that in adding it he removed the necessity for the second principle of intelligence. Without realizing what he had done he may have suggested to the literary consciousness of our day the basic principle of an adequate ethic. Perhaps in the concept of love is found the key to the ethical solution for the moral issues of the present and possibly of the future.

Love has a psychological foundation. It is a fact of human nature as well as a generally conceded *ought* of human conduct. Interpretations of it vary, refinements of the term "love" in psychology are yet to come, but it is a concept of apparent permanence in the systematic investigation of human nature. It is an ingredient, at least, of the more complex aspects of human behavior. Generally considered, moreover, love involves such a variety of psychological foundations as intelligence, emotion, feeling, conation, sentiment, and attitude. Its wider base than that of intelligence as a principle of ethics is thus evident.

Further, love is a recurrent theme in the history of ethics, a repeated element in the methods of ethics. It appears in Plato. It occurs in Jewish morality. It is basic in the early Christian morality. It is the queen of the theological virtues in the early medieval period, to say nothing of its eminence in the mature medieval systems like that of Aquinas. It finds prominence in modern ethics at the hands of the penetrating Butler. It is important to the thorough Sidgwick.

Again, the concept of love lies deep in the moral consciousness of the contemporary West and in parts of the Orient, as far as general, non-technical observation can disclose. It is the avowed or the implied morality of the countless organizations for the inculcation of morals and the service of mankind throughout the civilized world. It is possible that a technically controlled study of "current opinion" would verify the prominence of the concept that is claimed for it in this paragraph. Surely it is referred to in the recent radio address by Sir William Bragg, President of The Royal Society of London[3]:

> Now comes the really important point. How are we to behave in the face of this growing knowledge of the world in its material aspects? I believe that most will trust to the observance of the fundamental rules of Christianity. I do not argue the question as to whether these rules are to be found in Christianity alone: that is outside my province today. Here is to be found the incitement to right action. After that comes wisdom, based on an understanding of the influence which natural knowledge has had and will have upon our lives. We have to acquire skill in the use of what we discover, and skill is not acquired in a day.

[3] See *Science News Letter*, May 6, 1939.

Here is indication of the possibility that the ethic of love will furnish considerable, perhaps indispensable, help in formulating a contemporary ethic which will be not only technically sound but practically effective.

Most important of all the observations to be made upon the possibilities lying in the concept of love is that it has found prominence in the reflections of a thinker versed profoundly in the philosophy of science. In fact, he finds in the concept of love the solution in ethics of a problem of the greatest possible importance for the philosophy of science: individuation. He finds in it the deeper principle which he feels Royce was seeking in his presentation of loyalty, the deeper principle which would make loyalty no longer necessary. He finds it there by virtue of the essence of the concept of love itself: *love individuates*.[4]

Here, then, in the concept of love is an ethical principle which history repeatedly proposes, which issues from the careful analysis of Sidgwick as a possible ultimate, which challenges refined technical devices for ascertaining its width and depth in current moral opinion, which survives, in the most rigid thinking, against a background of the philosophy of science. Here, then, is a concept which can reasonably be emphasized as an ultimate ethical principle, a basis for moral action, and a promising problem for the most careful consideration on the part of the contemporary ethicist.

[4] E. A. Singer, Jr., *Modern Thinkers and Present Problems*, especially pp. 290-99.

THE CULTURAL FUNCTION OF RELIGION

JOHN KNIGHT SHRYOCK
Dean of the Convocation of North Philadelphia

IT HAS long been recognized that human activities may conveniently be grouped under the three headings of science, morality, and art. Each of these three has its own ideal, and each ideal, by its nature, is a limiting concept which may be continually approached, but never completely reached. Human progress therefore proceeds along these three roads, though not necessarily at a uniform or coördinated rate.

The fundamental postulate of science is that no purpose exists which the scientist is obliged to respect, save his own, and this applies both to mechanistic and purposive sciences.

In the mechanistic sciences, such as physics and chemistry, the scientist conventionally limits his view of the universe so as to consider all objects as structural. In such a universe, purpose apparently has no place, and yet there is one purpose which cannot be eliminated—the purpose of the scientist himself.

The view that all objects are structural only is not forced upon the physicist, but is a deliberate and arbitrary assumption. It is not demonstrated by experience, but on the contrary, the experience of the physicist is interpreted by means of this postulate. The physicist himself, however, stands apart from the machine he has created, no matter how earnestly he argues that he has shut himself within it. Such a structural universe is his creation, which he has conceived because such a universe could eventually be brought under his control. This conception of the universe has proved exceedingly useful by enabling man to predict, and thereby control, events; but the success of prediction based on this postulate has been approximate only, and does not apply to certain classes of events. In any case, the purpose of the scientist himself must be regarded as transcendent to the structural universe his purpose has created, and it is a purpose which the scientist himself is obligated to respect. He cannot make such an assumption as that the universe is undetermined without destroying his own purpose, and therefore that assumption would be repugnant to him, even though he might not be conscious why it was repugnant.

In the purposive sciences, such as biology, purposive behavior is recognized and studied, and this involves the corollary that the cause of such an event should lie in the future. A few years ago, a doctor's dissertation is said to have been presented on the thesis: "Reasons for the shape of the stomach of the female dragonfly." Without entering into a discussion of this burning subject, it may be said that whatever the reasons for the shape of the lady's organ were, those reasons lay in part in the future. The stomach had a certain function to perform, and was obliged to meet certain environmental conditions, so that the solution of its problem involved the assumption of a certain shape.

The biologist recognizes the existence of purposes other than his own, but is not obligated to respect them. He studies the stomach of the female dragonfly, but when his own purpose demands, he does not hesitate to destroy it. The extremes to which this principle is carried may be seen in medicine, where the observer may inoculate himself with a disease in order to study its effects. He destroys his own purpose as an organism in order to satisfy his purpose as a scientist. Here also the scientist is obligated to respect no purpose save his own scientific goal.

This ruthless disregard of all purpose save that of the scientist is the peculiar characteristic of science, and is the element which unites the various and otherwise unconnected scientific disciplines. It is altogether different from the postulate which lies at the base of morality.

The moralist not only recognizes the existence of other purposes besides his own, but assumes that he is obligated to respect them as his own. Those purposes are conventionally limited in our culture to other human individuals, but this is not necessary.

In the *Jatakas*, the Buddha is represented as having once existed as a rabbit. While wandering through the forest, he met a hunter sitting disconsolate beside a fire, with no food to cook. The moral duty of the Buddha was obvious, and without hesitation he leaped into the fire and cooked himself. But before he did so, he shook himself three times, lest in his immolation he should destroy other life than his own. The question of the Buddha's duty to himself is not discussed, but since his purpose was the attainment of Buddhahood, it may be assumed that there was no inconsistency.

In Western culture, the duty toward lower forms of life is not felt to be so insistent, though a certain amount of obligation is recognized, as in the prevention of cruelty to animals. But in general, the moralist confines his obligation to respect purposes other than his own to human individuals, and respects the purposes of animals only so far as those purposes do not conflict with his own.

The cultural reason for morality is the need for help from contemporaries. While in theory the scientist may control his structural universe unaided, in practice, his task requires all the assistance he can secure. Science is the creation of many men, and of many generations. The accumulation of scientific knowledge is so great that one individual can master only a minute portion of it, and the scientist is continually dependent upon aid from others. His knowledge and his ability are so limited that without such aid he is largely helpless.

Many men have made the assumption that they need not respect the purposes of other men, regarding them only as tools for the achievement of their own purpose. But history indicates that whenever it has become apparent that an individual is acting upon this assumption, the result has been the eventual frustration of the purpose of the individual making the assumption. Sometimes a temporary success is achieved, especially where the individual disregards the purposes of only a part of the number of his contemporaries. A Roman gentleman felt no respect for his slaves, but did respect other patricians. Yet an absolute monarchy, in which the monarch assumed that he need respect no will save his own, cannot be judged a success. It is doubtful whether it has ever been fully realized in practice, and the nearer it has been actually approached, the more unsatisfactory it appears.

Slavery and war illustrate the attempts which have been made to apply the assumption of science in the realm of human intercourse, and neither can be considered as an empirical success. Both carry inescapable defects which undo their benefits, and the longer the period of time considered, the more apparent these defects become.

Therefore the degree to which the individual achieves his purpose depends in part upon the help he receives from his contemporaries, and this help will be denied him if it becomes clear that he has adopted toward men the attitude he has adopted toward animals and inanimate objects.

But many men have endeavored to disguise their real attitude, and while they have actually regarded other men merely as tools, have pretended to respect them as purposive individuals. Such hypocrisy is typical of those who aspire to be dictators, and has been expressed and defended by Machiavelli. These men are really scientists in their dealings with their fellows, but pretend to be moralists, using morality as a cloak because the circumstances demand such a disguise.

"One prince of the present time, whom it is not well to name, never preaches anything else but peace and good faith, and to both he is most hostile, and either, if he had kept it, would have deprived him of reputation and kingdom many a time."[1]

The leaders of men have often regarded their followers as well as their opponents much as a hunter regards the animals he pursues. The leader is obliged to consider the purpose of the victim, but only in order to thwart it in the achievement of his own purpose. Yet because the leader of men depends upon men, he pretends to a respect for them which is not real.

Such an attitude would generally be considered immoral.

[1] N. Machiavelli, *The Prince*, trans. by W. K. Marriott. Everyman's Library: London; Dent, 1908, p. 145.

But is that, in itself, any reason why it should not be assumed if science is the only goal of man? If man be obligated to respect no other purpose than his own, yet in the achievement of his purpose is obliged to appear to respect others, is not such hypocrisy itself respectable? The consideration of this question involves the third of the three categories of culture.

Art is more difficult to define than either science or morality, but its essence lies in the phrase, "Art for art's sake." The characteristic of art is that the artist enjoys his task for its own sake, and not for the sake of something else. The scientist labors to secure power over his environment, and the moralist endeavors to attain good, not only for himself, but for others, yet both may find their work disagreeable in itself. The artist, however, loves his work for its own sake, and not as an instrument. He may be engaged upon the creation of a tool, but in his work, he forgets the instrumental nature of that work in the joy of the work itself. That tool, at least for the moment, becomes an end in itself, and in his creative task the artist loses all thought of self and of his fellows.

Such a conception means that art is an essential element in the life of every man, and is not limited to those who are considered artists in a technical sense. The fine arts are conventional disciplines in which the artist is arbitrarily limited in his means of expression in order that he may be more effective within those limits. The musician not only limits himself to effects produced by sound waves, but is further restricted in the types of these waves. Within arbitrary limitations he strives for effectiveness by means of variety, originality, tone, coherence, and other factors, the final decision resting with the pleasure produced by the sound itself. The other fine arts would permit of similar analyses, and all would show that the conventional limitations incidental to each fine art are made for the sake of increased effectiveness within those limitations, with no thought of any purpose beyond the fine art itself. But art cannot be limited to these conventional disciplines, nor the term artist to those who so restrict themselves. Any man working for love of his work is an artist, even though his task may not lie in any of the fields customarily regarded as art.

It is apparent that both the scientist and the moralist may be artists. Indeed, they must be artists if they are to achieve real and permanent success, for unless they love their work for its own sake, their full purpose can hardly be fulfilled.

The scientist is obliged to undergo rigid self-discipline. He is not only a scientist, but a man, and it is characteristic of men that they can limit themselves to one purpose only by great effort. Why should the scientist make such an effort, when it demands the refusal of so many things he would like to enjoy? The power over environment which he seeks, even under the most favorable circumstances, can be his only for a short time, and will be exercised chiefly by others to whom, by his characteristic assumption, he feels no obligation. And it frequently happens that the achievement of a scientific purpose involves the destruction of the scientist, or the risk of such destruction, before the results of the achievement become apparent. Only a man who loves his work for its own sake will make such sacrifices. Yet the scientist who loves his task is more than a scientist; he is an artist, for he has added the ideal of art to the ideal of science. Not only does he strive to master his environment, but he loves that struggle for mastery.

The same reasoning applies to the moralist who must, if he is to achieve his purpose, be more than a moralist. Morality consists of rules designed to permit men to achieve their separate purposes through the life of the group, receiving aid from their fellows in return for which they sublimate or suppress certain of their own desires. Yet nothing is more oppressive than a moralist without charity, and those who have exemplified a bare morality, like the Pharisees and the Puritans, have been generally condemned and eventually have become ineffective.

The good scientist not only loves his struggle with environment, but often comes to love that environment for its own sake. The moralist, however, must love men for themselves, or his purpose is certain to fail. The most efficient method of making men moral which has yet been discovered—notwithstanding our continued reliance upon criminal law and a penal system—is to love them, and no amount of moral preaching and example is, as St. Paul pointed out, of much use without charity.

Yet the ideal of science does not include a love of science, and the ideal of morality does not include a love of men. Only when the scientist and the moralist have borrowed the ideal of art can they fully achieve their own ideals.

Both the scientist and the moralist may object that the love of their work is included in the ideal of that work, but this is not true. The purpose of the scientist is the control of environment, not a love of environment, and he may come to love his work, not because he is a scientist, but because he is inevitably more than a scientist. Morality consists of rules governing the relations of the subject toward other men and himself regarded as an object, and it is possible to obey rules which are disagreeable. If the moralist loves men, he is including in his ideal something beyond morality, for love laughs at regulations.

But if the scientist and the moralist must include the ideal of art with their own characteristic ideal, because they are men, it is also true that each man must be loyal to all three ideals. The scientist makes science his goal, but he cannot ignore the ideal of morality any more than he can ignore that of art. As a scientist he respects no other purpose than his own; but since he depends upon help from others, he is obliged to have intercourse with them, and this requires his allegiance to the rules developed in order that social intercourse may be carried on successfully. The physician is a scientist, but all physicians take an oath which is concerned, not with the ideal of science, but with the ideal of morality.

The moralist, in like manner, must concern himself with science. It is useless to tell men that they should obey moral rules when they do not have enough to eat, or are living under economic conditions which make moral, as well as physical health, impossible. It is now recognized that science and morality are connected to a degree that has led some to hold that morality is merely a branch of science, and that science alone can cure all moral evils. But there is an essential difference between the ideals of science and morality, and there is no reason in science itself why the scientist should be concerned with the welfare of others, save as it concerns the efficiency of his tools.

In the same way, the artist must concern himself with science and morality. Leonardo da Vinci was a scientist as well as an artist, yet his greatest work is now only a memory because he neglected to paint upon lasting material. A man who does not devote himself to one of the fine arts, but endeavors to live artistically, must consider whether the work he loves has a reasonable chance of success under the operation of the laws of science.

Artists rebel against morality, feeling they have no concern with it, and resenting the restrictions which a strict morality occasionally endeavors to impose on the fine arts. The essence of art is enjoyment, while the essence of morality is duty, and so there have been conflicts between artists and moralists, each group maintaining a distrust of the other.

Yet no self-respecting painter would sign his name to a picture executed by another, or represent his own work as that of a great painter of a past generation. Why should such practices be disparaged, if the artist has no ideal save the standards of art? If a millionaire is not sufficiently educated to tell a Rembrandt from its copy, why need he be undeceived? Honesty is the concern of the moralist, not the artist, and if the artist has no relation to morality, why should he attempt to incorporate moral qualities and rules in his own canon?

A man may devote himself to the pursuit of science, or morality, or art. Yet because he is a man, he cannot entirely ignore the two he has not chosen, and usually features of those two are incorporated in his chosen ideal. The scientist may maintain that as a scientist he works for the welfare of humanity, and endeavor to make the structures created by science into objects of beauty. The moralist may feel that sanitation, good housing, and adequate wages are a part of morality, and speak eloquently of the beauty of goodness. The artist studies the medium in which he works as a part of his art, and creates his own moral standards even while he rejects those of the majority. Each may think that such borrowings are a part of his own field, being unconscious that they have been taken from another branch of culture.

Yet the assumptions and ideals of science, morality, and art are separate, and in themselves unconnected. The scientist need not be either moral or artistic as a scientist. The illusion of many scientists that they necessarily work for the good of humanity is being lost by the realization that the triumphs of science can be used against humanity quite as easily as for it. The physician is usually sincere in his love for mankind, but that does not alter the fact that his knowledge could be used to poison as well as to heal. The engineer may erect a building which is stable and convenient, but which the artist would prefer to have enshrouded in perpetual darkness.

The moralist has frequently quarrelled both with the scientist and the artist. He always insists that his rules take precedence over every other consideration. The Polynesians must wear European clothes, because only European clothes are moral, even though such costumes are not suitable from a scientific point of view on the islands of the South Seas, and if one may judge from the moving pictures, are certainly not so effective artistically.

The artist may not only ignore the laws of science, but he may, if he wishes, make a lack of science appear attractive and desirable. And he can suggest and encourage immorality as effectively as he can morality, for the indecency of the subject has no relation to the greatness of the art which portrays it.

If the scientist, the moralist, and the artist are obliged to borrow from each other, it is not because of any necessity in their separate fields, but because each is more than a specialist. The activities of men may be divided among these three categories, each of which possesses its own characteristic assumption and ideal. But no man can limit his activities to one or two of these fields. As a man, he must to some extent be active in all three.

Since the ideals of science, morality, and art are separate and not necessarily connected, any union among them must come from without. Attempts to include morality and art within science, or science and art in morality, or science and morality

in art, are foredoomed to failure because of the necessary restrictions of each field.

Yet man, if he is to be rational, and conceive his relation
to the universe as intelligible, must in some way unify the
ideals of these categories of his activities. It is not enough to
have separate and discrete ideals in science, morality, and art,
for man must have an ideal and a purpose, as man, which will
unite and harmonize the ideals of his several spheres.

The necessity for this unifying conception is not only theoretical, but practical as well. To a degree impossible in any other
form of life, man has the capacity for education, and for accumulating the results of his experience. He has also the ability
to adapt these results to changed circumstances. These results
of cumulative education, which man can use in controlling
himself and his environment, are called culture, or civilization.

Because man's culture is cumulative, it is possible for civilization to advance, and such advances are necessarily made in the
three categories of man's behavior. All progress in culture can
be analyzed as a progress in science, morality, or art. The invention of a new machine such as the radio, and the realization
of an obligation in social relations such as the abolition of
slavery can easily be classified, but it is more difficult to realize
how advance can be made in art. Such progress does not imply
that greater works of art should be produced in the conventional disciplines, but rather that man should increasingly acquire the ability to enjoy his work for the sake of the task
itself; that the average man should increasingly become an
artist in whatever he undertakes. In order that man should
advance toward the ideal of art, it is not necessary that genius
should improve upon Phidias, or Rembrandt, or Homer, or
Bach; but it is necessary that mankind as a whole should increasingly enjoy life, and the tasks of life.

Yet history shows that dangers are involved in cultural advance. For progress in civilization to be permanent and safe,
it is necessary that the advance should be fairly regular and
even along all three roads. And whenever advance is made
along one of these, while culture stands still in the others, the
result is catastrophe. Such advances are necessarily uneven, but

the greater the disparity in progress in the three directions, and the longer this disparity is permitted to remain, the greater the danger becomes. History shows that eventually there is a general collapse of civilization, even in the field where advance has been made.

Without entering all three fields, one illustration may be given of the way in which this cultural law operates. It is probable that the armies of Justinian represented the highest point in military science reached in the ancient world, whether or not we regard Belisarius and Narses as greater than Hannibal and Alexander. Yet this very efficiency in military technique was in itself one of the causes of the collapse of ancient civilization, and the century following the wars of Justinian was the darkest in the history of Europe. The period which ended with Justinian, while it showed advance in certain branches of science, was hopelessly defective in the degree to which men might enjoy life for its own sake, for the men of that period shared a common pessimism, while the only hope was in a future existence. And curiously enough, the efficient armies of Justinian were succeeded by the crude and unwieldy levies of the Dark Ages. The average morality of the succeeding age was low, and it was not until men once more learned how to coöperate and to enjoy life that progress again became apparent. Moreover, the lack of emphasis upon progress in science during the Middle Ages may have been due to the debacle caused by a one-sided emphasis upon science during the preceding period.

Each of the three categories of human behavior is motivated by certain inherent human desires which cannot be eliminated, or safely suppressed. Whenever one or two of these sets of desires are suppressed in a civilization for any length of time, they break out in abnormal ways which may eventually cause the disintegration of that civilization.

Therefore it is apparent that the need for a unifying ideal which will harmonize and maintain the balance among the separate ideals of science, morality, and art is not merely academic. It is not that human curiosity, represented by the philosophers, desires a simplified conception of the universe, and of man's place in it. Rather it is a necessity, if culture is not to degenerate and collapse, that some force should be found that will act as a gyroscope of civilization, preventing it from toppling to one side.

Such situations are not new, and it would be strange if man had not already discovered some answer to this question. No solution that could be offered would operate mechanically, and each generation would be obliged to apply the solution afresh to its own peculiar situation. But mankind has generally held that the most efficient balancing force in culture is religion.

The scientist assumes that he need respect no purpose save his own. The moralist assumes that he is obligated to respect the purposes of other men as he does his own. The artist assumes that life is worth living. But the fundamental assumption of the religionist is that a purpose underlies and controls the universe, and that it is the end of man to fulfill the purpose of God for man.

The postulate of God as the end of man, and as the controlling power behind the universe, unifies the ideals of science, morality, and art by including them in the purpose of God.

The scientist respects only his own purpose in mastering environment, but his power is limited and often thwarted. His control over Nature, such as it is, is obtained by means of a knowledge of laws of Nature. Those laws are either the invention of the scientist, or they are the laws of God; and perhaps one may be pardoned for preferring to conceive God as the perfect scientist, rather than an imperfect scientist as God.

The moralist insists that men must respect each other, but the answer that this is merely a matter of convenience would generally be considered immoral. If the existence of God as an approachable ideal is not assumed, however, convenience becomes the only reason for morality, while the lives of those regarded as the best of men become meaningless. But the moment the assumption of God is made, man's duty to his neighbor becomes reasonable as part of his duty toward God.

If man alone in the universe exhibits purpose, his plight is so tragic that it is hard to conceive how any thoughtful man could enjoy living, or feel it to be worth while. Life is so hard, even under relatively favorable circumstances, that some more-than-human purpose is needed to make it either rational or joyful.

The assumption of religion is a unifying conception which not only includes the separate and limited ideals of varied human behavior, but unites them into the common ideal of the purpose of God, and makes reasonable a conception of life as a continuous approach to this single ideal.

Within that ideal each of the limited ideals has its place, from which it may not be removed. The scientist, moralist, or artist who neglects the other branches of human behavior is neglecting also his duty to God. The scientist and the artist are equally obligated to be moral with the moralist, even though morality is not their special field of interest, because it is a part of their duty as men.

Since each of these three ideals is preserved inviolate within the ideal of religion, religion becomes a force which tends to maintain a balance among them. That religion is not always as efficient in this task as it should be, is partly due to an imperfect conception of religion by a given group, and partly because men's minds are set, not upon their pursuit of the ideal of man, but upon one or more of the lesser and discrete ideals.

Religion tends to maintain a balance among science, morality, and art by insisting that each man, no matter how specialized his activities along one of these lines, cannot neglect the other two. The experience, both of individuals and of groups, indicates that culture requires that such a balance be maintained.

But does not philosophy consider the ideal of man as a whole, and is not philosophy more satisfactory to a man of culture, in that it does not involve the necessity of such an assumption as the existence of God?

There is, however, a difference in interest between the philosopher and the religionist which results in their possessing different values for the preservation and advance of culture. The most cherished assumption of the philosopher is the postulate of intellectual liberty. A philosopher, as such, demands that he be free to assume any intellectual position he desires, provided his thought be logical and coherent. He is interested primarily in the intellect, and only secondarily in conduct.

On the other hand, the religionist reverses this attitude, being practical rather than academic. His interest is not primarily in the intellect, but in the will. Consequently he denies the postulate of the philosopher that there should be freedom to assume any intellectual position whatever, and maintains that only such intellectual positions may be taken as will safely direct the will.

The philosopher, with his academic attitude toward life, may look philosophically upon the ruin of the individual and the collapse of civilization. There are certain positions in philosophy, which all philosophers as such insist can logically be taken, which make the destruction of culture of relatively little importance. If such a philosopher feels regret at such a situation, it is not because of his philosophy, but because his philosophy cannot prevent his being a man.

But the religionist cannot regard the fate of culture lightly, for he is a behaviorist in the sense that he is interested, not in what men think, so much as in what they do. He has assumed a philosophic position, not for its own sake, but in order that men's wills may be safely directed.

Safely directed toward what? Toward God defined as the end of man, and as including the discrete ideals of science, morality, and art. But science, morality, and art, taken together, and without consideration of an essential unity among them, make what we call culture. Progress toward God must be a balanced progress in science, morality, and art, and therefore an adjusted and proportionate advance in culture means an advance toward God. A religionist cannot look upon individual or social degeneration from a philosophic point of view; he cannot be a detached spectator. Consequently he is of greater cultural value than the philosopher.

The point may be illustrated by the deaths of Socrates and Jesus. Socrates could be detached and unaffected by his fate. Jesus was equally unaffected with regard to his own end, but he was affected by the fate of mankind in a way that Socrates was not, and so there are tragic elements in the Cross which are not apparent in the death of Socrates.

The significance of the two deaths for the future of culture was very different also. The death of Socrates, splendid though it was, has had relatively little effect upon culture; but the death of Jesus has changed the whole history of civilization.

It may be concluded that religion is a greater force in the development and preservation of culture than philosophy. In religion a philosophic position is assumed, but it must be a position which will safeguard the accumulation of the results of human experience which we call culture. In philosophy, the intellect is supreme and free; in religion, the intellect is secondary to the will, and to the fruits of the will in culture.

Yet scientists, moralists, and artists claim that they find no need in their separate fields for the assumption of the existence of God. An agnostic or atheistic scientist may make as successful prophecies as one who is religious. David Hume was more moral than most of his critics. Few men have enjoyed life as successfully as Epicurus.

And this contention is true as long as science, morality, and art are considered merely as separate and unconnected ideals. In order to be a successful scientist it is not necessary to believe in God. But no man can be a scientist only, nor a moralist, nor an artist. He is first of all a man and with his end, as man, these limited fields do not deal. It is the practical necessity, both for individuals and groups, of a unifying and balancing concept, which furnishes the cultural function of religion.

Occasionally some scientist, moralist, or artist goes farther, and claims that evidence presented in his field indicates that the postulate of the existence of a purpose behind the universe is untenable. The scientist may hold that the universe is structural only; or the moralist may argue that a good God could not permit the evil which is only too apparent, or the artist may maintain—as has been maintained in India—that life is not worth living.

Such claims are very old—as old as Democritus, Job, and the Upanishads. It would be out of place to discuss them here, beyond saying that if these arguments were valid, mankind would have discarded religion many centuries ago.

In every field, knowledge and experience must be preceded by certain postulates, in the same way that Euclid begins with unprovable axioms, such as the definitions of point, line, and plane. These fundamental postulates can neither be proved nor disproved by experience, because experience depends upon them for its interpretation. Among such postulates are the primary assumptions of the scientist, the moralist, the artist, and the religionist; and the postulate of the existence of God is no more difficult than the postulate of the existence of a human individual. Indeed, there are much better reasons for believing in God than for believing in one's own soul. The universe would be irrational without God, but it could get along quite well without man.

The survival of religion, in spite of the claims of scientists, moralists, and artists that they do not need it, or can invalidate it, indicates that religion has a permanent function in culture. It is not a drug for the individual, but a balance wheel for society, harmonizing and uniting man's separate ideals. That religion has been opposed so often has been partly due to the claim sometimes made, that religion, instead of being a unifying conception, was itself a separate and limited ideal, in competition with the ideals of science, morality, and art.

The assumption of the existence of God has led to a special field of philosophy dealing with the corollaries and implications of this postulate. The religionist has defined certain moral rules as possessing a divine sanction, while other rules do not. Art has been divided into the religious and the profane. Behavior directed toward God has been considered differently from social behavior. Religion has been held to offer a separate road of approach to the ideal not necessarily connected with science, morality, and art. This claim is urged particularly by the mystic, who may find in his peculiar experience a direct and immediate union with the ideal.

It cannot be emphasized too strongly that religion does not offer a separate road of cultural advance. No matter how religious a man may be, if he is to approach closer to the ideal, he must do so by means of science, morality, and art, harmonized by religion. There are no new discoveries in religion, save in the sense that every new discovery in science, morality, or art is a discovery of religion. There are three ways of approaching God, and they are the three roads of cultural advance. Even the mystic must travel these roads, and the glory of the mystical experience is the full realization of the joy of living in union with God.

Religionists can make no greater mistake than to suppose that they can be religious without being scientific, moral, and artistic—using these words in their widest sense. The religious man is not one who leaves these things behind, but rather, one who approaches God by these three roads simultaneously.

Unfortunately, the term religion is used in two meanings. It is used for the harmonizing concept in culture, and it is also used for a special section of culture dealing with the development and implications of the initial postulate of religion—with such matters as theology and cult. Yet even in its narrower significance, religion should not be considered a separate avenue of progress. The work of a priest is only his specialized function in society, and that function may be classified in one of the three ways. By means of religion, the priest helps men to approach God through respecting themselves, through respecting others, and through living so that they may enjoy life.

In performing its function as a harmonizing and balancing influence in culture, it is sometimes necessary for religion to restrain the urgency of one specialty in order that the others may not be ignored, and religion may incur the enmity of those who are so restrained. At present, the interest of men is concentrated largely upon science, and this concentration has already endured for so long that civilization itself has become unstable.

There is no objection to the progress made in science, and every triumph has brought man nearer to certain of the attributes of God, such as omniscience and omnipotence. Progress toward the ideal of man must be made through science, and a neglect of science would eventually impede and nullify advance along any other road. But the advance in culture must not be limited to science, for if morality and art are neglected, science itself will develop the seeds of degeneration, and it is apparent that this has already begun.

The jubilant optimism of scientific writers today sounds too like the joy of Procopius over the military science of Justinian; and as in the time of Justinian, it is military science which is receiving most attention at present. Yet history indicates that absorption in the art of war has generally forerun a collapse of culture.

For centuries, man has been interested chiefly in the mastery of his naturalistic environment, and relatively little in the mastery of himself, or in the art of living. The new forces he has let loose, he does not fully understand, and cannot yet adequately control. An attitude of mind has been developed which relies upon science to solve all problems, even when those problems are caused by the neglect of morality and art. Man has temporarily forgotten that only morality can insure the beneficial use of the power generated by science, and that only art can make possible the enjoyment of our machinery.

In such a situation, it is the function of religion to restore equilibrium among the forces of culture. There is no reason in science itself why the scientist should be moral, or enjoy life, and so the restraining factor must be the concept which unites and includes all three.

Man's interest must be shifted, not to the detriment of science, but to the improvement of the other factors in culture. There have been crises in which religion has failed to perform this function until it was too late. Men have despaired of securing intelligent coöperation and of living happily, and have degraded religion into a mere means of escape. But the cultural function of religion is not to hold out the hope of a future world when this one has become too difficult; it is rather to mold the forces of this world so that man may advance continuously toward his ideal, and that his society may grow into the Kingdom of God.

III

AESTHETICS

ESTHETIC OF MUSIC AND THE RATIONAL IDEAL

JOHN STOKES ADAMS, JR.

Department of Philosophy, University of Pennsylvania

IN THE history of philosophy, the muddle that is esthetic, or philosophy of art, has had a career that quite belies the importance now assigned to it. Kicked around among the philosophic disciplines, relegated to the backstairs for centuries, the highlights of its history are so feebly discernible that many a respectable historian of philosophy can safely neglect it altogether. And even today when, though by acclamation only, it seems to be permitted a position coördinate with other philosophical studies, the energy with which it is pursued by some is by no means proportionate to the degree of care exercised in the scrutiny of its basic propositions. One wonders, it is true, whether it may not be part of the order of nature that philosophers shall remain uproariously insensitive to the challenge of art, but who shall blame them when it is seen that all artists appear united in a conspiracy to foreclose philosophy?

The reasons for this war of nerves are coming to be better understood; but whatever the reasons, on its account the history of esthetic has turned out to be but a scanty thing. Aristotle lays down certain inalienable principles, of course only as integral with his general system. Two thousand years pass. One historian discovers in this span a collection of Hegelian trinities, another a cluster of desultory observations concerning art; but in the eighteenth century Baumgarten still finds beauty "ein verworrener Begriff " Kant at least lays down the foundation for a sound investigation, but this investigation proceeds so coolly that in sheer desperation "feeling" must be invented to take up the residue. A host of new difficulties naturally arise, and as though to endow this mysterious esthetic feeling with a semblance of reality, interesting labels are attached to it, such as "qualitative Reflex-gefühle," and finally that masterpiece of confusion, *Schein*—invoked to stand apparently for anything whatever, and to signalize the poverty of philosophers in the realm Kant had hoped might become a science. Meanwhile, the psychologists get hold of the field, and in their artless way spend more than a century piling data on data, with an enthusiasm so great as to excuse the impression that progress consists in permitting them to keep on their way.

But if this questionable agglomeration is all the dialectic the history of general esthetic has to show, it is still a very pattern of logico-historical precision compared with the story of the unfolding of its subordinate field, the esthetic of music. Here the philosophically unconscious theorist has run the gamut of caprice. Libraries have been filled with glib vivisections of the "meaning of music," all attesting the most rudimentary conception of the meaning of definition. Esthetic is equated with the analysis of form, and in a welter of structure worship a Beethoven symphony is reduced to a complex arabesque. The formalist, not content to make the most even of the little he has, goes on to "science," raking it over from geometry to sociology, and chews the leavings into a pulp of verbiage entitled the Appreciation of Music. At this the artist is aghast and the layman shudders—but the philosopher's back is turned. The dogmatic assertions of a Schopenhauer, the one-sided observations of a Hanslick or a Hartmann, have all served to obfuscate an issue already embarrassed by philosophobia. And when one reads what a Wagner has to say, one wonders whether it would not be better to abandon the investigation altogether, for how can purity be expected downstream when it is not discernible at the source?

The contemporary situation in esthetic of music is a jungle of myopic hypotheses and blustering cross-purposes. One camp advances a theory of art that cannot be taken to include music, another a theory of music that cannot be couched with reference to the other arts. There are the fervently professional analysts of form, distinguished by preference for appearances, contempt for causes, and great skill in the technique of music— a race of careful dullards, unaware of the far-flung conceptual possibilities of their art. There are those to whom esthetic is altogether nonexistent, its problems chimerical, and their pursuit an infraction of the spirit of art. There are the performing musicians with highly flexible fingers who either play as automata without thinking, or think without knowing what they are thinking about. There is the occasional articulate composer who, mistaking the recorder of laws for the lawgiver, pays homage to "new" psychology as to a cult. There are the professional critics, to whose advantage it is that music be left undefined; these thrivers on mysticism know that unlocking the gate will throw out of work all who make their living by pointing out the beauties of the wall. And finally, there are some conscientious philosophers who have heard of music, have noted that it undeniably has a palpable effect on the bulk of mankind, and who then, with as much courage as they can summon, include mention of it in their forthcoming formulation of the universe of esthetic discourse.

That this situation has a genesis and a history does not render it the less intolerable. And here and there evidence is not wanting that the toleration of it has run its course. A musician will point out that formal contemplation of music must not be at the expense of the deeper insight in which man senses the presence of the creative spirit; that to wait on skill, and more skill, with no hint of the force which underlies, conditions, and justifies it, is to stultify the rational ideal; and finally that recourse to "ineffability" is no proper device for the true inhabitant of these animated and antiromantic times.[1]

And again, a philosopher will be seen to formulate the conditions whereby this clowning confusion must and shall cease. Professor Singer has scant patience with it.

Perhaps he is not to be envied a smoothness the fountain of whose ease is want of experience; but for the same reason, neither need those cherish themselves who, lacking his feeling for science as he theirs for art, imagine themselves saving their esthetic souls by refusing to think. For one who would relinquish with equal sense of loss what in sudden insight and what in brooding reflection

[1] Cf. Paul Krummeich, "On the Nature of Music," *General Magazine and Historical Chronicle*, XXXV (October, 1932), 1.

he had seized on, the only provident thing to do is to keep as long as his grasp will let him his hold on both. . . . So it is with many of us who, having lived the moment to our soul's capacity, have thereafter with what was left of our science struggled to recover our powers of reflection, sensible there could be no continuing satisfaction in dumfounded bewilderment.[2]

Had Singer chosen music as his sole field of illustration in the subsequent pages of this article, he could not have done better. The fear of philosophy has made men wary of trying to define music functionally. In music, of all the arts, the ravening persistence of the ateleological definitions is what has obstructed the development of esthetic. Not until rational man puts something of *his* own into the inert framework of a Pythagorean ratio or a classical contrapuntal form, does it come into *its* own. Thus inspired it begins to function, and its purpose stands defined when its function is understood. And yet for these two thousand years, the Pythagorean ideal has endured, whether in some new theory of "dynamic symmetry," or in attributing unconscious counting[3] to Bach because a frequency-ratio of 5:6, and not 4:5, would suit his *Weltschmerz*, the better to produce a *Mass in B minor*, and not in B major.

And yet the effort to define musical beauty teleologically brings us to wrestle with that superb and unfathomed group of problems Singer envisages, the avoidance of which is the ostrich hope of all ateleological definers. To find the intrinsic worth of music, but then to find its worth for man! "To find the X such that to be an X-server is to be beautiful!" Any public apologist for music has his stock-in-trade of answers to the question, "What is the purpose hereof?" "To inspire," he will croon, knowing this will silence all but the most intransigent. "To march as to war," some archaeologist will say, leaving a host of cross-vistas unexplored. A modern Plato might say, "To promote escape," or, more readily today, "To encourage irrationalism." And yes, there is always, "To be expressive."

A naive investigator of music's purpose might hurriedly con-

---

[2] E. A. Singer, Jr., *On the Contented Life*, Chap. I, "Esthetic and the Rational Ideal," p. 5. Subsequent references are to this article.
[3] Leibniz's phrase.

clude it is simply, "To be a good servant" to some end precon-
ceived.

What beauty may be claimed for a new invention in sewing-
machines, carpet-sweepers, toilet-equipment, so obviously measures
nothing but some enhanced fitness of these "beautiful" devices to
their defining ends, we are inclined to wonder whether any but a
salesman could bring himself to prostitute so divine a word to so
low a use.[4]

Consider the frightful and sinister possibilities of "enhanced
fitness" there were in music for that man of whom it was said
he permitted his radio to continue its blare while he was out
of the house, to the end that he might not have to endure that
awful moment of silence between his unlocking the door and
rushing in to turn it on again! And recently a perfume company sold its product put up in miniature merry-go-rounds
which played faintly corrupt airs by Louis XVI, presumably to
emphasize the delightfully decadent character of the merchan-
dise. "But there is nothing vulgar about the beauty of a tiger's
fangs, any more than about the ugliness of a tiger's snarl; and
no one is trying to sell the former, nor to drive the latter off
the market."[5] There is nothing vulgar about Grieg's *Papillon*
or Debussy's *Cathédrale*. It is granted that these had not the
purpose merely of invoking such images: the images were but
the *occasion*. "Yet if this beauty be not that of the *good* servant,
this ugliness that of the *bad*, what meaning can either have?
And, in fact, those fangs are wonderful good servants of the
tiger; that sneer bodes ill enough for man."[6] To make things
worse, Socrates is said to have argued, on the premise that the
useful was beautiful, that his broad nostrils and capacious
mouth must necessarily be beautiful. And many an antique
cosmologist, in defining the useful in terms of Nature's purposes, has shown everything, beautiful or ugly, to be equally
useful, as furthering God's plan! On the whole, the perception
of the useful has entered upon the scene of the esthetic judgment only to confuse it. If, for example, it is seen that an artist

[4] Singer, *op. cit.*, p. 12.
[5] *Ibid.*, p. 12.
[6] *Ibid.*, p. 12.

has been challenged by a utilitarian situation, our joy in his work is supposed to rise in proportion to the success of his solution. If on the other hand the possible utility-values have been flouted or neglected by the artist, we are supposed to feel as though we had been duped. Yet our understanding of this, particularly in the crafts, is dependent on information to be supplied by the anthropologist—for an outlandish utensil may have a use known only to the outlander. The present mode in "functional architecture" exploits this feeling for the primal call of utility. It is not that the functional architect desires to neglect all extra-utilitarian demands on the part of the beholder; he wishes to convert these impulses back into an additional feeling for utility. It may be that the mind will always tend to find a use for what is beautiful, but a single instance of failure ought to be sufficient to confound the functionalist. Another prominent, and no more sensible, case of this confusion grew out of the Darwin-Spencer controversy over the origin of music, as being connected somehow with the song of birds. But merely to push back the problem by several aeons is not to solve it.

And so Professor Singer approaches, only in order to reject, his own tentative definition, the grasping of which has as its condition the understanding of purpose in general: That beauty may be "the quality of a more perfect means to an end presupposed."[7] This he admits makes only the means beautiful. But are there no beautiful ends? With finality he, and we, can dispose of the *petitio principii* that art is its own end: too many generations of critics have revealed themselves philosophical dilettanti by that device.

No, what makes us suspect we have as yet (in this definition) done scant justice to art and its works of beauty, is not the hurt outcry of the fine artist on learning that some use has been found for his output. It is just the selectiveness of the man-in-the-street when in making a useful purchase he pauses, hesitates; be it knife or fork, platter or cup he would have, he compares, chooses; and from among many samples of each, *his choice is not always the best-adapted.*[8]

[7] *Ibid.,* p. 15.
[8] *Ibid.,* p. 16.

In his choice of this tune rather than that, it is not always the one he can whistle, nor always the one he can identify by name, nor the one with which he can sell a bottle of perfume, or impress the world with his goodness, or command the attention of listeners or lull his own to sleep—there are tunes *equally useful* in all these offices, but does he not still choose among them?

We do not as yet pretend such esthetic beauty to reside in useless objects, we ask only whether it do not distinguish values in *equally useful* ones.[9] . . . The superiority that lends "technical beauty" may be calculated with respect to as many ends as there are teleologically defined classes; "esthetic beauty" can have but one.[10]

What is the one? Even if it be still insisted that art is for art's sake, beauty for beauty's sake—still, what *is* this sake? What, for instance, is the part of beauty in the teleology of music?

Well, for one thing, beauty is not the sole preoccupation of music. No great acquaintance with its history is needed to press home this observation. How do the ateleologists meet it? Their apologetic would proceed as follows: the history of music has been a history of increasing complexity in the chordal ratios, with higher and higher numerical values for the tonal elements thereof along with the increasing conspicuousness of their incommensurability; with this has come, on the psychological side, an increasing toleration of such complex ratios on the part of the listener. Therefore ugliness, at any one moment in this history, is a function of the degree of violation to which the proportional conventions of the moment may be subjected. This is all very well, and accounts for the well-known structural facts in the history of music and in the history of listening. But such a process suggests a limit—no "absolute," indeed, but such a limit as Kant may have had in mind in the *transscendentale Logik*. The teleologist recognizes this difficulty. He does not go so far as Plotinus, to identify beauty with form and the totally ugly with the totally amorphous. He is apt to pass over this problem, or at least to postpone it, and travel to a greater one:

[9] *Ibid.*, p. 18.
[10] *Ibid.*, p. 21.

what is it that beauty and ugliness, apart from subjective vari-
abilities, may be considered as serving equally well?

Wearily we must take notice of those long episodes in the
history of art when it was the *good* these were expected to serve.
There are many possible relations between the good and the
beautiful, but that of master and servant cannot be one of
them, save for those who would filibuster the discussion of
esthetic's central problem. To trace the vicissitudes of this relationship is beyond the scope of the present inquiry, but one
thing is noticeable: there was a time, perhaps a little after the
beginning of the Hellenistic Age, when the relative inseparability of these two became an embarrassing burden to each, and
in itself a vicious tendency. In Homeric times, and in the
Greece up to Pericles, it was an ingenuous but above all a
harmless convention to make heroes beautiful and villains ugly,
and such survivals of this convention as one sees today may be
equally harmless—only they are too often done in another
spirit, namely that which threw its shadow over the later Athens,
over Alexandria, over Rome, over Florence, and over Paris, the
spirit according to which the persistent identification of beauty
with goodness was itself an evil, leading to "injustice." The
child, who fears an ugly relative as though she were a ghoul,
and who adores a beautiful one, is analogous to the earlier
tendency, which created the Nature religions and peopled
heaven with deities who were good-beautiful and bad-ugly. But
the later tendency, though continuing the identification, for-
sook the child's innocence and took on a new turn some have
chosen to regard as vicious. Plato's *Charmides* may be taken as
foreshadowing this; that the handsome youth could be other
than excellent in character was unthinkable to the entire company assembled. And in the Greece of the decadence, as in the
Egypt of Cleopatra, the only sin was ugliness. The Ugly
Duckling theme runs through the time. The black sheep is
errant *because* he is black. The spirit of the *Charmides* achieved
its supreme expression in the *Thousand Nights and One Night*,
where beauty is right, and all sin vanishes in the presence of a
ravishing poem recited at an auspicious moment; but wickedness is materialized in the person of a hag, whose head must be

forfeit if the singing is to go on. But since these times, we have "grown up" and the matter has become diffuse. After the Renaissance a beautiful maiden might conceivably have hidden a cloven hoof under her gown, and conversely a monstrous hunchback might so come to have embodied the principle of virtue that the faithful were adjured to put themselves in the way of passing monsters. With such polar varieties as these, and presupposing the relationship of service as between the beautiful and the good, how can we wonder that the Puritans came to consider beauty as serving evil, and music as "that lost and depraved art"? As to beauty in the service of good, the old errors persist. The series of injunctions in the *Republic* about the moral effects of certain kinds of music may have varied in detail or application, but not in principle, over the last twenty-five centuries. To Plato, the flute was sensuous, therefore unsettling and orgiastic; today it is the embodiment of classic restraint; its very use suggests a prim elegance. For in truth the flute has outgrown its panic implications as thoroughly as it has outgrown its military uses in the old-fashioned fife. Yet many Platos today say of saxophones and marimbas what he said of flutes; and though no one any longer condemns the Lydian mode on moral grounds, yet many there are who will not even listen to Strauss' *Salomes Tanz* or Stravinsky's *Sacre du Printemps*, for fear of personal corruption, on moral grounds alone.

The abandonment of the good seems as requisite as that of the useful in the rating of beauty among music's purposes. And the *true*, be it a concept ever so charming to the philosopher, must suffer similarly. And why, one wonders, is it that the esthetician, readily handling the problem of the relation of truth to art in general, becomes so self-consciously appalled when this problem is swung over into music? The fact is, not that the problem is profound, nor that it does not exist, but simply that from a teleological angle it is not important. Aristotle, in awarding a high place in the enjoyment of beauty to the pleasures of recognition, started a hundred generations speculating as to the place of "realism"; but truth does not of itself make the esthetic experience, nor is it even a necessary ingredient. But considering for a moment what part it does play, that part need not become obscure in the case of music. Pure music of course cannot deal with object-images: indeed, because of its apparently spontaneous inception, it cannot be attached to the retinue of any external power. The transformation of auditory data into musical sounds is immediate, and no intrusion of object-images can deflect the flow. But this does not cancel the possibility of truth judgments. The background of pure music is probably pure kinesthesis, which furnishes no object-data; and hence the composer can neither recognize nor express his own past in terms of objects. But expressing himself in tone, he has the keenest knowledge of the essence of his message. Pure music represents the dynamic residue of the composer's acquisitions, reorganized into temporal images and crystallized in tone; representing the *essentia* of events, it cannot give the attributes pertaining and indispensable to their spatial appearance. And yet it may represent these *essentia* truly or untruly, be it never so little concerned with three-dimensional imagery. Anyone who has been at all moved by pure music must have seen that it is a kind of type-thinking, which must not be perverted by a reduction to the specific; anyone, other than an extreme nominalist, must then grant truth (or untruth) to music.

But here again, having explored this path, we find it leads nowhere along the line of the main problem. All these various servings by beauty in the cause of this utility, that good, the other truth, might interchangeably have occurred in the cause of the inutile, the evil, the false. And has, over and over again! The question has been unmercifully begged. Any servant, if paid enough, will serve any master. Our inquiry is, what does beauty do with her time when she is free? Lapse into purposeless desuetude? If so, let us have done at once with the whole problem, eliminate beauty as a separate concept, and abolish esthetic. But Professor Singer is not ready to do quite this. His fourth postulate takes the leap:

(4) *Only the art whose purpose is to change the purposes of the beings to whom it is addressed is fine ("free," or "freeing") art.*[11]

[11] *Ibid.*, p. 26.

And his own comment: "All our previous teleological definitions . . . have set their classes to *winning* ends; art only wins
its purpose by first *losing* us, i.e., loosing us from old ends."
The purpose of art is a revision of purposes. Not, however, in
the homiletic sense known to any teacher (for teachers are also
purpose-changers), not merely to produce the *conviction* that
our purposes should be changed, but also to see that something
is *done* about it. The artist aims not merely to produce a state
of mind—his aim is also to throw us into a mood of doing; as
Emerson said of books, "that one is great which puts me in a
working mood"—if it were not for this, "Apollo is an imbecile."
But *working*—working for change toward new ends:

the new for whose sake [art] emancipates from an old love must
not be merely another of the same kind, must not be the same
heaven sought by better means or suddenly lost by worse ones; the
movement art sets free must be *toward a new heaven*, a new end
or kingdom of ends . . . free from all shadow of returning.[12]

The physician, the preacher, the penitent all have as their task
the altering of purposes, but always with them somehow it is
an altering back to old ones.

(5) *The* [complete] *artist must be a messenger of discontent*—
what more he may be remains to be seen.[13]

Again, the pioneer in science, in contributing to progress by
substituting new hypotheses for old, may be thought to have
the task not only of abandoning the old, but also of guarantee-
ing no return; yet the scientist *specifies* the new, and even ex-
pounds its meaning. This art does not do—for art may not
teach.

(6) The artist, after having inspired us with discontent, advo-
cates no new ideal wherein contentment may be found.[14]

And finally, lest it be thought that, so far, the philosopher
might share all these attributes with the artist, one more postulate is required. For philosophy is not art, no more than is
science. The philosopher, it is true, creates new ideals, and he

---

[12] *Ibid.*, pp. 34-5.
[13] *Ibid.*, p. 26.
[14] *Ibid.*, p. 38.

creates them *for* us; but the artist creates *in* us the mood to create.

(7) The artist creates no new ideals; *he creates the creator of ideals.*[15]

Music is an arena of illustration for the testing of this set of postulates: it seems to be the purest of all agencies for that strange purposiveness without purpose—what Kant called *das interessenloses Wohlgefallen*—that Professor Singer subtends in his discussion. The inertness of the products of the graphic arts renders them susceptible to willful violation of the principle of art as a messenger of discontent. The desire to acquire or possess the object, so pathetically displayed by art collectors, can only contaminate the esthetic experience, by shattering the divine discontent inspired by art, and by advocating the return to some old ideal, embodied in the image of an antique talisman. But in music, one *may not* have a personal interest in the object. The dead hand of a Croesus, a Lorenzo, or a Hearst has never been successfully laid on this realm. Their activity may have a place in the teleology of the world, but it is not a place favorable to Art the changer of purposes. Theirs is simply the spirit of the woman of property who, cautiously investing her money in government bonds, said to her agent: "These at least are perfectly secure?" "I should not say that," was his guarded reply, "but they will be the last things to go." Music will not brook this easy spirit. The contemplation of it involves that disinterestedness which is the condition of any change of ideals. There seems to be no adequate reason why we should give up Bach because we no longer perform his fugues on a clavichord. And if the artist is to create the creator, his product is better not incarcerated in museums.

The common experience of men seems also to be that of all the arts, music, whatever else it may commit or omit, *moves,* and moves men most out of themselves and least back into themselves. The former moving is surely the clue to esthetic beauty, the latter to technical beauty—and although sheer technicians may exist with respect to music they have a worse

[15] *Ibid.,* p. 40.

time than the technicians of other arts, because they may take
no refuge in mere craft. A carpenter is at least an honest laborer
and constructive, but a tune-juggler must be a mountebank if
for no other reason than that, though he constructs, he constructs in order to juggle.

In reference to art's changing one's purposes, and changing
not merely as transferring but as transforming, the "complete"
musician is necessarily defined in these terms. It may be supposed for argument that a certain famous musical idiom of the
eighteenth century reached its ideal expression in Mozart. In
the hands of Haydn, as any property in the hands of a bourgeois,
this was transferred; but in Beethoven's it was transformed into
something new in kind, not recalled, not reverted, but set
toward "a new end or kingdom of ends."

The apologists for swing music are equalled in philosophical
ineptitude only by those who seek to answer them. But
equipped with this view of art's purpose, the answer should
be ready. Such dire sterility as can only find outlets through
warmed-over "classics" invested with a searing, grinding ham-
mer-beat is the nadir of an art transferring and not transforming men's purposes, and transferring them back to an infantility
certainly not that of the race (for primitive music was never
such), not even reminding us of the instinctive things of the
world (for the truly passion-swept soul is no narcotist), and not
expressive of the times (for today's rhythms are intricate).

And further, this transformation shall be no mere shift in
coördinates. Proposals for further subdivision of the scale, experiments with polytonality and atonality, venturing (with
Schoenberg) upon an n-voiced polyphony or (with Scriabin)
upon a no-voiced mysticism, are devices not likely to affect the
progress of men's purposes, particularly as it is usually dis-
coverable that such devices have already been exploited to the
full, either by the Chinese, or by the medieval Church.

Professor Singer's peroration, though perhaps without explicit intent, is a paean of hope for esthetic of music. The old-
style esthetic was essentially an integral thing, and historians
were content that it remain so. But in the presence of music,

esthetic must become differential, given to the calculating of experience as a flow, and not a fund. In estimating the chances of attaining any artistic goal, *mood* is indispensable—and it must be definable. In music, mood is no static lump of soul-states: it is a process, a "limiting ratio," whose coefficients tie all variables into some systematic relation between structure and function. The terms of this relationship are for future esthetic to discover.

If there is anything in Schopenhauer's view to which we would defer, it is his definition of music as unconscious philosophizing. We need not approve the first word in this phrase as much as the second. But just as art is the most difficult of all activities in which to build on a rational foundation, music is the most difficult of all the arts in this respect. Yet there it is, awaiting the application of this ideal. That Beethoven is not a jumble of random play-impulses, but conceivably embodies an ethical message; that music is not an orgy of visceral jolts, but conceivably represents the significant tonal projection of the idea in temporal form—these are matters just coming to be granted.

It is not that the rational is to be defined in terms of the esthetic. A rotten egg is disgusting, but the chemist still feels no disgust toward hydrogen sulphide. It is rather that "the esthetic motive presupposes a rational ideal."[16] It is the function of the moralist to set the standards at which man may be expected to aim. It is the function of the scientist to state the mode of approaching, and lay down the conditions for attaining, these standards. It is the function of the artist, through his mastery of moods, to *impel* men to the attainment of the ends set by the moralist, through the means stated by the scientist—by making it seem "worth while."

But Professor Singer does not insist that these activities be successive and in that order. "We may have a sense"—a mood —"of changed direction *before* we realize to what new thing our change may tend! . . ."[17] Before the vision of a new time can shape itself in the intellect, the sense of repulsion"—the

[16] *Ibid.*, p. 54.
[17] *Ibid.*, p. 51.

breath of discontent—"that had all along been upon us takes on an assurance of constancy: whithersoever we tend, *we know we can never turn back*. This I call the tragic moment."[18] But not of itself is the tragic moment tragic,—only when it is inspired of beauty. ("Sois belle! sois triste!" says Baudelaire.) "When, then, art has brought us to the moment we have called *the tragic*, the moment when a movement out of the old self and its time-out-of-joint has 'set' in the sense of never-returning, then if the mood is heroic, its energy creative, I call the work of art *beautiful*."[19] This job of the artist is inseparable, then, from the heroic mood of new creating. And if, as Pater claimed, all art is constantly aspiring toward the condition of music, we cannot escape the implications for a new esthetic.

[18] *Ibid.*, p. 52.
[19] *Ibid.*, p. 53.

SHAPER, THINKER AND VISIONARY:
A PROBLEM IN AESTHETICS*

Louis W. Flaccus

Department of Philosophy, University of Pennsylvania

THE man of the street is apt to think lightly of both artist and philosopher. He himself is a shaper and thinker as he builds a factory, organizes a business, and shrewdly sets thought to work to gain practical success. To him the artist is a child and the philosopher, a grey pedant. He may become an art patron and collector of pictures, but it is too often only to be known as such or to invest in paintings as one would in stocks. The artist naturally resents both neglect and exploitation. Nor does he feel kindly toward philosophy. He does not like to see art pocketed in a thought-system. The philosopher, as trained abstract thinker intent on his world formula, stands within the shadow of what he builds. Even when he is less single-minded and more observing, he rarely sees much of the art that is all about him and fails to respond to the force, direction, and form of a life of which even his thought-pattern is a part. To him the artist is either a mere entertainer or the creator of something, the purposes and meanings of which, philosophy alone can set forth.

Is this clashing disharmony necessary? If not, how can it be ended? The answer seems very simple. Make the artist thoughtful, sensitize the man of the street, and force the philosopher into a living contact with art. Have them meet within the walls of a museum of Fine Art. But easy answers are too often the signs of an easygoing temperament. This problem demands a study of the nature of that shaping and thinking from which both art and philosophy spring. It calls for an understanding of art as outer reshaping, called pattern, and as inner reshaping, emotional, imaginative, and intellectual—all this in a

* Reshaped, in part, from a lecture given at the Philadelphia Museum of Fine Art in 1936.

world of seeming. Whatever may be thought of man, singly or in the mass, he must be granted two admirable qualities—courage and enterprise. From crude beginnings he has risen through persistent shaping and thinking. Life, without and within, was either formless or alien and hostile. His was the task of gaining a gradual technical mastery of nature and of himself—by energy, skill, and thought.

The varied range of this shaping is enormous: the chipping of an arrow head, the fashioning of a thole pin, the tying of a knot, the damming of a river, the ordering of a tribal hunt, the making of a dynamo, the shaping of raw materials, the disciplined patternings of industry and commerce. The purposes involved are trivial or important, generic or specialized, of interest to either individual or group.

Whoever has trimmed a hedge or cleared a woodland patch knows something of the wild, irrepressible life of Nature, which must be mastered. It takes energy to become civilized. It is not a matter of pebbles smoothed and rounded by the sea of time. All this shaping, technical or not, is creative of values.

Not only does man shape—he thinks, and this thinking is bound up with his shaping. He reflects, devises means, thinks things out. He examines, weighs, judges. Everywhere in the forming of his experiences and the gaining of his purposes thought plays a part, and appears in a thousand variants. It is a technical device, serving man in what he plans and in what he shapes.

There are, however, ways of shaping and thinking that go beyond the matter of practical control and show energies and values of their own. The one is art; the other, philosophy. They are not the late flowering of a complex civilization which has gained leisure and repose through a slackening of the pressure of need. The caveman of northern Spain lived precariously and crudely, yet created and enjoyed art. The earliest folklore reveals man as a seeker of cosmic meanings.

The problem of how philosophy is related to that other abstract thinking—science—lies far afield. While the scientist is content to order and relate facts within a special range, the philosopher is mastered by a totality complex. As he builds, he aims at an all-inclusive system of relations. This is true of the early Greek philosophers, of metaphysicians like Plato or Spinoza; it is true also of thinkers who, more modest, reduce philosophy to a method or develop a general theory of experience. Everywhere the single living experience of the artist and the common man is devalued, reshaped, revalued in terms of a totality of relations.

In some ways the philosopher and the artist have much in common. Imagination works in both. They are reshapers and organizers. A system of thought, like a work of art, may have applied to it the tests of harmony, balance, and economy. But I suspect that widening the term aesthetic in this way and claiming that it inheres in all experience is itself the biased gesture of the philosopher—a gesture that reveals a deep-going difference between the shaping that is art and the thinking that is philosophy.

This difference may be understood by following the philosopher as he develops a theory of aesthetics and fits it snugly into his system of thought. Often he turns his face to the sea of speculation, casts his weighted net, catches and hauls in the swift, brilliant thing called beauty as he has hauled in those other creatures of the deep—truth and goodness. He carries it home in his net of relationships. Plato, Kant, Hegel, and Croce are given to such netting. Or he may have come to distrust metaphysics. He then turns his back to the sea and faces the world of art as it exists in surprising variety in a picture, a statue, a mask, a fetish, a canoe prow, a jar, an arrow-smoother, a cathedral, a group dance. In some of these, art seems to exist for its own sake, in others it reflects the processes and uses of life. This art, either by the piece or in the bulk, may be superficially enjoyed; it may be understood and critically tasted and tested or it may be speculated about. To stop with the first is bad; it is a cheap way of missing what is one of man's greatest rights: the search for quality. The second offers the chief problem of aesthetics. The philosopher inclines toward the third. He is apt to put in the place of a sympathetic understanding of the nature and quality of art a thinking about, a tracing of contexts, a wide-flung generalizing about culture and experience. This is like marking laboriously the pattern of the filaments in a spider's web and neglecting the spider.

The obvious thing about shaping is that it involves work, craftsmanship, skill. The fitting together of the parts of an intricate machine, the making of a fishing rod, the weaving of a rug, the cutting of a diamond, the creation of a lithograph, the interlocking of movements or sounds in a dance or a symphony, the fashioning of a dagger or canoe paddle—all reveal man as an efficient shaper.

As he achieves control in all these processes he gains incidental pleasures—of expressing himself as a skilled worker, of perfecting, of lingering within what he has done. However, neither craftsmanship alone nor the pleasures incidental to it serve to give the quality of the shaping that is art.

An attempt to mark off this quality may be made by considering five things: a hotel, a watch, a Malayan kris, the Parthenon frieze, and a picture by Georgia O'Keefe, called "Cowskull and White Roses."

A hotel is a physical object. It is made up of other objects—rooms, furniture, linen, china, cutlery. Its meaning lies in their functional togetherness. They all contribute to the purpose of the hotel, which is to be a sound investment with a money yield gained from catering to the comfort of its guests. From that angle it interests us not merely as a physical object, but as expressive of special ambitions and purposes. But there may be a hotel man who is not merely a money-maker and efficient manager, but a dreamer with a vision of an ideal hotel to be realized through incessant shaping and reshaping. Myron Weagle in Sinclair Lewis's *Work of Art* is such a man. He has a vision and a mastering impulse to gain it through action. In a broad sense he may be called an artist, and what he aims at might be called "work of art." Such uses are misleading. As Myron passes from hotel to hotel, organizes, becomes dissatisfied, gives his ambition a wider fling, he is at all times the restless seeker. His activity throughout is forward looking, functional, comparative: better, better, better hotels. Even if his best could be realized, it would in meaning be only a smoothly running organization in a factual world. This is what separates the loose use of the term "artist" from the true one. The shaping of the artist is not forward-looking and comparative, and he is not in that sense a seeker of perfection. He rests, and asks us to rest, in the individual picture or poem or building. What he creates is not merely a new functional assemblage of forms, colors, sounds, emotional experiences, but new forms and new values. These go beyond function and craftsmanship; and are to be understood only as related to a world of seeming, or semblance.

A watch, too, is a physical object of such and such a size, shape, weight, material. Its interior is an ingenious relating of parts to make it go. It is meant to be a timepiece. As a mechanism it may be of one or the other of many patterns. Likewise, all airplanes are meant to fly, but they may be monoplanes, biplanes, autogiros. The primary use and the secondary ones of durability, cheapness or costliness, ease of carrying determine the form of the watch. The difference between the original stubby, high-bodied Ford and the newer streamline models can be traced in part to functional needs—more space for a powerful engine, lessened wind resistance, and so forth. But there is an aesthetic plus in the automobile and the watch. Ford, no lover of art, confessed that in order to compete with other makers of cars he was forced to cater to what might be called a public demand for beauty. In the watch there is, apart from the matter of efficiency, an artistic shaping in the filigree work of the hands, the quality of the dial face and numbers, the cutting into the gold rim or back. It is largely because of this that a watch becomes an object of individual interest. Apart however from this ornamental elaboration, over against it, and in sharp contrast to it, is this fact: a watch is, first and last, a timepiece, a tool of practical control.

A Malayan kris was given me by the grandson of a man who brought it from Java. It is a short sword fitted to a wooden sheath. I like to look at it. There is no sentimental interest nor do I ever expect to draw blood with it. Yet there is pleasure in the thought that it is a serviceable weapon. The kris may be put into the sheath in either of two ways. One allows a hair-trigger speed in pulling it out. The hilt is of heavy wood, for balance, and the part to be gripped is carved into straight ridges to allow a firm hold. The blade as it curves to a point shows edges going in low curves. An uglier wound can be made by such a blade than by a straight one. Functional adaptation—is this all there is to be said? A straight blade with a few jagged projections would make even an uglier wound. Whoever has examined halberds, maces, and other old weapons must have noted the grotesque shapes fitted to inflict the severest hurt by piercing, hacking, and clubbing. They are irredeemably ugly to the eye. But this Malayan blade is a rippling play of lines. It is alive as it moves from the hilt to the point like a snake. This is not a fancy of mine, but an observable living delight in form and line an artist has put into a useful object. The sheath is plain, with only a decorative touch or two. I like to run my fingers along the surfaces to get the feel of its sensitive model-ing. On the blade near the hilt are a few simple, variational lines. It is because of such an artistic plus that the kris as I look at it impresses me as something personal and individual.

The Parthenon frieze shows the Panathenaic procession: youths, maidens, magistrates, sacrificial animals afoot, men rid-ing or walking or pausing. Honor is to be done to the seated gods. As such it is a note in that full-toned harmony of civic and religious art—the Parthenon. The birth of Athena, her guardianship of Attica, the battle with centaurs, the colossal statue within were all symbols and carriers of love and fear of gods, and of civic pride. A grand theme with thematic varia-tions! of unusual interest to whoever, impatient of art for art's sake, sinks art into a functional theory of cultural values. But devoutness and love of country do not account for either the creation or the enjoyment of religious and civic art. Something crude or brazenly ostentatious might have served equally well to carry deep and sincere feeling. There is a direct art quality about the frieze, as there is in that other procession cut in low relief on the stairway of the Great King in the royal palace at Persepolis. That, too, is commemorative and patriotic in theme. There a procession is shown—a symbol of the might and span of Persia—tribute-bearers leading camels or oxen or carrying fruit, soldiers and guards on the march. Suppose we forget about temples and palaces and ceremonial and for the moment respond directly to Athenian youth and horse, to cameleer and camel. Here is no naturalistic copying; here is no large social meaning. Rather is there art for art's sake. In the strength and delicacy of line, the effective spacing, the simplifying of surfaces, the way plane cuts into plane and line meets line, the perceptual image is enjoyed for its own sake—a luxury life seldom allows. This quality of design and felicitous shaping is found not only here and in the sculptural work of widely different cultures, such as Assyrian, Egyptian, Gothic, Mayan, it is manifest in a Greek coin or vase and in a line time has chipped from the poems of Sappho.

Four objects have been considered: hotel, watch, Malayan kris, and the Parthenon frieze. In the first, the hotel, the meaning lay in practical purposes and social conveniences, and the shaping was functionally pointed. Any interest in the hotel as a sense object is speedily translated back into the thought of what a hotel ought to be. The point of view is comparative and the response is not to something individual. The Parthenon frieze is part of a religious and civic symbol. To the artist it was something other—a sensuously alive, vividly imagined and delicately wrought design. To the art lover, also, it ought to be that—an unending delight to the eye.

The fifth example is to be a picture. This choice serves a double purpose. A picture is set off from its surroundings by a frame, offers itself as a sense object and is, often, created for its own sake. We can respond to it directly and enjoy it slowly at our leisure. Here art is not sunk into something functional and social. A painting is, of course, socially conditioned. The canvases of Boucher and Fragonard reflect a frivolous, graceful, and artificial court life. But that has little to do with their art quality. The choice of a painting then makes it more difficult for the social-minded thinker to misinterpret in his favorite way. He is more easily found out than in his comment on a tribal dance, a patriotic poem, or the Parthenon. Again, may we not, in turning to a picture, discover that there is to art something more than shaping for the sake of a pattern—something that is vision, inner reshaping, emotional and imaginative, all expressed in and through a design? I believe there is.

Georgia O'Keefe's "Cowskull and White Roses" is an effective and startling picture—effective through its individuality and patterned quality—personal because of the strange objects built into the design. The triangle of the front of a bleached cow's skull is the main architectural form. Harmoniously related to it are the curved shapes of the roses. There are contrasts between textures—brittle and waxen—and between whites and greys. This picture lives, as all pictures ought to live, first of all, as a sensuously shaped design. But there is more to art than pattern. It takes creative imagination to bind into a sensuous unity objects which appeal so differently to our senses and are so unlike in their thrust into our emotional and imaginative life. You may, after a hard winter, see the bones of cattle strewn along the desert highlands of Wyoming. If you are observing, you may see how nature turns them to dust and covers them with the living grey of sage brush. If you are thoughtful, you may reflect on this cycle of life and death. Or you may turn to white roses. In direct presence and associations they differ from red or yellow roses. As you think about them you may in the end reach their calm pure note in the massed variety of funeral flowers. In all these instances the togetherness of life and death has been reached indirectly, ponderously through reflection. But in the picture it strikes directly. Depth is given to the design. The psychic seems to live within the pattern. Life and death—death and life! The skull is given a living quality, the roses are held immobile within the frame; the two are given a new, shared meaning in and through art.

This is something other than patterned shaping. Something new has been created for imagination, feeling, and thought by the artist as his visions take form. It may be urged that this inner seeing and shaping while manifest in a painting is absent in a rug or an unadorned vase. There is something vicious in a theory which argues that since pattern is essential to all art there is nothing essential to art but pattern. Granted that there is less of the psychic in a rug than in a picture or a drama, it cannot be flattened to a mere bit of wallpaper patterning. Not only is it self-complete, but in it is a spirit—the breath and vision of the artist—from which the art lover cannot escape.

Turning from painting but keeping to the theme of life and death, three examples of poetic vision may be given.

Benét in his American epic *John Brown's Body* comes to the thought that modern industrial America has sprung from the Civil War. He forms this into verses short, variable, expressive, ecstatic. These verses carry a vision that is strange, violently opposed to common sense, imaginatively and emotionally his own—a vision from the world of art. Here are a few lines:

> Out of his body grows revolving steel,
> Out of his body grows the spinning wheel
> Made up of wheels, the new, mechanic birth,
> No longer bound by toil
> To the unsparing soil
> Of the old furrow-line,
> The great, metallic beast
> Expanding West and East,
> His heart a spinning coil,
> His juices burning oil,
> His body serpentine.
> Out of John Brown's strong sinews
>   the tall skyscrapers grow,
> Out of his heart the chanting buildings rise,
> Rivet and girder, motor and dynamo,
> Pillar of smoke by day and fire by night,
> The steel-faced cities reaching at the skies,
> The whole enormous and rotating cage
> Hung with hard jewels of electric light,
> Smoky with sorrow, black with splendor, dyed
> Whiter than damask for a crystal bride
> With metal suns, the engine-handed age. . . .[1]

Robinson Jeffers, visiting the home of his ancestors, exclaims

> But I in a peasant's hut
> Eat bread bitter with the dust of dead men.

This is bold inner reshaping. As in a vision he sees the mingling

[1] From *John Brown's Body*, published by Farrar & Rinehart, Inc. Copyright, 1927-28 by Stephen Vincent Benét.

of death and life—the battleground and the field, the soil soaked with blood, the broken spear, the crumbling bone, the living grain.

As Hamlet addresses the skull of Yorick, there is softness in his mood, for he was fond of this jester of his father's. As he elaborates, his thought by some strange alchemy of art comes to mean more to Hamlet and to us than mere memory of loss or mere fact. In art even thought is given new values; it serves, not truth-speaking, but emotional vibration and imaginative vision.

The question whether the artist is a thinker as well as a shaper cannot be answered with a yes or no. Some artists are incredibly naive and childlike in their thinking; others, like Dante or Goethe, are searching and profound. Some create with little thought, others, like Rodin, reflect as they fashion. But to regard art as a bit of thinking, to be tested as the practical man and the scientist test it, is to misconceive utterly the part thought plays in artistic reshaping. A work of art is not an item of information nor an intellectual construct. Art recreates thought in its own image—in that of a world of seeming in which it moves and has its being.

The step toward a world of semblance is the third and hardest. The first and second steps to an understanding of the meaning of art were: patterned shaping and an inner psychic reseeing and reshaping within the pattern of a design.

The view that art is semblance, seeming, illusion, make-believe, shadow play is a very old one. Plato held to it, and it has reappeared in Schiller, Lange, Vernon Lee, Parker, and others. Plato used it to discredit art. Intent as he was on the real, in the sense of the perfect and the permanent, he came to regard Nature as she appears to our senses as the great illusionist shifting colors and shapes, transforming and distorting. The philosopher sees through her tricks. This world of the senses the artist flattens out and distorts still further. A painter, he puts colors on a flat surface and tricks us into the perception of a solid object; a sculptor, he shapes stone to a seeming man, but this man cannot move, cannot breathe, cannot express himself in word or deed. In principle there is no difference between this and the view that poetry is a pack of lies.

In the illusion theory of Lange, art is not censured as being shallow and misleading. It is held to be playful self-deception; an enjoyable make-believe in which vivid actuality and unreality either oscillate or blend. But still what seems is tested in terms of what is.

This is true also of the third of these unsatisfactory theories of semblance, that which moves art work close to dream work and interprets dreams, after the fashion of Freud, as subconscious wish fulfilment. The formula runs something like this: "Art is the imaginative expression and realisation of a wish." Life as we live it is imperfect, chaotic, filled with disappointments, marked by frustrations. Dreams and art are our way of getting even with life. We put into them our yearning for something ordered and satisfying. It must be admitted that many dreams can be rationalized in this manner, and that some art is a romantic escape of this sort. But the essence of dreams is capricious, irresponsible, roving, chaotic fancy. They are unlike the disciplined shaping and imagining of the artist. Again, art creates its own wishes. A sex-starved consciousness may paint a luscious nude, but only a wish rooted in art can make of that nude a fine picture. Renoir is a case in point. The Freudians might cite a comment made by one of his friends: "To paint a woman excites him more than if he were caressing her." But what of this remark of Renoir's: "Some of our servants have had admirable figures, and have posed like angels. But I must admit that I am not hard to please. I would just as soon paint the first crock that comes along, as long as she has a skin that takes the light."

A reference to Keats's ode "On a Grecian Urn" may serve to point the criticism of this Freudian view and lead to a true interpretation of the world of semblance. Keats takes as material for his poem a sculptural relief. The sculptor had gained his matter from life: a dance, a youth pursuing a maiden, a musician, bits of religious ceremony and group life. In the actual world of human experience all such persons and incidents have their meaning in time, in change, in yearning aimed at fulfillment, and in the expressing and redirecting of effort. The music begins and ends and begins again, the dance may be

repatterned to a new ecstasy, the maiden may be caught and
kissed, there may be new gatherings at the shrine of some god.
Observe what the sculptor has done. He has called a magic halt
to all the movement, the forward thrust of wish and purpose so
typical of life as experienced and wished for. Everything has
been frozen to one moment of stone. The dancers will never
move, the piper will be forever silent, the youth can never
catch his maiden. What we wish for in life, even as we are
poised in pausing, is not here imaginatively fulfilled, in fact, it
is denied. It has been denied so that something other, something peculiar to art may be affirmed. These stone semblances
fall into space patterns, and in place of the arrested movement
of life there is the flowing movement of design. In this way
Keats responds to the sculptural relief. Everywhere his pattern,
movement, and vision are superimposed on those of the sculptor. The zest and yearning, the flurry and warmth of life had
disappeared in this "cold pastoral" of chiseled stone. These
images are given a new life through Keats's rich, detached imagination, creating and moving within a world of seeming.

Here are parts of the poem:

> What leaf-fringed legend haunts about thy shape
> Of deities or mortals, or of both,
> In Tempe or the dales of Arcady?
> What men or gods are these? what maidens loth?
> What mad pursuit? what struggle to escape?
> What pipes and timbrels? what wild ecstasy?

II

> Heard melodies are sweet, but those unheard
> Are sweeter; therefore, ye soft pipes, play on;
> Not to the sensual ear, but, more endear'd
> Pipe to the spirit ditties of no tone.
> Fair youth, beneath the trees, thou canst not leave
> Thy song, nor ever can these trees be bare;
> Bold lover, never, never canst thou kiss,
> Though winning near the goal—yet do not grieve;
> She cannot fade, though thou hast not thy bliss,
> For ever wilt thou love and she be fair!

III

Ah, happy, happy boughs! that cannot shed
　Your leaves, nor ever bid the spring adieu;
And, happy melodist, unwearied,
　Forever piping songs for ever new;

* * * * * * *

V

O Attic shape! Fair attitude! with brede
　Of marble men and maidens overwrought,
With forest branches and the trodden weed;
　Thou, silent form, dost tease us out of thought
　As doth eternity; Cold pastoral!

At the very end of the poem there is a false note. The phrase is often quoted: "Beauty is truth, truth beauty" by its stark abstractness breaks the spell Keats has woven.

But may not the poem be, after all, a daydream into which Keats has put wishes life never grants—eternal love, never changing youth, deathless spring, unwearied strength, soundless music "for ever new"? A distinction must be made between two types of daydreams. According to Freud, Rebecca in *Rosmersholm* builds subconscious dream work around the wish to supplant Mrs. Rosmer; Macbeth's dream of kingdom, subconsciously formed, springs forth into murder. Peer Gynt's inflated ego dreams wishfully of royalty. A social worker envisages slum clearance or the cutting down of disease. In all these cases, the daydream is pointed toward self-satisfaction gained through actual change. "I will be a king, a Kaiser," exclaims Peer Gynt. But the dream Keats conjures up is not of this type. Art dreams many dreams—of heaven and hell, of Kubla Khan, of trolls, ghosts and monsters, of Lazy Man's Paradise, of Gargantuas, Tom Thumbs and Calibans. In this second type of dreaming there is no self to be satisfied; no sense of factual change; no anticipation of possible attainment. Imagination creates visions, forms, and realities of its own.

The fault with the illusion theories of Plato and Lange and

with the Freudian dream and wish theory lies in applying an actuality-control to art. Here are examples of what is meant by such a control. As I look at trees growing at the edge of a pool and turn to their reflection in the water, I may check off the image as a distorted mirroring of the trees. Suppose I see a desert image of a cluster of palms and a spring. Can I reach that spot and find shade and water or is it nothing but a mirage? Such actuality-controls are needed for an effective ordering of experiences. Imagine them applied to art. I count the stars on an American flag in a painting, find them incorrect in number and therefore call the picture bad. Or I say of a Matisse: "How ridiculous, the man has moved everything to a frontal plane, he is ignorant of actual space relations." Such responses are absurd.

This criticism may be put constructively by saying that in art we are held within the semblance. As Vernon Lee puts it, we pass from the thing to the shape; from the intellectual, factual, and practical to a surface play of color, line, light and shade, texture, sound, and visual and auditory form. The approach of the artist is, first and foremost, a sensuous and perceptual one. A soul-span separates the troubled, blazing, mystical art of Van Gogh from the rich, decoratively wrought, naive art of Keats, but in both there is an ecstasy of color, of texture, of Nature as sensuous image.

Semblance in art is partly perceptual—passing from an object to a shape, partly psychic—passing from the inner experiences of real life to simulated thoughts, feelings, moods. The first offers the lesser difficulty.

Suppose I pause in the act of striking a match and think about and observe the box I have taken it from. I remember where I bought it, how much it cost, reflect on how useful it is. As such it is simply one of a kind: there is nothing individual about it. As an object it has an inner, partially filled space which I know about but do not see. This space is within six planes set at right angles. The planes differ in area, color, color edging and texture. As I move the match box about it assumes different shapes. As I hold it tilted the visual angles are no longer right angles. Instead of thinking about it as an object,

I have now received it directly as a more or less interesting
visual image. The factual—curiosity and purpose—has disappeared.

In like manner I may reduce to a play of line, shape, color,
and texture the grouped table, reading lamp, and easy chair
that serve my needs and minister to my comfort. Again I may,
from the window of a high building, look down on intersecting
streets busy with traffic. There are automobiles, people hurry-
ing, walking slowly or stopping, lights changing and controlling
the streams of traffic. I may respond to all this as an artist would
and feel it as a rhythmic pattern. This is how, with a little
training of our senses, we may detach ourselves from self-
concern, from the factual and practical, and respond aesthet-
ically to life; this is what the artist does consistently; and this
is what we must look for in art—semblance and design, or
rather design within a world of seeming.

Two objections must be met. I may be accused of making of
art something dreamy, unreal, insubstantial; or I may be blamed
for having made of it a trifling play in which the substantial
interests and spiritual values of life can find no place.

The first of these objections requires no extensive answer.
Is there anything dreamy or unreal about any of the shapes of
the match-box? or about the reflections of trees in water? or
about the color and sound in Keats's "To Autumn"? or about
the men and women in a drama whose reality is semblance and
nothing but that, whose actions, feelings, and thoughts spring
from and rest in the imagination of the poet? But what of an
acted play or a dance recital or the building the architect has
set down foursquare as an object in the physical world? There
is here a rather naive confusion between the physical material
and art product—the stone of the building, the actor, the body
of the dancer and the aesthetic object. Kicking against the
stones of the Parthenon, impressed with its physical thereness,
seeking a mathematical formula, speculating in the spirit of the
historian or social student on the when, where, whence, and
whereto—this is to neglect aesthetic qualities of design and
spirit which inhere even in a photograph and persist even in
the silence of all social meanings.

A second objection accuses the semblance theory of reducing art to shallow, irresponsible play. Back of this are thoughts like the following: life is a serious matter of purposes, interests, values, ideals—no sharp line can be drawn between technology and fine art, skill and purpose marking both—life has a right to expect of art what is found useful and valuable in living— art has from the first been conscious of this demand, hence it has worked functionally in a building, a vase, a mask, a rug or a dance, inspirationally in a commemorative statue, and has expressed and sanctified the inner life of man in poem after poem. Has an aesthetic theory the right to neglect all these implications?

It cannot be denied that many art objects are created with reference to specific purposes, and that these purposes are manifest in their forms. Purpose, again, seems to point directly to a world of actualities. What then becomes of the theory that art is semblance? and that aesthetic appreciation moves within this seeming? A distinction must be made. We naturally respond to skill and functional adaptedness when examining an intricate bit of machinery—a watch, a combustion engine, an electrically controlled system of locks in a vault. In all such cases we find satisfaction in the presence of skilled workmanship, in comparing part with part, tracing relationships, responding, not to a mere sense object, but to an ingenious, efficient mechanism adapted perfectly to useful functioning. Suppose we are contemplating a building or a picture. Here, too, are to be found skill and functional adaptation. Each part functions in relation to all the others. But if we respond to skill merely as skill or follow purpose beyond what is built into the sense impression, we are in danger of losing the aesthetic object altogether. The more thoroughly I enter into the details of a combustion engine, the farther I shall be from an interest in the sense form as it appears—my mind will be filled with thoughts of use, efficiency, and type. In art, purpose may be a source of pleasure, but only when it is held contemplatively and functions constructively and centrifugally within a self-complete appearance. Like the other values of life, it must be taken into a world of semblance.

What of the inner life of man? Feelings and moods experienced, thoughts aiming at truth, spiritual ventures, goods prized and ideals cherished—are they to have no place in art? Is art merely a kind of wallpaper patterning? The fear of such psychic emptiness leads to the mistaken view that what we prize in real life must find a forceful and persuasive voice in art, and that it is this we must respond to and enjoy.

The artist is not a sense-intoxicated child. He is a shaper, a designer, and he creates new forms in that relatively formless thing we call life. He is a spiritual interpreter and creator as well.

Art is far from being shallow. It is rooted in the personality of the artist, and has room within it for all the spiritual values of mankind. It is human—and deeply human. Dante is a great plastic poet, with a marvelous sense of the quality of sound and light. But his *Divine Comedy* is art spiritually enriched.

It must, however, be insisted on that human values as they appear in art are held within a world of seeming and are expressed in relation to design. They are simulated and transmuted. Here, too, an actuality-control is out of place.

Joy and sorrow, love of home and country, moral and social ideals, pity, courage, a sense of honor or justice, strength of muscle or spirit—all these have their place in art. But the art may be either good or bad. The mere worthwhileness of something in real life does not of itself mean excellent art. Few will deny that the El Greco "Christ on the Cross" is a more spiritual and imaginative painting than that of Rubens. But here, as in all good art, the spirituality is expressed and given a new meaning through color, light and dark, line and mass. The constant use of factual and moral tests has made much of Ruskin's aesthetics valueless. Some years back there appeared in a reputable art journal an article which professed to give the art credo of the writer. Two pictures were shown, one an old Dutch painting of a drinking bout at an inn, the other with the composing of the *Marseillaise* for a subject. The first was called low and bad, the other, noble and good, and this was offered as aesthetic criticism! It must be admitted that in the world of factual value carousing is less honorable and desirable than working for the freeing of mankind. In art there is a different world—Falstaff, Gargantua, Lady Macbeth, and many a night-mare shape from painting are among its immortals. The fact that the artist simulates feelings, moods, and values does not mean that he is dishonest, and that we remain unmoved. Through psychic empathy on his part and ours shadow shapes become enriched with new qualities and with recreated, revalued mean-ings for the imagination.

Here is where the economist, the Marxist, the humanitarian art critic go wrong. They fail to see that to carry art into the street, the factory, the slum and into the conflict of classes is one thing, and to carry these into art is quite a different thing. They impose on art an impossible spiritual and social burden. They censure the artist or decorate him with the order *pour le mérite*, for their work is supposed to be his. I remember a bit of Russian propaganda, conveyed by means of drawings em-bodying sound advice to the farmer. He was to bring his grain to the Soviet markets, avoid the profiteer, patronize community eating houses, steer clear of shady entertainers, sharps, and pimps to be found at public gatherings. In this case the propa-gandist happened to be a good artist. What sticks in the mem-ory is the quality of his line drawing, the all pervasive gusto and sympathy of his character sketches. Walt Disney's *Big Bad Wolf* comes to a bad end. The *Three Little Pigs* do not. A moral lesson? something in praise of cleverness? Perhaps. But what the artist has given and what we enjoy is a wolf, riotously alive and self-expressive, and three little pigs that are not merely good and innocent and clever—three little pigs of a rollicking imagination. Social-minded critics are so deadly in earnest, so dogmatic, so saturated with moral ideals. They mean to tear art from its world of semblance and expect it to be nothing but the turmoil, the stress, the aspirations, and the remedial measures of real life. But they cannot kill art.

Art may glorify God, but it is not above or below treating the Devil with loving kindness. Caliban, Iago, Falstaff as living persons would call forth disgust or fear or contempt. Art carries them beyond life into a realm where they have a reality given them by an expressive and sympathetic imagination. They are not measured by moral standards. To express evil or to share it emotionally in life is bad; to be just or unselfish is good. Clytemnestra was a very wicked woman, but in Aeschylus she is a great poetic figure. The moralist is right in distrusting imagination which runs over fair and foul alike, and of which a bad man often has more than the good man. He is wrong, however, in subjecting the artist to the test of limiting himself to the sterling qualities and substantial interests so highly prized in fact. The source of the error lies in not observing the psychic distance that marks all art. Design is one way of establishing that distance. When Tolstoy retold *King Lear* in bald prose and called it a silly play, he was guilty of foolishly dragging art across the line. Another is connected with the recreating and reinterpreting of the inner life. Anger, jealousy, grief, heroic courage, loyalty, deep religious feeling, as experienced in ourselves and observed in others, interest us in terms of cause, turmoil, and feared or hoped for result. But hate in Iago, jealousy in Othello, turmoil in Lear, courage in Hotspur are in their causes and effects mere semblance—psychic material within the form and spirit of fiction. We can, therefore, contemplate them in their essential quality. Is it not strange that joy and anger, which are directly experienced—who would laugh or scowl before a mirror?—are when projected into art and contemplatively enjoyed given visual form and new meaning? Is it not strange that moods, which are haunting and changing in their silences, are re-created for the ear in the tone structures of music? Mere sound is made to vibrate with psychic meanings.

The world of semblance has a splendor and a being of its own. It is ringed with barriers no heavy-footed moralist or actualist can safely pass. He may turn back and exclaim: "This is only a city of dreams." Its splendor, it is true, is, first, for the eye and the ear, but it is not, therefore, that of a soap bubble or a butterfly's wing. The city of art is also a city of the mind where everything human may find a new home and a new value.

We have swung back to our starting-point—to the artist, the philosopher, the public, and their lack of accord. Art has been interpreted as design, as reshaping outer and inner, as personal vision, as seeming or semblance. Society has always and will always seek to put art to its uses. Like everything else in life, art is a challenge to the thought-hunger of the philosopher and to the practical-mindedness of the public. As long as the philosopher is a mere theorist and as long as the public is sunk in actualities or swayed by ideals to be realized in living, there cannot on their part be an understanding of art. The artist, in turn, must not be "arty" and shallow—he must be aware that art is deeply, richly, and widely human, and that he is to hold with his designs something of the expressive varied semblance of the psychic life of man.

ATELEOLOGICAL THEORIES OF
AESTHETIC

MILTON C. NAHM

Department of Philosophy, Bryn Mawr College

THE significance of Aesthetic for the philosophical system of
Empirical Idealism is presented by Professor Singer in
Esthetic and the Rational Ideal, an enquiry proceeding from
an examination of the terms "art" and "beauty" to the fundamental problem of the import of the experience made possible
for us by the artist. Aesthetic, Professor Singer holds, "presupposes a rational ideal." The end of art is to be found neither
in discoveries in science, religion or morality nor in the estab-
lishment of novel philosophical systems. The artist, rather,
"creates the Creator." It is the "Creator" who fashions "a world
more rational, not a world more beautiful."

It is in the light of this hypothesis that man's artistic activity
and his experience of the products of that activity are given
their teleological significance. The artistic is no less indispensable than are man's scientific and moral efforts to the progress
which Professor Singer envisages as "the measure of man's co-
operation with man in the conquest of nature."

In establishing his view of the purpose of art, Professor
Singer examines and subjects to general criticism the diametri-
cally opposed ateleological interpretation of art and of beauty.
Ateleological aesthetic, however, has appeared in many forms
and it is of value to examine the cogency of the predominant
types developed in the history of theoretical aesthetic. In "Form
in Art,"[1] an initial analysis of the problem was made. In that
article, however, I was primarily intent upon an examination
of the difficulties inherent in the ateleological theories which
have their bases in analyses of "abstract" forms offered by Plato
and by Kant. In the present essay, I propose to examine the

[1] Published in *Art: A Bryn Mawr Symposium,* Bryn Mawr Notes and Mono-
graphs, IX.

validity of ateleological theories of "concrete" forms. To establish the position and to justify the terminology employed, it will be of value to recall certain views presented fully in the previous essay.

Not all ateleological theories of aesthetic are theories of form in art nor are all formal theories of art necessarily dissociated from the idea of an end. It may be argued, however, that the most cogent ateleological theories of aesthetic are dependent upon an analysis of form. The reasons for this dependence may be indicated by a brief reference to Plato's dialogue, *Hippias Major*. Plato, searching for the meaning of "beauty," treats "form" as "the something identical which makes them [i.e., particular beautiful objects] to be beautiful, this common quality which pertains to both in common and to each individually."[2] Plato is not content, however, to allow "form" to remain merely the proper means to the end of beauty nor is he content to leave unanswered the question whether or not this means is beautiful. An added connotation is given to the term "form" and it is one which has been widely retained in philosophical speculation upon beauty. This connotation is given in the definition of form as "the something of such art that it will never appear ugly anywhere to anybody."[3] Form, in this sense, is no longer merely the "common" nor is it simply a means to an end. Indeed, if that were its original status, the means has become beautiful. In effect, form has become the absolutely beautiful—absolute in the sense that its beauty is neither relative to nor dependent upon time, place, use, or personal taste.

Two consequences of this analysis are of interest: In the first place, it follows that all works of art, i.e., products of the maker's technique, which do not accord with the "form" are necessarily denied status in the aesthetic universe of discourse. This denial has resulted at one time or another in the exclusion from the aesthetic field of tragedy, comedy, representative or imitative art, and of distortion.[4] In the second place, it follows

---

[2] *Hippias Major*, 300 A.
[3] *Op. cit.*, 291 D.
[4] Cf. "Form in Art."

that once the beauty of the formal object is taken to be "absolute" and "not relative," art is defined ateleologically, i.e., without reference to purpose. There is introduced at this point into aesthetic a fundamental distinction* between the formal theory of art and those theories which attribute the aesthetic factor in the work of art to one of three possible relations of means to end. On the teleological hypothesis, the work of art is potentially definable in terms of a non-aesthetic end, an aesthetic end or some combination of non-aesthetic and aesthetic ends. Upon the ateleological or formal hypothesis, the work of art must have a certain delineation, shape, contour, sequence of parts, or it must accord with a certain ratio, proportion or dimension. It may be the best means to an end such as pleasure, exaltation, or rationality. Despite their divergences, all formal theories of the type described agree in this, that the objects are defined without reference to unique aesthetic purpose. They diverge in two ways: The form or the common may be mathematical or non-mathematical and it may be "abstract" i.e., non-sensuous or "concrete" i.e., sensuous.

Two important results of the analysis of "abstract" formal theories in "Form in Art" bear directly upon the development of the present problem of "concrete" form. It was shown, in that essay, that the "abstractness" of the objects selected by Plato and Kant as "absolutely beautiful" involves the treatment of "form" as if it were a term susceptible to complete separation from "matter," the very term which gives it significance. Granted that "form" and "matter" may be treated separately in the logical field, it is quite impossible to accept their separation in the empirical realm, in which objects are for us sensuous and productive of sensations in us. The theory of "abstract" form is and must be in aesthetic a characterization of a difference in the degree of the formal elements in relation to the non-formal elements. It may never be a characterization of a difference in kind.

It was further demonstrated that within the aesthetic systems of Plato and Kant, the most rigorous formalists in the history of the subject, "form" as the "common" is in reality the conception of unity. It may be held, therefore, that our present analysis may proceed upon the assumption that if there be absolutely beautiful forms, limiting the aesthetic universe of discourse and defined without reference to a unique aesthetic purpose, the theory which supports their validity must rest upon the proof that there are "concrete" or sensuous unities of this kind.

The theory of ateleological, concrete forms may be stated in the following manner: "Beautiful objects," both spatially and temporally considered, are limited to specific complex "varieties in unity" and their selection is governed by the principle of the subordination of the parts to the whole. Their beauty is taken to consist in their form i.e., in the complete unification of their parts in conformity to a mathematical principle or in the coherence of their parts on analogy to the coherence of the parts of a living being.[5] These forms are held to be beautiful without reference to specific aesthetic function or purpose, although they may in other connotations have ends or purposes i.e., as flowers, plants, or living men. No abstraction of sensuous or material elements is demanded and, consequently, the integration of the form may be produced by means of color, composition, or sound. One form is ordinarily taken to be the most beautiful and the principle accepted in explanation of its beauty is applied to the beauty of nature and art.

It has been a recurrent and, perhaps, natural development in aesthetic theory that, once form and unity are identified and there has been introduced into the conception of formal aesthetic the analogy in art and in nature of an organic unification, the hypothesis of sensuous or concrete forms should be developed largely with reference to the beauty of the most highly developed and evolved organism—man.[6] Again and again in the history and theory of art, the beauty of the human form has been taken to be the exemplar of the perfectly beautiful form. Find the *measure* applicable to the relation of the parts of the whole of the structure called "man" and the prob-

[5] The suggestion of an organic whole in art may be found in Plato's *Phaedrus* 264. It is amplified by Aristotle in *Poetics* viii 4. The unity attributed to the concrete whole is not one of homogeneous parts. The parts are, rather, "in a manner agreeable to each other and to the whole," as is suggested in *Gorgias* 504.

[6] Cf. Plato's *Timaeus* 30 *et seq.* and 44 D.

lems of beauty and of form are solved—or so the ateleological
theorists have held from the earliest times. Small wonder, indeed, that Dürer said that he would rather be shown what is
meant (by a canon of proportion) than behold a new kingdom.[7]
With the canon, we shall primarily be concerned, for it is in
the various attempts to secure its proper formulation that the
theory and practice of art meet to the degree most suitable for
the analysis of the general hypothesis of concrete form.[8]

A. The Ateleological "Concrete" Mathematical Hypothesis: Plato and the Canon of the Human Form.

Let us attend to the formulation of the ateleological theory
of sensuous form, undertaking the task in the light of a controversy reflected in Plato's Sophist. In the discussion of art in
that dialogue,[9] Plato divides imitative art into that of making
"likenesses" and that of "phantastic art or the art of making
appearances." The particular problem under discussion in the
dialogue follows upon an investigation of perspective in sculpture and painting. The contrast is drawn between "likeness-
making," in which there is produced "a copy which is executed
according to the proportions of the original" and "phantastic"
art "in works either of sculpture or of painting, which are of
any magnitude." In the latter art,

there is a certain degree of deception; for if artists were to give the
true proportions of their fair works, the upper part, which is farther
off, would appear to be out of proportion in comparison with the
lower, which is nearer.

The conclusion is reached that sculptors and painters who follow the "phantastic" mode "give up the truth in their images
and make only the proportions which appear to be beautiful,

[7] The Literary Remains of Albrecht Dürer, ed. Conway.

[8] Professor Rhys Carpenter, in discussion, indicated his general agreement with
the position maintained in the analysis of the canon, but suggested that the
practising artist used the canon as a "rule-of-thumb," a rule kept roughly in
mind to be followed in general and to be altered when necessary. There can
be little doubt of the truth of this contention. It may be pointed out, however,
that men like Vitruvius and Dürer specify certain theoretical problems and solutions in their treatment of the canon and, also, that once the empirical "rule-of-
thumb" is examined by theorists like Plato and Kant, it becomes the basis for
a formal principle of beauty.

[9] Sophist, 234-36, ed. Jowett.

disregarding the real ones." The suggestion has been made[10] that Plato believed that artists could display the truth by following a true canon of proportion. Schuhl[11] holds that Plato is expressing his adherence to one of the great traditional theories of the "most beautiful forms"—the Canon of Polycleitus[12] which is ordinarily supposed to have been incorporated in the *Doryphore*. This canon of proportions had been altered by the newer artists, Lysippos and Euphranor.

Plato's defense of the Polycleitean Canon is but one of the many enunciations men have made of their faith in the possibility of discovering the clue to "perfect beauty," i.e., to a beauty explicable through form alone with no reference to function. The search has not been limited to sculpture. The Platonic-Polycleitean tradition has found its way into the theory of architecture by way of writings as diverse as those of Vitruvius and Hambidge, among others, and into painting through theories proposed by Leonardo and Dürer.

[10] P. M. Schuhl, *Platon et l'Art de son Temps*, pp. 6 *et seq*.

[11] *Ibid*., pp. 8-9 *et seq*.

[12] Polycleitus' Canon, defended by implication by Plato, is neither the first nor the last of attempts of this nature. The earliest-known canon is the *Sanskrit Silpa Santra* in which the length of the hand is contained in the body seven and one half times. See B. C. A. Windle, *The Proportions of the Human Body*. The Egyptians, according to Diodorus Siculus, 1.98 (Cf. C. Blanc, *Grammaire des Arts du Dessins*, chap. 7) had developed a canon which was presumably so accurate that two sons of Thocus each working separately constructed by means of it a single statue which was integrated perfectly. However, although not the first, the Canon of Polycleitus is of particular importance not alone because of the quality of the sculpture produced in this period but because it is the beginning of a great tradition and one of the standards of comparison in classical times. See Schadow, *Polycleitos*, p. 11, particularly the quotations from Galen *De Temperencia*, 1.9: "Carvers, painters, sculptors, and artists in general, strive to paint and represent the most beautiful forms they can find, whether of human beings or animals. Such a form is exemplified by the 'Canon' of Polycleitus. The statue owed its name to the fact that its parts are of perfect proportion, and in harmony." Cf. Cicero, *De clar. orat.* c. 86. Concerning the practice of the artists, compare Eugene Guillaume, "Doryphore" in *Monuments de l'Art Antique*, p. 4; and R. Carpenter, "The Spirit of Classic Art," *Historical Aspects of the Fine Arts*, pp. 9-11. Of the context of the Canon there are some traces. Cf. C. Blanc, *op. cit.* chap. 7, quoting Galen, *De Hippocratis et Platonis decretis* (ed. Ven., 1563) liv. 5, p. 255: Pulchritudinem vero non in elementorum sed in membrorum congruentia, digiti vidilicet ad digitum, digitorumque omnium ad palmam et ad manus articulum, et horum ad cubitum, cubiti ad brachium, omnium denique ad omniam positam esse censet; perinde atque in Polycletis norma litteris conspicitur.

Dürer's faith[13] in the canon is but one instance of the belief that theorists may find by the science of mathematics the answer to the problem of an absolute beauty. But the most significant fact concerning the Canon was that its measures were disregarded in practice and that Plato was opposed to the very innovations which tended to alter the Polycleitean norm.[14] In Cicero's *Ad Brut.* (c.2), for example, there is the significant statement that

other artists did not allow the perfections of such statues as those of the Olympian Jupiter and the Doryphorus to discourage them from the attempt to produce something greater.

It is precisely against such innovations in practice as those introduced by Lysippos and Euphranor that Plato inveighs,[15] although the newer sculptors are merely displaying once again the empirical impossibility of a complete dependence upon a rigorous rule for the production of the absolutely beautiful form. This is shown by reference to Lysippos whose chief contributions to the art of sculpture Pliny[16] tells us were

in his vivid rendering of the hair, in making the heads smaller

[13] Despite his conviction that only God is beautiful and that the Fall of man resulted in the destruction of the "perfect form," Dürer retains faith that a geometrical demonstration of such beauty may be possible: "It seemeth to me impossible for a man to say that he can point out the best proportions for the human figure. . . . Howbeit, if a man can prove his theory by Geometry and manifest forth its fundamental truth, him must all the world believe, for one is so compelled." (*Op. cit.,* p. 245.)

[14] Cf. Guillaume, *op. cit.,* pp. 13-14: "Mais ce serait une erreur de croire que, tout en étant une règle par excellence, il fût considéré comme étant la règle absolue. La type qu'il formulait ne pouvait s'appliquer à tout. Les Grecs ne cherchaient point à établir une unité que eût été la ruine de l'art. Certes, ils étaient capables de concevoir l'absolu, mais la liberté leur était nécessaire, et ils ne pouvaient la sacrificier à aucune règle particulière, si parfaite qu'elle fût." See also, Carpenter, *op. cit.,* pp. 9-10: "Although some of our sculptors may have honestly believed that it was possible to find the one, single, and perfect embodiment of the naked beauty of our race and kind, a sort of unsurpassable formula for pose and proportion and muscular articulation, none the less I notice that even these sculptors sought their ideal by improving on their predecessors and not by merely copying and recopying a purely traditional standard and concept of perfection. Even if we believed that beauty could be reduced to its true forms and hence to formulas, still we never said that such formulas were inert, unchanging abstractions."

[15] Schuhl, *op. cit.,* p. 8.

[16] *The Elder Pliny's Chapters on the History of Art,* in the *Historia Naturalis,* trans. K. Jex-Blake. xxxiv. 65.

than older artists had done, and the bodies slimmer and with less flesh, thus increasing the apparent height of his figures. There is no word in Latin for the canon of symmetry which he was so careful to preserve, bringing innovations which had never been thought of before into the square canon of the older artists, and he often said that the difference between himself and them was that they represented men as they were, and he as they appeared to be.

Euphranor, too, while he first gave "heroes their full dignity, and mastered the theory of symmetry," ignored the canon. "He made the body, however, too slim and the head and limbs too large."[17]

Although actual practice of this kind does demonstrate that the artist ignores theory if theory is inadequate, there persists the hope for the production of a mathematical rule adequate to the expression of perfect beauty. What was desired by the proponents of the *Doryphore*, in Guillaume's words,[18] is perhaps the hope of all ateleological theorists whose proposed solutions to the problem recur:

. . . le Doryphore avait un intérèt plus considerable encore: c'est qu'il avait été pour ainsi dire, construit d'après une règle mathématique. Il constituait un système de proportions tel que l'on pouvait conclure des dimensions de l'une de ses parties aux dimensions de tout et réciproquement du tout à la mesure de la moindre de ses parties. C'est que les Grecs appelaient la symétrie.

If, however, the force of Plato's dialectical skill loses itself as it is directed to the practice of sculpture, the tradition he upheld sways the imaginations of later theorists by the very promise of the rigor which Vitruvius believed would offer the clue to the "perfect buildings" of the ancients and which Leonardo sought to ascertain in painting by the application of the "divine number." It will be of value to examine, even briefly, this tradition.

Vitruvius reverts to the Greek conception of the work of art as analogous to the unity of the organism.[19] This organic whole, he holds, may be analyzed mathematically. The source

17 Pliny, *op. cit.*, xxxv, 128.
18 *Op. cit.*, p. 7.
19 *De arch.*, Bk. iii, ch. 1, trans. M. H. Morgan.

of the "fundamental ideas of measure" are derived from the members of the body: "These they apportioned so as to form the perfect number."[20] The architectural standard is that based upon the proportions of "a well shaped man." The most important element, presumably, is that "The head from the chin to the crown is an eighth."[21]

This passage from Vitruvius' work Leonardo da Vinci quotes with approval[22] and in turn attempts to apply the canon to the art of painting: "The length of the hand," he writes, "is 1/3 of a braccio and this is found nine times in a man. And the face is the same and from the pit of the throat to the shoulder, and from the shoulder to the nipple, and from one nipple to the other, and from each nipple to the pit of the throat."[23] Leonardo's belief in the efficacy of the canon of the absolute beauty of the human form seems, on the whole, half-hearted. Richter[24] says that

the sketch (accompanying the measurements), as we see it, can hardly have been intended for anything more than an experimental attempt to ascertain relative proportions. . . . The proportions of this sketch are not in accord with the rules which he usually observed.

A very simple explanation of Leonardo's view is possible. It may be granted that the Italian's interest in science and mathematics led him to the assumption that a canon of this nature was possible. On the other hand, his skill as an artist must equally have convinced him that an irrevocable standard was impossible to attain and to maintain. It is clear that in practice two serious problems presented themselves to Leonardo. The first is noted by Schadow.[25] It concerns the fact that while

[20] *Op. cit.*, iii, 1, 5 and 9. Cf. Book i, 2.1. "Order gives due measure to the members of a work considered separately, and symmetrical agreement to the proportions of the whole. It is an adjustment according to quantity—by this I mean the selection of modules from the members of the work itself and, starting from the individual parts of the members, constructing the whole work to correspond."

[21] *Ibid.*, iii, 1.2.

[22] *Trattato della Pittura* (ed. J. P. Richter), Sect. 343.

[23] *Ibid.*, Sect. 309. Other proportions are given by Leonardo in the sections which follow in the *Trattato*.

[24] *Ibid.*, note to Sect. 313.

[25] *Op. cit.*

the dimensions of length may be determined, those of thickness and breadth cannot be so determined owing to the immense variety of nature (*immensa misteriosa natura*). The second difficulty is sufficiently clear from Leonardo's own words:[26]

These rules are of use only in correcting the figures;—but if you try to apply these rules in composition you will never make an end, and will produce confusion in your works.

More important, however, is the fact that Leonardo's theory is at fault. He suggests his problem as follows:[27]

therefore take a man of three braccia in height and measure him by the rule I will give you.

But, he adds, to meet criticism,

If you tell me that I may be mistaken, and judge a man to be well proportioned who does not conform to this division, I answer that you must look at many men of three braccia, and out of the larger number who are alike in their limbs *choose one of those who are most graceful and take your measurements.*

It is evident that Leonardo is using as a mere average the canon which Vitruvius thought to be a standard so absolute that it corresponded to ten, the "divine number." Moreover, Leonardo is not unambiguous with regard to the "measure." He holds that "Every part of the whole must be in proportion to the whole,"[28] and while he strives to interpret "whole" as the "whole" of the figure, it is evident that the proportions are also relative to the "whole," i.e., to the entire composition in which the figure appears, except in the case of a single statue in relief.[29] Of more importance is the fact that Leonardo is

[26] *Op. cit.*, Sect. 18.
[27] *Ibid.*, Sect. 309 (*italics mine*).
[28] *Ibid.*, Sect. 366: "*Every part of the whole must be in proportion to the whole.* Thus, if a man is of a stout short figure he will be the same in all his parts; that is with short and thick arms, wide thick hands, with short fingers with their joints of the same character, and so on with the rest. I would have the same thing understood as applying to all animals and plants; in diminishing (the various parts), do so in due proportion to the size, as also in enlarging."
[29] Cf., more particularly, Michelangelo's statement that "the artist must rely on his own eye as surest guide to correct proportion." Michelangelo actually painted some of the stooping figures in his compositions as much as twelve "heads" in height.

using a standard other than mere "measure." His selection involves at the outset only the choice of "many men of three braccia" in height. He later stipulates, however, that *in addition* the selection must be made of "those who are most graceful," i.e., most beautiful by reference to a factor over and above the physical measurements obtained by the application of the canon.[30]

Of the tale of Dürer's attempt to succeed in the task in which Leonardo fails, little need be said. Like Leonardo, Dürer was interested in Luca Pacioli's *De divina proportione* (Venice, 1549) and also, like da Vinci, he turned to Vitruvius for inspiration.[31] Of the Latin writer's theory, Dürer wrote that Vitruvius "has brought the human limbs together in a perfect proportion, in so satisfactory a manner that neither the ancients nor moderns are able to overthrow it." But the application of Vitruvius' theory is no less difficult for Dürer than for Leonardo. Despite the care exercised in his adaptation of the canon,[32] difficulties arise. He writes,[33] for example, that "no two figures have the same form; anyone who searcheth among men will find that out . . ." The painter attempted to derive the measures from groups but he soon abandons the method for that adopted by Leonardo:[34] "Further, in order that he may arrive at a good canon whereby to bring somewhat of beauty into our world, thereunto it were best for thee, it bethinks me, to form thy canon from many living men. Howbeit, seek only such men as are held beautiful and from such draw with diligence." Recognizing clearly his own failure to formulate a canon for the perfectly beautiful figure but accepting his defeat with a

[30] *Op. cit.*, Sect. 309.

[31] *The Literary Remains of Albrecht Dürer*, p. 165.

[32] Dürer proceeded on the hypothesis that the figure of a normal man is seven of his own heads in height. He divided the body into three principal lengths: from the neck to the hip, the hip to the knee, and the knee to the end of "shin bone" and suggested that the first length is to the second as the second is to the third. The details of Dürer's canon are given by T. W. G. Foat, "Anthropometry of Greek Statues," *Journal of Hellenic Society*, vol. 35, pp. 225-30.

[33] *Op. cit.*, p. 239.

[34] *Ibid.*, p. 246. Cf. p. 179.

liberality reminiscent of Plato, Dürer at last hands on the task of finding the perfect form to future artists:[35]

"Good" and "better" in respect of beauty are not easy to discern, for it would be quite possible to make two different figures, one stout the other thin, which should differ one from the other in every proportion, and yet we scarce might be able to judge which of the two excelled in beauty! What Beauty is I know not, though it dependeth upon many things. . . . I do not highly extoll the proportions which I here set down, albeit I do not believe them to be the worst. Moreover I do not lay them down as beyond improvement, but that thou mayest search out and discover some better method by their help.

A sufficient number of instances of the mathematical concrete ateleological "forms" have been given to indicate clearly the difficulties involved in finding "the most beautiful figure." For the most part, these difficulties have arisen from empirical sources. It is significant that both Leonardo and Dürer deviate from their own canon. It is equally significant that Vitruvius' canon is susceptible to empirical exception and that the writer on ancient buildings offers an unconscious refutation of his own attempt to derive a canon for the most beautiful form.[36] No canon has been evolved that has not undergone an alteration believed to be essential by practising artists. It may be argued, indeed, that this is no serious objection to the hypothesis, for it might be assumed that some artist-mathematician may evolve the perfect canon. A telling objection, however, has been found in the hypothesis that a perfect unity may be

[35] *Ibid.*, p. 179.
[36] D. S. Robinson, *Greek and Roman Architecture*, p. 149: "The subject of proportions is always difficult and elusive, but this temple [of Athena Polias at Priene] will illustrate the general character of 4th century and Hellenistic design. The architecture seems to have aimed at a proportion of length to breadth approximating to 2:1. It is mathematically impossible to produce a stylobate of exactly these proportions, without abandoning the principle of the equality of all intercolumniations but a peripteral scheme of 6 by 11 (in which the number of intercolumniations of the flank is double that on the fronts) gives one of the nearest possible approximations to this relation." Cf. pp. 156-57: "Some ancient architects have asserted that sacred buildings ought not to be constructed of the Doric order, because false and incongruous arrangements arise in the use of it. . . . It is not because this order wants beauty, antiquity (*genus*), or dignity for form, but because its detail is shackled and inconvenient from the arrangement of the tryglyphs."

evolved. It has been seen that the artists and theorists themselves have not derived the actual "beauty" of their art from the measures involved. Leonardo held, for example, that we must select a "well-shaped man" as our model. Clearly, the principle of beauty is a presupposition of the very instrument whose application was intended to reveal it.

It is evident, also, that the significance of the phrase, the "most beautiful form"—and here we may use the canon of the human form as an illustration—has not been defined with sufficient strictness. For the most part, the various canons have ignored variations of race, age, and occupation, as well as the differences in the proportions of male and female figures.[37]

It may be reiterated that these difficulties are not insuperable. It should be argued, rather, that they reveal a systematic problem basic to any attempt to discover an absolutely beautiful form or unity and to this systematic problem we may now turn. It is apparent that the canon of human beauty results from collections of the proportions of a large number of individuals of a given type, age, height, and race. It is apparent, also, that these proportions represent the *average* proportions of that group of individuals. There need be little doubt that the figures offered by Leonardo, for example, are accurate. There is, moreover, no doubt that a statistical average may be absolutely accurate. The probability is that the proportions agreeable to the greater number may be given exact expression. This probability is precisely the object of Vitruvius', Dürer's and Leonardo's search. But deviations from the average must be expected in the individual case, precisely as deviations in the individual case must be anticipated with respect to the accurate statistical death-rate. The unity sought by Polycleitus, the retention of which was demanded by Plato, and which was the object of interest among mathematically-inclined artists— this absolutely beautiful form is simply and solely the *norm*. The statement of such an average or *norm* can be given with exactitude in mathematical terms, i.e., in terms of measured probability.[38]

---

[37] Cf. Schadow, *op. cit.*, and Kant, *K. d. U.*, Sect. 17.
[38] Cf. Singer, *Mind as Behavior*, pp. 64-68.

The very factors which have often been taken to deny the exactitude demanded by the ateleologist are in reality support for the teleological hypothesis. The deviations from the *norm* which Vitruvius, Leonardo, and Dürer encountered are indicative of a rule holding for averages governing the beauty of human figures. Within these averages will be found the most pleasing form. What the earlier theorists expressed in somewhat inexact language or, rather, what may be inferred from their failure to discover one absolutely beautiful form may be stated precisely by reference to the more exact expression of formal theory in modern times by writers like Fechner and Hambidge.[39] In Hambidge's hypothesis of dynamic symmetry, for example, the task is undertaken to supply a principle to account for "some correlating principle which could give artists a control of areas." As such, the principle is opposed to "static symmetry or proportion." The primary requirement of dynamic symmetry has been concisely put by Carpenter.[40]

For the curvilinear area of a vase a simple rectangle is substituted. This is the containing rectangle, of which the sides are parallel to the vertical axis and the base-line of the vase. It is, as it were, the smallest rectangular frame into which the whole vase will fit. . . . If this rectangle can be split up into rectangles of similar and related shape and if these smaller rectangles can be used to determine recognizable elements of the vase, the occurrence of dynamic symmetry is held to be established.

The requirement is "that the whole rectangle may be completely subdivided into squares and rectangles similar to the original rectangle or of closely related shape."

The hypothesis of dynamic symmetry is propounded as the means by which the sculptor constructed his figures. It is implied not that this is a theory of aesthetic experience but that within this symmetrical arrangement will be found a beautiful form constructed on the principle of an organic whole. Upon examination, however, as Carpenter has carefully pointed out, the hypothesis of dynamic symmetry reduces to a reitera-

[39] See *Vorschule der Aesthetik* and *Dynamic Symmetry*.
[40] "Dynamic Symmetry: A Criticism," *American Journal of Archaeology*, 1921. Series 2, XXV, p. 19 *et seq.*, arranged.

tion of the ratio approximating 5:8 which "has in all ages been a recurring favorite in artistic composition and artistic design. It is the famous 'divine section' or '*Phi* proportion'—Somewhere in the neighborhood of that ratio man has an inveterate tendency to localize his sense for beauty of proportions."[41]

The most significant portion of Carpenter's statement is to be found in the words "in the neighborhood." Hambidge has given one more example of the artist's awareness that it is the "*phi* proportion" which experiment has indicated will produce the highest average reaction, as is shown by statistics formulated most clearly by Fechner. Hambidge has shown that the artist—probably unconsciously—constructs vases on the proportion 5:8, while Fechner has found that this proportion represents the probable *norm* of appreciation, based upon experiments involving large numbers of observers. Fechner, conducting the experiments with care to avoid idiosyncrasies of personal taste and taking his individuals from varied groups, secured an empirical test of the proportion for which most but not all of the individuals would express their preference. Deviation from the *norm* was not only expected but demanded.[42] Moreover, the statement that the preference falls in the neighborhood of the proportion 5:8 is a simple statement of fact. It is what happens under certain controlled conditions.[43]

It must be emphasized, however, that such norms or averages are mere descriptions of what happens and that, as descriptive, they offer no complete answer to the philosophical problem, the "why" this or that average proportion pleases or why

[41] *Op. cit.*, pp. 34-35.

[42] C. Birkhoff, *Aesthetic Measure*, p. 11: "Such aesthetic comparison of which the aesthetic measure M is the determining index, will have substantial meaning only when it represents the normal or average judgment of some selected groups of observers." Cf. p. 47.

[43] Something, however, must be added concerning the objects ordinarily subjected to the measurement. In the investigations by Hambidge and by Birkhoff, the measures are not limited to the actual object but in the case of vases, for example, include the spaces under the lip of the vase. Cf. Carpenter, *op. cit.*, p. 23. Hambidge presents us with "an orthogonal projection of the vase upon a single vertical plane." This involves the inclusion of "rectangular airspaces with others which overrun the edges of the vase." This tendency to include in the ratio elements that go beyond the aesthetic object is to be found in Vitruvius, as well as in the writings of modern ateleological theorists.

this or that rough average pleases more perceivers than does that of another group of objects basic to another set of figures. The philosophical analysis begins with the realization that such statistical averages are statements of measured probabilities. The probability, however, that a certain number of individuals will prefer a form of a given kind or proportion, with the proper compensation for deviation in the statistics, is not a description of the kind of automatic behavior implied by a Plato in his argument[44] that "pure pleasure" inevitably results from the perception of an absolutely beautiful object or by a Kant[45] in his intended proof that the forms which are the objects of the judgment of taste are universally beautiful because all men cognise and the faculties involved in the experience of beauty are basic to cognition. It is, rather, a description of teleological behavior, a statement that the artist in a given instance succeeds in constructing a work of art which produces an effect "for the most part" and for an average of individuals. But, as the ateleological, non-mathematical, and "concrete" hypothesis of form presents itself as an alternative to the mathematical, the most important point emerges. Form as unity may not constitute a strict limitation to the aesthetic universe of discourse. This follows because art objects are units or wholes which may be unified not by the identity or similarity of their parts but by reference to end or purpose. This may be shown briefly by reference to Kant and to the post-Kantian philosophers.

B. *The Ateleological, Non-mathematical "Concrete" Hypothesis: The Post-Kantian Interpretation.*

As has been shown ateleological aesthetic has selected frequently the human figure as the most perfect form, beautiful without reference to unique aesthetic function. But, as was also indicated, Kant who formulates a non-mathematical aesthetic, holds the human figure to be inadmissible as an object of the judgment of taste. The reasons offered are complicated by Kant's view that a judgment upon a work of art or a natural

---

[44] See *Philebus*, 51.
[45] *Op. cit.*, Sect. 9.

object of this kind would rest upon empirical and, therefore, a posteriori principles and would not be universally valid. The strongest criticism offered by Kant, however, of the factors basic to so many canons of perfect beauty is that "the stature of the beautiful man" is the average obtained by the imagination reconstructing a thousand separate individuals as one—the "form constituting the indispensable condition of all beauty, and thus merely correctness in the (mental) presentation of the race." Kant holds that the pleasure associated with such a presentation is a consequence not of taste but follows solely "because the presentation contradicts no condition under which alone a thing of this kind may be beautiful."[46]

Yet, the possibility that an ateleological, non-mathematical form, manifested in the human figure, may solve the aesthetic problem of beauty presents itself to the post-Kantian idealists in aesthetic. It is in one of the most profound of the philosophical treatments of art that the rejection of the possibility is found. Hegel finds that, in the evolution of the art-stages through which *"Geist"* proceeds dialectically and which he interprets to be its manifestations in concrete sensuous *Gestalt*, form and content are completely united for the first and only time in the history of art in the representation of the human body in the sculpture of the classical Greek period.[47] In sculpture, Hegel holds, the classical form of art has found "the free and adequate embodiment of the *idea* in the shape that, according to its conception, is peculiarly appropriate to the *Idea* itself."[48] It is in the artistic representation of the human form that the *Idea* thus manifests itself most integrally as form and content in art.

Such perfection and union, one might suppose in the light of the claims made for the Canon of the Human Figure, should represent the epitome of artistic endeavor in the achievement of the perfect form. But Hegel—and it is not alone for systematic reasons—sees that classical art, with its dependence

---

[46] *Op. cit.*, Sect. 17.

[47] "We must claim for sculpture, that it is in it that the inward and spiritual are first revealed in their eternal repose and essential self-completeness." *The Philosophy of Fine Art* (Bosanquet's trans.), Introduction, p. 199.

[48] *Ibid.*, p. 184.

upon the human body for its effect, is inadequate. Two reasons are offered for the inadequacy. In the first place, there is required too great a limitation upon the external manifestation or, in other words, upon the scope and extent of art itself. Secondly, there is required too great a limitation upon the spiritual content manifested in that shape.[49]

Hegel's hypothesis is that the human form, because of its "externality," "alone is capable of revealing the spiritual in sensuous guise."[50] From it, as the summation of *Idea* and technique, has been eradicated all that is accidental and incongruous. However, as Hegel says with reference to the gods who are manifested in classical sculpture,[51]

The seriousness of the gods becomes a grace, which does not agitate with violence or lift a man above his ordinary existence, but suffers him to persist there tranquil, and simply claims to bring him content.

Hegel implies that the profound feelings essential to the experience of art are not awakened by these lifeless forms. Thought is "dissatisfied in a reality which is no longer adequate to express it."[52] The movement, strength, and variety of the objective world force themselves upon the artist. Human emotion and thought demand expression and even the most perfect technique in sculpture cannot reveal them nor, by implication, can the form of the human body in its highest artistic exemplification display them. It is true that behind Hegel's assertion that the most beautiful form does not represent the highest stage of art lies the entire philosophical system and method which he employs. When Hegel, however, proceeds to accept into his aesthetic the work of the Dutch painters, the sublime and, by implication, the ludicrous, the comic, and the grotesque, there is seen the end of ateleological defining. No longer may art be limited by the search for an absolutely beautiful form

[49] *Ibid.*, p. 186. "The outer shape must be purified in order to express in itself a content adequate to itself; and, again, if the conformity of import and content is to be complete, the spiritual meaning which is the content must be of a particular kind."

[50] *Ibid.* (Osmaston's trans.), vol. 2, p. 177.

[51] *Ibid.*, p. 259.

[52] *Ibid.*, p. 260.

accompanied by the demand for the complete accord of all art objects with it. The primary characteristic of art may be unity, as the ateleologist insists. Certainly, the foremost contribution of ateleological aesthetic derives from its recognition of the necessity for unity and coherence in the object of art. Nevertheless, the arguments put forward by the ateleologist to demonstrate that unity is necessary are insufficient to prove that this necessary condition is also a sufficient one for the explanation of all of the *phenomena* of art and of the aesthetic experience.

It has been shown that both the non-mathematical theory of "concrete" form and the analogous mathematical formulation convert "form" into unity. It has also been argued that the ateleologist who maintains that the artistic universe of discourse may be limited to absolutely beautiful forms must hold that unity is both a necessary and a sufficient condition for beauty. Whether or not the universe of discourse called artistic or aesthetic may be limited to absolutely beautiful unities becomes the problem at issue. It is well to recall that the ateleological view rests upon the conversion of the "common" to the "absolutely beautiful." But the original search by the ateleologist for the "common" continues despite the interpretation of the term as the "absolutely beautiful." In consequence, an examination of the adequacy of "unity" as the "common" to serve as a strict limitation upon the aesthetic universe of discourse will make evident the fundamental ambiguity of ateleological and formal aesthetic.

"Forms" which owe their unity to the reiteration of a given "measure" or to a given proportion and "forms" which are unified by the relation of their parts to the whole upon analogy to an organism represent limited classes of unities. Variety may be unified not only by ratio or boundary,[53] by complex variations of ratios and proportions but also by the end or ends subserved by the object of art. The elements of a particular work of art may be bound together, indeed, by the repetition of a common "measure." This may not constitute a strict limitation upon the aesthetic universe of discourse, however, since the elements of a particular art-object may be bound together

[53] Cf. "Form in Art."

by their collective subsumption under one end. To call the "measure" beautiful or "absolutely beautiful" is a natural mistake of ateleological aesthetic. The parts of a work of art are beautiful only if the part of the particular work of art subsumed under an end is considered to be a whole in itself. Plato is a sounder aesthetician in his suggestion[54] that the eyes of the statue need not be painted a beautiful color because it is the beauty of the whole that is desired than he is in his attempt to limit painting and sculpture to measures of the canon or to deduce in *Philebus* the forms which he takes to be absolutely beautiful.

It is this ambiguity in the term "form" as it is interpreted to signify "unity" and as the ateleological hypotheses make evident, that has led theorists to assume that objects of art may be limited to those which display a common measure. It is evident, rather, that "unity" as a strict limitation upon art is not a tenable hypothesis. It is also evident that to use the term "form" as unity is merely to demand that coherence be a necessary presupposition to the aesthetic experience. Because of this ambiguity, the hypothesis that "an art-object must have a certain form; it may have a certain purpose," is untenable. The alternative hypothesis, "an art-object may have a certain form; it must serve a certain purpose," must be investigated. It may be said, further, that at the outset the teleological principle places no limitation upon the objects which may be found to serve the purpose which binds the diverse parts together.

Certain further consequences which follow from the analysis of "form" are of interest. As a statement that the diverse must be unified, no a priori limitation may be laid down for the conditions which will satisfy this requirement. Specifically, no demand may be made for unification in terms either of complex proportions derived from the relation of the parts to the whole of the human figure or in the coherence of the parts on analogy to the coherence of the parts of a living being. Nor may it be said that objects unified by either of these means are beautiful because of such unification.

Granted this, it follows that in terms solely of "form," all

[54] *Republic,* iv.

that may be said is that the object must be unified, whether in terms of proportion, organic integration, or of end. It may be held that the object may be distorted or irregular in proportion and that the elongated limbs of a figure by El Greco and the exaggerations of a statue by Epstein may be potentially beautiful for the same reason that the regularity of the lines of a Madonna by Raphael or the classical proportions of a Polycleitian statue may be beautiful. It may be said, furthermore, that art may be representative, imitative or symbolical since, on hypothesis, mathematical measure or proportion or non-mathematical coherence of parts on analogy to the organism occupy a status as unifying principles not one whit higher or more relevant than pedagogy, morality, perfection or desire as means to the end of the unification of art-objects. If these latter ends be inapplicable to the description of art, it must be because an unique end of art may be demonstrated and not because "form" delimits the universe of discourse.

It follows, from the analysis of "form" as a norm, that there are no absolutely beautiful objects.[55] Form is, in effect, the name for a problem. It indicates in its demand for unity the necessary condition for aesthetic experience. To that necessary condition must be added the sufficient condition or conditions for the aesthetic experience. That addition is to be found in the designation of the unique function of art.

[55] It follows, moreover, that there can be no universally valid judgment of taste if by that is implied an infallible and accurate predictability that a particular object will be judged to be beautiful. In aesthetic judgment and experience, there are not only errors of perception to be considered. There are periodic alterations in the taste commended in a given culture, in consequence of changes in religion, in morality, and in science recognized as desirable by the culture in which the art is judged. Moreover, taste seeks novelty, as well, and artistic usage "stales." The test of profound art is to be sought in recurrence of interest rather than in either unbroken uniformity of judgment or continuity of taste. But, ultimately, the judgment of taste is not universally valid because it is not describable in mechanical but, rather, in teleological terms.

THE EXPRESSION OF MEANINGS AND EMOTIONS IN MUSIC

MELVIN GILLISON RIGG

Department of Psychology,
Oklahoma Agricultural and Mechanical College

I

IN FORMULATING the rules for his ideal republic, Plato forbade the use of the Lydian and Ionian modes, since he believed them to be suggestive of sorrow and dissoluteness. On the other hand, the Dorian and the Phrygian modes were approved because they were thought to stand for courage and for temperance, respectively. Plato likewise sensed a moral difference in rhythms; a "good" rhythm typified the courageous and the harmonious, while a "bad" rhythm signified meanness, insolence, or fury.[1]

Plato is not alone in this assumption that music can suggest that which is beyond its immediate realm. It is almost universally assumed that a composition can express emotions, that it can be joyful or sorrowful, exciting or restful, that it can depict triumph or yearning. Many persons would go farther and claim that music can present definite meanings, that it can portray the spring, the early morning, a brook, a spinning wheel; or the composition may recount the various escapades of an outlaw, his apprehension, condemnation, and execution. Program commentators and music critics make their living by retailing such ideas, and so great is the trade demand that if the composer leaves no interpretation of his production, it is usually not long before one is invented.

Perhaps this desire to read non-musical significance into music is but one instance of a more widespread tendency of the fine arts to encroach upon each other. Such terms as tone in a picture, and color applied to music, while understandable

[1] *Republic,* Book iii.

as synonyms for intensity and timbre, seem to be evidence of this overlapping. As against the tendency, Lessing has stated in his *Laokoön* the conviction that poetry should not try to paint a picture nor painting to depict action. Should music become a party to a similar non-aggression pact?

But any effort to resist aggression must involve a delineation of exact boundaries. Just how far does the sphere of music properly go? To what extent is it possible for music to express meanings and emotions?

It is first necessary to note that a composition may occasionally imitate natural sounds. In his *Siegfried*, Wagner produces effects similar to the songs of birds; Strauss likewise, in *Don Quixote*, simulates the bleating of sheep by means of muted brass. Perhaps the most conspicuous example of all is Rimsky-Korsakoff's *Flight of the Bumblebee*, a clever bit of orchestration which is useful as an encore number to afford some relief to non-musical members of the audience.

Next may be considered the significance which comes as the result of association. Music enters readily into associative bonds. A piece which the writer practiced as a boy always suggests Egypt to him, since he was reading a book at the time dealing with that country, although the composition is, as a matter of fact, Polish, and has nothing Egyptian about it. Such a connection is an individual affair; this selection would not mean Egypt to anyone else. But in the case of other works, associations may be widespread in the popular mind, and if the traditional meaning is known, it is easy to feel the appropriateness of the musical setting. Mendelssohn's *Wedding March* arouses the thought of orange blossoms, and the *Star Spangled Banner* that of patriotism. We have never heard the music of the latter in its original form as a drinking song. Also we fancy that the *Moonlight Sonata* really depicts moonlight and that there is something swanlike in the familiar piece by Saint-Saëns.

Even more troublesome are the conventional meanings which have become attached to certain detailed features of music. Boats move traditionally in 6/8 time whether they be gondolas, sailing vessels, or canal boats; the *Barcarolle* from the *Tales of Hoffmann* is a familiar example. Horses are suggested by phrases in triplet rhythm, such as are found in the *Erlkönig*.[2] Even in Mendelssohn's *Elijah*, the horses which come down from above to carry the prophet to heaven, and are neither trotting nor galloping but *flying*, are revealed to us by these conventional triplets.[3] Since in these cases the association is not with the entire opus but with a detail only, this same characteristic occurring in a work entirely new to the listener may suggest its accustomed meaning, and may thus establish a conviction that the significance is intrinsic.

II

The composer is usually accorded a privileged position in the interpretation of his own works. If he announces that his symphony represents the restless striving of the human spirit against the decrees of Fate, then for any other musician to fail to find this meaning becomes a confession of musical insensitivity. It may be suspected that we have here a case analogous to that of the Emperor's clothes, no one daring to reveal that he does not see a non-existent significance.

The value of an experimental approach to this problem seems obvious. How accurately are the intended meanings of composers actually conveyed to listeners by the music alone? The present writer decided to ascertain what would be the results of such an investigation in his own classes.[4]

Eighteen Victrola records[5] were accordingly selected and

[2] In the symphonic poem *Phaëton* by Saint-Saëns, passages in triplet rhythm alternate with those containing a closely similar figure of two sixteenth notes and an eighth.

[3] I am indebted to my former teacher, Professor H. A. Clarke, for pointing out to me both of these conventions.

[4] Melvin G. Rigg, "An Experiment to Determine How Accurately College Students Can Interpret the Intended Meanings of Musical Compositions," *Journal of Experimental Psychology*, v. 21 (1937), pp. 223-29.

[5] These records were: *Siegfried's Funeral March* (from *Götterdämmerung*), Wagner; *Butterfly's Death Scene* (from *Madame Butterfly*), Puccini; *Swedish Cradle Song* (Victrola record No. 3004-B), folk song; *Elegy*, Massenet; *At Dawn* (from *William Tell Overture*), Rossini; *Adagio Lamentoso* (from *Symphonie Pathétique*), Tschaikowsky; *King's Prayer* (from *Lohengrin*), Wagner; *Garden Music* (from *Faust*), Gounod; *Turiddu's Farewell* (from *Cavalleria Rusticana*), Mascagni; *Fatal Stone* (from *Aida*), Verdi; *Moonlight*, Debussy; *Farewell* (from *La Bohême*), Puccini; *Elizabeth's Prayer* (from *Tannhäuser*), Wagner; *Good Friday Music* (from *Parsifal*), Wagner; *Death of Boris* (from *Boris Godounow*), Moussorgsky; *Omphale's Spinning Wheel*, Saint-Saëns; *Serenade* (from *Don Giovanni*), Mozart; *Death and Transfiguration*, Richard Strauss.

played to seventy-four college students. The records were heard at two different sittings to avoid fatigue. Each auditor was provided with the following outline for his guidance:

I. Sorrowful, serious, religious, etc.
    A. Death
        1. Death scene
        2. Funeral march
        3. Elegy
    B. Sorrow
        4. Sorrow in general
        5. Farewell
    C. Religion
        6. Good Friday music
        7. Prayer
II. Joyful (love, activity, nature, etc.)
    D. Love
        8. Love song
        9. Serenade
    E. Activity
        10. Spinning song
        11. Cradle song
        12. Dance
    F. Nature
        13. Morning
        14. Moonlight[6]

The auditors were asked to judge first whether the music was predominantly sad-serious or joyful, and they entered either I or II on the blanks provided. Then they were to try to make a more accurate judgment and tell whether the piece portrayed death, sorrow, religion, love, activity, or nature. This they did by entering on their reports one of the capital letters from A to F. After that a still finer discrimination was to be attempted and the students were to indicate whether the composition represented a death scene, a funeral march, an elegy, etc., by using the Arabic numerals from 1 to 14.

In any such experiment it is of course necessary that the titles or traditional meanings of the selections be unknown to the

[6] This outline was made to accommodate the actual selections that were used; it is not designed as a universal system of classification for music.

persons serving as judges. The observers were consequently asked for each item if they had heard the composition before, and if so, what was the name of it. Most of the music was not recognized, and in only one per cent of the cases could the name be given correctly. When a student knew the title, his reply to this item was not counted in the data. Occasionally a word or two of the songs would be discriminated, but most of the vocal numbers were in foreign languages, and the one which was in English was sung by a foreigner, so this source of error was not extensive. The student was asked, when he heard a significant word, to record the fact, and his response to this number was likewise left out of the tabulation.

The results of the experiment were that 73 per cent of the time the auditors could tell whether the music was intended to be sad or joyful; 41 per cent of the time could further classify the pieces into the categories death, sorrow, religion, love, activity, and nature. Only 25 per cent of the time could they make the still finer classification as indicated on the outline. The percentages are in each case better than chance, but in only the first discrimination is there a majority of responses for the right category.

There was naturally a great variability among the different compositions. In the third or finest discrimination the *Swedish Cradle Song* was correctly classified by 64 per cent of the group, the *Garden Music* from *Faust* by 56 per cent (perhaps because it is a duet for soprano and tenor), *Omphale's Spinning Wheel* by 50 per cent (probably because of the rhythm), and the *Serenade* from *Don Giovanni* by 38 per cent (possibly because of the characteristic accompaniment). Strauss' *Death and Transfiguration* was correctly placed by 36 per cent and called a funeral march by another 34 per cent.

On the other hand, Massenet's *Elegy* was considered to be a love song or a serenade. If grief was intended to be represented, the attempt was not in this case successful. *At Dawn,* a portion of the *William Tell Overture,* was by more than half of the judges regarded as expressing some sort of sorrow. Twenty persons (28 per cent) identified the *King's Prayer* from *Lohengrin* as a prayer, but nineteen others (26 per cent) thought it was a serenade. *The Farewell* from *La Bohême* was put down by almost half of the auditors as a love song; the sorrow of the selection was not recognized. In the case of the *Good Friday Music* from *Parsifal*, 18 per cent of the listeners thought it a serenade; only 15 per cent said that it was religious and only 7 per cent classified it as Good Friday music. This latter figure represents merely the chance distribution.

In spite of the instances of correct placement, the percentage of success for the experiment as a whole seems low, especially in view of the fact that the students were supplied with outlines which gave them a clear idea of what was coming. It might be too much to expect anybody hearing music at random suddenly to realize that a selection would be appropriate, let us say, for Good Friday. But when the category "Good Friday music" is one of the fourteen terms of an outline, the small number of correct responses appears as a more serious failure.

The question as to the influence of training upon any sort of musical judgment is a constant one, and in this instance an answer was sought by dividing the listeners into three groups on the basis of their education in music. The high and low groups were then compared, and it appeared that those with the most training could make correct placements (in accordance with the composer's intention) only slightly oftener than those with the least training. In the first discrimination, for instance, the highly trained group had a percentage of 75 against a percentage of 71 for the relatively untrained group. This difference is too small to be reliable,[7] and it seems doubtful if training makes any practical difference in the ability to judge the emotional significance of a selection.[8]

The negative results of the experiment are surprising to many persons. The objection has been made that the observers

[7] The ratio of the difference to its own standard error is .33, which means that if the experiment were repeated 100 times we could expect the slightly trained group to excel the highly trained group in 37 instances.

[8] This result is in agreement with a similar conclusion announced by Hevner to the effect that trained musicians are able to judge the emotional significance of the major and minor modes only slightly better than untrained observers. Kate Hevner, "The Affective Character of the Major and Minor Modes in Music," *American Journal of Psychology*, v. 47 (1935), pp. 103-18.

must have been insensitive to music. It is true that they were not conservatory students, but they were enrolled in a college which is superior to the average for American institutions of learning; moreover, some of them had studied music for many years. It is consequently hard to escape the conclusion that the intentions of composers usually do not "get over" in any specific way to the cultured strata of our population.

III

Several of those who communicated with the writer with reference to the experiment just described have maintained the position that at least the more general moods may inhere in compositions. Perhaps the *Moonlight Sonata* does not necessarily suggest moonlight, but it is more appropriate for moonlight than such a piece as the *Stars and Stripes Forever*. After learning what the intention of the composer was, it is often possible to realize that the mood is suitable, although the meaning could not have been conveyed by the music alone.[9]

Undoubtedly the problem is not an all-or-none proposition; it is a question of how much and in what directions, and the next step would seem to be one of analysis. Some of the difficulty of judging a work occurs from the fact that it may not be in the same mood throughout. Strauss' *Death and Transfiguration*, for instance, contains a theme in marked contrast to the rest of the composition. But even if attention is centered on a single phrase, just what features of this phrase account for its emotional significance?

An elaborate attempt to analyze music with the purpose of identifying such characteristics has been made by Erich Sorantin.[10] After a study of numerous works in which the intentions of the composer were evident from text or title or were otherwise known, he has selected certain features as being symptomatic of five different emotions, as follows:

[9] This is what the writer understands to be the view of Mr. Deems Taylor, who discussed this experiment on his New York Philharmonic broadcasts for February 20 and February 27, 1938.

[10] Erich Sorantin, *The Problem of Musical Expression,* Nashville, Marshall and Bruce, 1932.

Lamentation	*Joy*
slow tempo	accelerated tempo
descending minor seconds in melody	ascending fourths in melody
minor mode	major mode
legato phrasing	staccato notes
trochaic rhythm	iambic or anapaestic rhythm
dissonance	simple harmony
low register	forte dynamics

Sorrowful Longing	*Hopeful Longing*
melodic intervals and chords of seventh or ninth combined with features of lamentation	melodic intervals and chords of seventh or ninth combined with features of joy

Love

dolciata S curve melody[11]
thirds and sixths in treble
major mode
moderate tempo
legato phrasing
melodic intervals and chords of seventh or ninth

Sorantin has presented no experimental proof that persons who hear the above musical patterns actually sense these emotional qualities. The present writer, in an attempt to supply such evidence, has performed five additional experiments, in all of which short musical phrases were played to auditors, who recorded their impressions of each passage. The number of judges varied in the experiments from 84 to 105. These were for the most part college students, who naturally possessed varying degrees of musical training. The five experiments were concerned with 129 different phrases and involved 15,739 separate judgments.

The first experiment[12] was concerned chiefly with examples from the literature of music selected by Sorantin to illustrate his theories. However, some of the phrases were made to order

---

[11] A dolciata S curve melody is one having an upward and downward oscillation.
[12] Melvin G. Rigg, "Musical Expression: An Investigation of the Theories of Erich Sorantin," *Journal of Experimental Psychology,* v. 21 (1937), pp. 442-55.

by the present writer by a process of putting into them every-thing that was called for by one of the patterns and of exclud-ing everything else. This experiment seemed to show that Sorantin's theories for lamentation and joy are well substan-tiated, but that the theories for sorrowful longing, hopeful longing, and love are less certain. Strangely enough, the phrases written for the experiment confirmed the theories better than did the passages selected from the classics. This outcome does not mean that these original phrases are better music, but evidently results from their custom-built method of composi-tion.

The chief limitation of the experiment was that it merely tested Sorantin's theory for each pattern as a whole. If a phrase combined all of the lamentation characteristics, descending minor seconds, minor mode, dissonance, etc., the data showed that it did actually suggest lamentation. But there was no evi-dence as to which of these features were the most important; indeed some of them might have had no effect at all, or might possibly have exerted an influence which weakened the total emotional significance of the phrase. The next step in the research was to determine the influence of the several char-acteristics, both individually and in various partial combina-tions.

The four subsequent experiments[13] all involved variations of the same five phrases, which are identical with (or closely similar to) original phrases used in the first experiment. The second in the series of investigations is called the Single Varia-tion Experiment, since each additional phrase was modified from its original in one feature only. For instance, the original phrase designated as A-1 embodies the seven lamentation char-acteristics previously enumerated. Each additional phrase em-bodies a modification of one of these seven features, the other six remaining the same. The third investigation is called the

[13] Experiments II and III have been published jointly. M. G. Rigg, "What Features of a Musical Phrase Have Emotional Suggestiveness?", *Publications of the Social Science Research Council of the Oklahoma A. & M. College*, No. 1, 1939. Experiment IV was published as, "Speed as a Determiner of Musical Mood," *Journal of Experimental Psychology*, v. 27 (1940), pp. 566-71. Experiment V ap-peared as, "The Effect of Register and Tonality upon Musical Mood," *Journal of Musicology*, v. 2 (1940), pp. 49-61.

Cumulative Experiment. The phrase A-11, for example, differs from A-1 in two features (it has no dissonance and possesses ascending seconds). The phrase A-12 differs from A-1 in these two respects and also in one other characteristic, and each subsequent phrase varies in one additional feature until all seven of the characteristics of A-1 have been contradicted. The fourth research is the Tempo Experiment, each of the five original phrases being played at six different metronome speeds. Experiment V was concerned with register and tonality; each of the phrases being shifted (1) either up or down an octave, (2) either up a fifth or down a fourth to the key of the dominant, (3) up one half-step, (4) down one full step.

In Experiments II to V the auditors were assisted in making their judgments by the same check list. This is a matter of importance, since to a certain extent replies are determined by the categories the list contains. From Experiment I it appeared that the most valid discrimination is between the happy and the sad. Consequently the students were first asked whether the phrase was primarily sad-serious, designated as X, or pleasant-happy, designated as Y. After this judgment the observers were to attempt a finer discrimination by classifying the phrase under subheadings. The complete outline is as follows:

X Serious-sad	Y Pleasant-happy
1. Solemnity	6. Hopeful longing
2. Sorrowful longing	7. Love
3. Melancholy	8. Revery
4. Lamentation	9. Gaiety
5. Agitation	10. Joy
	11. Triumph

These terms were chosen with two purposes in mind: (1) to include all the categories used by Sorantin so that his theories might have ample opportunity to prove themselves; (2) to include certain other terms suggested by the participants of a preliminary tryout. It was explained to the auditors that for these experiments melancholy meant something less intensely sad than lamentation, while gaiety was less intense than joy.

The five experiments showed in their results a consistency which was beyond expectation. Some of the conclusions are summarized:

The most important feature, in so far as emotional suggestiveness is concerned, appears to be tempo. Fast tempo weakens the effect of lamentation; a phrase which when played at ♩ = 60 meant lamentation to 55 persons, suggested this emotion to only 12 persons when played at ♩ = 108. Slow tempo destroys the joy-effect; a different phrase, suggesting joy to 49 judges when played at ♩ = 160, attracted only 8 responses for this category when played at ♩ = 72. So important did this finding appear in Experiments II and III that Experiment IV was devoted to tempo alone. The five original phrases, two of which had been established as sad and three as happy by the previous investigations, were played, each at six different metronome speeds. The general rule was found to hold that an increase of speed meant progress along the dimension from sadness to happiness. Sometimes the evidence was in the sub-headings, changes in the number of choices for lamentation or joy, but for the most part it was clearly registered in the shifts of the X and Y responses.[14] The different features are of course interdependent and the emotional quality of the phrase is the result of the total pattern. Fast tempo may weaken the lamentation effect, but it is not enough by itself always to make a phrase happy. In the case previously cited where the lamentation replies went down from 55 to 12, nevertheless the responses remained overwhelmingly on the X side of the outline.

Staccato notes also furnish a good example of this interdependence of factors. Introduced into a phrase containing characteristics of sorrow, the staccato notes suggest agitation; embodied in another phrase devoid of sorrow features, the staccato notes make it happier and tend to suggest gaiety.

The major mode has an influence away from lamentation and in the direction of the Y side of the outline, but is not enough by itself always to make the phrase happy. On the other

[14] The only partial exception to this result was that for the phrase C-1, somewhat sorrowful in character, there was no significant change between two adjacent slow speeds (♩ = 60 and ♩ = 80).

hand the minor mode has a tendency away from joy and in the direction of the X side of the outline, but is not enough by itself always to make a passage sad. Mode is on the whole not so important as tempo.

Changes in register were found to be very important, a shift up producing results in the direction of joy, while a shift down made the phrase sadder. If the difference was as 'much as an octave, this rule held without exception. Changes of approximately half an octave, transpositions up a fifth or down a fourth to the key of the dominant, produced results somewhat less consistent; out of ten instances the rule held in eight cases and the variations in response were usually slight. The effect of joy was also enhanced by a trill at high register, but in this case the speed of the trill was no doubt an important additional influence.

However, for many details of the Sorantin theory no evidence could be found. One of the features of lamentation was supposed to consist of *descending* minor seconds, but it apparently made little difference whether these seconds went up or down. Joy is supposedly suggested by *ascending* fourths, but descending fourths seemed to produce about the same results. Longing and love were both associated in the theory with intervals and chords of the seventh, but when these were omitted, the results were not materially changed. The thirds and sixths in the treble and the dolciata S curve melody, both features of love according to the theory, likewise seemed to have little significance.

With regard to another matter, not a.part of the Sorantin theory, the evidence was also negative. Musicians have attached enormous importance to the matter of tonality. The different keys have been assigned distinctive characters, so that the selection of a key for a new composition is regarded as requiring a fine perception of fitness. In Experiment V, by transposing the phrases down one step or up one half-step, large changes in tonality were produced, although the changes in register were slight. There were ten such shifts in the fifth experiment, and in eight instances no changes of any consequence in the distribution of replies could be observed.[15] Therefore, this investigation lends no support to the view that different keys possess peculiar qualities.

IV

But to return to the positive results: there are certain characteristics of music which really seem to suggest sadness, joy, agitation, and perhaps triumph. The most important features appear to be tempo, staccato notes, mode, and register.[16] How may these results be interpreted?

In the first place, to what does the emotional quality belong? It is a common experience to realize that the mood of the music is different from one's own. "That is happy music," you may say, "but I am not happy, and it irritates me." Is the emotional quality then in the music? There would be many who would hesitate to accept the metaphysical implications of this position. "Joy and sorrow, agitation, and triumph, these," they would say, "are conscious states and can inhere only in a sentient being." And such persons could probably construct for themselves a satisfactory theory based upon the principles of association and empathy. Through long experience, they would claim, we have connected some features of music with joy and others with sorrow, and in certain ways we reinforce these connections by putting ourselves into the music.

Perhaps the joy-picture is illustrated by the little child bubbling over with the exhilaration of living and apparently possessing boundless energy. He jumps and skips with the eager spontaneity of all young animals. We have thus come to think of rapid tempo as one of the features in the pattern for happiness. Our connection of high register with joy may be similarly explained, since laughter and shouts of merriment

[15] In the other two instances the results were as follows: One change from C major to B flat major produced a 17 per cent loss for joy and a 12 per cent gain for gaiety. The other change from F minor to E flat minor brought about a 19 per cent shift from melancholy to sorrowful longing. None of these shifts is *statistically* significant in the sense of having a critical ratio of 3, although in one case the ratio is 2.9. In view of the inconsequential results from the other eight instances, it is questionable whether any conclusion can be drawn from these two cases.

[16] These lists are not of course exhaustive. They are merely the results of the present series of experiments.

make use of the higher degrees of pitch.[17] The sorrow pattern is on the other hand that of restraint, with actions slow or forced; we may visualize an old man sitting dejectedly and occasionally uttering low moans of despair. And since it is desirable to get away from the conventional and to approach the natural, can not additional confirmation be secured from the actions of animals? Sigmund Spaeth has told the writer that hounds start to bark in a higher pitch when they have picked up the scent of the fox. The happy dog also frisks around at a lively rate, barking excitedly, while the dejected dog slinks away, tail between legs, and his inquiring whine is in a lower register. A similar contrast may be observed between a patient in the manic phase of manic-depressive insanity, who jigs and sings, and the same patient in a later depressed phase, sitting in a drooped position and moaning.[18]

It should be remembered that the effect of any feature is varied by the influence of other features which may be present. There is no implication that all emotions involving rapid rate or high pitch are pleasant in character. The writer found that a sad phrase played fast, while it became less sorrowful, tended to suggest agitation. Perhaps hysterical grief is to be viewed as sorrow plus agitation. Recent research has also indicated that fear and anger as expressed by actors in speech are both characterized by high pitches.[19] Since these categories were included only in the check list used in Experiment I, no evidence of any value with regard to these points has been collected by the present writer.

Staccato notes introduced into a sad passage may well remind us of the quick, jerking movements of agitation; in a happier setting the staccato notes may suggest laughter or dancing.

The features of speed, pitch, and staccato notes also undoubtedly depend for their effects upon empathy as well as association. Some persons will tap out a lively tune, humming

[17] There may also be another explanation in the fact that the higher pitches involve more rapid vibration rates. Thus register may ultimately be reducible to speed.

[18] Low, rumbling thunder also seems sad to certain persons, perhaps because it has been associated with gloomy days.

[19] Grant Fairbanks and Wilbert Pronovost, "Vocal Pitch during Simulated Emotion," *Science*, October 21, 1938, v. 88, No. 2286, pp. 382-83.

the melody. Many others will feel the impulse to move at a rapid pace, and to hum subvocally. Perhaps the reason why happy music seems so irritating in moments of depression is simply that we feel impelled to make these joyful movements, which are in conflict with our prevailing mood.

But why does the major mode suggest joy and the minor mode sorrow? The major triad is a combination of a major third and a minor third, with the major third below. The minor triad is the same combination with the major third above. Or if only the major and minor *thirds* are considered, instead of the complete triads, why do two notes whose frequencies have the ratio 4:5 suggest joy, while two other notes with the ratio 5:6 suggest sorrow? It is true that the major third is slightly more consonant than the minor third, and slightly more agreeable, as determined by laboratory experimentation, but the differences are hardly great enough to account for the divergence in emotional effect.

Some persons hear the howling winter wind in a minor key. It is perhaps actually nearer to the chromatic scale than to the minor; however, most persons would say that the chromatic scale is closer to the minor than to the major. It has also been claimed that wolves howl in minor, and so for both these reasons the minor mode may have been connected with loneliness and the unpleasant.

It has, however, been suggested that our interpretation of the minor mode is a mere convention. Heinlein[20] determined that only 7 per cent of pieces for beginners are in minor; consequently these are set off in the child's mind as something abnormal. Most of these, moreover, were found to have descriptive titles suggesting the weird or the gloomy. An explanation for this convention may be that the somber qualities of the words sung to the old ecclesiastical modes have left their stamp upon the minor keys, which to a certain extent resemble them.

However these explanations may be regarded, it appears from the experimental evidence that music can portray at least

[20] C. P. Heinlein, "The Affective Character of the Major and Minor Modes in Music," *Journal of Comparative Psychology*, v. 8 (1928), pp. 101-42.

the emotions of joy, sorrow, agitation, and perhaps triumph. No doubt additional evidence will reveal other similar emotions which belong with these four. But the attempt to go beyond this general area places the matter on extremely uncertain ground. Music, it is here contended, can portray general moods, but not definite ideas. The writer would be inclined to agree with an extension of Lessing's position, and hold that music should try neither to paint a scene nor to tell a story. A composition may be lacking in vigor and convey a certain indistinctness, but does it represent moonlight? Another selection may have something in the nature of a "sweeping dignity" perhaps, but does it suggest a swan moving down a river? As a matter of fact, the mood of a piece may be appropriate to a great many different situations; it may be impossible to tell whether the intention is to represent the rustle of spring, the maiden's dream of love, or a state of religious ecstasy.

This viewpoint does not condemn the employment of music as an accompaniment or setting, and used in this way it may reinforce the various emotions presented. A happy poem should have a happy musical setting; for a tense moment in the opera the music should be agitated or "stormy." But the ideas of the poem or the story of the opera, we should obtain, not from the music, but from the words.

Is it not true that persons for whom a wealth of non-musical interpretation seems essential are those who find it difficult to understand music *as* music, and are thus impelled to seek beyond its confines that significance which within it they can not find?

IV

HISTORY

ΦΑΝΤΑΣΙΑ IN PLOTINUS

Gordon H. Clark

Department of Philosophy, Wheaton College, Illinois

THE high metaphysical topics of the One, the Divine Mind, and the Soul; the perennially interesting religious problem of mysticism; and such broad subjects as the origin of evil or the nature of beauty are those which, naturally, have received the greatest attention in the study of Plotinus. The value of a man's thought, however, can often, and often better, be measured by his application of the general principles to questions of detail. Here is undertaken an examination of the detail, *imagination.*

The first section of this article is an Introduction, consisting of a brief historical paragraph and a survey of Plotinus' usage; the second section is an annotated translation of the most important chapters; and the third is an index.

Because of the paucity of references and the lack of developed theory, Plato can hardly be considered to have inaugurated the study of imagination or representation. In the *Sophist* 263D–264B he discusses thought, opinion, and representation. After practically identifying the first two, he describes representation as the condition of thinking when sensation is its cause. Representation, therefore, is a mixture of sensation and opinion.[1] So far as the word itself is concerned, Plato does not go far beyond colloquial usage.

Aristotle takes pains to indicate that with him imagination will have a new meaning; and this is natural because, when Platonic reminiscence is replaced by Aristotelian abstraction, representation in the form of imagination becomes technically important. Freudenthal has admirably studied the Aristotelian theory. But it is to be noted that even in Aristotle the word has also the wider uses of sense presentation and of thoughts of intellectual objects.[2]

---

[1] Cf. *Tim.* 52A; *Theaet.* 193B, 195D; *Philebus* 38B–39C.
[2] Cf. Bonitz, *Index Aristotelicus, sub voce.* Also Hicks, *Aristotle De Anima,* p. 460.

The materialism and the empiricism of the Stoics obviously require a strict interpretation of representation, seeing that one type, the comprehensive, is the criterion of truth. Yet not all representations are sensible and come through a sense organ; some are rational, as for example, the representations of incorporeals.[3] In fact a proposition may be called a representation. Thus we see that the history of the word before the time of Plotinus does not force a limitation of its significance either to memory-image, since it may occur during sensation, or to any image strictly speaking, since there are representations of non-sensible objects.

When one comes to study Plotinus, who, by the way, does not discuss the subject separately but is involved in it mainly because of the discussion of memory, not only does colloquial usage produce a range of meaning not easily gathered into a single formula, but, further, Plotinus' metaphysics prevents the drawing of any hard and fast line between imagination and the activities above and below it. Unlike Aristotle with his clean-cut distinctions, Plotinus merges each faculty with the next; and while the notion of faculty is frequently found, and while there is an apparent tendency to hypostatize each function into a separate little spirit, the faculty psychology is perhaps farther removed from his system than from that of Aristotle. In fact, it seems that Plotinus had to defend, against the questioning of the more traditional Academicians, his allegiance to the Plato who so sharply separated sensation from reason. But, however he may have satisfied the Platonists, the levels of consciousness are in reality more like the continuity of an inclined plane than the discrete steps which Aristotle's theory suggests.

To develop the subject a survey will be made of the various meanings which Plotinus gives to this word, imagination.

False notions, particularly the false notion that bodily beauty and musical ability contribute to happiness, are representations or imaginations.[4] Again, some passions are the result of opinions, as when the opinion that death is imminent causes one to be fearful. "Now imagination takes place in the soul, both the former,

---

[3] Arnim, *Stoicorum Veterum Fragmenta*, II No. 61, p. 24, 1, 15; and No. 65, p. 25, 1, 15 ff.

[4] I i 9, 8; I iv 15, 12. (The number after the comma is always the line in Bréhier, *Plotin Ennéades*.)

which we call opinion, and also (the latter), its derivative (fear)
which is no longer an opinion but something like a vague opinion
or uncritical representation occurring in the lower part of the
soul."[5] Not only are sense objects, such as the sun and the stars,
objects of representation or imagination, but even the Good itself
is capable of being imagined or represented.[6]

Thus, it is seen that with respect to merely literary usage the
range of objects falling under the power of representation is very
wide and cannot be restricted to sense image or memory image,
but includes emotions, universals, and judgments.

There is in the *Enneads* no formal definition of imagination, but
one passage stands out as more explicit than the others, and besides leads on to other considerations which advance the study.
In discussing the freedom from evil of the soul which is not in
contact with something inferior to her station, the question, not
only of desire, fear, and anger, but of representation also arises.
Representation or imagination is then denied to the pure soul on
the ground that "imagination is an impact from an irrational,
external object, and (the soul) receives the impact when it is not
indivisible."[7]

This phraseology, apart from the whole Plotinic background,
may seem to resemble and to be based upon Stoic materialism.
But Plotinus frequently enough guards against, not only Stoic
materialism, but also the materialistic or behavioristic traces in
Aristotle. In addition to the general refutation of these two schools
in IV vii, a more particularized account occurs in III vi 1–3.
Toward the end of a discussion defending the impassibility of the
soul, he asserts that while the soul causes fear, shame, and blushes,
it is the body and not the soul which experiences these effects.
Then, in a summary which both Heinemann and Bréhier believe
that Porphyry added, but which in any event is thoroughly Plotinic, imagination is explicitly mentioned. "Imaginations are not
like imprints (of seals) in wax."[8] The notion of an imprint is again
rejected in IV vi 1. Sensations, he says here, are not imprints, and
consequently memory cannot depend on the conservation of im-

[5] III vi 4, 18–21.
[6] V viii 9, 5; VI viii 13, 46.
[7] I viii 15, 18.
[8] III vi 3, 30.

prints. The remainder of the passage makes the matter perfectly clear. In seeing we grasp an object at a distance. Whatever impression there may be occurs, not in our soul, but at the place in which the object seen is.[9] If there were an image in the soul, how could the soul assign a distance to the object? It could not see as separated from itself what actually was in it. Again, the soul recognizes the dimensions of the object seen; but if seeing took place by means of imprints in the soul, how could the extent of a very large object be recognized? And there is the further objection, the most fundamental of all, because it is essential to a realistic epistemology: if we can see only imprints or images, then we do not see the objects themselves.

Representation or imagination, therefore, must not be regarded as a dead impression with depressions and elevations as in wax; nor even as a qualitative change in the organ; but as an activity of the soul in grasping the object.

Whatever is said against materialism or behaviorism, when Plotinus is speaking of sensation, applies with even greater force to imagination, for imagination is on a spiritually higher level than sensation.[10] And Plotinus clearly indicates that in sensation one is dealing with an activity of the soul and not with a necessary result of the law of inertia by which impressions are preserved in material stuff. In III vi 1, 1, sensation is called an ἐνέργεια as opposed to πάθος, and both here and in IV vi 2 sense is said to pronounce judgment. In IV vi 3, 15–16, the soul illumines sense objects, which perhaps is an echo of the ancient notion that the eye of the mind resembles a lamp or searchlight. And again, VI vii 7 asserts that sense objects are images of intelligible objects and literal sensation is more obscure than the perception of the intelligibles; in fact sensations are faint intellections, and intellections are clear sensations.

Although Plotinus is thus careful to refute materialism and behaviorism, he is by no means blind to the physical conditions,

[9] A passage which seems to contradict this is found in I i 7, 9–14: "With respect to the soul's power of sensation, it does not have to do with sense objects, but grasps the impressions arising from the sensation in the living being, for these are already intelligibles. External sensation is an imitation of this, but this is in reality more true, for it is an impassive contemplation of forms." The confusion arises because Plotinus has here called this higher activity sensation. Cf. below on VI vii 7.

[10] IV iii 29, 22 ff; IV vi 3, 27ff; IV iii 23, 31 ff.

causes, and accompaniments. Discussing freedom and volition,[11] Plotinus remarks on the instability of right self-determination apart from right reason and sound knowledge. With nothing but a correct opinion one's freedom would be precarious, for chance and imagination are not dependable guides to duty. "And since imagination is not in our power, how can we class as free agents those who act under its influence? For by imagination we mean imagination strictly speaking, viz. that type excited by bodily passions. For lack of food and drink produces imaginations . . ." Plotinus continues in this chapter to insist that imagination depends on the condition of the bodily organs.

Frequently he is not so physiological as Aristotle, and speaks only of a disturbance or shattering of a mirror, rendering images impossible. Nothing too scientifically exact is found in IV iv 17, 12 ff. Something a trifle more explicit is given in IV iv 20. This latter chapter argues that desire, at least bodily desires, originates in the living body—of course not in inanimate things—when the body requires for its self-preservation some contrary state. This desire produces a more perfect one in that "nature" which, being the lowest extremity of soul, has been the animating cause of the living body. Next, sensation experiences a representation after which the soul decides to satisfy or to deny the desire of the body.

A final illustration of the dependence of imagination on bodily conditions may be taken from IV iv 28. A certain bodily organization inclines one to anger; sick people are more irritable than the healthy. Following upon such emotions we have sensation and representation, and by taking cognizance of these the soul decides upon the proper reaction. Not only does the line of causation proceed from below to the soul; the reverse also is possible. The soul, using reflection and perceiving some evil, stirs to anger the hitherto quiet body.[12]

Not too far removed from the bodily conditions of imagination, and occurring with sufficient frequency to justify separate mention, emotion is named as a result of imagination. The imagination of imminent death causes fear.[13] Imagination gives to those who have

[11] VI viii 3.
[12] Cf. IV iii 23, 33.
[13] III vi 4, 19 ff.

that faculty the knowledge of what they are suffering.[14] Emotion and imagination, as antithetical to true freedom, are mentioned together.[15]

Consequently, from Plotinus' ethical and mystical standpoint, imagination involves pollution and necessitates purification. To rise to the higher world one must rid the soul of the representations of things here below.[16] The end of IV iii 31 with chapter 32 does not specify the complete eradication of all earthly experience because they describe a process not yet completed; but the following chapter, IV iv 1, which Bréhier edits so that it begins in the middle of a sentence—so close is the connection with the preceding—entirely erases the memory of earthly events. To the same effect is the consistent placing of intellection on a higher level. "Intellection is superior to imagination, for imagination stands between the (physical) imprints of nature and intellection."[17] Thus, imagination is not the lowest stage in the cosmic hierarchy, not the lowest even among the conscious activities of the soul; nor is it the highest.

So far most of the references cited occur in passages where Plotinus mentions the subject more or less incidentally. The theory itself, as it relates imagination to sensation, to intellection, but chiefly to memory, can best be explained by analyzing the few short chapters which bear directly and intentionally on the subject. This will involve a translation, for various reasons; first, Plotinus has written so explicitly that he ought to be reproduced in full; second, the existing translations are not quite satisfactory, as comparisons will show; and finally—a fact which will prevent this new translation also from being satisfactory—the difficulties of Plotinus' language[18] both force a translation to assume the role of an interpretation and render it expedient that an interpretation approximate a translation.

---

[14] IV iv 13, 14 ff.

[15] VI viii 2, 8 ff; VI viii 3, 7 ff.

[16] III vi 5; I viii 14, 5.

[17] IV iv 13, 12–13; Cf. I i 2, 28; V v 6, 18.

[18] Paul Elmer More, *Hellenistic Philosophies*, p. 174, says bluntly, "His handwriting was slovenly, his spelling and grammar faulty . . . his style so crabbed that the best scholar of his day found it unintelligible and the modern Grecian reads it with agony." His philosophy matches his language: "a meaningless answer to an impossible question raised by a gratuitous hypothesis." P. 223.

Translation of IV iii 23.

Each part of the body illumined and animated by the soul participates in the soul in its own peculiar manner. And according to the fitness of the organ for its work the soul gives it a power suited to that work. Thus (5) the power in the eyes is that of sight; the power of hearing is in the ears; of tasting in the tongue; of smelling in the nose; and the power of touching is present everywhere, for with reference to this type of perception the whole body is present to the soul as an organ.[19]

Since the organs of touch (10) are in the primary nerves, which also have the power of moving the living being and from which this power distributes itself; and since the nerves have their origin in the brain; that is where [medical men] place the origin of sensation, desire, and in general all functions of life; on the assumption that where the (15) organs take their rise, there is to be situated that which uses them. But it would be better to say that the origin of the activity of the power is there, for it is at the point at which the organ begins to be in motion, that the power of the operator, that power which is suited to the tool, must, so to speak, exert its force; or rather, not the power, for the power (20) is everywhere; but the origin of the activity is there where one finds the origin of the instrument.

Accordingly, the powers of sensation and appetition, since the soul is a sensitive and imaginative[20] nature, have reason above them, just as the soul by its lower part neighbors on that which it is above.[21] Thus the ancients placed the soul (25) in the uppermost part of every living being, in the head, as being not in the brain but in that principle of sensation by which reason[22] is seated

[19] Bréhier's translation omits the phrase on smelling, and the explanation of the omnipresence of the power of touch.

[20] It is to be noted that while, in the references from diverse sections, φαντασία includes all forms of representation, when Plotinus comes to the main discussion of the subject, it is imagination more strictly which is considered. Thus he follows Aristotle rather than the Stoics.

[21] The general principle by which each power or faculty neighbors on the next higher and next lower is frequent in Plotinus. Bréhier translates this particular phrase, "la raison, qui, par sa partie inférieure, est voisine des parties supérieures de ces facultés." But since γειτονοῦσα is feminine, it must be the soul, or faculties, which neighbors. Mackenna has, "downward, it [the soul] is in contact with an inferior of its own."

[22] Bréhier makes ἐκεῖνος refer to soul, which is impossible; and since αἰσθητικῷ is neuter Mackenna is right in referring it to λόγος four lines back.

in the brain. Something must be assigned to body, especially to that which most of all receives the activity of body;[23] but also something that has no community with body whatsoever must participate in that (30) which is a form of soul, of soul capable of accepting the perceptions which come from the reason.[24]

[Such must be the relative positions of these factors] because the faculty of sensation is a sort of judge, the faculty of imagination is quasi-intellectual, and appetition and desire follow upon imagination and reason. Accordingly, discursive reason is not in the brain as in a place, but because what is there participates in it. And the meaning of (35) localization with respect to the faculty of sensation has been explained.[25]

Translation of IV iii 29

Are we then to refer memory to the faculty of sensation so that the faculty of memory and the faculty of sensation will be the same? But if the shade[26] remembers also, as was said, the faculty of sensation will be double, or if the faculty of sensation is not the (5) faculty of memory, but is another faculty, then that which remembers will be double. Again, if the faculty of sensation also deals with things learned, it will be the faculty of concepts too.[27] Certainly these two must be different. Shall we then assume a common faculty of perception and give to it the memory of both [sense objects and concepts]? Now if it is one and (10) the same thing which perceives sensibles and intelligibles, this suggestion might amount to something, but [since this reverts to the notion that concepts could be sensed] if it must be divided into two, there will none the less be two faculties. And if we give both to each of the two souls[28] there would then be four.

---

[23] Mackenna has the impossible rendering, "the activity of reason."

[24] The something assigned to the body is the work of the organs, including the sensory and motor nerves. The soul itself is the other something, which participates in reason, its Form.

[25] The remainder of chapter 23, dealing with the vegetative functions, is omitted.

[26] I. e., the shade or ghost of Hercules in Hades, while his spirit at the same time is with the gods.

[27] Concepts could then be perceived by sensation.

[28] The two souls are either the ghost in Hades and Hercules with the gods, or the soul in the body and the soul detached and purified. The latter pair is more in keeping with the general context. The *two* which precedes and the *four* which follows must be faculties, and not memories, as Bréhier supposes.

And in general, why is it necessary to assign memory to that by which we sense, so that both should belong to the same (15) power; and why must one assign the memory of things reasoned about to that by which we reason? Those who reason the best are not the same as those who best remember. Those who benefit equally by sensation do not remember equally well; some have keen senses, but others remember although their sensation is not so sharp.

Now, in the next (20) place, if each of these faculties is distinct, and if the one is to remember the things which sensation has previously grasped, does it not follow that memory must sense what it is to remember? [Not exactly.] Rather, nothing will prevent the sense-image's[29] being a representation-image to that which will remember it; so that memory and retention belong to the faculty of imagination which is a distinct faculty.[30] For (25) sensation culminates in imagination; and when the sensation no longer exists the visual image is present to the faculty of imagination. If, then, the imagination of an absent object is already in this faculty, it is remembering, even[31] if it endures but a short time. If it remains a short time, the memory is brief; when the image remains longer, they remember better, since the imagination is then stronger and does not readily change so as to unseat and throw off the memory. Memory, then, belongs to the faculty of imagination, and such are the objects we remember.[32]

We should explain the differences among memories either by the differences among the powers themselves, or by exercise or the lack of it, or by bodily admixtures (35) inhering or not, which do

---

[29] αἴσθημα . . . φάντασμα.

[30] Cf. Arist. *De Memoria*, 450 a 22 ff. Bréhier, *Notice in loc.*, p. 31, remarks that chapters xxix–xxxii present the character of a scientific research after the fashion of Aristotle's *De Memoria*, "que Plotin a eu probablement sous les yeux en rédigeant ces chapitres." In chapter xxv Plotinus appeals to a definition of memory which is often repeated elsewhere; and most naturally makes memory deal with the past—hardly an Aristotelian discovery however; and IV vi obviously involves the Aristotelian treatise; but it cannot be said that Plotinus faithfully follows the Aristotelian theory.

[31] Mackenna omits this relatively important clause. A textual problem is involved.

[32] Bréhier translates: "The memory of sense objects belongs, therefore, to imagination." It is true that so far only sense objects have been mentioned; the emphasis however, is not on sensation, but rather on images. Therefore, the word *such* refers, not to sense objects, but to images, and the question of the memory of concepts is left open for discussion in the following chapter.

or do not cause qualitative changes and disorders. But these matters are discussed elsewhere.

Translation of IV iii 30

But what about [the memory] of reasonings? Does the faculty of imagination deal with these also? If indeed an imagination follows upon every act of thinking, then, perhaps, when such an imagination, like an image of an object of thought, endures, there might thus be (5) memory of the thing known. But if not, another explanation must be sought. Perhaps that which is received into the faculty of imagination is the verbal formula[33] which accom-

---

[33] The difficulty in this passage centers in the word λόγου, which Mackenna translates as *Reason Principle*. This meaning is frequent in Plotinus; cf. above IV iii 23, 23, 31 and 32. The notion is still clearei in the cognate word τὸ λογιζόμενον. In I vi 2, 15 and 17, it is a divine *reason*. In I iv 3, 17, it is *species* and therefore nearly Idea. This latter passage continues by ascending from the Idea of Beauty in nature through the Idea in the soul, particularly the wise soul which the Idea illuminates, on to a still superior λόγος which does not descend into thin&s but exists in itself, and is more properly termed νοῦς. In the same vein I iv 2, 25–27 and the context shows that above sensation there is something which judges, and this is λόγος or νοῦς. Obviously the meaning is reason. But, unfortunately, in the passage to which this note is attached, reason makes no sense, for discursive reason itself can hardly be received into the faculty of representation. Therefore Mackenna found it impossible to translate the γὰρ of line 7. This γὰρ, and the exigencies of Plotinus' system as well, require some result of discursion to be received into the faculty of imagination or representation; and Bréhier with a stroke of genius translates the λόγου as *formule verbale*. Whittaker, also, in *The Neo-Platonists* (2nd ed. p. 51), very briefly makes the same suggestion. Since there are many passages in which Plotinus uses λόγος in the sense of word, definition, or argument, no grammatical reason can oppose Bréhier's translation.

It may be a stroke of genius on the part of Plotinus also, for the question of the memory of concepts was one which Aristotle did not fully answer. For Aristotle, memory depends on the preservation of a sensible affection, and not on a concept. Further, the continuance of the affection results, not from the activity of the soul, but from the physical condition of the organ. Summarizing 450 a 22 ff. we find that memory is a function of that part of the soul to which imagination belongs, and all sense objects are immediately and properly objects of memory, while concepts are objects of memory *per accidens*.

It is interesting to note how closely Plotinus follows Aristotle in details while coloring them by a foreign metaphysic, and to note also how Plotinus makes more definite some matters left vague by Aristotle. Perhaps the earlier philosopher's theory is sufficient to explain the memory or recollection of the concept *horse;* no difficulty arises from basing it on the image of a particular member of the species. Plotinus, however, with his Platonic orientation, apparently has in mind more complicated notions. What image could be pointed out as the stimulus to the recollection of the meaning of logarithm?

Modern psychologists, in order to preserve the theory that no thought is possible without images, have not only added auditory, gustatory, etc. to visual images— quite properly—but have also, when the other forms of imagery failed to sustain their conclusion, extended the notion of imagination to kinaesthesia. The word

panies the concept. For the concept is indivisible, and not yet externalized; it remains internal and escapes our notice. But speech, by unfolding it and leading it from the state of a thought to the faculty of imagination, exhibits the thought as in a mirror, and thus (10) we have the perception of it, its conservation, and memory. And therefore, since the soul is always thinking, we have perception whenever it arrives at this stage. For thinking is one thing, but perception of the thinking is another; and while we always think, we do not always perceive. This is because the recipient not only receives thoughts from above, but also sensations from below.

Translation of IV iii 31.

But if memory belongs to the faculty of imagination, and both souls are said to remember, there will be two faculties of imagination. When the two are separate such is the case, but when they are the same thing in us how can there be two and in which of them does imagination occur? For if it occurs in both (5) there

---

image, however, in the phrase kinaesthetic image, has lost all its literal meaning, and even a gustatory or olfactory image would be difficult to define. It may have been by reason of such vagueness that Plotinus was not willing to subscribe wholeheartedly to the proposition that every act of thought involves an image.

For Plotinus, there are two sorts of imageless thought. First, faced with the difficulty here outlined, he still holds that there should be something akin to an image—a substitute for an image, by which memory and thinking take place. The faculty of discursive reasoning in the soul judges on the basis of images derived from sense. Cf. V iii 2, 7, ff. and V iii 3, 6. Sensation is the necessary means of consciousness, cf. I iv 10, 2. Accordingly, when a concept cannot be imaged, there must be some other method of externalizing it. The reason is given in IV iii 30, 7 ff. Discursive reasoning, by means of verbal formulae, is, therefore, one type of imageless thought. One may note that for Aristotle images are natural, and the same for all men, while language is conventional.

The second type of imageless thought is more properly called such, and to it the above explanations do not apply. The theory above holds for conscious, discursive reasoning. A few lines below the point at which this footnote began Plotinus says that we always think, though we do not always perceive. Sensation, as stated above, is necessary for consciousness, but since mind and soul are prior to sensation, they may act unconsciously. The body is a sort of mirror to the action of mind and soul, so that in sleep or in insanity when the mirror is to a greater or lesser extent disturbed, there is either no consciousness at all, or a confused consciousness. Cf. I iv 10. When, on the other hand, the bodily organs are properly disposed, the activity of νοῦς is mirrored and we have sensations and images. But the images are not a necessary condition of the thinking which causes them.

This unconscious activity is more noble than sensation and imagination. A person who is intent on reading will not be conscious that he is reading. The best courage, and the best artistic activity, are unconscious. Consequently, consciousness and imagination weaken the acts which they accompany.

will always be two imaginations, for it is not true that one of them deals with intellectual objects and the other with sensibles. For such an arrangement would in every case result in there being two persons[34] having nothing in common with each other. If, then, in both, what is the difference?[35] And how is it we do not perceive the difference? [There are two possibilities.] When the one is in agreement with the other, so that the (10) faculties of imagination are not separate, though the better dominates, there is but one image, with a sort of shadow accompanying in the other [faculty], like a dim light merging into a greater. But when they conflict and discord arises, the lesser becomes perceptible by itself; but we fail to notice that it is in another (15) because also in general we fail to notice the duality of the souls. For the two form a unity in which the one drives the other. The one sees all things and when it leaves [the union with the other soul in the body] it retains some images from the lower stage but dismisses others, just as we remember little of the conversation of our inferior friends after we have changed to others of higher rank (20), whom we keep in mind very well.[36]

AN INDEX

The student of Plotinus has no aid for his work comparable to Bonitz' *Index Aristotelicus*, or even to Ast on Plato. Both Creuzer and Bréhier provide an index for a few important passages. For example, in addition to an *Index des Références dans les Notes*, an *Index des Textes Cités par Plotin*, and an *Index Analytique des Matières*, Bréhier has an *Index des Mots Grecs* in which he lists six references for φαντασία, one for φάντασις, five for φάντασμα and one for φανταστικός. The following will give some idea of the possibilities; it is intended to be complete.

[34] *Persons* here is the translation of ζῷα. Zeller, *Die Philosophie der Griechen* (3te Aufl.), III 2, p. 583, is mistaken. "Es ist aber eine doppeete Einbildungskraft zu unterscheiden, die der niederen und die der hoheren Seele; jene bewahrt die sinnlichen Bilder, diese die Gedanken . . ."

[35] Mackenna paraphrases: "And if both orders of image act upon both orders of soul, what difference is there in the souls?" Bréhier has it: "Si donc la mémoire est dans les deux imaginations, en quoi diffèrent les deux images?" Perhaps the conditional clause is better given by Mackenna; but that it is Bréhier who has correctly understood the question is seen in the fact that Mackenna's question receives no answer. Plotinus explains that we do not notice the duality of the images because we are not aware of the distinction between the souls.

[36] Cf. III vi 5, 26 mentioned above, and I viii 14, 5.

φαντάζω

I i 8, 15; ii 2, 25; vi 1, 7; 3, 9; 4, 10; viii 1, 11; 9, 13;

II v 4, 12; ix 9, 63;

III v 1, 36; 4, 17; vi 5, 11; 7, 17; 7, 21; 7, 23; 7, 26; 13, 17; 14, 14; 14, 26; 15, 22; vii 1, 21; 2, 5; viii 9, 14;

IV iv 3, 7; 13, 15; vi 2, 24;

V viii 4, 23; 5, 22; 9, 33;

VI iv 12, 32; v 9, 15; 9, 23; vi 3, 33; 3, 38; vii 15, 27; 15, 30; 29, 27; viii 3, 14; ix 3, 29; 6, 14; 10, 15.

φαντασία

I i 9, 8; ii 5, 20; iv 10, 19–21; 15, 12; viii 14, 5; 15, 18;

II ix 11, 22;

III i 7, 14; vi 3, 30; 4, 19; 4, 21; 4, 45; 4, 46; 5, 10; 5, 26; 15, 12; 15, 16; 18, 33;

IV iii 23, 33; 29, 27; 30, 3 (twice); 31, 5; iv 3, 7; 4, 6; 8, 3; 8, 18; 13, 12 (twice); 13, 13; 13, 14; 17, 9; 17, 12; 20, 17; 28, 41; 28, 48;

V i 10, 26; iii 3, 6; v 6, 18; vi 5, 15; viii 9, 5; 9, 8;

VI iii 12, 13; vi 3, 39; 12, 5; 12, 6; viii 2, 8; 2, 17; 3, 7; 3, 8; 3, 11; 3, 13; 3, 16; 11, 17; 13, 46.

φάντασις

III vi 7, 23; 13, 52; 17, 6.

φάντασμα

III v 7, 8; vi 5, 3; 6, 67; 7, 13; 14, 17;

IV iii 29, 23; 31, 11;

V iii 11, 7; viii 9, 12; 9, 14;

VI vi 17, 10.

φανταστικός

IV iii 23, 22; 23, 32; 29, 23; 29, 31; 30, 2; 30, 7; 30, 10; 31, 1; 31, 2; 31, 10.

KANT AND THOMAS AQUINAS ON THE PROOFS FOR THE EXISTENCE OF GOD

FRANCIS P. CLARKE

Department of Philosophy, University of Pennsylvania

IT IS generally assumed that in his criticism of the proofs for the existence of God Kant has given such a logically complete analysis that quite apart from the historical setting of any earlier treatment, no attempt to establish a "natural" or "rational" theology, other than that which he allows, is permissible.

It is the purpose of this paper to state first the arguments of Kant, then those of Thomas Aquinas, and then to see more clearly the bearing of the former on the latter. It will be maintained that the disagreements are not as thoroughgoing as is usually assumed; and that, while real differences remain, much of the disagreement is purely verbal.

Kant reduces the possible proofs of the existence of God to three: (a) the physico-theological, based on the definite constitution of the world as we experience it; (b) the cosmological, based on the general idea of experience; and (c) the ontological, based not on experience but on the mere concept of God.

Following the order of Kant's discussion, we consider first the ontological. In this the concept of a supreme being, that is, an absolutely necessary and unconditioned being, is taken to include its necessary existence. "God exists," or "There is a God," is taken as an a priori, analytical proposition. But in fact all existential propositions are synthetic. Existence indeed is not properly a predicate at all, that is, it is not a concept which adds any note to what has previously been defined and considered as possible only. Existence is given only in experience and with the determining conditions there found, and beyond the field of experience cannot be asserted. The concept of a supreme being then is a mere idea which cannot in any manner enlarge our knowledge of existence.

The cosmological argument proceeds: "If anything exists, an absolutely necessary being must also exist. Now I, at least, exist. Therefore an absolutely necessary being exists." The proof, then, starting from experience leads to a necessary being. But what characteristics would a necessary being have? For this we must turn to pure reason, for we find in experience no particular being which we can call necessary. But the ideal of a supreme being which reason affords is only regulative, not constitutive of experience. We are in fact again concerned with the ontological argument. We must indeed look upon the world as if it originated from a necessary cause; but this necessity belongs to the formal demands of reason, not to the external world. The principle of causality has no application outside the realm of sensible experience. Hence no cause considered as necessary can be hypostatised as an existent beyond the realm of experience.

The physico-theological argument proceeds from the world as experienced to a cause taken to be sufficient to account for the observed order. It can, at best, however, lead to an architect who is hampered by the material in which he works, and not to a creator to whom all is subject. For this, which is to show that all in Nature is contingent, one must invoke the cosmological proof. This argument does not then establish the existence of a supreme being; for that one must again fall back ultimately upon the ontological proof.

These proofs all involve the speculative use of reason, and its application to a realm beyond that of possible experience. Theology then cannot be based on Nature where cause and effect hold sway; there remains, however, one possibility: the practical use of reason. The speculative use of reason, however, is valuable in correcting and making consistent with itself whatever knowledge may be derived elsewhere. It establishes the supreme being as an ideal without a flaw, a concept which completes and unifies the whole of human knowledge.

The attributes of necessity, infinitude, unity, existence apart from the world (and not as a world-soul), eternity—free from conditions of time, omnipresence—free from conditions of space, omnipotence, and others, are purely transcendental predicates; and thus the accurate conception of a Supreme Being which every theology requires is furnished by transcendental theology alone.*

The idea of God is for pure reason a regulative principle only, and consequently while we can recognize the necessity of the principle, we cannot know the source or the ground of the necessity as it is in itself. Nevertheless we are justified in thinking this principle in terms which properly speaking are applicable only in the world of sense, that is, in analogy with the objects of experience, and this may be extended to certain anthropomorphisms.

The speculative reason then is impotent to establish the existence of this supreme being, though forced by its own requirements to use it as the unifying principle of experience; but what the pure reason cannot do, the practical reason can accomplish. Or more accurately, since it is the same reason operative in both capacities, in its practical aspect reason establishes what in its speculative activity it must leave an open question. Thus there is no conflict, no contradiction.

The grounds on which the practical reason proceeds are found in the analysis of the *summum bonum*. Two elements are seen to be necessary: virtue and happiness. These must be considered in a relation of cause and effect. Therefore either the desire for happiness is the motive to virtue, or the maxim of virtue the efficient cause of happiness. But both of these seem impossible: in the first, if the will be determined by the desire of personal happiness, it is not moral at all; in the second, the practical determination of cause and effect in the world depends on the knowledge of the laws of Nature and not on the moral dispositions of the will. Thus arises the antinomy of the practical reason. But only one of the elements of the antinomy is absolutely false, the other not necessarily so. For it is only in so far as virtue is considered as a cause in the world of sense, that no necessary connection can be established between it and happiness. But if the will may be considered as

* *Critique of Pure Reason* (Meiklejohn's Trans.), Dial. Bk. II, Ch. 3, Sect. 7.

belonging not only to the sensible world but also to the purely intelligible, then at least mediately it may be a cause. Thus morality is the supreme good, and the first element in the *summum bonum*; happiness as morally conditioned, the second. Because the practical reason commands us to seek this complete *summum bonum*, it must also conceive it as possible. Therefore, it must also conceive the necessary conditions for its attainment: namely the existence of a supreme being as the author of the sensible world and thus the ground of the relation between virtue and happiness. The moral law, then, must postulate the existence of God, as the necessary condition of the possibility of the *summum bonum*. The admission of this existence results then from our consciousness of duty, but the admission is an act of the speculative reason. But this admission in no manner enlarges our speculative knowledge. The conception of God then belongs to morals rather than to physics: to the practical reason, not to the speculative.

St. Thomas Aquinas enumerates five proofs for the existence of God. Before developing these, however, he considers the a priori arguments, or the claim that the existence of God is self-evident. Among these is the argument of Anselm which Kant calls the ontological. This Aquinas rejects, on the ground that we do not know the essence of God; and on the ground that even granted a concept of God as that than which nothing greater can be thought, it does not follow that there must exist *in rerum natura* a being corresponding to our concept. What we can know of God can be derived only from the effects which we observe, hence all proofs must be a posteriori.

The first three proofs rest on similar principles, and are frequently viewed as variations of one fundamental proof. The first form is the argument from motion to an unmoved mover. There is strictly speaking no self-mover: nothing can be the cause of its own motion; for motion is the actualising of the potential, and nothing can be at the same time both potential and actual in the same respect. Therefore the cause of motion (which is actual) must be other than that which is caused to move (which is potential). This mover is in turn either unmoved (that is not caused to move by something outside itself) or it in turn has a mover. If the former we have reached the unmoved mover, which we call God. If the latter, we have either an infinite regress, or the series ends in an unmoved mover. An infinite regress is impossible, because the secondary movers move only by virtue of the first mover, and if there is no first then there is no motion at all; but we started with the observed fact of motion.

The second proof derives from the analysis of efficient causation. We find an ordered series of efficient causes in the world. Nothing can be the efficient cause of itself; neither can there be an infinite regress of efficient causes. Therefore we must come to a first efficient cause, which we call God.

The third proof proceeds from the merely possible, or contingent, to a necessary being. Again experience shows us that there are contingent beings in the world. But not everything can be contingent, for that which is contingent is at some time or other non-existent. But if all things were contingent, then nothing would be existent now; for the non-existent must receive existence, and it can only do so from the existent. Therefore there must be a necessary being which does not derive its existence from elsewhere, and this we call God.

The fourth proof derives from the degrees of value (the good, the noble, and the like) found among things. But a greater or less good, etc. presupposes the highest as the point of reference and the cause of the rest. Therefore, there must be the highest good, etc., which we call God.

The fifth proof proceeds from the order of nature. But things lacking intelligence can be ordered to an end only by an intelligent being. Therefore there must be an intelligence which orders nature, and this we call God.

It must be noted that the impossibility of an infinite regress does not refer to a temporal series, for Thomas holds that the Aristotelian teaching of the eternity of the world is free from contradiction. It is the impossibility of an infinite regress in an ordered series that is maintained.

One must note also the nature of the demonstration afforded. It is a demonstration "that" and not one as to "what"; that is, the demonstration proceeds from effects to a cause, the exact nature of which is not directly known but only inferred. Strict demonstration proceeds from the essential definition, but of God we can give no definition properly speaking. For the definition involves genus and properties, neither of which apply to God. Even the term *summum bonum* is applied to God not in the sense of a highest genus but in the sense of a cause; and even there the meaning is not univocal; for God is the cause from which all other goods flow, but God is good in a more excellent manner than any derived good; the good is present in him *eminenter*.

We do not then acquire a knowledge of God as he is in himself. In fact it is impossible for any created intelligence to comprehend God. Even the supernatural knowledge of the beatific vision falls far short of that; and no purely natural knowledge can even attain the essence at all. Since all our knowledge is rooted in sensation, it cannot directly apprehend any reality which is purely intelligible. All knowledge of such is analogous.

A term which is "analogous" or one of proportion (or proportionality) is between one purely univocal and one entirely equivocal. The validity of the use of analogy to give us some insight into the nature of the first cause is upheld by Thomas, attacked by Kant. In this use of analogy we must distinguish between what is signified, and the manner of signification. The latter is rooted in our experience, but we may legitimately transcend experience in respect to the object signified, and this without surreptitiously assuming that it *is* an object of experience.

And Kant also is forced to admit that analogy must be used to formulate our description of God: God is not an object of experience; both Thomas and Kant agree on this. Our terms of science and of discourse in general are based on experience: both Thomas and Kant agree on this. The very act of thought necessarily carries itself beyond itself to what must be its ultimate ground; do not Thomas and Kant also agree on this? Kant says such a ground is regulative only for the speculative reason, and not constitutive. But this only means it is not itself another item of knowledge as an object of experience. Unlike the categories, it does not get its content directly from experience. And it is precisely for this reason that it must be described by analogy from experience. If "knowledge" be restricted to objects of experience, then we have no "knowledge" of God. For Kant, it is not the requirements of the reason as speculative, but as practical (i.e. the requirements of moral consciousness) that establish the existence of God, but it is the speculative reason which acknowledges these requirements, and it must be the speculative reason which sets forth the nature of God. But in analyzing the nature of a "necessary" being whose existence has been established by the argument from contingency, it is difficult to see how the "ontological" argument is involved. Kant has confused the question of proving the existence of God, and the further problem of establishing in more detail the nature of God. Nor is it clear why the demands of the speculative reason are not as exigent as those of the practical reason.

Another difference between Thomas and Kant is in the interpretation of the nature of the practical reason. For Thomas the practical differs from the speculative only in the end toward which it is directed; Kant seems to say the same thing. But for Kant the practical reason and the will are identical; for Thomas they are not. The presuppositions of morality, just as those of the speculative order, are principles of reason, not postulates of the will. It follows then for Kant that the principle of contradiction is fundamental also for the will (as practical reason). This is expressed in the "categorical imperative" as the foundation of morality; for this reduces to the principle of contradiction.

It would seem, then, that the major difference between Kant and Thomas lies in the answers given to the question, does analogy yield knowledge? Or, stated in another way, the difference lies in the definition of knowledge itself. If knowledge be restricted to that of which we have immediate experience, or where at least experience is an immediate constituent element, then such use of analogy, since one term transcends experience, cannot yield knowledge. It yields, for Kant, "regulative" principles only; but it is impossible even for science, or "knowledge," to proceed without such principles. And since this is so, Thomas calls such inevitable conclusions from experience, also "knowledge."

THE CATEGORIES OF ARISTOTLE

ISAAC HUSIK

*Department of Philosophy, University of Pennsylvania**

*H*ABENT *sua fata libelli.* Thirty-four years ago I published a paper *On the Categories of Aristotle* in the *Philosophical Review.*[1] Like the case of the proverbial Irishman who desired to be buried in a Jewish cemetery because that was the last place the devil would look for an Irishman, so it seems that the *Philosophical Review* at that time was the last place that an Aristotelian scholar would look for a literary-historical article on the *Categories* of Aristotle. And so the article was stillborn. No European student of Aristotle knew about it and it did not find its way into the bibliographies of the subject. Dupréel, whose article on the same subject appeared five years later,[2] does not refer to my article and shows no knowledge of it. That the article did not merit such complete neglect is proved by the fact that my teacher and colleague, the late Professor William Romaine Newbold, an expert Aristotelian, was completely convinced by the arguments advanced therein in favor of the authenticity of the treatise and regarded the question as settled. The late Charles S. Peirce similarly agreed with me and made very flattering comments on the article, except that he disagreed with me on the last six chapters of the treatise, the so-called *Postpraedicamenta*, which he thought were not genuine, though on what grounds he did not say.

Now after thirty-four years, the question, it seems to me, stands

---

* Professor Husik, for many years a colleague of Professor Singer in the Department of Philosophy at the University of Pennsylvania, had accepted an invitation to contribute to this volume. His death occurred before the proposed article was completed. The editors, feeling that this volume would not be complete without an article by Professor Husik, have taken advantage of the fact that he prepared, for the December 1938 meeting of the American Philosophical Association, a brief paper upon the *Categories of Aristotle*. This paper, accompanied by comments of Sir William David Ross, Provost of Oriel College, Oxford, was published in the *Journal of Philosophy* (August 3, 1939). In this article, Professor Husik brought up to date a study *On The Categories of Aristotle*, printed in the *Philosophical Review* of September, 1904. The editors have taken the liberty of coördinating the two articles to make available to Aristotelian scholars a contribution of importance.
(¹) Vol. XIII (1904), pp. 514–28.
(²) *Archiv für Geschichte der Philosophie*, Vol. XXII (1909), pp. 230–31.

exactly as it did then. None of those who wrote on the subject
since then has added anything very significant except Dupréel,
and none has answered my arguments, which indeed they did
not know. Accordingly, I thought it would be valuable to revive
the question of the authenticity of the *Categories* by way of sum-
ming up the situation as it now stands.

The present writer has the unenviable position of being in a
minority of one in regarding the entire treatise, including Chapters
X–XV, as genuine. The others divide themselves as follows:
Waitz,[3], Zeller,[4] Maier,[5] Gomperz,[6] and Ross[7] hold that the
first nine chapters, with the exception of the conclusion of chapter
IX, are genuine, while the last six chapters were added by some
later author. On the other hand, Spengel,[8] Prantl,[9] Rose,[10]
Brandis,[11] Gercke,[12] Dupréel,[13] and Jaeger,[14] regard the whole as
spurious. Of these, Rose, Dupréel, and Gercke maintain the unity
of the book. What the rest of this group think regarding this
question I do not know.

[The argument of my article of long ago follows:]

The little treatise of Aristotle which stands at the head of the
Organon has caused a great deal of difficulty to students, both
ancient and modern. The bulk of the discussion has centered about
the question of its place in the *Organon* and in Aristotle's system,
and the character of the ten categories to which the greater part
of the book is devoted. But there have been found also critics
who expressed a doubt as to the authenticity of all or part of the
treatise in question. To say nothing of the ancient commentators
of Aristotle, the earliest attempt in modern times to cast a doubt

[3] *Organon*, I, p. 266.
[4] *Die Philosophie der Griechen* (3d ed.), II, pt. 2, p. 67, n. 1.
[5] *Die Syllogistik des Aristoteles*, II, 2, p. 291 and note.
[6] *Griechische Denker*, III, p. 402, Zu Buch VI, Kap. 4, beginng.in
[7] *Aristotle*, pp. 9–10.
[8] *Münchener Gelehrte Anzeigen*, 1845, Vol. XX, No. 5. pp. 41 sq.
[9] *Zeitschrift für Altertumswissenschaft* (1846), p. 646; *Geschichte der Logik*, I, p. 90,
n. 5.
[10] *De Aristotelis librorum ordine et auctoritate*, p. 234 sq.
[11] *Abhandlungen der Berlin. Akademie* (1833), "Ueber die Reihenfolge der Bücher
des Aristotelischen Organons," etc.
[12] *Archiv für Geschichte der Philosophie*, IV (1891), pp. 424–41.
[13] See n. 2.
[14] *Aristoteles*, p. 45, note.

on the genuineness of the work seems to be that of Spengel in *Münchener Gelehrte Anzeigen* (Vol. XX (1845), No. 5, pp. 41 sq.). He was followed by Prantl in *Zeitschrift für Altertumswissenschaft* (1846, p. 646), and in his *Geschichte der Logik* (I, p. 90, n. 5), also by Valentinus Rose in *De Aristotelis librorum ordine et auctoritate* (p. 234 et sq.). Zeller, on the other hand (*Philos. d. Griechen*, 2nd ed., II, pt. 2, p. 67, n. 1), decides in favor of the genuineness of the first part of the work, the *Categories* proper, and against the so-called *Postpraedicamenta* from Chapter X to the end.

Before I take up the examination of the evidence adduced by the scholars just mentioned, it is important that I dispose of an erroneous statement which has, to my knowledge, remained unchallenged from the time it was written down by Brandis in 1833 to this day. I refer to his article in *Abhdl. d. Berlin. Akademie* (1833), entitled "Ueber die Reihenfolge der Bücher des Aristotelischen Organons," etc. He there (p. 257) argues that the *Topics* was written before the *Categories*, for in the former (VII, 6, p. 153a 36) we find the statement ἐπειδὴ ἀνάγκη τὰ ἐναντία ἐν τῷ αὐτῷ ἢ ἐν τοῖς ἐναντίοις γένεσιν εἶναι whereas in the *Categories* (ch. 11, p. 14a 19) the theory of ἐναντία reached a more developed stage and the case is stated as follows: ἀνάγκη δὲ πάντα τὰ ἐναντία ἢ ἐν τῷ αὐτῷ γένει εἶναι ἢ ἐν τοῖς ἐναντίοις γένεσιν, ἢ αὐτὰ γένη εἶναι; i.e., opposites must be either in the same genus or in opposite genera, *or be themselves genera*. The addition of the third possibility in the *Categories*, which was omitted in the *Topics*, is, to Brandis, a proof of the priority of the latter.

Waitz (*Org.*, I, p. 266), fearing that yielding this point would make it easier for the critics to attack the authenticity of the *Categories*, cannot answer it otherwise than by dividing the *Postpraedicamenta* from the first part, and while giving up the latter to Brandis to do with it as is right in his eyes, saves the kernel of the treatise from attack—"quae feruntur Postpraedicamenta ab ipso Aristotele Categoriis adjecta esse haud probabile est."

In the case of Brandis, it looks very much as if his argument was the result of a chance lighting on the particular passage above quoted; and if by chance he had hit instead on page 127b 10, ἐπειδὴ τὰ ἐναντία ἐν τοῖς ἐναντίοις γένεσιν, we may presume his argument would have been considered still stronger as showing the *Topics* to be two steps behind the *Categories*.

As a matter of fact, however, we find this threefold classification of ἐναντία fully developed in the *Topics* and with more definiteness and detail than in the *Categories*, and it is strange that it should have escaped Waitz.

P. 123b 1 sq., Aristotle points out how we can examine the correctness of a given genus by reference to opposite species. If a given species of which the genus is in question has an opposite, then the investigator must proceed as follows: (1) If the given genus has no opposite, we must see whether the opposite of the given species is in the same genus as the given species. *For opposites must be in the same genus*, IF THE LATTER HAS NO OPPOSITE. (2) If the genus in question has an opposite, then we must see whether the species opposed to the given one is in a genus opposed to the genus in question. *For the opposite must be in an opposite [genus]*, IF THE GENUS HAS AN OPPOSITE. Finally, (3) the species opposed to the given one may not be in a genus at all, but be itself a genus, as, for example, the good. In that case, *the given species cannot be in a genus either*, BUT MUST ITSELF BE A GENUS, as is the case in the "good" and the "evil," neither is in a genus, but each is itself a genus. Ἔτι ἂν ᾖ ἐναντίον τι τῷ εἴδει, σκοπεῖν. ἔστι δὲ πλεοναχῶς ἡ σκέψις· πρῶτον μὲν εἰ ἐν τῷ αὐτῷ γένει καὶ τὸ ἐναντίον, μὴ ὄντος ἐναντίου τῷ γένει. δεῖ γὰρ τὰ ἐναντία ἐν τῷ αὐτῷ γένει εἶναι, ἂν μηδὲν ἐναντίου τῷ γένει ᾖ. ὄντος δ' ἐναντίου τῷ γένει, σκοπεῖν εἰ τὸ ἐναντίον ἐν τῷ ἐναντίῳ· ἀνάγκη γὰρ τὸ ἐναντίον ἐν τῷ ἐναντίῳ εἶναι, ἄνπερ ᾖ ἐναντίον τι τῷ γένει. φανερὸν δέ, τούτων ἕκαστον διὰ τῆς ἐπαγωγῆς. πάλιν εἰ ὅλως ἐν μηδενὶ γένει τὸ τῷ εἴδει ἐναντίον, ἀλλ' αὐτὸ γένος, οἷον τἀγαθόν· εἰ γὰρ τοῦτο μὴ ἐν γένει, οὐδὲ τὸ ἐναντίον τούτου ἐν γένει ἔσται, ἀλλ' αὐτὸ γένος, καθάπερ ἐπὶ τοῦ ἀγαθοῦ καὶ τοῦ κακοῦ συμβαίνει· οὐδέτερον γὰρ τούτων ἐν γένει, ἀλλ' ἑκάτερον αὐτῶν γένος.

It will be seen that not only is the threefold classification found here in full, but the circumstances are defined which accompany and determine every one of the three possibilities. If there is a development between the *Categories* and the *Topics*, it is undoubtedly in the direction of the *Topics*.

But how are we to explain the omission of the third condition in the passage cited by Brandis, and the omission of both the second and third in 127b 10? The explanation will be evident if we refer to 124a 1 sq. In 123b 1 sq. Aristotle enumerates the various lines of argument which the disputant must have ready to attack the genus named by the opponent. In 124a 1 sq. he names the lines of argument to be followed by anyone who wishes to establish the genus of a given species. If the genus he wants to establish has no opposite, he must show that the species opposed to the given species is in the same genus as the given. If the genus has an opposite, then he must show that the opposed species is in the opposite genus. The third possibility is naturally left out here, for in that case he has no genus to establish.

ἀναιροῦντι μὲν οὖν τοσαυταχῶς ἐπισκεπτέον· εἰ γὰρ μὴ ὑπάρχει τὰ εἰρημένα, δῆλον ὅτι οὐ γένος τὸ ἀποδοθέν· κατασκευάζοντι δὲ τριχῶς, πρῶτον μὲν εἰ τὸ ἐναντίον τῷ εἴδει ἐν τῷ εἰρημένῳ γένει, μὴ ὄντος ἐναντίου τῷ γένει· εἰ γὰρ τὸ ἐναντίον ἐν τούτῳ, δῆλον ὅτι καὶ τὸ προκείμενον. . . . πάλιν ἂν ᾖ ἐναντίον τι τῷ γένει, σκοπεῖν εἰ καὶ τὸ ἐναντίον ἐν τῷ ἐναντίῳ· ἂν γὰρ ᾖ, δῆλον ὅτι καὶ τὸ προκείμενον ἐν τῷ προκειμένῳ.

127b 10 is evident at once, for the condition is stated at the beginning of the paragraph which determines the first of the three possibilities—Ἔτι ὅταν ὄντος καὶ τῷ εἴδει καὶ τῷ γένει ἐναντίου τὸ βέλτιον τῶν ἐναντίων εἰς τὸ χεῖρον γένος θῇ, συμβήσεται γὰρ τὸ λοιπὸν ἐν τῷ λοιπῷ εἶναι, ἐπειδὴ τὰ ἐναντία ἐν τοῖς ἐναντίοις γένεσιν . . . If we now go back to the passages quoted by Brandis, 153a 36, we shall have no difficulty in explaining the omission of the third condition. Chapter III deals with the topics necessary for *establishing* a definition (153a 6—ἀναιρεῖν μὲν οὖν ὅρον οὕτως καὶ διὰ τούτων [chs. 1 and 2] ἀεὶ πειρατέον· ἐὰν δὲ κατασκευάζειν βουλώμεθα, πρῶτον μὲν εἰδέναι δεῖ. . .). The first element in the definition is the genus; we must therefore see that the genus is well established (*ibid.* 32, πρῶτον μὲν οὖν ὅτι τὸ ἀποδοθὲν γένος ὀρθῶς ἀποδέδοται). If the thing to be defined is not in a genus at all, but is itself a genus, it cannot be defined; and hence the third possibility is out of place here.

Alexander, in his *Commentary on the Topics* (Berlin ed., p. 506, 3–5), whom Brandis cites, saw the explanation. His words are: οὐκέτι δὲ προσέθηκεν "ἢ αὐτὰ γένη εἶναι," ὡς ἐν ἄλλοις λέγει, ὅτι μηδὲ χρήσιμον ἦν πρὸς τὸ προκείμενον τοῦτο προστιθέμενον· οὐ γάρ ἐστιν ἡ ζήτησις νῦν εἰ γένος ἐστὶ τὸ προκείμενον, ἀλλ' ὑπὸ τί γένος.

Having shown that there is no reason whatsoever for supposing the *Topics* earlier than the *Categories*, I will take up the arguments of Spengel, Prantl, and Rose to prove the spuriousness of the treatise. The purely linguistic peculiarities cited by Spengel and Prantl, Rose himself admits are not of great weight; hence I need not concern myself with them any further. The main argument, however, of all the three critics is the subjective one, that the diffuseness of style and the "senseless" repetitions of the *Categories* are unworthy of Aristotle and unlike him. This may be readily answered by the consideration that, though the style and general tone of the *Categories* is very different from that of the *Metaphysics* or the *Posterior Analytics*, it is so strikingly similar to that of the middle books of the *Topics*, both in tone, style, and method of treatment, that one cannot help feeling that they belong to the same period. The following passages in the *Topics* (106a 9–22, b 17–20; 107a 18–31; 108b 12–19; 122a 31 sq., b 18–24; 127a 3 sq., b 18–20; 129b 5–13, 30–130a 14, b 11–15; 141b 15–34; 145b 9–10; 146a 4–7, etc.) exhibit the same diffuseness and repetitions as the *Categories*, and Book V in particular is characterized by the same uniformity of formula and expression that Rose finds so "un-Aristotelian" in the *Categories*.

The title, πρὸ τῶν τόπων, cited by Simplicius, whether it goes back to Aristotle or not, represents a true notion as to the place of the categories in Aristotle's scheme, and it is the object of this paper by a more minute comparison than has hitherto been made of the two treatises in question, to prove this statement.

Besides the general similarity in tone and style, there are found single words and phrases common to the two works, though but rarely if at all found elsewhere, at least, in the *Organon*. For example, 3a 36: ἀπὸ μὲν γὰρ τῆς πρώτης οὐσίας οὐδεμία ἐστὶ κατηγορία, and 109b 4 ἀπ' οὐδενὸς γὰρ γένους παρωνύμως ἡ κατηγορία κατὰ τοῦ εἴδους λέγεται. κατηγορία in this sense is rare in Aristotle (cf. Trendelenburg, *De Arist. Categ.*, pp. 8–9; *Gesch. d. Kategorienlehre*, p. 5; Bonitz, "Ueber die Kateg. d. Arist.," *Sitzungsb. d. phil.-hist. Kl. d. Kais. Akad. d. Wiss. zu Wien.*, X, pp. 591ff., *especially* 602, n. 2, 620–23), and with the combination of ἀπὸ as above is sufficiently striking to argue identity of authorship.

Again, 8a 33, ὁ δὲ πρότερος ὁρισμὸς παρακολουθεῖ μὲν πᾶσι τοῖς πρός τι, οὐ μὴν τοῦτό γέ ἐστι τὸ πρός τι αὐτοῖς εἶναι τὸ αὐτὰ ἅπερ ἐστὶν ἑτέρων λέγεσθαι, and 125 b 24 ἴσως μὲν οὖν ἀκολουθεῖ δύναμις ἑκατέρῳ τοιαύτη . . .

οὐ μὴν τοῦτό γε ἐστὶ τῷ μὲν ἀνδρείῳ τῷ δὲ πράῳ εἶναι . . . Here again the phrase οὐ μὴν τοῦτό γέ ἐστι is rare, if at all found anywhere else, and in the passage cited, it is used in both instances with ἀκολουθεῖ or παρακολουθεῖ, in the preceding clause to express the difference between the real definition, which signifies the essence of the thing defined, and an attribute or property, which, while always present with the thing, does not represent its essence. (Waitz is no doubt correct in adopting in 8a 34 the reading given above, τοῦτο γέ ἐστι τό, in preference to Bekker's ταὐτόν γέ ἐστι τῷ as appears from the similar passage in the *Topics* [125b 26], though neither Waitz [I, p. 302] nor Prantl [*Ztschr. f. Altertumswissensch.*, 1846, p. 650], who, in fact, opposes Waitz's reading, knew of the passage in the *Topics*.)

The mean between the contraries is generally, though not always, in the *Physics* and the *Metaphysics* designated by the term μεταξύ; in the *Categories* and the *Topics*, in the former exclusively, by the term ἀνὰ μέσον; cf., for example, 12a 2, 3, 9, 10, 11, 17, 20, 23, 24; b 28, 30, 32, 35, 36; 13a, 7, 8, 13, and 106b 4, 5, 8, 10, 11; 123b 18, 19, 23, 25, 27, 29; 124a 6, 7; 158b 7, 22, 38.

Compare also ὁ κατὰ τοὔνομα λόγος, 1a 2, 4, and 107a 20; also 1a 13, τὴν κατὰ τοὔνομα προσηγορίαν with 107a 3, τῶν κατὰ τοὔνομα κατηγοριῶν.

1b 16, τῶν ἑτέρων γενῶν καὶ μὴ ὑπ' ἄλληλα τεταγμένων ἕτεραι τῷ εἴδει καὶ αἱ διαφοραί, οἷον ζῴου καὶ ἐπιστήμης . . . = 107b 19 ἐπεὶ δὲ τῶν ἑτέρων γενῶν καὶ μὴ ὑπ' ἄλληλα ἕτεραι τῷ εἴδει καὶ αἱ διαφοραί, οἷον ζῴου καὶ ἐπιστήμης.

The opposite of αὔξησις is the scientific and metaphysical works of Aristotle is invariably φθίσις, in the *Categories* (15a 13–14) and in the *Topics* (122a 28) it is μείωσις (cf. Prantl, *Ztschr. d. Altertumwiss*, 1846, p. 651). In one instance (320b 31) θφίσις is defined by μείωσις (ἡ δὲ φθίσις μείωσις), the less known by the more known, and this accounts very readily for the use of the latter in the *Topics*, which is a popular treatise, and the *Categories* is of the same character. The other kinds of motion not being mentioned in the *Topics*, there is no possibility of the *Categories* having borrowed it from the *Topics*.

Compare also 11a 2, τά γε κατὰ ταύτας λεγόμενα . . . ἐπιδέχεται τὸ μᾶλλον καὶ τὸ ἧττον, and 127b 20, 24 τὸ δ'εἶδος μὴ δέχεται [sc. τὸ μᾶλλον καὶ ἧττον] μήτ' αὐτὸ μήτε τὸ κατ' ἐκεῖνο λεγόμενον.

So much for purely linguistic similarities. When we pass over to matters of doctrine, it is surprising how many points of contact there are between the two works. I shall follow the *Categories* and point out the parallels in the *Topics*.

The homonyms, which are given a definition and an illustration in the beginning of the *Categories*, have a whole chapter devoted to them in the *Topics*, the fifteenth of the first book, where they are also called πολλαχῶς λεγόμενα. Of particular significance is 107a 18–20, for in 20 we seem to have a direct allusion to the definition in the *Categories*. We must see, Aristotle says, if the genera designated by the given name are different and not subordinate to one another, as, for example, ὄνος applies to the genera ζῷον and σκεῦος (which is therefore a homonym), for the definition of these genera as connected by the name is different (ἕτερος γὰρ ὁ κατὰ τοὔνομα λόγος αὐτῶν). The greater space given to homonyms in the *Topics* is not due so much to a development in doctrine as to the necessities of the subject. The object of the *Topics* is a purely practical one, to provide the disputant with ready arguments properly pigeon-holed, and a single general definition of homonyms is not adapted to such use. We must needs go farther and show in what different special ways homonyms can be detected. The *Categories* have more the appearance of materials gathered in the shape of preliminary definitions of necessary concepts.

Synonyms are referred to in the *Topics* 109b 7, 123a 27, 127b 5, 148a 24, and 162b 37. Of these, the first is the most important, since it states that the genera are predicated synonymously of their species; *for the latter admit both the name and the definition of the former* (καὶ γὰρ τοὔνομα καὶ τὸν λόγον ἐπιδέχεται τὸν τῶν γενῶν τὰ εἴδη), assuming it as established that this condition constitutes synonymity. This is neither more nor less than a silent reference to the definition in the *Categories* (1a 6)—συνώνυμα δὲ λέγεται ὧν τό τε ὄνομα κοινὸν καὶ ὁ λόγος ὁ αὐτός. Moreover, we have almost the very words of the *Topics* in another place in the *Categories*, 3b 2, καὶ τὸν λόγον δὲ ἐπιδέχονται αἱ πρῶται οὐσίαι τὸν τῶν εἰδῶν καὶ τὸν τῶν γενῶν, καὶ τὸ εἶδος δὲ τὸν τοῦ γένους. 148a 24 also gives the same definition of synonyms merely in passing. Aristotle is dealing with the definition, and makes a statement that if the opponent makes use of one definition for homonyms it cannot be a correct definition, for it is synonyms and not homonyms that have one definition connoted by the name (συνώνυμα γὰρ ὧν εἷς ὁ κατὰ τοὔνομα λόγος). He speaks of the definition as already known. Similarly in 162b 37, καὶ ἐν ὅσοις τὸ ὄνομα καὶ ὁ λόγος τὸ αὐτὸ σημαίνει is a definition of συνωνύμοις preceding, and the καὶ is epexegetic (cf. Trendelenburg, *Elemen. Log. Arist.*, 6th ed., 1868, pp. 126–27).

Paronyms also are made use of in the *Topics*, 109b 3–12, in a way which shows the definition in the *Categories* is not purely grammatical, as it may seem at first sight, but has a logical significance quite as important as that of the former two. Paronymous predication is predication *per accidens*, as contrasted with synonymous, which may be per se (cf. also Trendelenburg, *Gesch. d. Kategorienlehre*, p. 27 et sq. and 30). Here also paronyms are not defined. It is assumed that the reader knows what they are.

The difference between καθ'ὑποκειμένου λέγεσθαι and ἐν ὑποκειμένῳ εἶναι, stated in the *Categories* 1a 20 et sq., is assumed as known in the *Topics* 127b 1 et sq., ἔτι εἰ ἐν ὑποκειμένῳ τῷ εἴδει τὸ ἀποδοθὲν γένος λέγεται, καθάπερ τὸ λευκὸν ἐπὶ τῆς χιόνος, ὥστε δῆλον ὅτι οὐκ ἂν εἴη γένος· καθ' ὑποκειμένου γὰρ τοῦ εἴδους μόνον τὸ γένος λέγεται (cf. also 126a 3 and 144b 31). Strange to say, however, after these distinctions Aristotle himself uses them interchangeably in 132b 19 et sq.

Categories 3, p. 1b 10–15 expresses very much the same thought as *Topics* IV, 1, p. 121a 20–6. The former states that whatever is true of the species is true of the individuals under the species (ὅσα κατὰ τοῦ κατηγορουμένου λέγεται, πάντα καὶ κατὰ τοῦ ὑποκειμένου ῥηθήσεται), the latter that to whatever the species applies the genus does also (καθ'ὧν γὰρ τὸ εἶδος κατηγορεῖται, καὶ τὸ γένος δεῖ κατηγορεῖσθαι). They both involve the logical hierarchy of genus, species, and individual, and the two principles are: (1) The genus applies not only to the species but also to the individual; (2) to the individual belongs not only the species but also the genus. What is especially important to notice is that, in the *Topics*, the principle is stated as already known and is applied to the particular case, thus assuming the existence of another treatise where these principles are stated and proved for the first time.

The treatment of the difference develops gradually in the *Topics* in the following passages: 107b 19 sq., 144b 12 sq., and 153b 6. The first of these is word for word the same with the statement in the *Categories*, 1b 16 sq., and they were both quoted above. Moreover the way in which the passage in the *Topics* is introduced, ἐπεὶ δὲ τῶν ἑτέρων γενῶν, etc., makes it a direct reference to the *Categories*. Aristotle's doctrine concerning the difference so far is that of different genera which are not subordinated one to the other: the differences are different in species. In the second passage quoted above, 144b 12, Aristotle corrects this view by adding that the differences in the given case need not be different unless the different genera cannot be put under a common higher genus. In the third passage, 153b 6, Aristotle adds some more qualifications which make it clear that in the preceding statements the word ἑτέρων, in the phrase ἑτέρων γενῶν, must be understood as including contrary genera (ἐναντία). For there the case is different. If the contrary genera belong to higher contrary genera, their differences may be all the same.

The preceding examination seems to show very clearly that the *Topics* build upon the basis laid down in the *Categories* and carry the structure higher and broader. It would be a very absurd alternative to suppose that a later writer, making use of the *Topics*, found nothing else on the subject of logical difference than the first passage, which he copied verbatim in his treatise, where, besides, it has no particular reason for existence. As a thought tentatively suggested, with the view of further elaboration and insertion as a proper link in a chain, the passage in the *Categories* assumes a different meaning, and its lack of connection with the preceding and following ceases to cause us serious difficulty.

If the view of the *Categories* taken here is justified by the preceding arguments and by what is still to come, it might even be a legitimate procedure to make use of the *Topics* in determining a disputed reading in the *Categories*. And we have one at hand in the passage quoted above on the difference.

Of genera which are subordinated one to the other, there is nothing, Aristotle says, to prevent the differences from being the same. For the higher genera are predicated of the lower, so that all the differences of the higher are also differences of the lower (ὥστε ὅσαι τοῦ κατηγορουμένου διαφοραί εἰσί, τοσαῦται καὶ τοῦ ὑποκειμένου ἔσονται). The last statement is manifestly untrue if it means that all the differences of the genus are also differences of any of its species. For example, the differences of ζῷον are πεζόν, πτηνόν, ἔνυδρον, etc. But surely these are not all differences of ἄνθρωπος, nor is any one of them a difference of ἄνθρωπος; for a difference of any class is that which, added to the name of the class, restricts it to a lower species; but πεζόν added to ἄνθρωπος merely repeats it, so that it is not the difference of ἄνθρωπος.

To obviate this difficulty, the Greek commentators, Porphyry, Dexippus, Simplicius, and the rest divide differences into "constitutive" (συμπληρωτικαί) and "divisive" (διαιρετικαί) so that πεζόν, πτηνόν and ἔνυδρον are divisive or specific differences of ζῷον, because, added to ζῷον, they divide it into its various species; at the same time, πεζόν is a constitutive difference of ἄνθρωπος, as forming part of its definition. With this distinction the meaning of the text is supposed to be that all the constitutive differences of the higher are also constitutive of the lower. This is not satisfactory, for Aristotle does not use differences in this sense (cf. Waitz, I, p. 279). Boethus (ap. Simplic. Basileae, 1551 f. 14b) emended the text to read ὅσαι τοῦ ὑποκειμένου . . . τοσαῦται καὶ τοῦ κατηγορουμένου ἔσονται. This emendation was not adopted by the later commentators, but there is a passage in the Topics which may be considered to favor it—111a 25–29. οὐ γὰρ ἀναγκαῖον, ὅσα τῷ γένει ὑπάρχει, καὶ τῷ εἴδει ὑπάρχειν· ζῷον μὲν γάρ ἐστι πτηνὸν καὶ τετράπουν, ἄνθρωπος δ' οὔ. ὅσα δὲ τῷ εἴδει ὑπάρχει, ἀναγκαῖον καὶ τῷ γένει· εἰ γάρ ἐστιν ἄνθρωπος σκουδαῖος, καὶ ζῷόν ἐστι σπουδαῖον.

The ten categories enumerated 1b 25 sq., are very frequently referred to in the various Aristotelian writings (cf. the table in Prantl, Gesch. d. Logik, I, p. 207, n. 356) but nowhere do we find the complete number ten except in the Topics 103b 22 where they are given in the very same order as in the Categories. They are not defined, thus showing that they are not treated there for the first time.

The discussion (3b 10) whether οὐσία, and particularly δευτέρα οὐσία, is τόδε τι or not, is again referred to in Περὶ Σοφιστικῶν Ἐλέγχων, which, according to Waitz and Pacius, is the ninth book of the Topics. The passages are 169a 35, 178b 38, 179a 8. Here it is

difficult to tell which was written first. The view in the *Categories*,
that the δευτέρα οὐσία περὶ οὐσίαν τὸ ποιὸν ἀφορίζει, ποιὰν γάρ τινα οὐσίαν
σημαίνει, looks like a compromise, and, as such, might be supposed
to be later than the similar discussion in the *Sophistic Refutation*
which denies the character of τόδε τι to the universal: φανερὸν οὖν ὅτι
οὐ δοτέον τόδε τι εἶναι τὸ κοινῇ κατηγορούμενον ἐπὶ πᾶσιν.

One of the arguments that Prantl builds much on to prove the
Categories spurious is the corrected definition of the category of
relation, 8a 32: ἔστι τὰ πρός τι οἷς τὸ εἶναι ταὐτόν ἐστι τῷ πρός τί πως ἔχειν.
This definition is a proof to Prantl (*Logik*, p. 90, n. 5) that the
Categories was not written before the time of Chrysippus; for, he
continues, *what occasion could one possibly have had before Chrysippus
to ask whether* πρός τι *is the same as* πρός τί πως ἔχον? *The expression,*
πρός τί πως ἔχειν, he asserts further, *is never found again in all the works
of Aristotle.* In the first statement he has reference to the Stoic
division of existents into four classes, ὑποκείμενα, ποιά, πρός τι, and
πρός τί πως ἔχοντα. The difference between the last two is thus expressed by Simplicius (*ap.* Prantl, I, p. 435, n. 101): πρός τι μὲν
λέγουσιν ὅσα κατ᾽ οἰκεῖον χαρακτῆρα διακείμενά πως ἀπονεύει πρὸς ἕτερον,
πρός τι δέ πως ἔχοντα ὅσα πέφυκε συμβαίνειν τινὶ καὶ μὴ συμβαίνειν ἄνευ
τῆς περὶ αὐτὰ μεταβολῆς καὶ ἀλλοιώσεως μετὰ τοῦ πρὸς τὸ ἐκτὸς ἀποβλέπειν.
As examples of the former, he gives ἕξις, ἐπιστήμη, αἴσθησις, which,
while being related to something else, have a character of their
own; of the latter πατήρ, υἱός, δεξιός, whose very essence is exhausted in their relation to something else. Hence Prantl jumps
to the conclusion that the author of the *Categories* was a late
Peripatetic influenced by the Stoic doctrine.

But a little linguistic analysis will show that Prantl confused
cause and effect. Only on the assumption of the existence of the
Categories before the Stoics can we rationally explain the origin
of the division and the terms. In itself, πρός τί πως ἔχον ought to
signify a less strict relative than πρός τι; the effect of the πως would
be to weaken the force of the πρός τι, and if the Stoics were the
first to coin these terms, they would have probably changed them
about. But the process becomes transparent when we suppose
that the Stoics had the book of the *Categories* before them. Here
the restrictive force in the second definition lies not in the words
πρός τί πως ἔχειν. These are merely a repetition of the original

definition (6a 36), ὅσα αὐτὰ ἅπερ ἐστὶν ἑτέρων εἶναι λέγεται, ἢ ὁπωσοῦν ἄλλως πρὸς ἕτερον, where the genitive relation of ἑτέρων and the other relations of ὁπωσοῦν ἄλλως are briefly summed up in πρός τι πως ἔχειν. The restrictive force lies in the few words that precede, οἷς τὸ εἶναι ταὐτόν ἐστι τῷ πρός τι πως ἔχειν. Now the Stoics were of the opinion that the class of relation ought really to be divided into two classes, and they abbreviated the definition, and the result was the catchword (for that was all that was wanted) πρός τι πως ἔχον.

For the second statement of Prantl, that πρός τι πως ἔχειν is never found in the works of Aristotle, rash is a mild term. Waitz had already pointed out (*Org.*, I, p. 266) that, in the *Topics*, Aristotle makes use of this corrected definition, Zeller (*loc. cit.*) adds 247a 2, b 3; 1101b 13, and we may add also 170b 30, 39. ἐν τῷ τὸν ἀποκρινόμενον ἔχειν πως πρὸς τὰ δεδομένα . . . οὐ τῷ τὸν ἀποκρινόμενον πρὸς τούτους ἔχειν πως.

The two passages in the *Topics* where use is made of the second definition are 142a 29 and 146b 4. Of these both have the appearance of referring to something that is already known, particularly the second, where the form ἦν (ἐπειδὴ ταὐτὸν ἦν ἑκάστῳ τῶν πρός τι τὸ εἶναι ὅπερ τὸ πρός τι πως ἔχειν) is clearly a reference to another place. This can scarcely be an allusion to the first passage in the *Topics*, for there is no proof of any kind there; it is all assumed. The close connection of the *Categories* with the *Topics* is shown here again, for these are the only two that have the second definition. In the *Metaphysics*, Δ, 15, p. 1021a 28, the first alone is used.

The reciprocal relation obtaining between the relative and its correlative, and the care necessary to properly designate the correlative in order to bring about this reciprocal relation as treated in the *Categories*, 6b 28 sq., are again referred to in the *Topics*, 125a 5 and 149b 4 sq., 12. In both passages cited, this attribute of reciprocity or convertibility (πρὸς ἀντιστρέφοντα λέγεσθαι) is assumed as known, and the necessity of getting the proper correlative (πρὸς ὃ λέγεται) is, in the latter passage, deduced from this attribute of the category of relation.

Topics, Δ, 6, p. 127b 18–25, reminds one of the similar discussion and phraseology of the *Categories*, pp. 10b 26–11a 2. Particularly the phrase τὸ κατ' ἐκεῖνο λεγόμενον, used in the *Topics* without any further explanation, as a familiar expression, looks very much like a reminiscence of τά γε κατὰ ταύτας λεγόμενα in the *Categories*, which in turn is an abbreviated form, or at least is connotive of the phrase (10a 27), τὰ κατὰ ταύτας παρωνύμως λεγόμενα ἢ ὁπωσοῦν ἄλλως ἀπ' αὐτῶν, and of the illustrative passage following.

The distinction made between πρός τι καθ'αὐτό and κατὰ τὸ γένος in *Categories*, p. 11a 23–36, and the question which this naturally raises, whether it is possible for the genus to be in a different category from its species, are mentioned again—120b 36 sq., 124b 15 sq., 146a 36, 173b 2.

If we examine the treatment of ἀντικείμενα in the *Topics* (106a 36 sq., 109b 17 sq., 123b 18–124a 9, 124a 35 sq., 143b 35), there will be no doubt left in our minds that it is based on that of the *Categories* (11b 34 sq.), rather than on the discussion of the *Metaphysics* (1018a 20 sq., or 1055a 3 sq.). We find the threefold classification of ἐναντία as found in *Categories* (14a 19), viz.: (1) in the same genus; (2) in opposite genera; (3) not in genera at all, being themselves genera (see above). The mean between the two extremes is designated in the *Categories* exclusively, in the *Topics* all but exclusively (the only exception being 123b 14, 17, 18), by the term ἀνὰ μέσον instead of by μεταξύ, which is the term used in the *Metaphysics*, 1057a 21 sq. (cf. Waitz, I, 310), while in the first passage, 1018a 20, where the classification of ἀντικείμενα is given, there is no mention at all of the mean.

This mean, the *Categories* (12a 20) tells us, is in some cases designated positively (ὀνόματα κεῖται τοῖς ἀνὰ μέσον), in some negatively (τῇ ἑκατέρου τῶν ἄκρων ἀποφάσει), and examples are given to substantiate the statement. In the *Topics* (123b 20) the truth is made use of as one already known: ἢ εἰ ἔστι μέν τι ἀμφοῖν ἀνὰ μέσον, καὶ τῶν εἰδῶν καὶ τῶν γενῶν, μὴ ὁμοίως δέ, ἀλλὰ τῶν μὲν κατὰ ἀπόφασιν τῶν δ' ὡς ὑποκείμενον. An illustration is given but the meaning of the terms is not explained. The definition of στέρησις, in the *Categories* (12a 29), is referred to in the *Topics*, 106b 27: ὅτι δὲ κατὰ στέρησιν καὶ ἕξιν ἀντίκειται τὰ νῦν λεγόμενα [sc. αἰσθάνεσθαι] (ἀναίσθητον εἶναι], δῆλον, ἐπειδὴ πέφυκεν ἑκατέραν τῶν αἰσθήσεων ἔχειν τὰ ζῷα . . . and 143b 35 τυφλὸν γάρ ἐστι τὸ μὴ ἔχον ὄψιν, ὅτε πέφυκεν ἔχειν.

Another reminiscence of the *Categories* is found at 131a 14–15, where Aristotle, in speaking of ἴδιον, says that it is not proper to assign as ἴδιον of an object a term or phrase involving the ἀντικείμενον of the object or what is ἅμα τῇ φύσει with it or what is ὕστερον, since these last do not make the thing clearer, and it is for the sake of greater clearness that the ἴδιον is used. Now it will be noticed that these three topics, ἀντικείμενα, ἅμα, and ὕστερον are actually discussed in succession, though not in the same order, in the *Categories* (11b 16, 14a 26, and 14b 24).

The term ἀντιδιῃρημένον and the idea denoted by it, seem to be peculiar to the *Categories* and the *Topics*. In the former it is defined in connection with the treatment of ἅμα (14b 33), and in the latter it is made use of as a familiar term (136b 3, 142b 7, 143a 34). Another consideration which makes it unlikely that the author of the *Postpraedicamenta*, not Aristotle, based his work on the *Topics* is that in treating of ἅμα he does not include ἀντικείμενα as one class of ἅμα τῇ φύσει, whereas he must have done so if he had before him 131a 16 (τὸ μὲν γὰρ ἀντικείμενον ἅμα τῇ φύσει) or 142a 24 (ἅμα γὰρ τῇ φύσει τὰ ἀντικείμενα).

Finally another argument made much of by those who deny the authenticity of the *Categories* (cf. espec. Prantl, *Ztsch. d. Alterth.*, 1846, p. 651) is the mention of six kinds of motion instead of three, or at most four, as Aristotle gives in the *Physics* (cf. Waitz, I, p. 318 sq.). Since the kinds enumerated are the same here as in the *Physics* and the difference lies only in reckoning γένεσις and φθορά, αὔξησις and μείωσις (φθίσις) as two or as four, there would be little in the argument to stay our conviction of the authenticity of the work, but this very peculiarity seems to make my case stronger; for, in the first place, I have already shown above that whereas in the other works of Aristotle φθίσις is the contrary of αὔξησις, in the *Categories* and the *Topics* it is μείωσις, and it is not likely that it was borrowed in the *Categories* from the *Topics*, since the complete list of the kinds of κίνησις is nowhere given in the *Topics*. In the second place, it appears from two passages in the *Topics* that, at the time of its composition, Aristotle regarded αὔξησις and μείωσις (φθίσις) as two, and similarly, γένεσις and φθορά as two. The passages are 111b 7, οἷον αὔξεσθαι ἢ φθείρεσθαι ἢ γίγνεσθαι ἢ ὅσα ἄλλα κινήσεως εἴδη, and 122a 28, εἰ οὖν ἡ βάδισις μήτ' αὐξήσεως μήτε μειώσεως μήτε τῶν ἄλλων κινήσεων μετέχει . . .

Dupréel, as I said before,* is the only one who has made a considerable contribution to the question since my article was published. His argument has no point of contact with mine, for he compares the *Categories* not with the *Topics*, but with the *Metaphysics*, and finds that they do not agree in doctrine.

I have no reason to quarrel with Dupréel when he tries to show that the first nine chapters, the categories proper, and the last six chapters, the *Postpraedicamenta*, are a unit and the work of the same author, for my comparison of the treatise with the *Topics* has led me to the same conclusion.

Nor have I any special reason to oppose his idea that the purpose of the treatise is not merely a treatment of the ten categories, but of the fundamental notions of philosophy. The title πρὸ τῶν τόπων, which I favor in my article, is not necessarily opposed to this idea. It may very well be that the nine categories correspond to the συμβεβηκότα καθ'αὑτά of the *Metaphysics* and the *Postpraedicamenta* to the matters mentioned in *Metaphysics* B, 995b 20 sq. And Dupréel is quite right when he points out that the style and matter of the *Categories* do not exhibit the philosophic power and genius of the *Metaphysics*, that in comparison with the latter the *Categories* is extremely shallow and banal. But so is book Δ of the *Metaphysics* in comparison with the rest of the book. But this is not sufficient to question the authenticity of Δ.

The whole argument of Dupréel seems to be based on the difference in the meaning of πρώτη οὐσία in the *Categories* and in the *Metaphysics*. In the *Categories* it means the individual, in the *Metaphysics* the form of τί ἦν εἶναι. This is merely a difference in terminology and may be paralleled by differences in the meanings of other terms in different works of Aristotle admitted to be genuine. One need only think of the terms καθ'αὑτό and γνωριμώτερον ἡμῖν. The term πρῶτος has different meanings in Aristotle. After all, Aristotle's doctrine on the nature of reality is not clear-cut, and the τί ἦν εἶναι itself is not just a universal, but somehow identical with the individual. When Dupréel decides that some shallow and

* *Journal of Philosophy.*

obscure person who did not know of Aristotle's theory of matter and form, but had merely heard of the term πρώτη οὐσία and misunderstood its meaning, wrote the *Categories*, long after Aristotle, he is assuming something very improbable. One who knew as much about Aristotle's philosophy as did the author of the *Categories* (on Dupréel's own admission) could not have been ignorant of his theory of matter and form.

I naturally have no quarrel with the group which favors the traditional view that the *Categories* is a genuine work of Aristotle. But, as we have seen, all of them reject the last six chapters. And so far as I can gather, Brandis is supposed to have clinched the argument against the authenticity of the *Postpraedicamenta*. So at least says Zeller.[15] But I have shown at length that Brandis's argument is based upon a misstatement of the facts. When the facts are stated correctly Brandis's argument falls. Brandis attempts to prove that the *Topics* was written before the *Categories* because the *Categories* shows a more complete analysis of ἐναντία than the *Topics*. I have shown that that is simply not true, that the *Topics* has the complete analysis and with more explanation and detail than the *Categories*. To be sure, this statement may be regarded as a boomerang. If the *Topics* has a detailed analysis of ἐναντία, and the *Categories* contains merely the statement of the result, then, it may be said, the *Categories* merely copied the result from the *Topics* and left out the rest. I admit that that is possible. But this does not help Brandis, Zeller, and the rest of the group because they seem to be committed to the opinion that the treatise which has the more advanced view is the later one. In any case one cannot speak of any *proof* that the *Topics* is earlier.

I have no particular comment to make on Maier's[16] idea that the earlier part of the *Categories* is related to the *Sophist* of Plato, as that is, of course, compatible with the notion that the *Categories* is an earlier writing of Aristotle when he was closer to Plato than later.

As for the expression ἐν Λυκείῳ used twice in the *Categories* (chap. 4, p. 2a 2, and chap. 9, p. 11b 14) as an example of the category of place (ποῦ) on which Gomperz and Jaeger insist as indicating

(15) See n. 4.
(16) See n. 5.

that the *Categories* could not have been written in Aristotle's youth, when the school of the Lyceum was not yet in existence, Mure[17] answers the argument by saying that "the Lyceum was a haunt of Socrates."

Summing up it would seem that I may even now repeat what I said thirty-four years ago: "I have shown, I trust, not only that the treatise of the *Categories* is closely related to that of the *Topics*, but also that it was written before the latter and serves as a basis for it upon which it builds, very often going beyond the *Categories*. This applies to the first nine chapters, properly called *Categories*, in the same measure as to the *Postpraedicamenta*. The unity of the book of the categories as we now have it is also maintained by Valentinus Rose [we may now add Dupréel]. *Ergo*, the whole work is genuine, and its peculiar character is to be explained on the ground of its being one of the| earliest attempts of Aristotle."

(17) *Aristotle*, p. 268, note.

NEWTON'S NATURAL PHILOSOPHY
ITS PROBLEMS AND CONSEQUENCES

JOHN HERMAN RANDALL, JR.
Department of Philosophy, Columbia University

SIR ISAAC NEWTON was not technically a "philosopher." He was at once something less, and something more—one of those men, like Darwin, Planck, or Einstein, who succeed in formulating ideas that make philosophers necessary, and to whom philosophers should therefore look with a mixture of extreme annoyance and deep gratitude. It is safe to say that had Newton—or someone else—not published his *Principia Mathematica* in 1687, there is hardly a single subsequent thinker whose thought would not have been different. It might perhaps have been more sterile, perhaps less confused and more consistent; but at least it would have been profoundly different. The ideas formulated by Newton have been ever since an intellectual fact to be reckoned with, and his "natural philosophy" has been the starting-point of all attempts to understand Nature, whether men have accepted it as ultimate, or have attempted to get behind it to something more ultimate and real. Not till this generation have the facts amassed by inquiry seriously shaken its main outlines. This body of Newtonian ideas can be viewed objectively today, for, we are told, it has disappeared from our own rapidly shifting natural philosophy. The great Newtonian system—as contrasted with his specific scientific discoveries—which for two centuries passed as the truth about our world, has crumbled before our very eyes. It is now dead, we gather from any contemporary account of the physical world—so dead that most of our philosophical works discuss it interminably, and vie in pointing out just where Newton made the wrong assumptions. A strange kind of mortality, to be sure! Newton may be dead, but he is certainly not buried; and his ghost seems as healthy as ever, and busily engaged in haunting us. We cannot set forth what we now believe about Nature without first examining in detail what we no longer believe.

Newton became in his own lifetime the symbol of both a method and an idea. The method for which he came to stand was usually called in the eighteenth century the "geometric spirit." It meant the endeavor to find a deductive system of science, depending on initial axioms themselves discovered by "analysis." Inspired by his example, men set to work confidently to become the Newtons in every field, especially in the various branches of the science of man and society. They undertook an initial analysis of their complex subject matter to find the axioms involved—an analysis which not unnaturally usually confirmed their previous insights and prejudices—and then arrived at their conclusions by a dialectical development of the consequences of these principles. Newton's success in natural philosophy stamped this "geometrical" or "analytic" method as the one scientific method to be applied universally.

Newton stood also as the symbol of an idea, the idea of Nature as a rational and harmonious order, to be discovered by this method in any subject matter—an order in striking contrast to the confusion and irrationality introduced by previous men into their traditional ideas and institutions. The goal of thinking was the search for this rational order. What was rational was *ipso facto* natural, and what was natural was what appealed as reasonable to the enlightened common sense of the progressive thinker. The history of eighteenth century thought is therefore largely the story of the search for the rational order of nature, expressing itself in natural laws, natural rights, a natural religion, and a natural morality.

Newton won his reputation and influence as a symbol because he actually succeeded in realizing the ideal of the seventeenth century scientists: he was really able to formulate a mathematical interpretation of Nature, and, unlike Descartes, to do it in genuinely mathematical terms. Like Galileo and Descartes, he too regarded nature as a tissue of properties, precisely ordered, the connexions of which could be expressed in terms of mathematics. Like them, he aimed "to subject the phenomena of nature to the laws of mathematics"; but unlike

them he had succeeded. He had found the mathematical principles and techniques to fit the various observations of the
astronomers, like Kepler's three laws of planetary motion, and
the "two new sciences" of Galileo, into a single mathematical
system. He had done what had been predicted: he had furnished the mathematical proof that the universe was a perpetual
motion machine. And so he reaped the glory of a century of
patient work. No wonder Pope exclaimed,

> Nature and Nature's laws lay hid in night;
> God said, Let Newton be, and all was light.[1]

God had let a good many others be also; but Newton gained
the credit. His name became synonymous with science. The
eulogies ranged from Addison's sober prose, "the greatest
mathematician and philosopher that ever lived,"[2] to more imaginative heights of fancy:

> 'Twas thence great Newton, mighty genius, soar'd
> And all creation's wondrous range explored.
> Far as th'Almighty stretched his upmost line,
> He pierced, and thought, and viewed the vast design.[3]

> From Heav'n's unbounded depth, she cried, I stole
> Angelic fire and form'd a Newton's soul.
> Taught him the secret walks of God to tread;
> And twixt the starry worlds his spirit led . . .
> Yet when the suns he lighted up shall fade,
> And all the worlds he found are first decay'd,
> Then void and waste Eternity shall lie,
> And Time and Newton's name together die.[4]

Halley in his *Eulogy* went even farther:

> Newton, that *reach'd* th'inseparable line,
> The nice barrier twixt human and divine!

It is scarcely surprising that Newton's own thought turns out
on examination to be rather different from Newton the symbol,

---

[1] Pope, *Works* (Cambridge ed.), p. 135.
[2] *Tatler*, Aug. 30, 1710.
[3] William Melmoth, *Of active and retired life.*
[4] Aaron Hill, *Tears of the Muses, Epitaph.*

both in method and in idea. We propose to consider his method, in which he worked out a quite different conception of the nature and goal of science than that for which he came to stand in the popular mind, a conception elaborated by Locke, and developed in detail by Berkeley and Hume into the main stream of the British tradition. At the same time he both suggested and made inevitable a second interpretation of science and its goal, an interpretation destined to come down through the nineteenth century as the great rival philosophy of science to that of the British thinkers: the Kantian philosophy. We shall then examine Newton's idea of what he called "the real world." His notions, especially his ideas of mass, space, and time, created puzzling problems for scientists, theologians, and philosophers. They not only raised insuperable difficulties for Locke, Berkeley, and Hume, and for subsequent British empiricists to this day. In the hands of Euler and the German physicists they led straight to Kant. Together with his conception of God as a principle of mechanics, they determined the course of Protestant rational theology. They form the background of nineteenth century philosophic idealism, and they remain, one suspects, partly responsible for the present outburst of speculative theology on the part of contemporary British and American mathematical physicists.

To understand the double aspect of Newton's method, as well as the concepts in terms of which he suggested his thought about the "real world," it is necessary to remember something of the background these ideas had in the British scientific mind of the previous generation. There had been two main streams in British science, the one predominantly mathematical and allied to the Platonic tradition in its metaphysical presuppositions and its basic physical concepts, the other primarily experimental and not nearly so hostile to Aristotelian ideas. The former was much influenced by the speculations of Henry More and his fellow Platonists, and received scientific statement in the words of Isaac Barrow, Cambridge mathematician and Newton's own teacher. The latter was associated more closely with the "physico-mathematical experimental learning" of the Royal Society; it is illustrated in extreme form in Joseph

Glanvill, and represented most brilliantly in the outstanding British scientist before Newton, Robert Boyle. Newton himself was very consciously the heir of both these scientific traditions, the mathematical and the experimental; the characteristic ideas of both flowed together in his own inconsistent thought.

In his method Newton was closer to Galileo than to any of the other seventeenth century variations upon the method of the *Posterior Analytics*, and to those more experimental-minded Frenchmen who kept a critical attitude toward Descartes: to Roberval, Gassendi, and Pascal. He had not seen Descartes' vision of a universal mathematics, and while he hoped that all phenomena might be mathematically explicable as forms of motion, he was not certain: he lacked what More called Descartes' "inexsuperable confidence." He was delighted to have reduced the palette of color to a mathematical pattern: he always insisted that "the science of colors becomes a speculation as truly mathematical as any other part of optics."[5] But he carefully distinguished between mathematical and physical propositions. He thought it possible that some physical propositions might not be expressible in mathematical terms. On the other hand, while he was sympathetic to confirmed experimentalists like Boyle, and quite willing to lend the prestige of his name to the rather aimless fooling around with things that consumed the time of many of the members of the Royal Society, he insisted strongly that nothing could be called really scientific knowledge that was not mathematically demonstrable. He tried, indeed, to keep a proper balance between an unlimited confidence in mathematics unchecked by experience, and mere experimenting unaccompanied by mathematical analysis and demonstration. He was the harmonizer of the two main methodological currents that had come down to him, the compromiser rather than the extremist.

Hence the general statements of his method which he permitted himself to set down sound much like Galileo, or any other seventeenth century physicist: "From the phenomena of motions to investigate the forces of nature, and then from

[5] *Opticks* (1721 ed.), p. 218.

these forces to demonstrate the other phenomena."[6] Again: "To derive two or three general principles of motion from phenomena, and afterwards to tell us how the properties and actions of all corporeal things follow from those manifest principles."[7] But he gave this method an experimental coloring, more even than Galileo, who after establishing the laws of motion felt no need of checking by observation on any of the consequences mathematically deduced from them. Newton did feel the need for such a check. The logical inclusion of a proposition within a deductive system was not enough to provide full verification: there might always be exceptions! Hence on the one hand he agreed with all the seventeenth century scientists that mathematical deduction from first principles alone gives intelligibility and understanding, alone shows why phenomena are as they are, gives the *causa mathematica*. But he did not agree that it supplies in itself a sufficient logic of proof to establish a fact. With Newton, the experimental analysis of instances in Nature, direct observation, forms a part not only of the method of discovery, as it did for all his contemporaries, but enters also into the logic of proof. It guarantees the physical reality of what has been mathematically demonstrated. In the language of Locke, whose problems of knowledge reflect much more closely than is usually supposed the problems of Newton's own thought, it transforms "certain" knowledge into "real" knowledge.

This experimental emphasis Newton signalized in his Fourth Rule of Reasoning in Philosophy:

In experimental philosophy we are to look upon propositions collected by general induction from phenomena as accurately or very nearly true, notwithstanding any contrary hypotheses that may be imagined, till such time as other phenomena occur, by which they may either be made more accurate, or liable to exceptions.[8]

Mathematical principles, that is, are always open to experimental revision in the light of freshly observed facts. He feels, indeed, that experimental proof is needed even of the basic

[6] *Principia Mathematica* (Motte trans., 1803), Preface, p. x.
[7] *Opticks*, p. 377.
[8] *Prin. Math.*, Bk. III; II, p. 162.

principle of the uniformity of Nature laid down in the Second and Third Rules:

That it should be so [that the theorem of the uniform proportion of the sines applies to all rays of light] is very reasonable, nature being ever conformable to herself; but an experimental proof is desired.[9]

He distinguished carefully between the certainty attainable in mathematical demonstration and the certainty attainable in physical science, even when mathematics is employed:

I should take notice of a casual expression which intimates a greater certainty in these things, than I ever promised, viz., *the certainty of mathematical demonstrations*. I said, indeed, that the science of colors was mathematical, and as certain as any other part of optics; but who knows not that optics, and many other mathematical sciences, depend as well on physical sciences, as on mathematical demonstrations? And the absolute certainty of a science cannot exceed the certainty of its principles. Now the evidence, by which I asserted the propositions of colors, is in the next words expressed to be from experiments, and so but *physical*; whence the propositions themselves can be esteemed no more than *physical principles* of a science. And if those principles be such, that on them a mathematician may determine all the phenomena of colors, . . . I suppose the science of colors will be granted mathematical.[10]

The best statement of what may be called Newton's mathematical experimentalism is to be found at the conclusion of the *Opticks*:

As in mathematics, so in natural philosophy, the investigation of difficult things by the method of analysis, ought ever to precede the method of composition. This analysis consists in making experiments and observations, and in drawing several conclusions from them by induction, and admitting of no objections against the conclusions, but such as are taken from experiments, or other certain truths. For hypotheses are not to be regarded in experimental philosophy. And although the arguing from experiments and observations by induction be no demonstration of general conclusions; yet it is the best way of arguing which the nature of things admits of,

[9] *Opticks*, p. 66.
[10] *Opera* (Horsley ed.), IV, 342.

and may be looked upon as so much the stronger, by how much the induction is more general. And if no exception occur from phenomena, the conclusion may be pronounced generally. But if at any time afterwards any exception shall occur from experiments, it may then begin to be pronounced with such exceptions as occur. By this way of analysis we may proceed from compounds to ingredients, and from motions to the forces producing them; and in general, from effects to their causes, and from particular causes to more general ones, till the argument end in the most general. This is the method of analysis: and the synthesis consists in assuming the causes discovered, and established as principles, and by them explaining the phenomena proceeding from them, and proving the explanations.[11]

Newton's procedure may therefore be said to consist of three stages: 1) Analyse the observed facts, to discover the principles therein involved. This process Newton called "deducing principles from phenomena" to emphasize the rigorous sense in which they are to be found involved in the data of observation, and not added by thought as an explanation of what is observed—in which, as Aristotle would have put it, they are seen to be there by *Nous*. 2) Then make all the relevant phenomena of the field under investigation intelligible by fitting them into a mathematical system depending on these principles, as he had himself done with Kepler's laws. This is the process Galileo called "composition," and Descartes "synthesis." 3) Finally, verify the physical reality of these conclusions by experiment.

When this has been accomplished, we have a mathematical system or order of phenomena, resting on experiment: a system of mathematical laws experimentally verified. But we have not yet discovered the physical or mechanical *cause* of these laws. It remains to find the mechanism involved. For instance, when we have proved that bodies tend to approach each other with a force directly proportional to the product of their masses and inversely proportional to the square of their distance apart, we can still ask, Why do they act that way? What makes them do

[11] *Opticks*, p. 380.

it? From these phenomena of motions we must still investigate the "forces of nature."

At just this point, on the causes of mathematical laws, Newton's thought divides. He was convinced that he did know the cause of the laws of motion: it is the *vis inertiae* resident in all mass. He was equally convinced that he did not know the cause of the law of gravitation, or the force involved. So his confidence in having found the force lying back of the laws of motion led his incipient experimentalism back to the orthodox conception of seventeenth century science, demonstrative knowledge from causes; while his ignorance of the force involved in the law of gravitation led it on to a novel conception of the nature of science, from which the concept of causality ultimately vanishes. This is a fundamental methodological dualism in Newton's thought which has been reflected in Locke's difficulties and in most subsequent philosophy.

On the question of the causes of the laws of Nature, Newton was extremely cautious. He distrusted the unverified mechanical hypotheses in which Descartes and many of his successors had reveled, such as the mechanical explanation of gravitation in the Cartesian vortex theory, in Gassendi, Huygens, Hooke, and Boyle. He was much interested in such explanatory hypotheses suggesting possible mechanisms for the operations of Nature; he himself advanced several different versions of a plausible mechanism for gravitation, and worked upon the idea all his life. But he rigidly excluded from "experimental philosophy" or science such "propositions assumed or supposed without any experimental proof."

I frame no hypotheses; for whatever is not deduced from the phenomena is to be called an hypothesis; and hypotheses, whether metaphysical or physical, whether of occult qualities or mechanical, have no place in experimental philosophy.[12]

What Newton meant precisely by "hypotheses" in this pronouncement is clear from a letter to Cotes:

As in Geometry the word Hypothesis is not taken in so large a sense as to include the Axioms and Postulates, so in experimental

Philosophy it is not to be taken in so large a sense as to include the first Principles or Axioms which I call the laws of motion. . . . And the word Hypothesis is here used by me to signify only such a proposition as is not a Phenomenon, nor deduced from any Phenomenon, but assumed or supposed without any experimental proof.[13]

Generalizations ordering and describing observed phenomena, or "mathematical causes," are not called hypotheses but axioms or first principles. In other words, Newton is excluding physical explanations or causal hypotheses, not descriptive or coördinating hypotheses. The engraver well understood this distinction who expressed his admiration for Newton, on a picture in which he appears as "a star of the first magnitude," in the lines:

> See the great Newton, he who first surveyed
> The plan by which the universe was made;
> Saw Nature's simple yet stupendous laws,
> And proved the effects, though not explained the cause.

He would have been still more accurate had he said, "not yet explained the cause"; for that there was a mechanical cause of gravitation to be found Newton never doubted.

Hence Newton recognized two kinds of cause or force in Nature: the force of inertia, a real power inherent in matter, and deduced from phenomena; and the force of gravitation. What the latter might be, he never committed himself upon; experimental philosophy had proved the "cause" of motion to be the force of inertia, but as yet had found only the law, not the "cause" of gravitation.

We must . . . universally allow that all bodies whatsoever are endowed with a principle of mutual gravitation. . . . Not that I affirm gravity to be essential to bodies: by their inherent force (*vis insita*) I mean nothing but their *vis inertiae*. This is immutable. Their gravity is diminished as they recede from the earth.[14]

I use the words attraction, impulse, or propensity of any sort toward a center, promiscuously, and indifferently, one for another;

[13] March 28, 1713; cited in Rosenberger, *Isaac Newton*, p. 372.
[14] *Princ. Math.*, Bk. III, Third Rule of Reasoning; II, 162.

considering those forces not physically, but mathematically: where-
fore, the reader is not to imagine, that by those words I anywhere
take upon me to define the kind, or the manner of any action, the
causes or the physical reason thereof, or that I attribute forces, in
a true and physical sense, to certain centers (which are only mathematical points); when at any time I happen to speak of centers as
attracting, or as endued with attractive powers.[15]

I use the word attraction in general for any endeavor, of what
kind soever, made by bodies to approach to each other; whether
that endeavor arise from the action of the bodies themselves, as
tending mutually to or agitating each other by spirits emitted; or
whether it arises from the action of the aether or of the air, or of
any medium whatsoever, whether corporeal or incorporeal, any how
impelling bodies placed therein towards each other. In the same
general sense I use the word impulse, not defining in this treatise
the species or physical qualities of forces, but investigating the
quantities and mathematical proportions of them.[16]

And yet, despite this habitual caution, Newton allowed
Roger Cotes to write the preface to the second edition of the
Principia, making "attraction," a force acting at a distance, the
real cause of gravitation, a power in bodies attracting other
bodies. To be sure, as late as 1717, in the second edition of his
Opticks, he wrote:

To show that I do not take gravity for an essential property of
bodies, I have added one question concerning its cause, choosing to
propose it by way of a question, because I am not yet satisfied about
it for want of experiments.[17]

Yet this lapse from caution outraged every mechanistic conscience, called down the wrath of Huygens as "absurd," and
provoked Leibniz to dub it a relapse into the barbarism of the
occult qualities of the schoolmen, the negation of all science.
Nevertheless it became the orthodox interpretation; and a new
kind of physical cause, "attraction," entered the body of science
along with the contact of billiard balls.

Hence it is clear how Newton could have two distinct types

---

[15] *Princ. Math.*, Bk. I, Def. 8; I, 6.
[16] *Princ. Math.*, Bk. I, Prop. 69; I, 174.
[17] *Opticks*, Advertisement II.

of influence on ideas of the nature and method of science. The first was orthodox, conservative, realistic, continuing the seventeenth century versions of the Aristotelian doctrine of science: science is a logical system explaining facts by mathematical deduction from their causes. The second was radical, novel, and "positivistic": science is a description of the experimentally observed relations between phenomena, expressed in mathematical language. The one sprang from Newton's conviction that inertia is the real cause of motion, and fitted a new cause, attraction, into the traditional scheme. The other sprang from his realization that he did not know the physical cause of gravitation, and assimilated the laws of motion to the law of gravitation as mathematical statements of the observed mathematical relations between phenomena, without seeking the causes of those relations. The first view, that science is a deductive system of causes, when combined with Newton's insistence that it must be a system deduced wholly from phenomena, led in the more penetrating Newtonians, Keil, Friend, Euler, and the other German physicists, directly to Kant. The second view, that science is a description of the observed course of nature, led in Berkeley, Hume, Maupertuis, Condillac, and Diderot to the empiricism of Mill and the British tradition, and to the positivism of Comte and the French. Hence while the popular mind, following Newton's supposed example rather than his precepts, took Newton as the triumph of the rationalistic, deductive method, and his ideal of science as realistic, the discovery of "the plan by which the universe was made," those who bothered to read and study him made him the father either of the Kantianism of the continental tradition, or of the observationalism of the British empiricists. Kantianism took its rise in the confident possession of an exact science of nature, whose validity could not be experimentally established yet ought to be; empiricism, in the confession of an ignorance only too apparent.

Just because Newton was so cautious, so convinced that all the ideas he admitted to his experimental philosophy were "deduced from phenomena," he made a number of uncriticised assumptions that have persisted in the structure of physical science and in the general philosophy of Nature until this generation. It is well to be suspicious of all men who proclaim that they are making no assumptions, that their ideas are forced upon them by the obvious facts. In large part, to be sure, Newton's assumptions were those implicit in the whole method of seventeenth century science, in the mathematical interpretation of nature itself; and hence Newton can be said to have crystallized rather than originated them, though his own determination of the concepts of mass and inertia added further details, and his vacillation as to method created new presuppositions. Certain of the more famous of Newton's assumptions —like those of absolute time and absolute space, which awakened vigorous criticism in his own generation—were made more plausible by the theological background of his natural philosophy; but in general it seems fairly clear that Newton's theological ideas were determined by his scientific concepts rather than vice versa. Theology, indeed, rarely distorts science; but science, in the hands of modernists, is always corrupting sound theology.

Indeed, Newton was surprisingly conservative in his view of the nature of "the real world." He had played a major part in making the concept of "force" and the ideas of the calculus an essential part of scientific thought, and it might have been expected that he would make these notions fundamental in his interpretation of the structure of Nature. But he quite failed to develop the implications of his own discoveries; he assumed without serious question the main outlines of the geometrical world as they had been laid down by Galileo and Descartes, and his own novel concepts made little difference. This is especially striking if Newton's natural philosophy be compared with that of his contemporary Leibniz. Leibniz, operating with similar concepts of force and the calculus, did make them basic in his thought; and in consequence he gives today an impression of much greater insight and profundity. The German seems really to have thought in terms of the calculus, not in terms of the more traditional geometry and matter in motion.

The two great contemporaries in fact illustrated a difference in mentality which has persisted through the many adventures that have since befallen the two traditions on which each left so profound an impress. English thought has been dominated by the conception of knowledge as a matter of sense-images; German, by the view that it is an affair of equations. The English thinker has been unhappy when he could not picture a world of substances; the German has been quite satisfied with a world of functional relations. The English scientist has been unwilling to rest content until he has pictured a world he could imagine; the German has sought rather for a system he could conceive. Like Kelvin, British scientists have had to invent a mechanical model before they have felt they really understood, and they have frequently been held back by their refusal to admit the unimaginable. The empirical tradition, in which the elements of knowledge are invariably sensations or images, has proved ineradicable in British thought; the rationalistic tradition, with its emphasis on relations, concepts, and systems of laws, has been as characteristically German. It goes without saying that in the present state of physical science this British preference for the substantial and concrete is having a hard time of it. Image and substance seem to have disappeared from contemporary physical theory. No mechanical model has yet proved possible for the systems of radiation we now handle mathematically with such assurance; our physicists offer us a world that is certainly unimaginable, and, one sometimes suspects, may in the end prove inconceivable as well! Leibniz seems to have the upper hand over Newton; Einstein has vanquished Oliver Lodge, and Heisenberg, Bohr.

Newton's method we have characterized as a mathematical experimentalism; and in his actual procedure he certainly introduced as many mathematical postulates as he found necessary to build up a rational system of mechanics or optics—postulates which it remained for the eighteenth century physicists to disentangle and state precisely, in the manner which Kant elevated into a philosophy. But, like so many other Englishmen of the seventeenth century, and later, his own theory of the logic of science was neither rational nor experimental, but "empirical." That is, he was convinced that the ultimate subject matter of science—what empiricists call the "data of science"—can consist only of what is directly given in sensation, that the origin and justification of science, and of all scientific concepts, of all the properties of matter figuring in his experimental philosophy, must be sought in ideas received through the senses. This insistence that the ultimate validity of science lies in its foundations in sense is as cardinal an assumption for Newton as for Locke, an assumption which makes inevitable the "problem of knowledge" that has created so many technical difficulties for subsequent philosophical thought, and is the tragic guilt initiating the long drama of epistemology.

In Newton as in Hobbes or Locke, this empiricism may well be due ultimately to the strong persistence in English thought of the Ockhamite logic, coming down through the Schools from the late Middle Ages. In Newton's case it was certainly reinforced by the desire to defend himself against the charge of having reintroduced the occult qualities of the Schoolmen, especially the traditional scholastic "gravitation." He always insisted with great touchiness that the objects to which his calculations applied were not abstractions of thought, but were given directly in sense: that all the scientific concepts he employed were "deduced from phenomena." His *Hypotheses non fingo* states this empiricism negatively; it is put positively in the Third Rule of Reasoning:

The qualities of bodies which admit neither intension nor remission of degrees, and which are found to belong to all bodies within the reach of our experiments, are to be esteemed the universal qualities of all bodies whatsoever . . .

We no other way know the extension of bodies than by our senses, nor do these reach it in all bodies; but because we perceive extension in all that are sensible, therefore we ascribe it universally to all others also. That abundance of bodies are hard, we learn by experience; and because the hardness of the whole arises from the hardness of the parts, we therefore justly infer the hardness of the undivided particles not only of the bodies we feel but of all others. That all bodies are impenetrable we gather not from reason, but from sensation. . . . The extension, hardness, impenetrability, mobility, and *vis inertiae* of the whole result from the extension, hardness, impenetrability, mobility, and *vires inertiae* of the parts; and thence we conclude the least particles of all bodies to be also all extended, and hard, and impenetrable, and movable, and endowed with their proper *vires inertiae*. And this is the foundation of all philosophy.[18]

Newton was obviously not unacquainted with what Locke called "simple ideas."

Now Newton's actual mathematical procedure made it necessary for him to assume much that his empiricism could not justify; and in his ideas of "the real world" his scientific procedure and his empirical theory collide violently. What his procedure led him to assume as mathematical postulates his empiricism made him treat as real physical existents, at least potentially observable. So he was led to describe the real world as consisting of entities with properties which by definition ought to be observable, yet in fact were not; at the same time that he insisted that sense observation alone furnished the data and the validation of the science of the relations of these entities.

Newton's real world is therefore made up of absolute masses endowed with an absolute force of inertia, and perhaps with a force of "gravitation," in absolute motion in absolute space and time; while sense experience supplies no evidence for any of these concepts. They could of course all be justified as logical assumptions, as mathematical principles employed to make intelligible what is directly experienced, as the later Newtonians and Kant did justify them. But when one insists, as Newton does, that science is a system of the relations of physical existents which are potentially perceptible, which ought to be perceived, and yet which cannot be, there are obviously at hand all the makings for a perplexing "problem of knowledge."

Nature consists, then, of unobservable particles of matter, provided with those properties universally present in every object we do perceive.

It seems probable to me, that God in the beginning formed matter in solid, massy, hard, impenetrable, movable particles, of such sizes and figures, . . . as most conduced to the end for which he formed them.[19]

[18] *Princ. Math.*, Bk. III; II, 160, 161.
[19] *Opticks*, p. 375.

In this world as it came from the hands of the Creator were no sounds, no colors, no warmth, no odors. It is the Cartesian world of extended particles, to which have been added, however, the solidity, mass, hardness, and impenetrability which distinguish bodies from space: a world of masses endowed with the force of inertia and the other tangible qualities of experience. To these elementary masses moving in empty space are added, in the case of man, souls on the Cartesian model, joined to the human body in what Newton calls the "sensorium." Only by the sense of touch can we know the qualities of bodies as they really are, for mechanical contact is the only relation they can really have to us; but we see only images produced in the sensorium, hear only sounds, perceive only odors there generated, not the real things which produce these sensations in the sensorium.

What the real substance of anything is we know not. In bodies, we see only their figures and colors, we hear only the sounds, we touch only their outward surfaces, we smell only the smells, and taste the savors; but their inward substances are not to be known, either by our senses, or by any reflex act of our minds.[20]

Newton still insists that he is being strictly empirical; for his non-sensible ultimate particles have no qualities save those found by experience to belong to all bodies of which we do have sensible experience. Yet the very existence of such particles is of course a dialectical necessity of thought, not an empirical fact; for they cannot possibly be observed. There is no conceivable way of reaching these ultimate masses by the only method which Newton recognized, the analysis of what is given in sense, "deduction from phenomena." They can have no empirical standing and must remain dialectical postulates. Hence the real essences of the bodies we do observe remain unknown, especially the crucial force of gravitation. Yet science is of the relations of these essences. Locke had merely to elaborate Newton's assumptions to generate his characteristic problems. These particles or tiny billiard balls are not even necessary for the formulation of Newton's mathematical laws

---

[20] *Princ. Math.*, Bk. III, General Scholium; II, 312.

of motion. The whole *Principia* could equally well stand if taken as applying to geometrical points endowed with mass, as Berkeley showed.

Why then did Newton desert his professed empiricism, which Berkeley later carried out consistently as an interpretation of mechanics, for dialectic? Because his mathematical procedure made him assume certain concepts, like inertia, which his very empiricism made him regard as physical existents and therefore potentially observable. Mathematical causes, principles of intelligibility, must be for him physical forces, real causes, lodged in real substances. The real cause of motion must be a physical force, inertia; just as for Euler it was another physical property of the particles, impenetrability. And these ultimate bearers of force must be permanent substances.

While the particles continue entire, they may compose bodies of one and the same nature and texture in all ages; but should they wear away, or break in pieces, the nature of things depending upon them would be changed. . . . And therefore that Nature may be lasting, the changes of corporeal things are to be placed only in the various separations and new associations and motions of these permanent particles.[21]

"That Nature may be lasting" Newton assumes a plurality of fixed, unchanging, discrete substances, under the spell of the old Eleatic dialectic. Newton has surely gone a long way from his insistence that all the concepts of physics must be given directly in sense! Starting with a subject matter directly experienced, he was led to seek by dialectic its necessary conditions. He found them in a realm which his own method of verification, the direct appeal to sense, could not possibly reach. His absolute fixed masses or intrinsically immutable particles can be deduced from phenomena as perceived only as the logical presuppositions of experience, making it possible and intelligible. They cannot be perceived in sensation, yet they must be real and objective; and to be real and objective they must be somehow involved in sensation. Thus the whole Kantian position is clearly implicit in Newton's combination of the procedure of making mathematical postulates with the empirical

[21] *Opticks*, p. 376.

logic that they must be immediately involved in sense observation.

Nor is this all. These fixed masses must have fixed essences, that is, unchangeable properties, the permanent sensible qualities of solidity, mass, impenetrability, motion, and inertia. All change must be accidental and external, must affect only the relations of these masses, not their fixed qualities or essences. Scientific procedure thus deals with the mathematical relations between masses. Yet science is defined as demonstration from causes, and the causes of phenomena are the non-relational powers and properties of these masses, their real essences, which are inaccessible to scientific procedure. It would seem obvious that a science that deals primarily with relations must define its concepts relationally. Yet Newton was led to conceive the real world as a world of masses with non-relational powers and properties, unknowable in terms of his science. The causes, then, of the mathematical relations between bodies are to be sought in their real essences, and their real essences are by definition unknowable. Thus the whole Lockean position is clearly implicit in Newton.

Moreover by making, like Boyle, half the qualities of bodies relational, dependent, that is, on the interaction of bodies, and hence observable—the so-called "secondary qualities"; while the other half, the "primary qualities"—likewise all relational in present-day physical theory—were left as self-contained and absolutely inherent in absolute masses, Newton established a gulf between objects experienced and the objects of science, between the world men live in and what empirical theory still calls "the physical world." Unlike Boyle, he assumed the latter to be alone real, the former to be present only in the sensorium. Science is thus left with the task of demonstrating the relations between unknowable elements in terms of unknowable causes. No wonder Locke, reflecting on this state of affairs, was led to comment, "We can have a useful and experimental, but not a scientifical philosophy of natural bodies." Newton's procedure implied that the concern of science was with mathematical relations in the experienced world. Yet his empirical logic drove him to assume that the terms of those relations are not in the experienced world at all, and yet are the only reality. The absolute masses of classical mechanics, instead of being taken as mathematical abstractions or isolates, were regarded as the sole components of Nature. Here is a cardinal illustration of what Whitehead has called the "fallacy of misplaced concreteness."

Still further, the assumption that the mathematical constants involved in his system were physical existents led Newton frankly to abandon even his professed empirical method with regard to motion, space, and time. He had perfectly satisfactory notions of motion, space, and time, as relative to the observer's frame of measurement, and only this measurable, "relative" motion, space, and time are actually employed in the *Principia*, in the application of the laws of motion to astronomy, for example. Yet the definition of motion, space, and time from the relation they bear to sense is a vulgar prejudice. So he is constrained to assume the physical existence of an "absolute" motion, space, and time. Absolute space is a fixed container, "in its own nature, without regard to anything external, always similar and immovable." Absolute time is also a physical existent, "of itself and from its own nature always flowing equably without regard to anything external."[22] This space and time provide a fixed frame within which masses have an absolute and intrinsic motion and rest of their own, independent of any relation to any other body or observer. This is the true nature of absolute motion, space, and time—though we can never observe them, but can measure and use only relative motion, space, and time.

It is a standing question why Newton brought in these absolutes at all; and many are the answers that have been given. In the light of the totality of his thought, it seems clear that they are implied in his mathematical procedure. His very statement of the first law of motion is in terms of absolute motion: "Every body perseveres in its state of rest or uniform motion in a straight line, unless it is compelled to change that state by forces impressed thereon." Such absolute velocity and acceleration demand absolute positions and dates—i.e., these absolutes are the logical presuppositions of the laws of motion of fixed,

[22] *Princ. Math.*, Bk. I, Scholium to Definitions; I, 6.

independent masses. They are principles in terms of which the observed motions of bodies are made mathematically intelligible. This was pointed out by Maclaurin, the most penetrating of the British Newtonians: "This perseverance of a body in a state of rest or uniform motion, can only take place with relation to absolute space, and can only be intelligible by admitting it."[23] The same position was developed at some length by Leonhard Euler, the greatest and most original of the second generation of Newtonians. Absolute space and time are mathematical postulates, "ideas of reflection," and not physical existents. Yet they are objectively true, and not merely "ideal" or "imaginary"—Euler was a Newtonian compelled to defend himself against a scientific opinion in which Leibnizians predominated—because they are necessary to make the experience which is adequately described in the laws of motion intelligible.[24]

But Newton did not himself follow this line of thought, which points so clearly to Kant. As usual he was forced by his empiricism to assume that mathematical postulates must be at least potentially observable, must be physical existents. In this case he actually tried to obtain experimental proof of the existence of absolute rotary motion, of an absolute acceleration wherein absolute space and time would be directly implied, and as it were almost visible. He twirled a pail half-full of water, and in the resulting concave surface thought he beheld the immediate effect of absolute motion. To imagine that mathematical postulates must be given immediately in sense is a confusion typical of the whole empirical philosophy of science down to our own day.

It is also true that such physical absolutes were necessary if Newton's absolute massy particles were to remain unchanged. Without a fixed container of absolute space, any interaction between substances would of necessity result in internal changes —and Nature would not be lasting. Thus Leibniz, assuming a purely relative time and space, was forced to posit the ab-

[23] Colin Maclaurin, *An Account of Sir Isaac Newton's Philosophical Discoveries* (1748), Bk. II, Chap. I, Sec. 9.
[24] See L. Euler, *Réflexions sur l'espace et le temps*, 1748.

sence of any interaction; and Whitehead today, assuming both relativism and interaction, is logically compelled to make his elements or events parts of a system of internal relations, continually modifying each other ad infinitum. In other words, if the masses which serve as terms in Newton's equations are to be absolute physical constants, so must the rest of the concepts of the *Principia*. As Euler put it, whatever is necessary to validate the mathematical laws of motion is *ipso facto* a real element in the experienced world, even though it never be found directly in observation.

Thus Newton's natural philosophy ultimately purported to describe a world, every element in which was inaccessible to observation, yet was also potentially observable to a perfect mind, ought to be observed, and cried aloud for such a mind to observe it. Hence it is not surprising that he should have given all his absolutes a home in the mind of God. Absolute time and space are God's sensorium: by existing God constitutes them, as the container wherein all motions take place. This Divine Sensorium or Mind sustains the entire field of physics, just as the Divine Will, or ether, the vehicle of force, holds the system of moving masses together. This theological foundation of Newton's natural philosophy thus needs no extraneous religious reasons to account for its presence, though such reasons were undoubtedly influential in his background, and his pronouncements are strikingly reminiscent of Henry More. It is there primarily because such a world needed a Supreme Observer to constitute it and hold it together. The consequences of the necessity of such a constitutive mind have been momentous for the subsequent philosophy of physical science. In Kant's version, pure reason, a generalized form of the human mind, has replaced the mind of God; but the divine mind returned with the idealists, and throughout the nineteenth century down to our present-day gropings, the world of physics—the so-called "physical world"—when conceived in Newtonian terms as existing in sharp contrast to the world of human experience, has always craved a Supreme Mind to lend it structure and permanence. Despite all the drive towards positivism, such a mind, whether taken as God or Reason, has persisted in some form as an ultimate physical concept. Where such a constitutive mind has been wholly lacking, as in the empirical tradition, natural science has had little structure or permanence; and empiricists have been always committed to trying to persuade physicists that their science ought to be a far different kind of thing, and ought to have a far different kind of structure, from what it in fact is and has.

DAVID HUME'S CONTRIBUTION TO
SOCIAL SCIENCE*

WILSON D. WALLIS

Department of Anthropology, University of Minnesota

The Human mind is of a very imitative nature; nor is it possible for any set of men to converse together, without acquiring a similitude of manner, and communicating to each other their vices as well as virtues. The propensity to company and society is strong in all rational creatures; and the same disposition, which gives us this propensity, makes us enter deeply into each other's sentiments, and causes like passions and inclinations to run, as it were, by contagion, through the whole club or knot of companions. *Of National Characters.*

IN THE history of social thought two great periods challenge attention: the period of the Stoics, and (approximately) the latter half of the eighteenth century. The Stoics included human nature in their scheme of Nature; applied to man the laws which they found applicable to Nature; and did not make the mistake of supposing that the factors which explain Nature explain also human action and motives. They appreciated the part played in human affairs by historic setting, which they conceived as essentially of two dimensions: time and culture. The latter half of the eighteenth century offers a long roster of men justly famous for contributions to social thought: Kant, Schiller, Herder; Montesquieu, Turgot, Condorcet, Rousseau; Hume, Ferguson, Price, Paine. Their precursors from Bodin to their own times are, of course, many, and they contributed to the clarity and fullness of eighteenth century thought.

Eighteenth century social thought is inseparable, save historically, from a wider endeavor which was laying the foundations of subsequent intellectual disciplines: a theory of probability applicable to discrete phenomena; astronomy with a

* For a critical reading of this essay and helpful suggestions, I am indebted to Dr. Alburey Castell, of the University of Minnesota.

celestial mechanics bequeathed by Newton; zoology; botany; anthropology; chemistry. Observation became an art guided by science; systems of classification laid the foundations of present day biologic disciplines; and these permitted comparisons which later gave the bases and the rationale of the great theory of evolution formulated and elaborated by Darwin. Not all of these contributions were duly weighed by contemporaries. Thus Hume writes in 1776: "Never literary attempt was more unfortunate than my 'Treatise of Human Nature,' it fell *dead-born from the press*, without reaching such distinction as even to excite a murmur among the zealots." He might have written similarly of his subsequent contributions to social thought, as notably those made in various essays contained in the collection which he called *Essays Moral, Political, and Literary*.[1] Some of Hume's contributions to social thought preceded by more than a century the comparable work of other scholars; and some are still superior to present-day modes; for the technical philosopher has generally disregarded the feeble efforts of so-called social scientists. Few contemporary philosophers have given social thought and method even scant notice. They have been content to shrug their intellectual shoulders and pass by on the other side; or quietly thank their metaphysical stars that they are not as these benighted. Perhaps successful social science is more an art than a science; and possibly must content itself to remain such. If so, these presuppositions are a challenge.

It is probably not by accident that Hume's first essay in this collection deals with "Delicacy of Taste and Passion." It is certainly not by accident that he there indicates the strength and the weakness of both Stoic and Epicurean as arbiters of individual conduct. As Hesiod and Lucretius point out that social development brings greater ills along with greater goods, so Hume depicts the greater ills to which the more highly sensitive individual is subject, or to which, necessarily, he is subjected. For delicacy of taste, like delicacy of passion (emotion), "enlarges the sphere both of our happiness and misery, and makes

[1] Part I published 1742; Part II published 1752. In this paper I have followed the edition of 1777, as edited by T. H. Green and T. H. Grose, New York, Longmans, Green, 1907.

us sensible to pains as well as pleasures, which escape the rest of mankind." Delicacy of taste, however, "is as much to be desired and cultivated as delicacy of passion is to be lamented, and to be remedied, if possible." To develop taste, discrimination, is to be prepared to enjoy the greater pleasures—if only the philosopher can succeed in rendering happiness "entirely independent of everything external." Yet the greater taste for some things means, of necessity, the greater distaste for certain other things; it sharpens, and may intensify, the reactions of the more discriminating. Only the sensitive ear can be pained by discordances; only the appreciative eye twitches at the sight of ugliness; only those who gather roses are bothered by the thorn.

It is a theme to which Hume returns at the close of his essay on "The Natural History of Religion": "Good and ill are universally intermingled and confounded; happiness and misery, wisdom and folly, virtue and vice. Nothing is pure and entirely of a piece. All advantages are attended with disadvantages."

In the conviction "that politics may be reduced to a science," the title of one of his essays, Hume says: "so great is the force of laws, and of particular forms of government, and so little dependence have they on the humors and tempers of men, that consequences almost as general and certain may sometimes be deduced from them, as any which the mathematical sciences afford us." There are "eternal political truths, which no time nor accidents can vary." That the press should be free is one of them; that a democracy provides its own remedies is another; for free governments provide checks by which it becomes to the interest of even bad men "to act for the public good." "Effects will always correspond to causes; and wise regulations in any commonwealth are the most valuable legacy that can be left to future ages." "A constitution is only so far good, as it provides a remedy against mal-administration." "As Force is always on the side of the governed, the governors have nothing to support them but opinion." The extent to which government can manufacture and dispense opinion was not so well known to Hume as it is to us. Politics, then, or, let us say, social phenomena, can be reduced to a science. Yet up to

Hume's day scarcely anyone had attempted the task. Machiavelli, it is true, had laid down some principles; as Hume remarks, these are based on astute observations, yet are sometimes woefully amiss.

That Hume had a lively appreciation of many fundamental social problems is shown by the subjects which he selected for treatment, and by his keen analyses: money, interest, international trade, population, national characteristics, the development of the arts and sciences. One must look for causes; and one must not mistake the efficient, that is, the necessary and sufficient cause, for collateral causes; or confuse the immediate and necessary effect with collateral effects. Here he is conscious of a difficulty which confronts the social scientist at the present day: How control the experiment? How assess the weight of the contributing causes or distinguish accidental effects from inevitable, that is to say, necessary, effects?

A first step presupposes a distinction between kinds of phenomena: There are recurrent phenomena, in which a is linked to b, or a_1 to b_1, and these can be singled out for special attention; for the recurrence enables us to identify them as not accidental. A sheer accident which recurs frequently, nereby loses its character of sheer accident. The lightning which strikes every year in the same place is not wholly erratic lightning; and the place which thus attracts the lightning is recognized as partial cause of this recurrent phenomenon. When "secret and unknown causes" operate we term them chance; when causes operate which can be predicted because they inhere in circumstance, we call them causes. Secret and unknown causes have great influence on social phenomena, for they inhere in the personalities of the great men who advance the arts and sciences. Yet these causes are not wholly chance; for the possibility of their origin and operation inheres in the character of the civilization or culture in which they arise. Virgil is an unknown cause; he could not have been predicted and it follows that he cannot be wholly resolved into antecedent causes. If Greek and Roman culture had not existed he could not have been a great poet; and he could not have written an epic. Pre-Greek civilizations produced no epic; and the great civilizations of the Far East have not produced an epic. As a matter of fact, the civilizations which have utilized the milk of domesticated animals have produced epics; those which have not utilized this product have not produced epics. Here, I suppose, would be an example of what Hume means by the ease of confusing collateral with efficient causes. If epics and utilization of milk of animals are related otherwise than accidentally the nexus is not clear. But the nexus between Virgil and Homer and between Virgil and many other classical writers, is clear enough; and seems a necessary nexus. Literary traditions are historic causes and are presupposed by the existence of a Virgil; but they are necessary rather than sufficient causes, inasmuch as they are presupposed by the existence of every educated Roman of the day; yet only Virgil responded to them in the specific fashion which made this stimulus the inspiration of a genius. You may know the materials with which Virgil will work, as you know the medium of the tongue in which he will write, but you do not know the selection he will make and you cannot predict precisely how he will remake the materials. Nature works with less than a hundred chemical elements, yet affords endless delight and perplexity by the complexity and variety of her compositions, through all the realm of both the living and the non-living; and can paint in another dimension on this varied canvas a billion-year-old story of geologic and biologic evolution—not to mention the procession of cosmic phenomena. Culture, too, is capable of almost infinite variety, and enduring development; and always and everywhere the component individual is product of time and place, yet something more than this. If you do not know the culture in which a man lives you cannot predict the range of his personality and accomplishments any more successfully than you can predict the type of animal from its chemical composition when you do not know its species. To predict more specifically you must know his biography. Hume was well aware of the interdependence of individual and culture.

You can predict the course of the culture—within bounds, of course—but you cannot predict the specific character of component individuals. You cannot know how the drop of water will behave, in detail, when thrown into the stream; but you can predict the behavior of the stream if you have learned its biography. In a culture of ample bounds any given few individuals are but as drops of water in the great stream. It has flowed previously much as now it flows when they are part of it; when they are gone it will flow on in much the same fashion. Adjacent particles will be influenced; but distant ones will be very little affected. *"What depends upon a few persons is, in a great measure, to be ascribed to chance, or secret and unknown causes; What arises from a great number, may often be accounted for by determinate and known causes."* The variability in human behavior is such that only when we have a multitude of instances can we detect the underlying impetus which must counter a great variety of opposing or deflecting forces; for frequently these will prevent the result which otherwise would follow. Consider, for example, the matter of a die which has a slight bias. The factors which influence the fall of the die are so numerous and so delicate that they cannot be understood and so cannot be predicted for a given throw or for a few throws. But though the bias is weak, given a sufficient number of repetitions of the throw, the existence and character of the bias will be revealed. "This bias . . . will certainly prevail in a great number [of throws], and will cast the balance entirely to that side." Eventually the bias side of the balance sheet will outweigh any other side and will continue to outweigh any of them while the results of the experiment accumulate. The illustration is valid insofar as applicable. But in social phenomena frequently it is difficult to know that the die which we cast repeatedly remains essentially the same die; and that the bias does not shift position. When the ivory die is given a second throw it has, we presume, forgotten its behavior at the first throw, and is not influenced by previous performance; but when Caesar crosses a second fluvial boundary the crossing of the first Rubicon is somehow present in the subsequent venture. The die of social phenomena may start on its career according to specifications; but it may quickly become altered in surfaces, corners, and content.

The arts and sciences, Hume says, can arise only among a

people who "enjoy the blessing of a free government." Louis XIV would have thanked Hume; and there was Charles I and Cromwell; and Renaissance Italy. The reasons for Hume's conclusion are the following: There can be no social development without law; law provides security; amid security, curiosity is encouraged; from curiosity comes knowledge. "The latter steps of this progress may be more accidental; but the former are altogether necessary. A republic without laws can never have any duration."

"Nothing is more favorable to the rise of politeness and learning, than a number of neighboring and independent states, connected together by commerce and policy." The interchange of ideas leads to mutual cultural enrichment. History abundantly confirms this inference; acculturation has been one of the most important factors in the growth of civilization.

With Hume, the doctrine of the rise and fall of civilizations, a concept exploited by many writers from St. Augustine to the present day, is a dogma: *"When the arts and sciences come to perfection in any state, from that moment they naturally, or rather necessarily decline, and seldom or never revive in that nation, where they formerly flourished."* It seems "contrary to reason" but is "conformable to experience." For if men are endowed with essentially the same inherent abilities at all times and in all ages, as Hume is inclined to suppose the case, how can there be these limitations upon their actual and potential accomplishments? Can such limitations exist unless they are self-imposed? To these questions Hume gives no answer; for it is not an answer to aver, as he does, that, "the arts and sciences, like some plants, require a fresh soil; and however rich the land may be, and however you may recruit it by art or care, it will never, when once exhausted, produce anything that is perfect or finished in the kind." Even as analogy this is weak, indeed false; for, by his own assertion, human innate abilities remain the same; hence the soil of individual potentialities, in which the arts and sciences inhere, is not a poorer soil by virtue of the sustenance which they have previously yielded; the ability of a generation has, by hypothesis, not been impoverished by reason of the accomplishments of preceding generations. The children's teeth are not worn down because the fathers have overchewed their grapes. Hume's lame analogy is only a despairing lament; and yet I confess some sympathy for him in the dilemma which he poses: If men's abilities remain the same, or do not decrease in successive generations, why then cannot the arts and sciences proceed indefinitely in or on the same soil? Why must they either develop or decay? Does history play us false here? From recurrence of cycles shall we conclude that inevitably cycles lie ahead? Must civilizations have their death pangs even as, it seems, man the individual must die? Culture as a human achievement, it is true, may last, as human life outlasts the little day of the individual; but must cultures pass from the scene, to make way for weeds to refertilize the soil? There have been agrarian reforms; why not cultural reforms and regenerations? Why may not a culture live as long as mankind lives?

In the essay "Of National Characters," Hume indicates that assuredly national traits exist, despite the prevalent tendency to overemphasize the degree or kind of their peculiarity. In the various national groups some classes of people may behave much the same irrespective of the national character; thus priests are much the same in all European countries, however much some of these countries differ from others. Yet, in the main, when we cross national boundaries we pass from one atmosphere of manners and customs to a different social climate. What is responsible for national differences? Hume, writing before Montesquieu, rules out physical causes as an explanation. His reasoning is as good today as then it was original and fundamental. Briefly, the inadequacy of physical environment as explanation lies in the twofold fact that adjacent peoples who live in the same kind of physical conditions have contrasting customs; and peoples who occupy the same or a similar region may greatly modify their customs and accomplishments. Thus the modern Greeks differ greatly from the ancient Greeks; and the modern Greeks differ much from adjacent Turks. It is curious that Montesquieu, who must have known this essay, ignores the argument; whereas Turgot, likewise, no doubt, acquainted with the essay, uses the argument with telling effect. The origin of cultural differences lies within the field of culture. Some individuals show traits not exhibited to the same degree by their fellows, and these are copied by others. Thus an influence runs through the group and soon becomes a group trait. Political control brings together those who participate in a common government or are subject to a common authority; and thanks to a common political authority national traits become established and tend to maintain themselves. Hume's surmise is as good a guess as any; its correctness is abundantly illustrated by recent and contemporary events.

All sorts of men appear in all parts of the globe; but not necessarily with the same frequency. "It does not follow, that nature always produces them in like proportions, and that in every society the ingredients of industry and indolence, valor and cowardice, humanity and brutality, wisdom and folly, will be mixed after the same manner." Hence in a given society a peculiar mixture of these may suffice to give the character to national society; because men imitate their political fellows. "Persons in credit and authority" will have a considerable influence on the manners of the people. They "kindle the same passion in every bosom." Moreover, "whatever it be that forms the manners of one generation, the next imbibe a deeper tincture of the same dye; men being more susceptible of all impressions during infancy, and retaining these impressions as long as they remain in the world." The present-day historian of culture has no better interpretation of cultural phenomena. Cultural conditioning and the lasting effects of the influences of infancy are the twentieth century sesame to an understanding of human behavior. Thus "where a very extensive government has been established for many centuries, it spreads a national character over the whole empire, and communicates to every part a similarity of manners." Conversely, in small governments which are contiguous we may encounter a different atmosphere as soon as we step over the political boundary. From ancient Athens to Sparta was a short journey; yet one passed in a few hours from the Attic culture of Plato's day to the Dorian culture of Lycurgus. Today in any large Western city one can step directly from the twentieth century into the Middle Ages, despite the radio and the telephone. Scatter men abroad but allow them to maintain communication or cherish their former culture and in spite of intervening territory they remain essentially one culture group. For, as a present day anthropologist has said, echoing a sentiment of Horace, "the Englishman takes England with him, wherever he goes, and the Frenchman, France." Or, as Hume expresses it:

> Where any set of men, scattered over distant nations, maintain a close society of communication together, they acquire a similitude of manners, and have but little in common with the nations amongst whom they live. Thus the Jews in Europe, and the Armenians in the East, have a peculiar character. . . . The *Jesuits*, in all Roman-catholic countries, are also observed to have a character peculiar to themselves.

Language tends to establish community of manners because it fosters communication; and dissimilar languages are a barrier to cultural transmission. This deduction from history was also excellent prophecy.

The spread of cultural traits is facilitated by communication, whether by "policy, commerce, or travelling." Thus, to eastern nations, all Europeans "appear to have a uniform character . . . The differences between them are like the peculiar accents of different provinces, which are not distinguishable, except by an ear accustomed to them, and which commonly escape a foreigner." At a little distance, the local differences in European countries fade out, and the common underlying traits of the culture characterize the region as one culture area with local diversifications. This, too, is modern anthropology.

There are, perhaps, eternal truths; or some, at least, which seem capable of lasting out man's little day on the planet. Some of these truths were known to our preliterate forbears—more of them, it may be, than we commonly give preliterates credit for; many were known to the men of classical times; and not a few were appreciated by Hume. Even so he is a child of his day, if wiser than most of his contemporaries. He is the more a child of his day because he did not appreciate very acutely to what extent he reflected both time and place.

The historical perspective in which we see events was not so clear to Hume; the mosaic of cultures, ancient and modern, was, of necessity, as well known to him as to us. He oriented historic periods from the standpoint of a day which was a precarious present, and the end-product of preceding centuries and events. We orient the eighteenth century from the standpoint of a citizen of the near-middle of the twentieth century; and to us those eighteenth century creeds and problems belong to larger dimensions. Our culture falls into place in a spatial mosaic; psychologically we are the center of our geographic world; but reason as well as experience tells us that center and horizon shift with the standpoint of the observer. These orientations make a difference in all matters that pertain to social phenomena. I know what my ethnographical-minded friend meant when he averred that there was only one thing he longed to do with philosophers and philosophies, namely, to stick a red-headed pin on the map for each school of thought, with date indicated. It can be done; and, indeed, as a cultural phenomenon, it would have meaning. On such an imagined map the cultural significance of philosophy and philosophers is apparent. We are used to the idea that philosophic schools are historic phenomena; we are seldom conscious of them as cultural phenomena. Yet they are the latter no less insistently than the former. In the implied intellectual matrix which a system of thought takes for granted, rather than in the explicit principles which it formulates, rests the strength of a doctrine. The former saves it from being merely a few black marks on a white sheet. This is as true of minds as of morals. The unwritten constitution is more potent than the written; to commit it to writing invites a challenge to the exposed doctrine. As all anthropology can be subjected to the scrutiny and described under the categories of philosophy, so all philosophy is material for the anthropologist insofar as he is interested in cultural phenomena. The validity of the one procedure is equivalent to that of the other; the profit from the respective approaches is another matter. The philosopher will have the last word among philosophers; and among anthropologists he will be wise who speaks last and discourses about culture.

Hume would have been a better philosopher if he had been more acutely historical-minded and more astutely cultural-minded. In one of the editions of the essay "Of National Characters," for example, he added a footnote to this effect: "I am apt to suspect the negroes, and in general all the other species of men (for there are four or five different kinds) to be naturally inferior to the whites. There never was a civilized nation of any other complexion than white, nor even any individual eminent either in action or speculation." He supports this conviction by the assertion that "such a uniform and constant difference could not happen, in so many countries and ages, if nature had not made an original distinction betwixt these breeds of men." In this doctrine he has followers at the present day. Yet immediately afterward Hume observes:

The Greeks and Romans, who called all other nations barbarians, confined genius and a fine understanding to the more southern climates, and pronounced the northern nations incapable of all knowledge and civility. But our island has produced as great men, either for action or learning, as Greece or Italy has to boast of.

The implications of the Greek and Roman points of view as historic phenomena and as cultural phenomena seem to elude him, and he falls into the same type of error: the supposition that our measuring stick is absolute, not relative, and that the period in which we write is the end-point of world history. His conclusion may be correct; but his argument is as weak as that of the Greeks and Romans which he cites; indeed, it is their argument couched in English of the eighteenth century, and with the same presuppositions. Turgot appreciated historic depth and cultural dimension much more fully than did Hume; and Condorcet carried on the great tradition of Bodin and Turgot with better fruits for later generations than did Hume. Regarding the importance of the freedom of the press Hume says about all that is fundamental in Mill's discussion of Liberty; but he does not say it with Mill's insight into its significance for democracy. Despite the fact that Hume was a historian of some pretensions, he seems to have missed the import of historic forces. In contrast to the present-day view of them as deeply seated forces which sweep through generations, they are for him passing phases of human life, ephemeral and largely accidental or incidental. If he had seen himself and his times as part of a great flow of events containing influences from Greece and Rome, and from farthest Ind and Cathay; if he had contemplated the fact that the fundamentals of his civilization were developed in prehistoric times; if he had known how essential to one generation are the accomplishments of preceding generations; some of his reflections would have had richer issue in an ampler sweep of thought. For philosophy, no less than philosopher, is a child of its day; and as philosophy is oriented, so is its emphasis. For, "the human mind is of a very imitative nature. . . . If we run over the globe, or revolve the annals of history, we shall discover everywhere signs of a sympathy or contagion of manners."

In his *Natural History of Religion* Hume writes the first modern psychological interpretation of religion. Here he distinguishes between the rational and the psychological, the naive reactions to the world and the rationalizations of philosophers. It was not an easy distinction in that age of rationalism.

The psychological basis of religion he finds in supernaturalism. Phenomena which are out of the ordinary, seemingly disregardful of natural law and order, are phenomena to which all men, in the degree that they are untutored, react similarly.

Thus "convulsions in nature, disorders, prodigies, miracles, though the most opposite of the plan of a wise superintendent, impress mankind with the strongest sentiments of religion; the causes of events seeming then the most unknown and unaccountable."

Our present-day more extended knowledge of human nature obtained through acquaintance with peoples of various culture in all corners of the world confirms Hume's surmise. All preliterate peoples have an acute sense of the supernatural; and all of them see the supernatural in those phenomena which seem to defy Nature, which are extraordinary and therefore are feared.

Even at this day, and in Europe, ask any of the vulgar, why he believes in an Omnipotent Creator of the world; he will never mention the beauty of final causes, of which he is wholly ignorant. . . . He will tell you of the sudden and unexpected death of such-a-one; the fall and bruise of such another; the excessive drought of this season; the cold and rains of another. These he ascribes to the immediate operation of Providence: and such events, as, with good reasoners, are the chief difficulties in admitting a Supreme Intelligence, are with him the sole arguments for it. . . . For men being taught, by superstitious prejudices, to lay the stress on a wrong place; when that fails them, and they discover, by a little reflection, that the course of nature is regular and uniform, their whole faith totters, and falls to ruin.

Elsewhere Hume points out that the concepts of morality and religion must be kept separate; in this essay he points out that historically they have in practice often been kept separate, or intermingled variously.

Hume paved the way to much of our present day social science; and illuminated his exposition with many pertinent illustrations from modern and ancient history.

BIBLIOGRAPHY OF THE WRITINGS OF EDGAR ARTHUR SINGER, JR.

1896

"Physiology of sensation." Paper read before the American Psychological Association.

Book Review: *L'Hégémonie de la Science et de la Philosophie*, A. Fouillée. *The Psychological Review*, III, 4.

Book Review: *Lehrbruch der Allgemeinen Psychologie*, J. Rehmke. *The Psychological Review*, III, 6.

1897

Abstract: "The physiology of sensation," *The Psychological Review*, IV, 2.

Book Review: *Contributions to the Analysis of the Sensations*, Ernst Mach. tr. by C. M. Williams. *Science*, n.s. VI, 152.

1898

Abstract: "Immediacy and the concept of sensation," *The Psychological Review*, V, 2.

"Sensation and the datum of science," *The Philosophical Review*, VII, 5.

1900

Abstract: "Nature and choice," *The Psychological Review*, VII, 2.

Book Review: *Ueber Gegenstände hohere Ordnung und deren Verhältniss zur inneren Wahrnehmung*, A. Meinong. *The Psychological Review*, VII, 3.

Book Review: *La nouvelle Monadologie*, Ch. Renouvier et L. Prat. *The Philosophical Review*, VIII, 6.

1901

Book Review: *What is Thought*, James Hutchinson Stirling. *The Psychological Review*, VIII, 4.

Book Review: *Methodology and Truth*, J. S. Creighton. *The Psychological Review*, VIII, 6.

1902

"Choice and nature," *Mind*, n.s. XI, 41.

Abstract: "On final causes," *The Philosophical Review*, XI, 3.

1904

"On mechanical explanation," *The Philosophical Review*, XIII, 3.

"Note on the physical world-order," *The Journal of Philosophy, Psychology and Scientific Method*, I, 23 and 24.

1906

Book Review: *Erkentnis and Irrtum: Skizzen zur Psychologie der Forschung*, E. Mach. *The Philosophical Review*, XV, 6.

1909

"Kant's first antinomy," *The Philosophical Review*, XVIII, 4.

1911

"Mind as an observable object," *The Journal of Philosophy, Psychology and Scientific Method*, VIII, 7.

1912

"Consciousness and behavior, A Reply," *The Journal of Philosophy, Psychology and Scientific Method*, IX, 1.

"On mind as an observable object," *The Journal of Philosophy, Psychology and Scientific Method*, IX, 8.

1913

"Man and fellow-man," *The Journal of Philosophy, Psychology and Scientific Method*, X, 6.

1914

"The mathematician and his luck," *The Mathematics Teachers*, VII.

"The pulse of life," *The Journal of Philosophy, Psychology and Scientific Method*, XI, 24.

1915

Lecture: *Giordano Bruno*. Free Public Lectures, University of Pennsylvania, II.

"Mr. Knox on monasticism," *Old Penn*, XIV, 10.

1916

"Love and loyalty," *The Philosophical Review*, XXV, 3.

1917

"On sensibility," *The Journal of Philosophy*, XIV, 13.

1918

Lecture: *The Empiricism of William James*. Free Public Lectures, University of Pennsylvania, V.

1920

Lecture: *Progress*. Free Public Lectures, University of Pennsylvania, VII.

1921

Book Review: *Der Untergang des Abendlandes*. Oswald Spengler. *Educational Review*, 61, 5.

1923

Modern Thinkers and Present Problems. Henry Holt and Company.

1924

Book Review: *Scientific Method*, A. D. Ritchie. *The Philosophical Review*, XXXIII, 4.
"On pain and dreams," *The Journal of Philosophy*, XXI, 22.
Mind as Behavior, and Studies in Empirical Idealism. R. G. Adams & Co.

1925

"Logic and the relation of Life to mechanism," *Proceedings of the American Philosophical Society*, LXIV, 2.
"George Stuart Fullerton, '79," *The Alumni Register*, XXVII, 8.
"On Spontaneity," *The Journal of Philosophy*, XXII, 16.
Book Review: *University of California Publications in Philosophy*. G. P. Adams, J. Lowenberg, Editors, Vols. IV and V. *The Journal of Philosophy*, XXII, 17.
"George Stuart Fullerton," *The Journal of Philosophy*, XXII, 22.
Fool's Advice. Henry Holt and Company.
"Concerning introspection: a reply," *The Journal of Philosophy*, XXII, 26.

1926

Book Review: *Consciousness, Life and the Fourth Dimension.*
Richard Erickson. *The Philosophical Review*, XXXV, 1.
"Esthetic and the Rational Ideal," *The Journal of Philosophy*,
XXIII, 9, 10, 11.
Commencement Address to the Undergraduate Schools, University
of Pennsylvania. *The Pennsylvania Gazette*, XXIV, 32.

1927

Address, Newbold Memorial Meeting. *Proceedings*, R. G. Kent,
Editor. Waverly Press, Baltimore.

1929

"On the conscious mind," *The Journal of Philosophy*, XXVI, 21.

1930

"Confessio Philosophi," *Contemporary American Philosophy*. The
Macmillan Company, N. Y.
"Philosophy of experiment," *The Symposium*, I, 2.
"On Virgil and three magicians," *General Alumni Magazine*,
XXXIII, 1.
Méchanisme et téléologie. Paper presented to *La Société philosophique de la Sorbonne.*

1931

"Logic and the relation of function to mechanism," *Proceedings of
the Seventh International Congress of Philosophy*. Oxford University Press.
"On a possible science of religion," *The Philosophical Review*, XL,
2.
"On the subject of artists," *Junto* (Univ. of Penna.) December.

1932

"Concerning the artist's career," *General Magazine and Historical
Review*, XXXIV, 2.

1933

Book Review: *Les deux sources de la morale et de la religion.*
Henri Bergson. *The Journal of Philosophy*, XXX, 1.

1934

"On the contented life," *American Scholar*, III, 3.

"Beyond mechanism and vitalism," *Philosophy of Science*, I, 3.

1935

"John Locke," *Annals of Medical History*, n.s. VII, 4.

1936

On the Contented Life. Henry Holt and Company, N. Y.

1940

"The strength of gentle lives" [memorial address for Isaac Husik], *The Jewish Exponent*, April 12.

1941

"Logico-Historical Study of Mechanism," *Studies in the History of Science, University of Pennsylvania Bicentennial Conference*. University of Pennsylvania Press.